CARIBBEAN

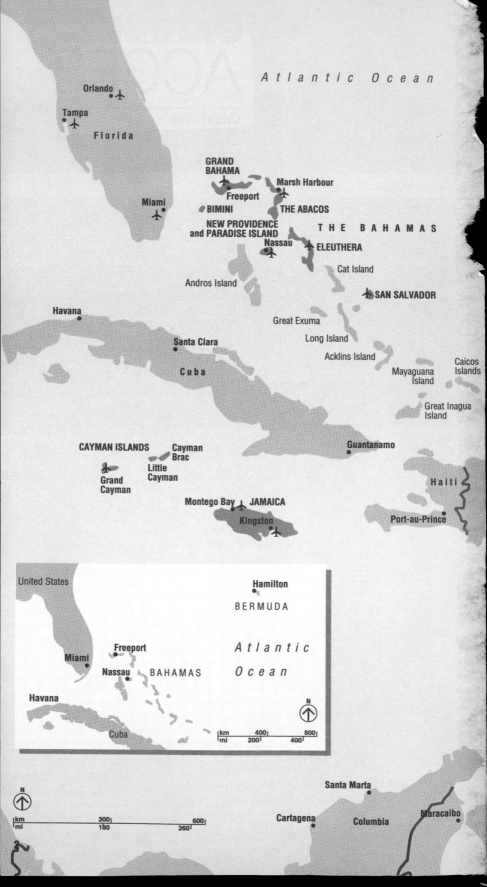

Images of gently swaying palm trees, deserted, sandy beaches, jade-green waters, and the lilting sound of a steel band are conjured up by one lyrical word:

Caribbean.
The Caribbean is the part of the world where the average temperature ranges from 78 to 90 degrees year-round, where the sea is calm, the sun is in abundant supply, and life is truly a day at the beach.

Spanning some 2,000 miles, this vast tropical playground of more than 300 islands can be narrowed down to less than 20 choice destinations—from the Caribbean's most enticing islands to the best of the Bahamas and beautiful Bermuda—which are all featured in the following pages.

In addition to the warm waters and the long, sparkling beaches characteristic of most of these vacation destinations, the Caribbean's **Cayman Islands** (Grand Cayman, Little Cayman, and Cayman Brac) and **Anguilla** are renowned for their superior underwater attractions for scuba divers, while history buffs are lured by the pastel Dutch "gingerbread" houses of **Sint Maarten** and the Spanish colonial forts and cathedrals in the 16th-century town of **San Juan** on Puerto Rico. High rollers prefer to spend their time

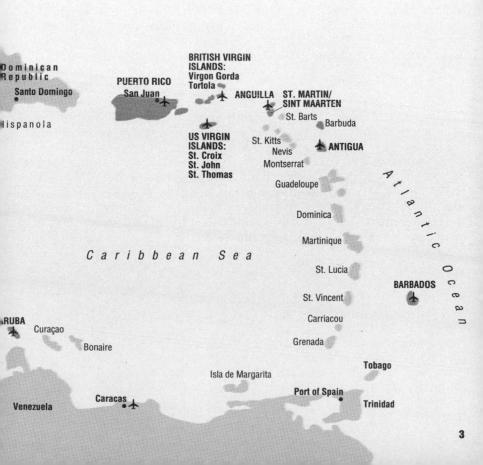

(and money) in the ritzy casinos on **Aruba, Antigua,** and **Puerto Rico,** and zealous shoppers like to hunt for those easy-to-find bargains on French perfumes, Swiss watches, crystal, and other imports on the islands of **Barbados,** St. Martin/Sint Maarten, and the **US** and **British Virgin Islands.** And then there's **Jamaica,** which, far more than any other Caribbean destination, is famous for its charismatic islanders and their smooth rum and reggae music.

Orientation

Only 30 of the 700 islands that make up the **Bahamas** are inhabited; the others remain natural and wild, much like they were when **Christopher Columbus** discovered them 500 years ago. This archipelago, just off Florida's southeast coast, is closer to the United States than any of the other islands (although geographic purists will tell you the Bahamas are technically in the Atlantic Ocean, not in the Caribbean). The seven most popular Bahamian islands—particularly **Paradise Island**—offer seemingly endless beaches, some of the region's top resorts, and ideal settings for water sports ranging from windsurfing to waterskiing.

About 800 miles north of the Bahamas (even farther into the Atlantic), **Bermuda** has earned its reputation as a premier honeymoon destination with letter-perfect service. The crown colony celebrates its British heritage with popular afternoon tea rituals and cricket games, a custom that distinguishes Bermuda from most of the other islands.

After Columbus discovered the Caribbean in the late-15th century, colonists from all over Europe (including Great Britain) settled on these far isles, bringing along their cultures, cuisines, and languages. Unlike many distant vacation retreats, the English language (with numerous dialects) prevails throughout most of this area, even though several of the islands have French, Dutch, or Spanish ties. The French island of **St. Martin** is the most challenging when it comes to communication; you may want to arm yourself with a French-English dictionary. But don't fret too much about potential language barriers. Tourism is the number one industry, and the islanders you meet will no doubt go to great lengths to understand your needs.

The diversity of the Caribbean islands is reflected more in the architecture than in the language. A number of buildings in Aruba look as though they were shipped straight over from Amsterdam, whereas the open-air architecture in Bermuda and the Bahamas reflects a more tropical-colonial style. In Puerto Rico, an island with a rich Spanish background, the exotic dwellings embellished with dramatic arches are reminiscent of what you might discover in the old Moorish capitals of the world. And on many islands the chattel houses, originally homes for the slaves who worked in the sugarcane fields and the gold mines until the mid-19th century, have been converted into everything from eclectic boutiques and gift shops to colorful clapboard homes.

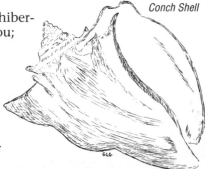
Conch Shell

Whether you study the architecture or hibernate in your resort, however, is up to you; tropical vacations are meant to be laid-back, where T-shirts, shorts, and swimsuits are the order of the day (along with a Mai Tai and a basket of conch fritters). So kick off your shoes (they're optional on most Caribbean islands) and dig your toes into the silky sand—life doesn't get much better than this.

Getting to the Islands

The Caribbean islands are mainly served through San Juan, St. Martin, and Antigua hubs by the following airlines:

Air Jamaica	800/523.5585
Airways International	305/526.3852
American Airlines	800/433.7300
Bahamasair	800/222.4262
BWIA International	800/327.7401
Cayman Airways	800/422.9626
Chalk's International	800/424.2557
Delta (Comair)	800/221.1212
Lufthansa	800/645.3880
Paradise Island Airways	800/432.8807
Riding Rock Inn Charter	800/272.1492
Trans World Airlines	800/892.4141
USAir Express	800/428.4322

Inter-Island Carriers:

ALM	800/327.7230
American Eagle	800/433.7300
LIAT	800/253.5011

Ferry Service

Although the notion of taking a ferry from island to island sounds like it might be an ideal way to explore the Caribbean, flying is really the better means of inter-island travel. The sea currents and distances (many of the islands are more than one hundred miles apart) have not made the ferry a popular mode of transportation. However, ferry service is available on the islands covered in this guide; your best bet is to call or stop by the local tourist office once you're in the Caribbean to find out which islands are easily accessible.

Getting around the Islands

Car Rentals

While some of the larger islands usually offer fleets of modern cars, don't count on it. Many islands only have cars that are several years old and in poor condition. It's best to rent a car with four-wheel drive if the island you're visiting is mountainous, and be prepared to drive on the left side of the road on the British isles. If the roads are poorly maintained or marked, you might be better off touring by bus or taxi. And don't expect to rent a car on Bermuda; the government prohibits rentals as a strict measure for controlling the number of automobiles on the island's roads.

None of the Caribbean islands have been developed in a grid format, so giving or getting directions can sometimes be confusing. Communities generally spread out from the boat docks. Consequently, islanders often give directions such as "the third building after the dilly tree" or "the shop in front of the yellow hibiscus." Some islands list beaches and bays instead of street addresses. Most of them, however, feature a major roadway fronting the sea that provides access to hotels, restaurants, and other attractions. So, prepare to get lost a few times; you can always ask again for directions.

How To Read This Guide

Caribbean ACCESS® is arranged by island so you can see at a glance where you are and what is around you. The numbers next to the entries in the following chapters correspond to the numbers on the maps. The type is color-coded according to the kind of place described:

Restaurants/Clubs: Red	Hotels: Blue
Shops/ 🌸 Outdoors: Green	Sights/Culture: Black

Rating the Restaurants and Hotels

The restaurant ratings take into account the service, atmosphere, and uniqueness of the restaurant. An expensive restaurant doesn't necessarily ensure an enjoyable evening; however, a small, relatively unknown spot could have good food, professional service, and a lovely atmosphere. Therefore, on a purely subjective basis, stars are used to judge the overall dining value (see the star ratings at right). Keep in mind that the chefs and owners often change, which sometimes drastically affects the quality of a restaurant. The ratings in this book are based on information available at press time.

The price ratings, as categorized below, apply to restaurants and hotels. These figures describe general price-range relationships between other restaurants or hotels in the region; they do not represent specific rates.

★ Good	$ The price is right
★★ Very good	$$ Reasonable
★★★ Excellent	$$$ Expensive
★★★★ Extraordinary	$$$$ A month's pay

Map Key

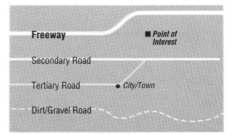

FYI

Accommodations

Island lodgings range from simple guest houses to luxury resorts. Condominiums and time-share apartments are rented by the day or week, and posh villas, with room for four to six people, are also available.

Orientation

On many of the islands, notably Jamaica, couples-only resorts have grown in popularity in the past few years. Another trendy resort plan is the all-inclusive program that includes the room, meals, liquor, wine, and cigarettes for one pre-paid price. Other resorts offer packages that combine accommodations, ground transportation, and airfare.

Room rates are generally lower off-season—in the late spring, summer, and early fall—and some of the major hotels close for maintenance or renovation from September through October.

Customs

United States citizens who have spent 48 hours outside of the country can bring $400 worth of duty-free, tax-exempt goods back home with them, provided this allowance hasn't been met within a 30-day period. Families traveling together can pool their purchases—and their exemptions. When the exemption has been exceeded, you will be charged 10 percent of the excess of any article priced up to $1,000.

Each American citizen over the age of 21 may bring home one carton of cigarettes and one liter of alcohol duty free. There are no limits on purchasing crafts made in the Netherland Antilles, antique goods (at least one hundred years old), foreign-language books, original works of art, caviar, or truffles.

The rules are a little different for Americans visiting the United States Virgin Islands. The limit is $1,200 worth of merchandise every 30 days, which may include five bottles of liquor (six if one is locally produced), five cartons of cigarettes, and one carton of cigars.

Every time Canadian citizens leave the country for more than 24 hours they may bring back $20 (Canadian currency) worth of duty-free merchandise. Once a year, they may return with C$300 in duty-free goods.

Canadians over the age of 16 may bring back 10 packs of cigarettes, five cigars, and two pounds of tobacco duty free. They may also return with 40 ounces of wine or liquor and two dozen 12-ounce cans of beer.

For more about these regulations, call the Customs Office listed in the government pages of your telephone directory.

Entry Requirements

Health or vaccination certificates are not required to enter (or leave) any of the islands featured in this guide.

Proof of citizenship and a return plane ticket are commonly required to gain entry onto a Caribbean island. And don't expect a driver's license to satisfy the citizenship requirement. In most cases a voter's registration card or a birth certificate with an official raised seal will do just fine, although a passport is your safest bet. Passports and passport information are available at main post offices and federal and state courthouses. The United States maintains passport offices in Boston, Chicago, Honolulu, Houston, Los Angeles, Miami, New Orleans, New York City, Philadelphia, San Francisco, Seattle, Stamford, CT, and Washington, DC.

Most airlines check for proof of citizenship before issuing a boarding card.

Since cruise ships hold on to passports until the cruise ends, passengers are issued identity cards when ships call at island ports. A ship identity card may also be required to reboard.

Money

Eastern Caribbean islands use the Eastern Caribbean dollar (EC$), but the American dollar and major credit cards are accepted throughout the region. For specific currencies of the various islands, see the introductions of the following chapters.

Telephones

Most Caribbean islands are in the 809 area code and are easy to reach by telephone. From North America, dial 1, then 809 followed by the local phone number.

Islands not in the 809 area code are Aruba (area code 297.8), St. Martin (area code 599.5), and Sint Maarten (area code 590).

Time

The Bahamas and Jamaica are on Eastern Standard Time (EST), the same as in New York and Florida, and so are the Cayman Islands, except during Eastern Daylight Saving Time (EDST), when the Caymans are one hour earlier.

Antigua, Anguilla, Aruba, Barbados, Puerto Rico, St. Martin/Sint Maarten, and all the Virgin Islands are on EST during EDST (from spring through fall), and an hour later the rest of the year.

Bermuda is always one hour ahead of the East Coast.

Tipping

As a general rule, service charges are added to hotel bills, eliminating the need to tip individual housekeepers (although you may always leave an additional tip for *service extraordinaire*). On larger islands 15 percent is also added to restaurant tabs. If you're not sure whether a tip has been added to your bill, don't hesitate to ask (the last thing you need to do on a vacation is to tip twice).

Tour guides are generally tipped about $2 per person. Those who hail a cab or unload your luggage typically get $1 or $2 (regardless of the number of bags), and taxi drivers receive 10 to 15 percent of the fare.

Cruise lines make their tipping policies clear to their passengers by equipping each of the cabins with information on the proper amounts to leave for the staff.

Tourist Offices

Free information on island activities may be obtained by writing (allow at least four weeks for a response) or calling these major New York offices:

Anguilla Tourist Information and Reservations Office
c/o Medhurst & Associates, Inc.
271 Main Street
Northport, NY 11768
800/553.4939, 516/261.1234

Antigua and Barbuda Department of Tourism
610 Fifth Avenue, Suite 311
New York, NY 10020
212/541.4117

Aruba Tourism Authority
521 Fifth Avenue, 12th floor
New York, NY 10175
800/862.7822, 212/246.3030

Bahamas Tourist Office
150 E. 52nd Street, 28th floor
New York, NY 10022
212/582.2777

Barbados Board of Tourism
800 Second Avenue, 17th floor
New York, NY 10017
800/221.9831

Bermuda Department of Tourism
310 Fifth Avenue, Suite 201
New York, NY 10017
800/223.6106, 212/818.9800

British Virgin Islands Tourist Board
370 Lexington Avenue
New York, NY 10017
800/835.8530, 212/696.0400

Caribbean Tourist Organization
20 E. 46th Street, 4th floor
New York, NY 10017
212/682.0435

Cayman Islands Department of Tourism
420 Lexington Avenue, Suite 2733
New York, NY 10170
212/682.5582

French West Indies Tourist Board
610 Fifth Avenue, Room 516
New York, NY 10020
212/757.1125

Jamaica Tourist Board
866 Second Avenue, 10th floor
New York, NY 10017
212/688.7650

Puerto Rico Tourism Company
575 Fifth Avenue, 23rd floor
New York, NY 10017
800/866.7827, 800/223.6530, 212/599.6262

Sint Maarten Government Tourist Office
275 Seventh Avenue, 19th floor
New York, NY 10001-6788
212/989.0000

United States Virgin Islands Division of Tourism
1279 Avenue of the Americas
New York, NY 10020
212/582.4520

Tourist Seasons

In recent years the Bahamas and the entire Caribbean region have enjoyed year-round tourism, but traditionalists consider fall and winter the prime time to visit.

Hotel rates are generally lower on the islands from April 15 through November 15, with many of the more expensive resorts offering special rates from Easter up to Thanksgiving. The best values are often available May through October, during the so-called shoulder season. Some resorts close during the months of September and/or October for renovation work.

Bermuda's peak season (the exact opposite of the Caribbean islands' and the Bahamas') kicks in the first week of April and continues through November.

Weather

The hurricane season runs from June through November, and major storms tend to hit toward the end of the year. Modern technology makes it much easier to predict storms, however. Anyone traveling in the Caribbean after June should stay informed of the latest forecasts by radio, television, or newspaper.

Bests

Bill Kofoed
Publicist, North Miami, Florida

The secluded **Dunn's River Falls** in **Ocho Rios** on **Jamaica**, which looks like a painting.

Port Lucaya on **Grand Bahama** island offers swimming with dolphins—a magnificent experience for touching and playing with these intelligent, gentle creatures.

Treasure Island, a day trip from **Paradise Island** in the **Bahamas,** is small and intimate, with excellent scuba diving and snorkeling spots. Even though there are daily excursions to the island, fewer than 20 people go there every day.

The **Grand Case Beach Club** on **St. Martin/Sint Maarten** is located on a beautiful beach and cove. This small resort is particularly appealing because it is adjacent to the village of Grand Case, which has many fine restaurants (some are even world-class).

The island of **Aruba** for its fine beaches. And don't miss boarding the **Atlantis** submarine for an underwater view of the reefs and fish.

Cheryl Andrews
Caribbean Public Relations Specialist, Coral Gables, Florida

The **Cotton Bay Club** on **Eleuthera** in the **Bahamas**—no casinos or nightlife, just pure relaxation and some great food.

The Buccaneer on **St. Croix** in the **US Virgin Islands** is known for its views of the pink sunsets over the Caribbean Sea and its great rum punch.

Walk to **Colombies Beach** on **St. Barts** in the Lesser Antilles; if you're lucky, you'll have the beach all to yourself.

Watching the sunrise over the British Virgin Islands and St. John from my bed or terrace at the **Point Pleasant** resort on **St. Thomas.**

Cayman Islands

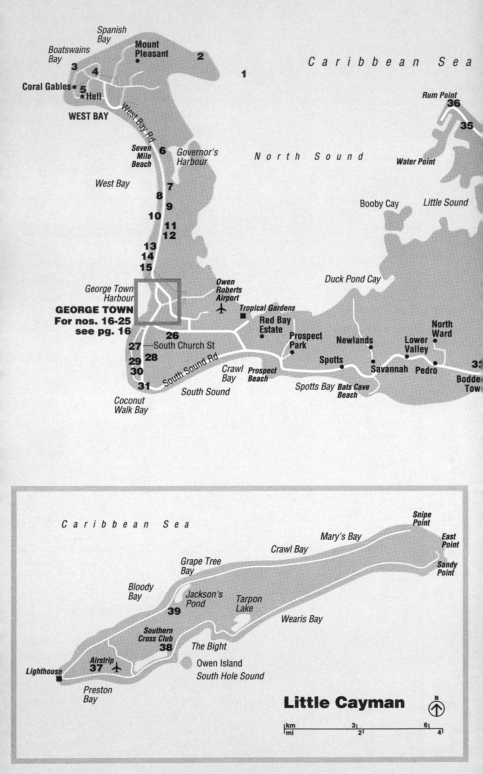

Spanish Bay
Boatswains Bay
3
4
5 Hell
Coral Gables
Mount Pleasant
2
1
WEST BAY
West Bay Rd
Seven Mile Beach
6 Governor's Harbour
West Bay
7
8
9
10
11
12
13
14
15
George Town Harbour
GEORGE TOWN
For nos. 16-25 see pg. 16
26
27 South Church St
29
28
30
31
Coconut Walk Bay
South Sound Rd
Crawl Bay
South Sound
Owen Roberts Airport
Tropical Gardens
Red Bay Estate
Prospect Park
Prospect Beach
Spotts Bay
Newlands
Spotts
Savannah
Bats Cave Beach
Caribbean Sea
North Sound
Rum Point 36
35
Water Point
Booby Cay
Little Sound
Duck Pond Cay
North Ward
Lower Valley
Pedro
Bodden Town
3

Little Cayman

Caribbean Sea
Snipe Point
Mary's Bay
Crawl Bay
East Point
Grape Tree Bay
Sandy Point
Bloody Bay
Jackson's Pond
Tarpon Lake
Wearis Bay
39
Southern Cross Club
38
The Bight
37 Airstrip
Lighthouse
Owen Island
South Hole Sound
Preston Bay

N

km
mi
3
2
6
4

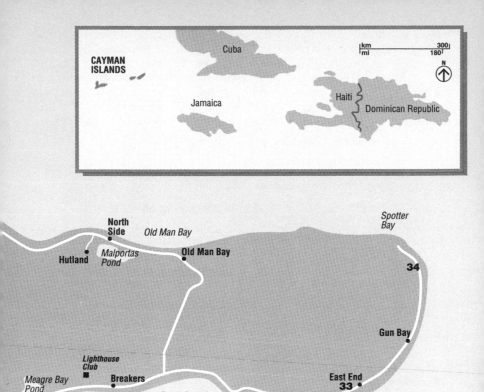

CAYMAN ISLANDS

Cuba

Jamaica

Haiti

Dominican Republic

km 300
mi 180

N

North Side

Old Man Bay

Spotter Bay

Hutland

Malportas Pond

Old Man Bay

34

Gun Bay

Lighthouse Club

Meagre Bay Pond

Breakers

East End
33

Pease Bay

Frank Sound

White Sand Bay

Bodden Bay

Grand Cayman

km
mi 2 3 4 6

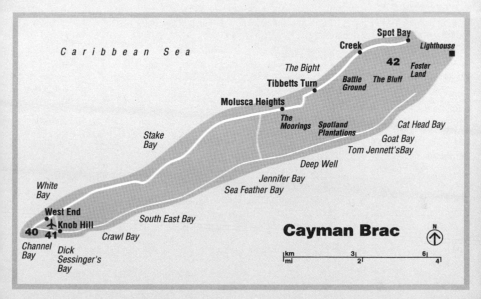

Caribbean Sea

Spot Bay

Creek

Lighthouse

The Bight

42

Foster Land

Tibbetts Turn

Battle Ground

The Bluff

Molusca Heights

The Moorings

Spotland Plantations

Cat Head Bay

Stake Bay

Goat Bay

Tom Jennett'sBay

Deep Well

Jennifer Bay

White Bay

Sea Feather Bay

West End

Knob Hill

40 41

South East Bay

Crawl Bay

Cayman Brac

N

Channel Bay

Dick Sessinger's Bay

km
mi 2 3 4 6

The Cayman islands—**Grand Cayman, Little Cayman, and Cayman Brac**—are renowned for their extensive coral reefs that lure scuba divers from around the globe and for their bustling financial centers. Nearly 600 banks conduct business in **George Town,** the capital of this tiny chain of three coral-covered mountaintops that have a combined population of 25,000. The Caymans lie 150 miles south of **Cuba** and 180 miles west of **Jamaica** near the **Cayman Trench,** the deepest part of the Caribbean at 24,720 feet below sea level. Until the 1960s, few tourists visited the isolated islands, but in the last three decades they have become the fifth largest financial market in the world and are considered one of the world's top five scuba-dive destinations.

Cayman Islands

Ten times the number of resident Caymanians visited the islands in 1990—250,000 business and leisure travelers with plenty of discretionary currency. Of course, the Caymanians benefit financially from this influx of foreign industry, so much so that the employment rate is nearly one hundred percent. While the Cayman islanders retain their West Indian heritage, at the same time they seem to embrace British domain. Other islands may opt for independence (such as nearby Jamaica), but the Caymans proudly remain a British crown colony, with all their pomp and circumstance intact.

Area code 809/94 unless otherwise noted.

Getting to the Islands

Airlines

American Airlines	800/433.7300
Cayman Airways	800/422.9626
Island Air	809/949.0241
Northwest	800/447.4747

Airports

Owen Roberts International Airport This Grand Cayman airport is two miles east of George Town and five miles southeast of Seven Mile Beach.

Gerrard-Smith Airport On the southern end of Cayman Brac, this airport is served by Cayman Airways and Island Air.

Edward Bodden Airfield Little Cayman's airport on the southern end of the island is served by Cayman Airways and Island Air.

Getting around the Islands

Buses

A private bus line runs between 7AM and 6PM from George Town and along Seven Mile Beach.

Car Rentals

Andy's Rent-A-Car	9.8111
Avis	9.2468
Budget	9.5605
Caribbean Motors	9.8878
Hertz	9.2280
Just Jeeps	9.7263
Payless	9.7074
Soto's Scooter Ltd.	7.4652

Driving

Influenced by British custom, cars have steering wheels on the right and they're driven on the left. Also, it's considered a courtesy on the Caymans to rarely honk your horn. Air-conditioned sedans and convertible Jeeps are your rental-car choices, as are motor scooters. Cayman laws require wearing a helmet when on a scooter, and having a Caymanian permit to drive any rental vehicle.

Taxis

Cabs are plentiful on Grand Cayman, and they are a reasonably priced option for traveling along Seven Mile Beach and in George Town. Once you head farther out on the island, the fares become quite steep and cost as much as a day's car rental. When you're in a taxi, however, you have the advantage of picking up some local lore from a charming Caymanian driver, and can imbibe at your destination without worrying about finding your way home.

FYI

Money

The Cayman currency was introduced in 1972 and includes six bills and four coins. American currency is accepted at most establishments. Banks are open M-Th 9AM-2:30PM; F 9AM-1PM, 2:30-4:30PM.

Personal Safety

Caymanians are justifiably proud of the island's reputation for being virtually crime-free and boast about leaving their cars and homes unlocked. Tourists may be just as fortunate, but it makes sense to exercise normal precautions with personal valuables and belongings. The Cayman gendarmes have no patience with drunk drivers and drug users, who are immediately taken to jail and must appear before a local magistrate for sentencing that, at its lightest, will include an order to get out of town immediately.

Phone Book

Fire 500

Hospital 555

Police 999

Visitors' Hot Line 9.8989

Visitors' Information Office 9.8342

Publications

Key to Cayman, published twice yearly, is an excellent magazine with information on restaurants, shopping, and nightlife. *Horizons,* an in-flight magazine for Cayman Airways, includes articles on island personalities and lifestyle, as well as tourist-oriented information. *The Caymanian Compass* is the islands' daily newspaper. American periodicals, including *USA Today,* the *Miami Herald,* and *The New York Times,* are available at most of the hotel gift shops.

Telephones

The area code for all three Cayman Islands is 809. To call from the United States, dial 1-809 and the local number. The prefix for numbers on the islands is 94, followed by a five-digit number. Within Cayman, simply dial the five-digit number; outside, you must dial 94 first.

Grand Cayman

Most bankers in the Caribbean conduct business on Grand Cayman, the largest of the three Cayman islands—20 miles long and four to seven miles wide. **George Town,** the capital city, consists of six major streets (most only one or two blocks long) where you'll find the government and civic buildings, banks, and many duty-free shops. **George Town Harbour** at Hog Sty Bay is where cruise-ship passengers arrive by the thousands, while adventurers in smaller numbers descend beneath the moored sailboats on submarine sight-seeing rides.

Most of the island's hotels and condos line **West Bay Road** and **Seven Mile Beach,** a five-mile-long stretch of coconut palms, populated beaches, and endless aquamarine horizons north of George Town. A few smaller resorts catering to divers are scattered along the **South Sound.** Beyond these two clusters of commerce lies the real Grand Cayman, which is located in tiny districts simply named **West Bay, North Side,** and **East End.** Traditional wood-frame Caymanian cottages with pink shutters, white picket fences, and raked sand lawns afford a backdrop for perfect snapshots along winding roads hugging the coastline. On the East End, waves crash into blowholes etched by nature into limestone caves and spray water 60 feet high in a spectacular show of force. Sea turtles propagate by the thousands at the **Turtle Farm** in West Bay, also the home of a bizarre geological attraction known as **Hell.**

Islanders and travelers alike gather under the feathery branches of Australian pines at **Rum Point** on the eastern shores of North Sound for afternoon barbecues and sunset cocktails by baby-blue bays. The relaxed Caymanian spirit is infectious at moments like this, when warm, tropical breezes carry the scent of spices and salt and the pulsing sounds of Caribbean rhythms and reggae throughout the island.

Caymanian Cottage

GARY L. GRIMAUD

1 Stingray City Imagine kneeling on white sand 12 feet underwater, stroking the silken underbelly of a stingray with a six-foot wing span, while other rays affectionately nuzzle you. Sound dangerous? Not at all. These

Cayman Islands

rays are so accustomed to human attention they swim toward dive boats with anticipation, knowing they'll be fed, petted, and loved once again.

Three local divemasters discovered this hangout for Southern stingrays (*Dasyatis americana*) in 1986 on their trips to the North Sound. They realized the rays were drawn to a shallow area where boat crews habitually cleaned their catch of fish and conch for lunch. The divers began visiting the rays regularly, feeding them bits of squid and dodging their whiplike, venomous tails—the source of their reputation as fearsome, dangerous creatures. Gradually, a community of 20 or so stingrays (mostly female) took up residence in the area and learned to get along with the humans.

Over the years the stingrays have come and gone, but their number stays fairly stable; divers, on the other hand, have increased and multiplied. As many as 200 divers and snorkelers visit Stingray City each day during the high season; tens of thousands in less than a decade. Almost all of Grand Cayman's dive operators offer trips to Stingray City—worth visiting for the view of these graceful creatures even if you're too terrified to try to swim among them.
♦ North Sound

2 Ristorante Pappagallo ★★★★$$$$ A-frame peaks of palm thatch jut out at angles from the roof of this decidedly romantic restaurant set on a natural lagoon in the midst of a bird sanctuary. Parrots, cockatoos, and macaws preen within the glass cages in the air-conditioned **Pappagallo Room,** while tropical breezes stir the palm fronds in the lakefront **Flamingo Room.** Start with the mouth-watering swordfish carpaccio, followed by lobster and shrimp flamed with Armagnac, or chicken breast sautéed with sausage and garlic. The only drawback is the restaurant's locale, about a 40-minute drive from George Town. The cab fare is steep, so you might reserve Pappagallo for a night when you've rented a car—though you'll need a designated driver, since the wine list is very tempting. Dress up a bit more than usual

(but still casually) for this special night.
♦ Northern Italian ♦ Daily 6-10:30PM. West Bay Rd (West Bay-Mount Pleasant). Reservations recommended. 9.1119

3 Cayman Turtle Farm Thousands upon thousands of green sea turtles in various stages of development flop about on top of each other in circular cement tanks at the only green sea turtle breeding farm in the world. Sea turtles were once a staple of the Caymanian diet, and were so prolific that **Christopher Columbus** first called these islands **Las Tortugas.**

But green sea turtles have been hunted nearly into extinction and are considered endangered in many parts of the world. A marine biologist on Grand Cayman came up with the idea of establishing a green sea turtle farm in 1968 as both a commercial and ecological venture. By 1978, turtles bred on the farm were being released into Cayman waters. Today, about 3,000 of the turtles raised here are sold for local consumption, while an equal or larger amount is released.

The farm is a fascinating venture well worth touring. A large gift shop sells just about everything you can imagine with a turtle theme, but remember, actual turtle products are not allowed into the US. A snack shop sells turtle soup and steaks, though you'd have to be a bit hard-hearted to chomp away while your lunch's relatives are in sight.
♦ Admission. Daily 9AM-5PM. West Bay Rd (West Bay-Mount Pleasant). 9.3894

4 Liberty's ★★★$ **Barbara** and **Grayson Liberty** prepare and serve hefty portions of native Caymanian dishes to crowds of locals and tourists willing to trek out to their small cottage in West Bay. You can get a good overview of the local cuisine at the Wednesday, Friday, and Sunday night buffets, where diners help themselves to conch fritters, boiled cassava, breadfruit, rice and beans, and curried chicken. By ordering from the menu on other nights you'll be able to try curried goat or oxtail, and Barbara's irresistable coconut cream pie. ♦ Caymanian
♦ M-Sa 11:30AM-3PM, 6-10PM. West Bay Rd (West Bay-Mount Pleasant). 9.3226

5 Hell A miniature Grand Canyon with jagged, blackened rock peaks that supposedly look like the charred remains of a fire in Hades, Hell is the ultimate tourist curiosity. There's a post office here so you can send postcards from Hell, gift shops with predictable slogans on their T-shirts, and a boardwalk from which to study the rocks. Hell is made of ironshore rock, a hard limestone that looks like black volcanic rock because of a coating of algae that secretes acid, eroding the rock in bizarre formations. ♦ West Bay Rd (West Bay-Mount Pleasant)

Restaurants/Clubs: Red   **Hotels:** Blue
Shops/ 🌳 Outdoors: Green   **Sights/Culture:** Black

6 Indies Suites $$$ One of the Cayman's most respected fishers, **Ronnie Foster,** created the islands' first all-suite hotel in 1990, with nearly instant success. Popular with divers, anglers, families, and business travelers, the complex has 40 suites with living rooms, complete kitchens with microwaves, and storage space for diving and fishing gear. Foster chose a wonderful stretch of nearly secluded beach for his hotel, and designed it to harmonize with the island's natural colors, using blue tile on the roof, and soft peach and periwinkle in the decor. All rooms face the courtyard pool and hot tub. Fishing and dive packages are available. ◆ West Bay Rd (George Town-West Bay). 7.5025, 800/654.3130; fax 7.5024

7 The Coffee Grinder If you like to have a few special treats in your room or are fixing meals in your condo, stop here for fresh-roasted coffees and fresh-baked croissants, Danishes, and brownies. Ice-cream addicts take note—there's also a Häagen-Dazs parlor. ◆ M-Sa 7:30AM-10PM. West Bay Rd (George Town-West Bay). 9.4833

8 Holiday Inn $$$ One of the first beachfront hotels on Grand Cayman, the Holiday Inn has undergone a much needed renovation, with a complete refurbishing of all 215 rooms. The outdated, drab decor has given way to bright tropical colors and local art lines the long hallways.

The restaurants and bars all have new, updated menus, but the management has wisely kept the popular breakfast buffet, renowned with locals and visitors for its abundant spread of made-to-order omelets, meats, potatoes, pancakes, waffles, and trays of tropical fruits. The hotel is known as a fun, festive place with plenty of water-oriented activities by the beach and at the large fresh-water pool. The **Barefoot Man Sand Band,** a Caymanian hallmark with 20 years of performing on the island, plays poolside W-Sa 8PM, for barefoot dancing under the stars. ◆ West Bay Rd (George Town-West Bay). 7.4444, 800/421.9999; fax 7.4213

Within the Holiday Inn:

Bob Soto's Diving Underwater adventurer **Bob Soto** opened the Caribbean's first dive shop on Grand Cayman in 1957. Soto, whose father was Cuban and mother Caymanian, grew up on the island, then served with the US Merchant Marines. When he returned home in 1957, few locals understood his enthusiasm for the new sport of scuba diving. By the time he sold his business to IBM exec **Ron Kipp** in 1980, diving was attracting thousands of tourists to the islands, and scuba diving had become big business. The Cayman Islands now have more than 30 dive operators, but Bob Soto's still stands out as a PADI four-star operation with a fleet of first-rate dive boats, excellent divemasters, and a full range of instructional programs. ◆ Daily 8AM-5:30PM. 9.2022, 800/262.7686; fax 9.8731

Coconuts Comedy Club What comedian would mind spending some time on Grand Cayman and performing before relaxed vacationers in sandals and shorts? Not many, that's for sure. The Comedy Club attracts the young talents who have acquired late-night talk-show fame, and a young, casual crowd ready to laugh. Occasionally, big stars who happen to be on the island will perform extemporaneously. ◆ Admission. W-Su 8PM-closing; showtimes 9PM, 10:30PM. Reservations required. 7.4444

8 Lantana's Restaurant and Bar ★★★$$$ When Lantana's opened in 1991, Austria-born chef **Fred Schrock** took the island by storm with his distinctive and wildly popular southwestern cuisine. Chef Fred studied in Santa Fe, New Mexico, then added an island flare to the grilled and roasted seafoods and meats. Grilled lamb comes with a red-onion marmalade; pork tenderloin is coated with jerk spices; and shrimp is served with cilantro pasta. The restaurant, located at the **Caribbean Club,** is decorated with cacti, terracotta pottery, and woven American Indian rugs. ◆ Southwestern/Caribbean ◆ M-F, Su 11:30AM-2:30PM, 6-10PM; Sa 6-10PM. West Bay Rd (George Town-West Bay). Reservations recommended. 7.5595

9 Hyatt Regency Grand Cayman $$$$ Regal, serene, and luxurious, the periwinkle-blue Hyatt Regency sits amid the emerald lawns of the **Britannia Golf Course** like a colonial British baron's Caribbean hideaway. The stately white columns, multipaned French doors, perfectly pruned palms, and abundance of blossoms will make you feel as though you should be dressed for a garden wedding or a spot of afternoon tea.

The hotel is located across the road from the beach, but has a fully equipped beach club with water toys, a pool, restaurants, and an excellent dive shop on the immaculate 266-foot-long stretch of talcum sand. A second pool on the hotel grounds has an unusual swim-up bar, surrounded by more stark white columns and a peaked roof. A color scheme that reflects the island's sunsets gives the 236 rooms and suites a calm, cool feeling. Villas worth settling into for the rest of your life line the golf-course greens. Naturally, you pay dearly for such elegance and comfort, especially during the high season. ◆ Deluxe ◆ West Bay Rd (George Town-West Bay). 9.1234, 800/233.1234; fax 9.8528

Within the Hyatt Regency:

Brittania Golf Course Designed by **Jack Nicklaus,** the only golf course on the island even has its own style of ball, lighter than normal to match the half-length fairways. The course is reminiscent of Scotland's Royal Troon and Turnberry courses, with grassy mounds and rolling dunes along the shores of lakes and the Caribbean. Brittania can be played three ways: as a nine-hole championship course, as an 18-hole executive course, or as an 18-hole Cayman

Cayman Islands

Ball course. The **Golf Club** restaurant (★★$$) is a pleasant spot for a leisurely lunch. ♦ Daily 7:30AM-6PM. 9.8020

Hemingway's ★★★$$ One of the prettiest spots for lunch or dinner is on the patio of Hemingway's looking toward the beach. Start with the Papa Doble, a daiquiri supposedly made just like Ernest Hemingway made his in Havana, with white and spiced rums and orange, pineapple, grapefruit, and lime juices. Rumor has it Papa Hemingway downed 16 of these potent daiquiris in one sitting. It's probably best not to challenge his record.

For a light lunch, have a Key West salad with crabmeat and palm hearts and a bowl of fish tea—an herbal bouillon with mussels, scallops, lobster, and shrimp. For dinner, go native with beer-battered coconut shrimp served with steamed yucca, or spicy jerk chicken with coconut rice and fried plantains. ♦ West Indian/Continental ♦ Daily 11:30AM-2PM, 7-10PM. 9.1234

Red Sail Sports Accomplished and personable divemasters and top-notch boats with shade, showers, tropical fruit snacks, and plenty of room to stash your gear are trademarks of Red Sail's operation. If you're planning to get certified on Grand Cayman you'll be well cared for by divemasters such as **Kate Copley,** who guide gung-ho, cowardly, handicapped, elderly, and youthful novices into the underwater world with ease. Experienced divers can take specialty courses in night, wall, and wreck diving, as well as underwater navigation. Total beginners can stick with resort courses that give them a brief intro to the wonders beyond, or stay abovewater on Red Sail's Hobie Cats, water-skis, windsurfers, and parasails. Anglers can go after blue marlin on air-conditioned yachts. Red Sail also has a small shop with a gorgeous selection of T-shirts, dive gear, books, and cards—all with an underwater theme, of course.

Whatever else you do, you must take a sunset cruise on Red Sail's 65-foot-long catamaran, *The Spirit of Ppalu,* named after the Polynesian god of navigation. The best seats in the house are on the hull, where the water rushes beneath six glass viewing

panels. The warm breezes will lull you into a complacent glow. Drinks and hors d'oeuvres are served by charming bartenders inside the teak cabin—try the Blue Ppalu, made with curacao, and you'll feel like you're one with the sea. Red Sail has snorkel trips to Stingray City and dinner cruises on the *Ppalu.* ♦ Dive shop: daily 8AM-5:30PM. Ppalu snorkel sail: Tu-Su 10AM-2PM. Sunset sail: M, W, F, Su 5:30-7:30PM. Dinner sail: Tu, Th, Sa 5:30-9PM. 7.5965, 800/949.7965; fax 7.5805

10 Lacovia $$$$ Of the many condominium complexes along Seven Mile Beach, Lacovia is repeatedly praised for being luxurious and serene. White two-story buildings by the beach feature 45 apartment units with air-conditioning, TVs, and telephones. The complex has hot tubs, tennis courts, saunas, and water-sports facilities. ♦ West Bay Rd (George Town-West Bay). 9.7599, 800/223.9815; fax 9.0172

11 Cracked Conch ★★$$ The rustic, nautical decor and low-key, friendly mood make the Cracked Conch a good spot for a reasonably priced steak, fish, turtle, or lobster dinner without the frills. Drive your cholesterol into oblivion with the coconut stew, or choose from the **Heart Wise** selections of healthy, fat-free foods. Musicians **Chuck** and **Barrie** perform Caribbean music on Thursday and Saturday nights. ♦ Caribbean ♦ Open daily from 11:30AM-10PM. West Bay Rd (George Town-West Bay). 7.5217

11 Lone Star Bar and Grill ★★★$ Down-home cooking, Texas-style barbecue, and a fun-loving attitude keep locals and travelers happy at the Lone Star. Past winners of the **Great Caribbean Chili Cook-Off** (imagine the competition), the cooks turn out mean barbecued ribs, grilled steaks, spicy Cajun dishes, and damn good fajitas. Diners gather around wooden tables while drinkers catch major sporting events on the satellite TV in the bar. This is a good place to meet those energetic, permanently tanned expats from all over the world working as divemasters, waitresses, and whatever else so they can live in paradise. ♦ Tex-Mex/Barbecue ♦ M-F 11:30AM-3PM, 5PM-midnight; Sa-Su 11:30AM-3PM, 5-11PM. West Bay Rd (George Town-West Bay). 7.5175

When Cayman Airways was established, one of the names considered for the airline was Cayman Island Airways. The founders worried, however, that an airline with the acronym CIA might have trouble flying over Cuba—a necessity for all flights traveling to and from the Caymans and the United States.

12 Golden Pagoda ★★★$$ Chinese favorites are available at a daily lunch buffet and at dinner, as well as for take out—ideal for a sunset picnic on the beach. Owner **Cece Delephena** is a gracious, accommodating hostess known for catering grand banquets. Try the shrimp in hot spicy sauce or the Mongolian beef. ◆ Chinese ◆ Daily 11:30AM-2:30PM, 6-10PM. West Bay Rd (George Town-West Bay). 9.5475

12 Galeria Plaza Several strip malls line West Bay Road between the clusters of hotels and restaurants. Most have branches of familiar fast-food chains, plus liquor markets and gift shops. Galeria Plaza is one of the largest of these centers, with plenty of parking and diversions for everyone. ◆ M-F 9AM-9PM; Sa 9AM-5PM. West Bay Rd (George Town-West Bay). 7.5231

Within Galeria Plaza:

Chests of Gold Artist **Kristin Anderson** does gorgeous things with cloisonné and gold—her glittering angelfish with emerald-green inlays are worth splurging on. The shop also has an impressive display of ancient coins (sold with certificates documenting historical authenticity) and heavy twisted, braided, and linked gold chains for displaying your treasure. ◆ M-F 9AM-5PM; Sa 9AM-1PM. 9.7833

The Dream Weavers Cayman Nan (aka **Nancy Smith**) weaves wall hangings and rugs on a large floor loom that dominates her small shop. Her sock-top rugs are similar to simple, colorful rag rugs, while her hangings include local shells, feathers, and beads. ◆ M-F 9AM-5PM; Sa 9AM-1PM. 7.5661

13 The Wharf ★★★★$$
One of the few restaurants right on the sands of Seven Mile Beach, the Wharf's **Ports of Call** bar is the perfect
spot for a sunset daiquiri, followed by dinner under the swaying coconut palms. Choose from Caribbean turtle, conch, and seafood dishes or traditional Continental fare such as French onion soup and lamb chops Provençale; be sure to order the seafood paella if it's offered as a special.

Chef **Werner Meyer,** a native of Austria, has a nice touch with seafood, stuffing dolphinfish (a meaty, flavorful fish called dorado in Mexico and mahimahi in Hawaii) with scallops and serving red snapper with a mango sauce. Don't miss his **Mohr Im Hemd,** a killer Austrian chocolate soufflé. The prices are more reasonable at lunch, when you can relax under a blue-and-white striped umbrella and watch the boats sail by. Air-conditioned dining is available, but it's a shame to miss the stunning view.

◆ Caribbean/Continental ◆ M-F noon-2:30PM, 6-10PM; Sa-Su 6-10PM. West Bay Rd (George Town-West Bay). 9.2231

14 Seven Mile Beach Most of Grand Cayman's tourist accommodations are clustered along this five-mile-long stretch of white sand beach running north from George Town to West Bay. No one seems to know the reason for the discrepancy between the beach's name and its geography. Locals point out that the beaches all belong to the queen, meaning they're open to the public. There is a wonderful absence of vendors along the beach, but a preponderance of jet skis and other water toys. Many of the dive boats leave from this area. ◆ West Bay Rd (George Town-West Bay)

15 The Almond Tree ★★★★$$$ Marinated as an appetizer or baked as a steak, conch is prepared at this restaurant (pictured above) with finesse. The turtle steak is more rare and flavorful treat—if it's your kind of dish, go ahead and order the **Reef Comber,** with turtle and lobster tail. The restaurant is also known for its exotic rum drinks. Try the Hurricane, a blend of light and dark rums, vodka, gin, triple sec, grenadine, and lime. Almond, breadfruit, and royal poinciana trees surround the restaurant's patio; a palm thatch roof covers the bar. The building is designed after the traditional village meetings halls on the Pacific Island of Yap, and is filled with artifacts and memorabilia from Africa, South America, and the South Pacific. Those in the know say the dessert chef makes the best Key lime pie on the island. ◆ Seafood/Steak ◆ M, W-Su 5:30-10:30PM. N. Church St (George Town-West Bay). 9.2893

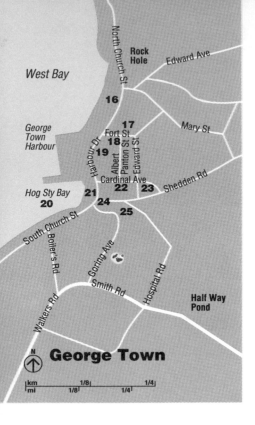

West Bay

Rock Hole

North Church St

Edward Ave

George Town Harbour

16

17 Fort St
18 Harbour Dr
19

Mary St

Albert Panton St

Edward St

Cardinal Ave **22** **23**

Shedden Rd

Hog Sty Bay **21** **24**
20

25

South Church St

Boiler's Rd

Goring Ave

Smith Rd

Hospital Rd

Walkers Rd

Half Way Pond

Ⓝ **George Town**

| km | 1/8 | 1/4 |
| mi | 1/8 | 1/4 |

16 Hog Sty Bay Cafe ★★★$$ A good choice for lunch or dinner during your tour of George Town, this cafe has nine tables on a wooden deck perched over the water. Much of the interior is taken over by dart players challenging each other to hit the bull's-eyes on the dart boards lining one wall. **Tom Keagy**, the proprietor, was once a partner at the enduringly popular **Crow's Nest** restaurant (see page 18), and has wisely capitalized on his past experience at his new cafe (opened in late-1991). The large Caesar salad topped with marinated conch is a satisfying meal in itself, especially when followed by the West Indian sundae—vanilla ice cream topped with banana fritters and rum raisin sauce. More substantial entrées include seafood pasta with a tangy citrus sauce, hamburgers with jerk sauce (for lunch), and snapper topped with tomatoes and feta cheese. The daily specials are a sure bet. The cafe is one of the few places near George Town that's open for lunch on Sunday. ♦ Caribbean ♦ M-F, Su 11:30AM-3PM, 6-10PM; Sa 6-10PM. N. Church St (George Town-West Bay). 9.6163

16 Fort George Built by the British around 1790 to protect Grand Cayman from Spanish invasion, Fort George no longer exists, but there is a plaque in its place. The **Old Fort Building** next door is a complex of gift shops. ♦ Harbour Dr (Mary-Fort Sts)

17 Legislative Assembly Building More modernistic and space age than most Cayman buildings, the Legislative Assembly Building is a formal place where you can watch how island law is created from a visitors galley over the Legislative Hall. The municipal government offices are housed in the plain-brick Peace Memorial Building next door. ♦ M-F 8:30AM-5PM. Fort St (Harbour Dr-Albert Panton St). 9.4236

18 Black Coral and... **Fort Street** is a good area for shopping, especially for jewelry. Even if you're not interested in purchasing a few gems to take home, try to stop by this gallery for a glance at the work of a true black-coral artist. Sculptor **Bernard Passman** retired to Grand Cayman more than a dozen years ago only to become the island's most famous black-coral artist, with commissions from the Cayman government, the British royal family, and a number of tourists who have fallen in love with his exotic work. Passman carves single pieces of black coral into willowy dancers and leaping dolphins. Laminated with gold, the coral is shaped into stunning earrings, bracelets, and rings. His shop is like a gallery, with each glass case holding another marvel. ♦ M-F 9AM-5PM; Sa 9AM-1PM. Fort St (Harbour Dr-Albert Panton St). 9.0123

19 Elmslie Memorial Church Captain **Rayal Bodden,** a prominent shipbuilder on Grand Cayman in the 1800s, designed this wood-frame, steepled church as the waterfront center of downtown. The interior ceiling is said to resemble the timber work Bodden used in the hulls of his sailing ships. Caymanians are respectful, decorous people; out of consideration to your hosts don't wear shorts or bathing suits into the church, or into the legal and government buildings of George Town. ♦ Su services 11AM, 7PM. Harbour Dr (Cardinal Ave-Fort St). 9.7923

20 Hog Sty Bay Known less colorfully as **George Town Harbour**, Hog Sty is Grand Cayman's main bay. Cruise ships dock outside the bay, disgorging thousands of passengers intent on splurging in the duty-free shops or submerging themselves along the island's world-famous reefs. There are a small park at the harbor and a tourist information booth that opens when cruise ships are docked. The **National Trust** has designated a self-guided walking tour of the historic sites in the area, explained in their map and brochure available at most hotels. ♦ Harbour Dr (Cardinal Ave-Shedden Rd)

While in the town of Hell on Grand Cayman, pick up a bottle of the zesty Hell Sauce, which is made with locally grown peppers, vinegar, tomatoes, and garlic.

Atlantis

21 Atlantis Submarines If you're afraid to scuba dive, check out the underwater scenery from your own porthole in a submarine traveling 50 to 150 feet beneath the sea in air-conditioned comfort. Gliding past the **Cayman Wall,** you'll see brilliant orange and yellow coral, and schools of tropical fish swimming past as if you didn't exist. These submarine tours are very popular, so make reservations early. Children under four are not allowed onboard. ◆ M, W, F-Sa 9AM-3PM; Tu, Th 9AM-8PM. S. Church St (George Town Harbour). 9.7700

22 Kirk Freeport Plaza Duty-free shopping is one of Grand Cayman's major attractions, particularly for cruise-ship passengers. Many of the duty-free shops are located in George Town, on Cardinal Avenue and Fort Street. Kirk's is a large complex with several small shops specializing in imported perfumes, jewelry, china, and crystal (including **Lalique, Waterford,** and **Baccarat**). ◆ M-F 9AM-5PM; Sa 9AM-1PM. Cardinal Ave (Harbour Dr-Edward St). 9.7477

23 Post Office The circular, cement-block Post Office, built in 1939, is a community gathering spot, since there is no mail delivery on the island. The islanders' 2,000 mailboxes are on the outside of the building, which is strung with colored lights. The Caymans' beautiful postage stamps make great souvenirs. ◆ M-F 8:30AM-4PM. Edward St (Shedden Rd-Cardinal Ave). 9.2474

24 Cayman Islands National Museum The **Old Courts Building,** a national treasure and landmark since the early 1800s, was transformed into a museum in 1990. The clapboard walls have a new coat of paint to match the white picket fence at the front of the two-story Cayman colonial building, an architectural marvel with porches, green shutters, and a flagpole once used to hold the lighthouse lantern. The museum's exhibits chronicle the island's shipbuilding, turtling, and rope industries, as well as its history of explorers, pirates, and shipwrecked sailors. ◆ Admission. Tu-F 8:30AM-4:30PM; Sa 10AM-5PM; Su 1AM-5PM. S. Church St (Goring Ave-Shedden Rd). 9.8368

25 Panton Square Cayman's version of Victorian architecture is exquisitely preserved in the homes around this grassy square. Note the frilly latticework along the upstairs porches, juxtaposed against the simplicity of the shuttered windows and plain porch railings. ◆ Harbour Dr (Goring Ave-Hospital Rd)

---

26 Eldemire's Guest House $ Budget accommodations with character are in short supply on Grand Cayman, but **Erma Eldemire** has done an admirable job of providing low-cost rooms with style for more than 20 years. Her Caymanian cottage, within walking distance of downtown and the ocean, has seven rooms, one studio, and one apartment, all simply furnished. Air-conditioning was added to the house in 1991, along with aqua-colored carpeting and refurbished bathrooms. ◆ Glen Eden Rd (S. Church St). 9.5387; fax 9.6987

Cayman Islands

27 Seaview Hotel $ The newly renovated aqua-colored Seaview is a welcome addition to the sparse selection of low-priced rooms on the island. Originally built in 1952, the hotel has 15 air-conditioned rooms (without televisions or phones) in two-story buildings around a freshwater swimming pool. The on-site **Cayman Diving School** offers resort and certification courses, dive trips, and equipment rentals. ◆ S. Church St (George Town-Bodden Town). 9.8804; fax 9.8507

PARROTS LANDING

28 Parrots Landing The vivid green and purple trim on the white cottage out front conveys the message that this is a lively place where the little details get special attention. Billed as a water-sports park, Parrots Landing doesn't have any splashing rides; the fun comes from snorkeling at four excellent spots just off-shore, diving the North Wall from shore, parasailing over the South Sound, or riding in a glass-bottom paddleboat. Hammocks hang between feathery Australian pines and Caymanian and Honduran parrots provide the appropriate background squawks for picnics and barbecues; the tables and grills scattered about the raked sand beach are available for public use.

The business end of the operation is an excellent dive shop specializing in serving small groups, and a large gift shop with skimpy swimsuits, neon scuba gear, and T-shirts emblazoned with purple and green designs. ◆ Daily 7AM-6PM. S. Church St (George Town-Bodden Town). 9.7884, 800/448.0428; fax 9.0294

29 Pure Art This pretty Cayman cottage with hardwood floors and sheer white curtains on the windows houses the island's best display of paintings, prints, sculptures, clothing, and crafts by local artists. Souvenirs with a Caymanian flair include handmade thatch brooms (some small enough to hang on a

Christmas tree), rosewood and purpleheart waurie boards used in a local marble game, Caymanian honey and preserves, rum cakes, and postcards and stationary with drawings of the local scenery, even underwater, by the shop's owner, **Debbie Van Der Bol.**

More significant mementos might include a lithograph called *Night Dive* by artist **Jan Barwick,** with a pastel, fantasy waterworld under a star-filled sky, or a copy of *In Our Own Write*, a collection of poetry and short stories by the Creative Writers Association

Cayman Islands

of the Cayman Islands. ♦ M-Sa 10AM-4PM (evenings by appointment). S. Church St (George Town-Bodden Town). 9.4433

30 **Sunset House** $$ The sunsets are particularly spectacular from the seaside deck of **My Bar** at this casual, friendly, low-key divers resort, one of the oldest hotels on the island. The original 1958 inn consisted of a wooden Cayman cottage and an eight-room addition; today the hotel has only 42 rooms in small, two-story cottages, all within one hundred feet of the water.

The simple peach-colored buildings have no more than a dozen rooms each, and are separated by lawns and palm trees. The waterproof and sandproof decor is more serviceable than picturesque, but the rooms do have air-conditioning and phones. Meals are served in a glass-enclosed dining room, but the favorite gathering spot is the bar, where sandwiches and snacks can be taken in with the view.

A limestone shelf extends from the hotel grounds over the water; stairs cut into the stone and ladders hung from the shelf give divers and snorkelers easy access to living reefs just offshore. The proximity to even larger reefs makes this a good spot for night dives—especially spectacular in the full moon. Most guests are divers on package plans, though the rates are very reasonable for non-divers. The dive shop (with four boats) and staff come highly recommended by scuba experts and publications in the US. ♦ S. Church St (George Town-Bodden Town). 9.7111, 800/854.4767

Within Sunset House:

Sunset Underwater Photo Centre

Professional underwater photographer, author, and teacher **Cathy Church** has a full-scale darkroom/classroom/rental operation here, with daily film processing, half-day, full-day, and week-long underwater-photography classes, and rental of high-quality cameras

and videos, including the Nikonos underwater camera. You can get a lot of tips on taking pictures underwater just by studying the incredible photos on the walls or by arranging for a photo buddy to go along with you on your dive. If you don't trust your photographic skills, you can purchase slides and prints taken by the pros. ♦ Daily 7:30AM-6PM. 949.7111; fax 9.7101

31 **Crow's Nest Restaurant** ★★★★$$ A veranda wraps around this traditional Caymanian house facing a secluded beach lined with palms and pines. All you can see from the road is a dirt parking lot and a quiet house, but walk around to the beach and there are tables draped in bright, tropical pinks, yellows, and blues on decks just over the sand. Listen to the Caribbean beat of Bob Marley or the Yellowbirds.

So popular it stays full even during the low season, the Crow's Nest does wonderful things with local flavors and seafood—spicy, deep-fried, coconut-battered shrimp with pineapple plum sauce; grilled swordfish with jerk mayonnaise; turtle steak with vermouth sauce. The grilled filet mignon with spicy jerk sauce is superb. Try to arrive before sunset, or take advantage of the sea view at lunch. ♦ Seafood/Caribbean ♦ M-Sa 11:30AM-2:30PM, 5:30-10PM; Su 5:30-10PM. South Sound Rd (George Town-Bodden Town). 9.9366

31 **Chef Tell's Grand Old House** ★★$$ Chef **Tell Erhardt,** a former television personality from Philadelphia, has created one of the most popular tourist restaurants on the island in a colonial-style plantation house by the sea. The screened veranda is the nicest spot for a candlelight dinner of crêpes, crab, and lobster. The ambience is more pleasing than the food. ♦ Seafood ♦ M-F 11:45AM-2:30PM, 6-10PM; Sa-Su 6-10PM. S. Church St (George Town-Bodden Town). 9.9333

32 **Bodden Town** The island's original capital, Bodden Town is named after Captain **Rayal Bodden,** a ship builder and architect who influenced much of Grand Cayman's development in the 1800s. Two cannons mark the entrance to the town, which sits at a good vantage point on a limestone bluff above the sea. A monument to Queen Victoria and a colorful cemetery overlook the water here. ♦ Bodden Town Rd (Pedro-Gun Bay)

33 **Cayman Diving Lodge** $$ Dedicated divers with little need for shopping and bar hopping are perfectly content at this small hotel far from the crowds in town. With only 15 air-conditioned rooms, the Lodge is the kind of place where guests and staff are on a first-name basis, sharing family style meals, playing cards on the communal patio, and exploring the underwater scenery along the shallow, horseshoe-shaped reef so close you can see it from shore. The Lodge is located at the **East End,** a quiet Caymanian community with far more churches than restaurants or bars. The water is equally uncongested, and divers have the opportunity to submerge themselves at more than one hundred dive sites along the **East Wall,** a nearly virgin territory where other boats rarely appear. ♦ Bodden Town Rd (Bodden Town-Gun Bay). 7.7555, 800/852.3483; fax 7.7560

33 East End The rugged coastline of the East End is pockmarked with caverns and caves, creating dramatic blowholes where geysers of sea water spray 60 feet into the air. Only one road runs along this part of the island, so it's impossible to get lost. East End was the first settlement on Grand Cayman. ♦ Bodden Town Rd (Bodden Town-Gun Bay)

34 The Lighthouse ★★★$$ This cobble-stoned lighthouse set on a solitary bench was taken over by **Roland Schoefer** and **Laurie Faust** in 1985 and transformed into a first-class restaurant that attracts discern-ing diners from all over the island. Chef Schoefer prefers to vary his offerings rather than work from a set menu, mixing West Indian cuisine—including the best conch fritters on the island—with German dishes such as sauerbraten and beef stroganoff. The oak tables are made of tree trunks, and the best seats in the house are at the banquettes along the screened windows overlooking the beach. The restaurant is about a 30-minute drive from George Town—a prohibitively expensive cab ride that costs more than a day's car-rental fee. ♦ German/West Indian ♦ Tu-Su 11:30AM-3PM, 6-10PM. Eastern Hwy (Bodden Town-East End). 7.2047

35 Cayman Kai $$$ Several varieties of villas and homes (called guest houses) are available as rentals at this 400-acre resort community on the island's quiet side. The nicest accommodations are in the **Garden Houses** on the beach and the **Island Houses** set in the landscaped gardens along a small cove. Some of the one-, two-, and three-bedroom houses have large screened porches and terraces; others are close to swimming pools; and all have full kitchens. The resort hosts a barbecue every Saturday evening. ♦ Rum Point. 7.9266, 800/336.6008; fax 7.9116

Grand Cayman's motto is "He hath founded it upon the seas."

36 Rum Point Considered by many to be the loveliest spot on the island, Rum Point pokes into the North Sound above **Booby Cay** on a limestone shelf nearly buried with needles from windswept Australian pines. Aqua-colored picnic tables dot the soft sand beaches, where crystalline water laps lazily on shore. A reef just offshore creates a natural wind-and-wave break so the bays are as calm as fish tanks. This is a wonderful spot for escaping the crowds.

Rum Point is bordered by an animal sanctuary and environmental-protection zone that helps

keep it unspoiled. There are a few hotels and resorts in the area, but many condos and private homes. Some snorkel and dive tours to Stingray City and the North Wall stop at Rum Point for lunch. ♦ East shore of North Sound

Within Rum Point:

Rum Point Club ★★★★$ This tiny take-out restaurant in a pine grove gets major points for ambience and attitude—about as tropically languid as you'll find anywhere on the islands. Reggae and calypso tunes play from an outdoor jukebox, regulars lounge about at the aptly named **Wreck Bar,** and first-timers spend as much time snapping photographs as eating their conch sand-wiches (which befits the situation, since the setting is far more pleasing than the cuisine). Flames flicker in oil lamps as day turns to night, giving the isolated point the feel of an undiscovered paradise.

If you've got wheels, spend a Wednesday evening at the weekly barbecue, but take care driving back to your hotel on the dark roads. It seems most of the island's expats and citizens gather here Sundays, away from the outsiders on the more tourist-oriented beaches; join them and you're likely to imagine staying forever. ♦ Daily noon-5PM. Wreck Bar: noon-midnight. Barbecue: W 6:30-9:30PM; F-Sa 6:30-9PM. 7.9059

Surfside Watersports The main office for this dive operation is down in George Town, and there's a boat leaving from the west side with the rest of the scuba flotilla. But the Surfside shop here on the point is a great launching spot for Stingray City, plus the sites along the North Wall, including **Tarpon Alley,** where you'll usually encounter several four-foot-long tarpon floating in a coral canyon. **Bob Carter,** the manager of the Rum

Point shop, is on a first-name basis with the eels and rays in the area, and is an expert underwater photographer, so bring your camera or rent one here. The divemasters and shop staff are amiable, amusing, and given to grinning at the slightest provocation—probably because they know they've got the dream jobs of a lifetime. Surfside also has a shop at **Indies Suites** (see page 13), one of the most popular dive-oriented hotels on Grand Cayman. ♦ Daily 7:30AM-5PM. 9.7330, 800/543.6828; fax 9.8639

Little Cayman

Ten miles long and only one mile wide, Little Cayman is a spit of limestone, coral, and salt marsh 70 miles northeast of Grand Cayman. More parrots and iguanas populate Little Cayman's nature reserve than there are sunbathers on its beaches. The island is more than 98 percent undeveloped, making it a refuge for rare native and migrating birds, including West Indian whistling ducks, which favor **Tarpon Lake**. People come to Little Cayman for refuge as well, and for spectacular diving and sportfishing. Anglers find tarpon and bonefish in abundance, while divers encounter virgin reefs and incredible drop-offs, especially at the dramatic **Bloody Bay Wall,** which plunges 1,000 feet below the surface and where visibility reaches 200 feet.

Civilization officially moved onto Little Cayman in 1990, when the island's 27 homes and businesses were illuminated by electric light. Until then, the residents (who now number somewhere around 20) used gas generators to power their refrigerators, ovens, and fans. Telephones arrived soon after—20 of them—replacing the four radios used to communicate with the outside world. Planes from the sister islands still land on a grassy airstrip, but the word is that condo and hotel developers are eyeing the island with lust. For now, there are precious few guestrooms on Little Cayman, but the islanders' generous hospitality makes up for the lack of luxury. And should these shores someday be overrun with tourists, there's always **Owen Island,** two miles out in the South Sound. The owners of Owen Island swear their 11-acre patch of sand and palm trees will never be sullied by civilization.

The Cayman Islands' flag incorporates the British flag and a white disc with the Cayman coat of arms, which was granted to the colony on 14 May 1958. The coat of arms consists of three green stars representing the islands, wavy blue lines for the Caribbean Sea, the lion of England for the motherland, a pineapple for the period when the Caymans were a dependency of Jamaica (then a British colony), a turtle for the national symbol, and a piece of rope for the islands' thatch industry.

Restaurants/Clubs: Red   **Hotels:** Blue
Shops/ ♣ Outdoors: Green   **Sights/Culture:** Black

20

37 Pirates Point Resort $$$ With only six rooms on five acres of beachfront property, Pirates Point feels like a private retreat. Owner **Gladys Howard** is a gourmet chef, which makes the all-inclusive rates a real bargain (the meals are superb). Diving and fishing trips are available, but not included in the rate. ♦ East of the lighthouse. 8.4210

38 Southern Cross Club $$ The largest resort on the island, the Southern Cross has 10 rooms on a thousand-foot-long white sand beach. When it opened in the 1960s, it was the first hotel on the island, catering to adventurous anglers and divers seeking absolute isolation. The large rooms were recently refurbished in bright whites and yellows, and are cooled by ceiling fans and sea breezes. Meals are included in the room rates; fishing and diving excursions are extra. ♦ S. Hole Sound. 8.3255, 317/636.9501(US)

39 Sam McCoy's Diving and Fishing Lodge $$ A family run operation devoted to diving, Sam McCoy's has six air-conditioned rooms, a duplex for small groups, and a cottage for families. The dive packages—with meals, air transfers, room, and diving included—are excellently priced, and the infamous **Bloody Bay Wall** is only a short boat ride away. ♦ North side of the island. 8.4526, 800/843.2177; fax 9.6821

Cayman Brac

Endangered Cayman parrots squawk in uninhabited woods and green sea turtles lumber to familiar beaches to lay their eggs in this natural paradise. Cayman Brac (89 miles northeast of Grand Cayman) is only 12 miles long and 2 miles wide, with a population of some 1,700 diehard Bracksters. In the spring a canopy of bright-orange royal poinciana tree blossoms seems to cover every road and trail, and rare orchids bloom beside mangoes and papayas. A few modern hotels and shops are clustered along the southwest side of the island near the international airport, and electricity, telephones, and satellite TVs are familiar commodities. But for the most part, the Brac remains classically, quietly Caymanian.

Bracksters tend to their yellow, pink, and white homes with care and devotion, planting periwinkles, bougainvillea, and palms in their sand yards, carefully raked of debris every day. Villagers gather to sweep and rake the cemetery every Saturday evening and to celebrate special occasions by cooking pots of coconut stew in outdoor kitchens called cabooses. Visitors tend to congregate along the southwest coast for the 50 or more spectacular dive sites. The north coast's limestone and coral beaches are best for beachcombing, while those near the hotels to the south are perfect for sunning and snorkeling. Once you've chosen to dive, swim, hike, or hang out in a hammock, you've pretty much made all your decisions for the day, which illustrates Brac's most endearing attribute—utter tranquillity.

40 Brac Reef Resort $$ Brackster **Linton Tibbets** combines the best of the island's culture, natural beauty, and hospitality with accommodations designed to captivate outsiders accustomed to certain luxuries. Air-conditioning was added recently to the 42 rooms, but it's far more romantic to open the windows and feel the sea breezes. The favorite gathering spot is a two-story, thatched-roof bar and deck at the end of a wood pier—though the pool and hot tub have their admirers as well. Caymanian specialties are a regular part of the restaurant's offerings, and are sometimes served buffet style on the beach. The resort has a full dive operation (called **Brac Aquatics**), with boats, equipment, and a luxurious dive boat for week-long trips to isolated reefs. ◆ Southwest tip of the island, about 3 miles west of the airport. 8.7323, 800/327.3835. Brac Aquatics: 813/932.1993 (FL), 800/458.2722

41 Divi Tiara $$$ A hideaway with creature comforts galore, Divi Tiara is first and foremost a diver's destination, though honeymooners find it idyllic as well. Expansions have transformed the Divi from a rustic inn to a full-scale resort with 58 air-conditioned rooms, satellite televisions, and telephones. Amenities include a freshwater swimming pool just off the white sand beach, tennis courts, a hot tub, and a restaurant and bar.

Naturally, the resort has a top-notch dive operation called **Dive Tiara**, with six high-speed boats and an underwater photo-and-video center called **Photo Tiara**. **Club Tiara**, a new addition to the complex, is a luxury timeshare-condominium setup. The resort is part of the Divi chain, with branches in Aruba, Barbados, Bonaire, and other Caribbean hot spots. ◆ Southwest side of the island, 3 miles west of the airport. 8.7313, 800/367.3584, 305/633.3484 (FL)

42 The Bluff The name Brac is said to be Middle English or Gaelic for bluff, referring to this 140-foot-high limestone plateau. Historians say the gray-white cliff must have been the first land **Christopher Columbus** spotted when he discovered the Caymans in 1503. It must have been a surprise, akin to finding a skyscraper in the Sahara. Pirates found its caves to be natural safe-deposit boxes for their loot; and today, treasure hunting and spelunking are popular pastimes for curious tourists. The Bracksters see the deep, solid caves far more practically as safe refuges from hurricanes and tropical storms. Wear sneakers or sturdy shoes when you climb about the bluff's slippery, steep paths, and stay away from the sheer cliffs to the north and south. More than 150 kinds of resident and migratory birds hang out on the bluff—dedicated birdwatchers can spot peregrine falcons and white barn owls. ◆ Northeast end of the island

Diving in the Deep

The Cayman Islands are to scuba divers what Disneyland is to kids, with the largest variety and number of dive sites of any Caribbean island. The Caymans have walls of extraordinary coral formations and more than 60 shipwrecks to explore, plus the water temperature stays a steady, comfortable 82 degrees and visibility is usually from 100 to 150 feet. As you dive among the sunken hulls, look for elephant-ear sponges and gorgonian fans flourishing in the coral gardens just a few feet from shore. Stingrays accustomed to human antics sometimes rub their silky underbellies against your body, while silvery barracudas with nicknames like Snaggletooth and Puff hover just out of touch. And then there are the French angelfish, creole wrasses, pufferfish, moray eels, spotted drums, peacock flounders, blue-striped grunts, eagle rays, and giant green turtles that pose for underwater portraits as if modeling for a tourist brochure.

Diving equipment can be rented on the islands, but if you've got your own gear, Cayman Airways allows three pieces of luggage per passenger to accommodate the big load. Hotels and resorts routinely offer packages with dive excursions, and more than two-dozen dive operators offer everything from beginner's certification courses to advanced deep-water diving, underwater-photography classes, and tips on diving among shipwrecks.

Grand Cayman's dive boats generally leave from Seven Mile Beach or the South Shore to sites just minutes away. Some companies have boats on the North Shore for trips to Stingray City and the North Wall. Most operators are members of the Cayman Islands Watersports Operators Association, which emphasizes safety, education, and conservation. There are decompression chambers and full medical emergency services on Grand Cayman, and the following businesses are some of the most established diving companies on this Cayman island:

Bob Soto's Diving 9.2022, 800/262.7686

Don Foster's Dive 9.8100, 800/833.4837

Eden Rock 9.7243

Parrots Landing 9.7884, 800/448.0428

Quabbin Dives 9.5597

Red Sail Sports 9.8745, 800/255.6425

Sunset Divers 9.7111

Surfside Watersports 9.7330, 800/543.6828

Treasure Island Divers 9.4456, 800/872.7552

Street vendors, called higglers by the locals, are outlawed on the Cayman Islands.

More than 250 permanent moorings have been installed along the coast of Grand Cayman to protect the coral reefs.

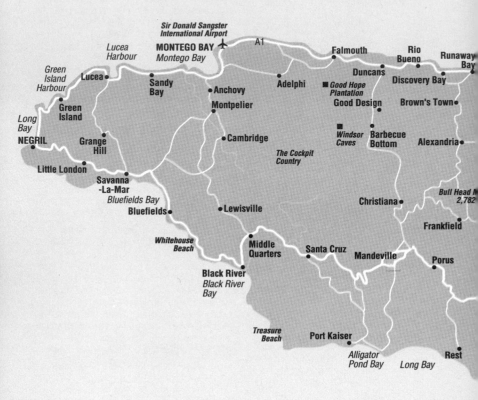

Sir Donald Sangster
International Airport

Lucea
Harbour

MONTEGO BAY ✈
Montego Bay

A1

Falmouth

Rio
Bueno

**Runaway
Bay**

*Green
Island
Harbour*

Lucea •

**Sandy
Bay**

Adelphi •

Duncans

Discovery Bay •

■ *Good Hope
Plantation*

**Green
Island**

Anchovy •

Montpelier

Good Design

Brown's Town •

*Long
Bay*

NEGRIL •

**Grange
Hill**

Cambridge •

*The Cockpit
Country*

■
*Windsor
Caves*

**Barbecue
Bottom**

Alexandria •

Little London •

**Savanna
-La-Mar**

Bluefields Bay

Christiana •

*Bull Head M
2,782*

Bluefields •

Lewisville •

Frankfield •

*Whitehouse
Beach*

**Middle
Quarters**

Santa Cruz •

Mandeville

Porus •

Black River
*Black River
Bay*

*Treasure
Beach*

Port Kaiser •

Rest

*Alligator
Pond Bay*

Long Bay

C a r i b b e a n   S e a

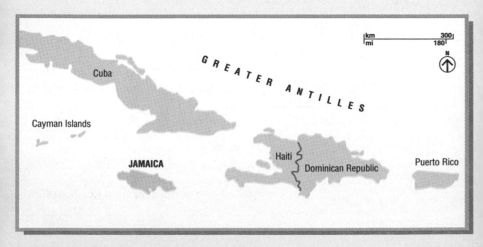

G R E A T E R   A N T I L L E S

km   300
mi   180

N
⊕

Cuba

Cayman Islands

JAMAICA

Haiti

Dominican Republic

Puerto Rico

Jamaica

Xaymaca (the land of wood and water) was the name given Jamaica by the gentle Arawak Indians who first inhabited this island. Rivers rush down the central mountains, feeding the rain forest and forming waterfalls and tributaries that turn the countryside green. Blooming tropical flowers provide vivid splashes of red, purple, yellow, and pink to the landscape. Add to this a blazing sun shimmering off the miles of white sand beaches and surrounding sea, and you have a dramatic canvas.

Jamaica is the third largest Caribbean island, and the people who live here are, for the most part, proud, opinionated, and fond of laughter. Their outgoing nature manifests itself in everything they do, from the street vendors who are among the most persistent on earth to the hotel waiter who introduces himself and shakes your hand, and the bartender who smiles and insists, "No mon, you don't want no scotch and soda. You try a Red Stripe. It's Jamaican beer, mon, the best in the world." Some tourists are taken aback by this gregariousness; others find it fun, interesting, and a memorable part of their island experience. If you feel hassled, just say so. Jamaicans expect people to speak their minds and respect those who do. Be clear, polite, and firm. Most likely, you'll be met with a smile and the response, "No problem, mon" (the words are virtually Jamaica's national slogan). Remember, tourism is the number one industry here; they want you to enjoy your stay and think well of their country.

Jamaica has three major tourist areas. **Montego Bay,** or "Mobay," as the locals call it, is the island's second largest city but the premier tourist destination. It's home to the **Great Houses,** grand plantation homes built during the 17th and 18th centuries; the **Marine Park,** a new underwater preserve for scuba divers, snorkelers, sailors, and windsurfers; and several championship golf courses. Mobay is also the starting point for a number of the most popular island tours, making it ideal for those who want great beaches, nearby sight-seeing, shops, and lots of nightlife without the complications of minibusing it to the resort towns of **Ocho Rios** or **Negril.** If you want to see museums and art galleries, take one of the day-long tours offered in the resort areas to **Kingston.**

Ocho Rios is the fastest growing resort area, with an active cruise port, duty-free shopping centers, and a number of straw-and-craft markets. Jamaica's newest deluxe resorts can be found along Ocho Rios' dramatic northern coastline. Horseback riding, golf, and sight-seeing excursions are popular daytime activities, as the beaches here tend to be small and water sports are best enjoyed in the mornings, when the sea is calm. An hour-and-a-half-long drive east on the northern coastal road will take you to **Port Antonio,** an out-of-the-way resort town where relaxing is a time-honored art.

True beach and water-sports lovers should consider Negril, an adult haven with a "kick off your shoes, anything goes" attitude. It's far away from the maddening crowd, with seven miles of spectacular beach and a sunset that sets the clouds afire with color. By law, no building in Negril is taller than the town's tallest palm tree. There are few modern distractions and not much sight-seeing nearby—which seems to suit the hippies turned Yuppies who flock here just fine.

As you choose among these destinations, keep in mind that Jamaica is the king of all-inclusive resorts. They took Club Med's method of operation and improved upon it a thousandfold. All-inclusive on this island means just that: upscale rooms, all meals and snacks, wine, bar drinks, water and land sports, nightly entertainment, taxes, tips, and airport transportation for one set price. It's a way of vacationing that is catching on throughout the Caribbean, but Jamaica still does it best.

Kingston, the seat of government and a business hub, is off the tourist track. Jamaica's largest and most populated city suffers crime and poverty rates that are much higher than in the tourist areas. Kingston is also the center of political unrest, whenever it occurs. Jamaicans are zealous about their politics and demonstrations can sometimes get out of hand.

Reggae music is another Jamaican passion, celebrated every summer (usually in July or August) at **Reggae Sunsplash,** one of the world's premier music festivals. Whether you're dancing to the rhythm of a reggae band or hiking through a rain forest, the best way to enjoy yourself on the island is to relax and adopt the Jamaicans' unofficial motto: "Don't worry, be happy." Then learn the word *irie* (pronounced *eye-ree*), which means "everything's okay," and believe it.

Getting to the Island

Airlines

Air Canada	800/776.3000
Air Jamaica	800/523.5585
American Airlines	800/433.7300
Continental	800/231.0856
Jamaican Express (from California)	408/452.0475
Jamaican Shuttle (from Orlando, FL)	800/526.2422
Northwest	800/225.2525

Airports

Donald Sangster International Airport Unless you're going to Port Antonio, try to fly nonstop into this Montego Bay airport. This way you won't waste precious beach time sitting on the tarmac in Kingston. To reach the airport, call 952.3801.

Norman Manley International Airport For information about this Kingston airport, call 924.8361.

Smaller airports are located in Negril, Ocho Rios, and Port Antonio. **Trans Jamaican Airlines** (952.5401/3) is the island's main air taxi, with daily flights between Jamaica's five main towns. Their planes, however, range from a small, single-engine plane to an 18-passenger aircraft; if you're easily unnerved, ask which plane is flying before you book a reservation, or stick to ground transportation.

Getting around the Island

Buses

Riding on a bus is an experience most tourists prefer to skip. The buses are old, uncomfortable, and crowded—not only with people, but also with luggage, crates of vegetables, and boxes of squawking chickens.

Car Rentals

In Kingston:

Avis	924.8013
Budget	924.8762
National	929.9190

In Montego Bay:

Avis	952.4543
National	952.2769

In Negril:

Vernon's Car Rental	957.4354

In Ocho Rios:

Avis	974.2641
Budget	974.5617
National	974.2266

In Port Antonio:

Eastern Car Rental	993.3624

Driving

Renting a car is a good way to get around if you can abide by the rules of the road. To begin with, you must be able to drive on the left, British style. Jamaicans like to get where they are going; they drive fast and will pass you at every opportunity. Driving at night between towns is not a good idea. If the car breaks down, you may well be stuck until morning. Or you may be deluged with well-meaning locals who swear they can fix anything mechanical. The roads are good, but they're filled with sharp curves and often have potholes, and wandering cows, goats, and chickens have the right of way. DO NOT rent a moped or scooter unless you have a large life-insurance policy or are interested in checking out the island's medical facilities. And leaving your car unlocked is akin to giving away whatever belongings you leave in it.

River Rafting

Thanks to the cleverness of actor **Errol Flynn,** who lived in Port Antonio, river rafting has become a popular Jamaican pastime. Flynn saw the sleek bamboo rafts carrying produce down the river and envisioned both a fun sport and a romantic excursion. Some say Flynn rafted down the river twice a day, each time with a different lady. The 26-foot-long rafts are built for two and are steered and poled like a gondola by a skilled "captain." The rafts drift toward the sea, passing cars backed into the river for washing, cavorting children, and hawkers selling fresh coconut juice. You can swim from the raft, bring a picnic lunch, be regaled by the captain's tales, or just hold hands while floating down the river. The best and longest rafting trip is on the Rio Grande.

The two-and-a-half-hour **Rafting on the Rio Grande** (993.2778) trip begins at Rafter's Rest in St. Margaret's Bay (15 minutes west of Port Antonio). Near Montego Bay is the one-hour-long trip on the **Martha Brae** (952.0527), offered by **Mountain Valley Rafting** (952.0527). As night begins to fall, torches light the way for an **Evening on the Great River** (952.5047/5097), which ends at a re-created Arawak Indian village where you're served dinner and drinks while being entertained by fire-eaters and a steel band. If you're staying in Ocho Rios, try the 45-minute trip down the White River with **Calypso Rafting** (974.2527). There's also an **Evening on the White River** (974.2619) with torches, dinner, and a show.

Taxis

The cabs range from modern, air-conditioned minibuses to beat-up old station wagons. If airport transfers are not included in your hotel package, take a **JUTA** (Jamaica Union of Travelers Association) cab if you're not going far. The fixed rate sheet isn't strictly adhered to, so be sure to agree on the fare before getting into the cab. Plan on spending $7 to $14 to get to the hotels in either Montego Bay or Kingston, and about $60 to get to Ocho Rios or Negril from Montego Bay, or to Port Antonio from Kingston. For more information about JUTA taxis, call 952.0813 in Montego Bay.

If you're headed away from Montego Bay (and not in a rush), you can save money by purchasing your seat from the **Tropical Tours** desk just outside the Donald Sangster International Airport's luggage area. The only drawback to their $16-per-person charge is that the minibus won't leave until it's at least half full.

Jamaican cabbies are friendly, patient, and often informative tour guides. Most will hire out for half a day, with rates running about $25 an hour.

When eating out in Montego Bay, call ahead; a number of restaurants in town offer free pick-up and drop-off cab service.

Jamaica

Tours

Jamaica's great diversity of landscapes lends itself to an incredible variety of tours. You can raft along a river, horseback ride into the hills, travel by train into the interior, hike into the Blue Mountains, take a jitney through a working plantation, or climb a waterfall (see "Dunn's River Falls" on page 36).

For a bird's-eye view of the island, contact **Helitours Jamaica Ltd,** in Ocho Rios at 974.2495 or in Kingston at 929.8150.

Sight-seeing, city, and shopping tours can be arranged through **Greenlight Tours** (in Montego Bay, 952.2200; in Ocho Rios, 974.2266; in Kingston, 929.9190), **CS Tours** (in Montego Bay, 952.6260; in Ocho Rios, 974.5934), **Tourwise Ltd** (Negril, 957.4223), and **JUTA** (Port Antonio, 993.2684).

Special-interest tours that focus on Jamaica's folk art, gardens, plantation houses, and exotic birds are offered by the **Touring Society of Jamaica** (952.9188). **South Coast Safaris** (962.0220 or 965.2513) offers photographic safaris, guided boat tours up the Black River, and fishing expeditions.

FYI

Money

The official currency is Jamaican dollars, but American money is accepted everywhere. In fact, many stores, restaurants, and cab drivers will quote you prices in American dollars. Banks are open M-Th 9AM-2PM; F 9AM-noon, 2:30-5PM. Some banks also are open Saturday mornings.

Personal Safety

Most of the crime in the tourist areas are crimes of opportunity, meaning theft. In an effort to curb this problem, the government has beefed up its police foot patrols. Use the same precaution you would at home: Don't wander down dark streets at night or leave personal belongings unattended on the beach and packages in open view on the front seat of your car—even if it's locked. Use the vault at your hotel to store your valuables. And if you choose to swim in a deserted cove, don't hang your bathing suit over the nearest tree to dry; it will likely disappear.

Jamaicans are to the Caribbean what New Yorkers are to the United States. The vendors will hound you with their goods, drive a hard bargain, and exasperate you with their persistence. Relax. If you want to buy something, bargain like mad, walk away, come back, and play the game. It's part of the Jamaican experience. If you want to be left alone, politely and firmly say "No" and keep walking.

Beware of the young men who insist you need a guide to walk with you around town. They expect a tip. If you feel harassed, remind them you are a tourist and they are giving you a bad impression of their country. This line almost always works because Jamaicans know how important tourism is to their economy.

It's unsafe to walk Kingston's streets at night. In fact, unless you're on a guided tour or need to be in Kingston for business, stay out of this city; it has the highest crime rate in Jamaica.

Ganja is marijuana, and it's grown on the island. If you're male, and between the ages of 18 and 50, you'll likely be asked if you want to buy some. It's illegal, but tourists are rarely bothered by the Jamaican police, especially in Negril. Smoking marijuana is prohibited on the street or in a public place, and expect to be arrested by the Jamaican authorities if caught importing or exporting even the smallest amount.

Phone Book

Ambulance 110
Directory Assistance...114
Fire 110
Police 119

Area code 809 unless otherwise noted.

1 Rick's Cafe ★★$$ College students flaunt their immortality by overimbibing and jumping from the cliffs into the sea more than a hundred feet below. Drinks and music flow and the time to see and be seen is about an hour before sunset, for this combination restaurant/bar pays homage to the setting ball of fire in a manner that's part pagan, part absurd, and all fun. ♦ West Indian/Seafood ♦ Daily noon-10PM. Lighthouse Rd. Dinner reservations recommended. 957.4335

2 West End Road Narrow, winding, and part dirt in places, this road is lined with cottages, small hotels, restaurants, and shacks selling T-shirts, straw hats, wooden sculptures, and Rasta berets. Ganja (marijuana) is sold openly, but no one should trouble you if you aren't interested. Several drum chicken stands sell jerk-seasoned chicken and pork. It's safe to eat, but watch the hot sauce, as even locals refer to it as "hellfire." **Archway Cafe** (★★$) serves pizza, while **The Hungry Lion** (★★★$) serves wonderful vegetarian shepherd's pie and steamed kingfish.

3 Charela Inn $$ For those who want to à la carte it, this is a good and reasonably priced alternative to the better-known all-inclusive hotels. Quiet and peaceful, it's on the beach, with an excellent on-premises restaurant and a circular pool set amid a garden. There's also a water-sports complex on the beach for sailing, diving, and windsurfing. Enjoy the family style hospitality. It's small, with only 39 rooms. ♦ Norman Manley Blvd. 957.4277, 800/423.4095

4 Swept Away $$$ This new and impressive couples-only oasis is geared toward fitness-and-health-loving duos. The big draw here is their 10-acre sports complex, with 10 tennis courts (clay, hard, and stadium), air-conditioned squash and racquetball courts, a state-of-the-art gym, a basketball court, and an outdoor jogging track. You're encouraged to improve your game by taking advantage of the free daily half-hour individual lessons offered by the resident pros.

A water-sports shack on the beach offers snorkel trips, sailing, and windsurfing—all with instruction. There's also scuba, with guests granted one free dive a day; however, the unaccommodating schedule is unusually frustrating.

The property is divided by Negril's main road, with the sports complex on one side and the accommodations and main body of the resort on the beach. The 130 veranda suites are tastefully minimalist in decor, with screened, wood-louvered walls, king-sized beds, terra-cotta tiles, and showers big enough for two. The enormous verandas double as sitting, breakfast, and sunning rooms. Noise addicts beware: there are neither TVs nor radios. Seekers of privacy, however, will probably feel uncomfortable in the ground-floor atrium rooms unless they keep the louvers angled at half mast—cutting down both the view and the light.

Both restaurants, as well as the beachside veggie-bar, feature health-oriented cuisine, with an emphasis on homemade pasta, fresh seafood, poultry, and Jamaican dishes. Several of the bars offer top-shelf liquor, while

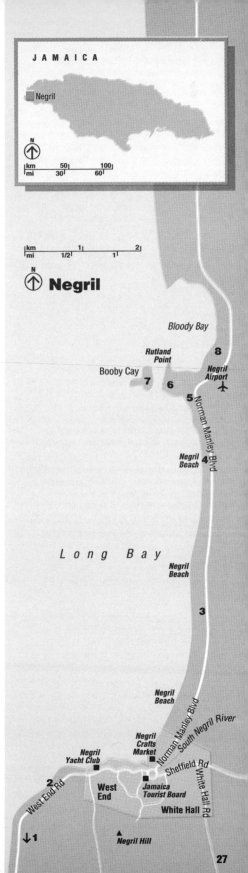

others offer carrot and fresh fruit juices. Their one-price-covers-everything policy makes this the vacation getaway for aging baby boomers who want to stay fit and young forever. ◆ Norman Manley Blvd. 957.4040, 800/526.2422

5 Sandals Negril $$$ Still the most romantic all-inclusive property in Negril, this couples-only resort is set amid lush foliage on Jamaica's largest stretch of private beach. Hammocks sway beneath the palm trees, while Jacuzzis just the right size for two are surrounded by high hedges. Classical music can be heard just as the setting sun turns the sky aflame with color. Casual is the

Jamaica

byword here, meaning a neat pair of shorts and a cotton shirt are fine for dinner.

Singalongs around the piano bar follow the nightly cabaret shows, but the real emphasis here is on water sports. Glass-bottom boat tours, waterskiing, snorkeling, scuba diving, sailing, windsurfing, and even aquatrikes built for two are included in the one-price-covers-all package. There are also tennis courts, two pools, a health club, shuffleboard courts, and a special croquet lawn. To top it off, there are exercise classes, plus daily activities that range from Pictionary contests to reggae-dance lessons. The 199 rooms are spacious and decorated in a soothing blend of salmon pink and forest green. (The bi-level suites are the most spectacular.)

There's also an offshore island for clothing optional sunbathing. Couples seeking a perfect mix of privacy, group activities, and fun will find it here. ◆ Norman Manley Blvd (Rutland Point). 957.4216, 800/726.3257

6 Hedonism II $$$ This hedonistic haven is true to its name, with a private stretch of sand on the five-mile beach of Long Bay. The 280-room resort was Jamaica's original answer to Club Med, but better executed. Anything goes at this free and easy, upscale sleepaway camp for adults only. Singles flock here, meals are mostly buffet style, and the action continues round the clock. The beach is divided into nude and prude, with each section equipped with its own bar. The disco hops all night and only closes when the last person either leaves or passes out. Head here for fun, every land and water sport you can think of except golf (horseback riding and even a circus workshop are included), and a vacation so casual that if you lost your luggage, all you'd need for the week is a bathing suit. ◆ Rutland Point. 957.4200, 800/858.8009 (US), 516/868.6924 (NY), 800/553.4320 (Canada)

Restaurants/Clubs: Red   **Hotels:** Blue
Shops/ 🌳 Outdoors: Green   **Sights/Culture:** Black

7 Booby Cay Kayak or motor launch over to this small offshore island popular with nude sunbathers and snorkelers. Several higglers have set up shop beneath the thatched tiki huts. Butterflies dance and flit over the verdant foliage and bathers disperse to find a patch of private sand. Several scenes from *Twenty Thousand Leagues Under the Sea* were filmed here. ◆ Free. Rutland Point, between Sandals Negril and Hedonism II

GRAND LIDO

8 Grand Lido $$$$ Here is the only hotel on **Bloody Bay,** a misnomer, as the two-mile crescent is unspoiled and backed by an impressive strand of palm and sea-grape trees. (The bay got its name from whalers who butchered their catch in these waters a long, forgotten time ago.)

The **SuperClubs** resort is geared toward burnt-out professionals age 30 and up, with pampering the agenda of the day and a one-price-covers-all policy. Accommodations are all bi-level junior suites housed in two-story Mexican-style buildings stretched along the beach. The rooms are a little dark until you open the French doors leading to the terrace or patio. Then sunlight fills the living room area, with its remote-controlled color TV and stereo cassette deck. Request whether you want a king-sized bed or two doubles. The *M/V Zein,* a former Onassis yacht, sits at anchor in the bay. Grand Lido guests can be married aboard (weddings are free), or take a sunset cruise.

The crowd is international and everything at this 200-room resort is top shelf, from the liquor to the white-gloved waiters at the gourmet restaurant. Dress ranges from chic casual to a required jacket at the **Piacere,** one of their four restaurants. The kitchen never closes and room service runs 24 hours. There's also a knock-out midnight buffet. (Late nights are standard here, with the nightly entertainment beginning at 10:30PM.) Amenities include two pools, five Jacuzzis, four tennis courts, a complete water-sports facility, a state-of-the-art fitness center, a plush video theater, a beauty salon, a disco, and numerous well-placed bars. There's a nude beach, but it's not private, and it's in an area where the sea is rocky.

The only drawback is that half the accommodations are built too close to the water-treatment plant across the road, and the smell (which varies with the direction of the wind) is definitely not upscale. On the plus side, the service is good and, since the property is spread out, there is never a feeling of being part of a crowd. ♦ Bloody Bay. 957.4010, 800/858.8009 (US), 516/868.6924 (NY), 800/553.4320 (Canada)

ANNIE KOOK

9 Rocklands Feeding Station Bird lovers and aficionados of the unusual flock to naturalist **Lisa Salmon's** sanctuary in Anchovy. Salmon regales her visitors with stories while Doctor Bird hummingbirds sip sugar water from her hand-held eyedropper. If you choose to participate, finches will alight on your hands to peck at the cupped birdseed. Be punctual, bring a camera, and wear lots of mosquito repellent. Children must be over the age of five. If you're not familiar with the roads, take a cab, it's hard to find. ♦ Admission. Daily 3-5PM. Anchovy, turn left onto Rte B8 south of Montego Bay. 952.2009

10 Julia's ★★★$$$ Splurge at this romantic enclave high in the hills overlooking the bay. The excellent Italian fare, Continental atmosphere, and spectacular view from the terrace make this a three-way winner. There are prix fixe six-course dinners, as well as an à la carte menu chock-full of favorites such as chicken cacciatore, red-snapper Française, and homemade pasta. Free transportation to and from your hotel is provided. Take them up on it as this restaurant can be tricky to find on your own. ♦ Italian ♦ Daily 6-10:30PM. Bogue Hill. Reservations required. 952.1772

11 Appleton Express Jeremy McConnell has put together this popular all-inclusive, day-long train tour through Jamaica's heartland. Historical trivia can be heard over a loud-speaker as the train rambles up into the hills. The bar car, serving free rum drinks, is the most popular place to sit, but also the most smoke-filled. The first stop is **Cadupa,** where children will greet you, their arms laden with wooden birds and straw placemats. The adults follow with bolts of brightly patterned cotton and polyester and samples of clothing that can be sewn to your measurements by the time the

train returns late in the afternoon. It seems preposterous, but order away with peace of mind. Better yet, bring along a dress or shirt you like, pick out some cloth, and let the clever seamstresses and tailors duplicate it.

A few drinks later, the train stops at **Ipswich Caves,** where there's an awe-inspiring limestone "cathedral" replete with formations that look like monks at prayer. Hawkers line the path leading to the caves, and it's a good place to bargain for sculpted wood birds, crocodiles, fish, and fruit. Lunch—a generous helping of curried goat, barbecued chicken, callaloo, jerk pork, and peas and rice—is held

in the rum-tasting lounge of the **Appleton Sugar Factory and Distillery.** A tour of the rum-processing facility follows. It's a good place to stock up on the famous Appleton Rums, although you may find better prices at the airport's duty-free liquor store. Make your reservations early, as the train only runs four times a week. ♦ Tu-F 8:30AM-4:30PM. Howard Cooke Blvd. Reservations required. 952.3692

12 Pier 1 ★★$$ This casual waterfront restaurant, popular with businesspeople, tourists, and yachting folk, is a good place to sip a tropical drink. Lunch is served on the outside deck, dinner upstairs in a classier setting overlooking the marina. Late Friday nights, this is the hottest spot in town, with dancing and music on the pier deck. Free transportation is arranged for diners. ♦ Seafood/West Indian ♦ M-Sa 10AM-midnight; Su 3-11PM. Disco: F 10PM-5AM. Howard Cooke Blvd, across from downtown Craft Market. Reservations recommended. 952.2452

13 Craft and Straw Market Rows of narrow stalls overflow with straw baskets, placemats, hats, and coasters, as well as T-shirts, swimsuit cover-ups, children's clothing, wooden carvings, dolls, and shell jewelry. The market bustles with shoppers and higglers—the local name for hawkers of merchandise. They are crafty, unlikely to sell you an item below the price they have in mind, and view the bargaining process as a game. ♦ M-Sa 8:30AM-5PM (some stalls open Su). Harbour St (Market St). No phone

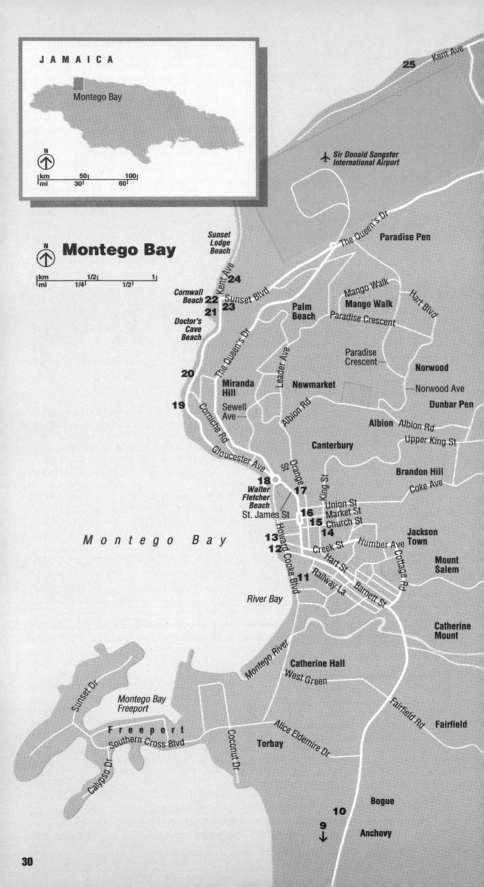

JAMAICA

Montego Bay

N

km 50 100
mi 30 60

N
Montego Bay

km 1/2 1
mi 1/4 1/2

25 Kent Ave

✈ *Sir Donald Sangster*
International Airport

The Queen's Dr

Sunset Lodge Beach

Kent Ave

24

Cornwall Beach 22
21

Doctor's Cave Beach

23 Sunset Blvd

The Queen's Dr

Leader Ave

Palm Beach

Mango Walk

Mango Walk

Paradise Crescent

Hart Blvd

Paradise Pen

20

19

Miranda Hill

Sewell Ave

Corniche Rd

Gloucester Ave

Albion Rd

Newmarket

Paradise Crescent

Norwood

Norwood Ave

Dunbar Pen

Albion Albion Rd

Upper King St

Canterbury

Brandon Hill

Coke Ave

18
Walter Fletcher Beach
St. James St

Orange St

17

16
15

King St

Union St
Market St
Church St
14

Humber Ave

Jackson Town

Cottage Rd

Mount Salem

M o n t e g o   B a y

13
12

Howard Cooke Blvd

Creek St

Hart St

11

Railway La

Barnett St

River Bay

Montego River

Catherine Mount

Montego Bay Freeport

Sunset Dr

Catherine Hall

West Green

Fairfield Rd

Fairfield

F r e e p o r t
Southern Cross Blvd

Coconut Dr

Alice Eldemire Dr

Torbay

Calypso Dr

Bogue

10

9 ↓

Anchovy

14 St. James Parish Church Built in 1775 to resemble a Greek cross, this Anglican edifice was badly damaged by the 1957 earthquake. It has since been restored and is one of Jamaica's most impressive places of worship. The building is only open to the public on Sunday, but the exterior architecture is of interest. ◆ Su service 11AM. St. Claver St (Church St). 952.2775

15 Gallery of West Indian Art Load up on unique holiday gifts for your friends at this small gallery. Owner **Liz Delisser** has collected the island's best hand-carved, hand-painted art. Animals carved from cedar and painted in gay colors and whimsical patterns greet shoppers from every shelf, tabletop, and window ledge. Purple-whiskered lions share space with red polka-dotted parrots and green-and-yellow striped angelfish. The walls mimic this carnival of color with canvases from top Jamaican and Haitian artists. The biggest plus of all: the prices are downright reasonable. ◆ M-Sa 9AM-5PM. 1 Orange St (Church St). 952.4547

16 Sam Sharpe Square House slave and part-time preacher **Sam "Daddy" Sharpe** is credited with starting the slave uprising known as the Christmas Rebellion of 1831. Sharpe's last words before he was hanged were, "I would rather die on yonder gallows than live as a slave." The revolution, albeit short-lived and bloody, started a chain of events ended seven years later with the abolition of slavery in Jamaica. In the northeast corner of the square is a tableau of five bronze statues: Sharpe preaching to a group of followers. Formerly called **The Parade,** the Sam Sharpe Square serves as a popular meeting spot. ◆ Gloucester Ave (Market St)

16 The Cage Constructed in 1806, this building once held runaway slaves. Today it houses the **Premier Tour Office.** ◆ St. James St (Market St)

16 Jamaican Tourist Board Their "Meet the People" program, which is free and extremely well organized, is the best way to experience the real Jamaica. Tourists are matched with Jamaicans by hobby, profession, interest, or just to meet a family. "The people in our program don't want anything except for you to have a good time and feel welcome," explains **Mrs. Hyacinth Ford,** the founder of Meet the People. "It's a way to come to Jamaica and leave with a friend." If you're interested in getting to know some Jamaicans, contact the board at least three days in advance. If you're simply curious about what the island has to offer, the office is a great place for information and brochures. ◆ Kent Ave (Cornwall Beach). 952.4425/8 (call in the afternoon and ask for Mrs. Ford)

17 Jenny's Citimart Pick up a supply of sauces and condiments to season your food back home, Jamaica style. Try the Picka-pepper, Hot Pepper (better known as "hellfire"), Scott's Jerk, or Gray's Spicy sauces. There are also marmalades, Blue Mountain coffee, pimento liquor (for marinating meat), and Busha Browne's spicy tomato-and-love-apple sauce. ◆ M-Sa 9AM-5PM. St. James St (CitiCenter Shopping Centre). 952.3313

18 Boonoonoonoos Beach Party Reggae-music lovers flock to this Friday night bash held on **Walter Fletcher Beach.** It's a tourist trap, but a velvet-lined one. The $34-per-person charge entitles you to a three-course Jamaican dinner; all-you-can-drink rum punch, Red Stripe beer, or soda; and a floor show that every Caribbean visitor should see at least once, the highlight of which is a torch-eating, fire-breathing dancer. Be sure

to bring your camera. ◆ F 7-11PM. Walter Fletcher Beach (Gloucester Ave). 974.2619 (ask for Carl Young)

19 Pelican Grill ★★$$ For more than 25 years the Pelican has remained one of Mobay's most popular dining spots. Business folk crowd in around noon; tourists and locals for dinner. The menu is a mix of Jamaican favorites, including escovitched fish (flavored, then sautéed with vegetables and sauce), curried goat, and American staples such as cheeseburgers and milk shakes. The adjacent **Pelican Cascade Room** (★★★$$) is a bit more expensive, but the seafood specialties and plush atmosphere are well worth it. It's open daily for dinner. ◆ West Indian/American ◆ Daily 7:30AM-11:30PM. Gloucester Ave, south of Corniche Rd. Dinner reservations recommended. 952.3171

20 Marguerite's by the Sea ★★★$$$ Dine on a terrace beneath the fronds of an almond tree and a canopy of Caribbean stars. The hills across the bay twinkle with lights, while the water laps at the terrace. The sophisticated menu includes the best smoked-marlin appetizer in town, fresh fish, Caribbean lobster, and several chicken specialties. Light jazz in the background gives way to a trio of musicians after 8PM. Free transportation to and from most hotels is provided for guests. ◆ Continental/West Indian ◆ Daily 6-11PM. Lunch, cocktails, and late-night supper 11AM-11PM at **Marguerite's Beer Garden.** Gloucester Ave (Belvedere Beach). Dinner reservations recommended. 952.4777/3290

Restaurants/Clubs: Red   **Hotels:** Blue
Shops/ ☂ Outdoors: Green   **Sights/Culture:** Black

21 Doctor's Cave Beach Mobay's most famous stretch of sand was once owned by **Dr. Alexander McCatty,** who helped promote the curative powers of sea water. He donated the beach to the town as a bathing club in 1906. It's now open to the public and is popular with local families, as well as with the tourists who are staying at the hotels across the street. While it may not cure gout, the crystal clear sea is both pleasant and placid. There are changing rooms, a snack bar, and a beach bar. ♦ Admission. Daily 9AM-6PM. Gloucester Ave, across from the Beach View Hotel

Jamaica

22 Mobay Night Out Every Monday evening, a part of Gloucester Avenue closes to traffic and becomes a rollicking street party. Come early and come hungry. Sample jerk chicken, meat patties, Ting orange soda, and the omnipresent Red Stripe beer. The sidewalks come alive with vendors, portrait artists, jugglers, costumed dancers, and tourists with cornrow braids in their hair.

This freebee is co-sponsored by the Jamaica Hotel Association and the Tourist Board. Mento (one of the oldest forms of Jamaican folk music) and steel bands enliven the crowd, locals show tourists how to dance to reggae, and the revelers party until midnight. ♦ Free. M 6PM-midnight. Gloucester Ave, between Jack Tar Village (Sunset Blvd-Kent Ave) and Pelican Grill. 952.4425/8

23 Pork Pit ★$ Easy on the wallet, this shaded outdoor restaurant is a good place to try a typical Jamaican lunch. Munch on spicy jerk pork or jerk chicken with sweet potatoes and rolls and wash it all down with a Red Stripe beer. Whatever meat you don't eat is eagerly swooped up by the resident egrets, while the pigeons make short order of the crumbs. ♦ Jamaican ♦ Daily 11AM-11PM. Gloucester Ave, diagonally across from Jamaican Tourist Board. No phone

Cuba: Hot Topic in the Tropics

With the release of *The Mambo Kings* in 1992, Cuba was reborn in the eyes of many Americans who viewed the country as nothing more than the home of Castro, Communism, and cigars. Images of a sensuous, flamboyant culture inspired many Americans to visit **Havana** and **Varadero,** cities officially designated "off-limits" by the United States State Department.

As long as **Fidel Castro** is in power, advises the federal government, Americans should not travel to Cuba. However, if you haven't the patience to wait for political change, it is possible to make a side trip to Cuba from Jamaica or the Bahamas (it's not illegal). Furthermore, many travel aficionados say it's safe. In fact, Canadians and Europeans have been vacationing on the island for decades.

Before 1959, Cuba was a popular tourist destination for Americans, who were lured by its beaches, mountain ranges, and fertile plains rich with sugarcane and tobacco. Cuba's culture is likewise compelling, and its Spanish ties in particular are reflected in the hearty cuisine and breathtaking colonial architecture, especially in Havana.

Before Castro came to power, Havana was considered the Caribbean version of Paris, the City of Light, with its wide, tree-lined boulevards and legendary nightlife. Even after more than a quarter century of Communism, Havana's Old World charm prevails in **Habana Vieja** (Old Havana), a square mile of palaces, plazas, and cobblestoned colonnades. One can easily imagine how a potent dose of capitalist entrepreneurism could restore this once vibrant city to its prerevolutionary splendor.

Varadero, another premier port of call, offers a wide selection of hotels, most of which are run by Span-

iards or Jamaicans. The city's 12-mile-long stretch of beach, 80 miles east of Havana, is the country's best and most popular resort area, with a wide variety of water sports and nightclubs.

Many people visit Cuba by hooking up with a tour company that takes care of getting you in and out of the country without complications and provides you with a thorough itinerary. **Caribic Vacations** (952.5013) offers three-, five-, and seven-day trips from Jamaica to Havana and Varadero. Prices start at $270 a person, depending on the hotel you choose and the length of your stay, and include airfare, a city tour, and breakfast and dinner every day. **Sun Holiday Tours** (952.4585) also flies groups from Jamaica to Santiago de Cuba every Wednesday for about $200. The price includes airfare, lunch, a visit to a sugarcane distillery, a tour of the city, and time for shopping and sight-seeing. You can also fly from Jamaica to Cuba on your own via **Cubana Airlines;** just make sure you have a tourist card, which is available from a tour operator or the Cuban consulate in Kingston.

From Nassau on New Providence, you can book two- or six-night tours to Havana through **Havana Tours** (328.0908); prices start at less than $300 per person for the two-day trip (including airfare, hotel, and breakfast).

When travel between Cuba and the United States becomes more accessible, a number of Caribbean-based cruise ships plan to add the port of Havana to their itineraries. Americans might even be able to fly to Cuba via Miami before the turn of the century; seminars in both the United States and Cuba are already addressing prospective problems for visitors, such as how to manage the anticipated crowds of tourists.

24 **Sandals Inn** $$ This all-inclusive, couples-only resort is tailored for twosomes who are on a somewhat restricted budget, yet enjoy the intimate atmosphere of a small inn. There are lots of activities and sports, but the beach is public and across the street. The big plus here is Sandals' "stay at one; play at all" policy. You can just hop on the free shuttle to Sandals Montego Bay to enjoy that resort's new Oriental restaurant, **Tokyo Joe's,** or the private beach and racquetball court.

The Inn's three-story, Great House design is built in a horseshoe around the lobby, a courtyard, and the pool. There are also a gourmet Jamaican restaurant, a small fitness center, and lighted tennis court on the premises. Cabaret shows are held outdoors. All the rooms were recently refurbished in a tasteful melange of sea-blues, pinks, and greens. The only difference between the standard and deluxe categories is the view. Ask for a room above the first floor. ◆ Kent Ave, a few blocks north of the Pork Pit. 952.4140, 800/726.3257

25 **Sandals Montego Bay** $$$ Hotelier Gordon "Butch" Stewart has worked his all-inclusive magic on six couples-only resorts in Jamaica. His concept is simple: Adam and Eve didn't need pockets in paradise, so why should guests visiting Sandals?

Literally everything is included in the one-price-covers-all package, from meals to bar drinks and tips. In fact, the only extra charges are for trinkets purchased at the gift shop, telephone calls, and cigarettes. This 243-room resort is geared toward discriminating couples who want to be pampered by outstanding service, yet prefer to wear shorts and a cotton shirt to dinner. It's perfect for those who want a festive vacation.

The amenities include restaurants, a disco, a late-night piano bar where everyone gets to sing along, a swim-up pool bar, and a first-rate fitness club that's open around the clock. Water sports are emphasized here, particularly scuba diving, windsurfing (with land trainers), aquatrikes, waterskiing, and glass-bottom boat rides. Their beach is the largest private stretch of sand in Montego Bay. "Playmakers" lead guests in a variety of activities, from pool volleyball to reggae-dancing lessons and toga-tying for weekly toga nights (sheets are provided, and there's absolutely no pressure to participate). There's also nightly entertainment followed by dancing. (Escapists can retreat to one of several secluded hammocks built for two.)

The only drawback to this resort is its proximity to the airport. When planes land or take off, the roar of the plane drowns out conversation. (At orientation, all couples are told that a Sandals tradition requires them to kiss each time they spy a plane. It's amazing how many couples cooperate.)

All of the rooms are decorated in soft tropical colors and feature king-sized beds, clock radios, color TVs, safe-deposit boxes, hair driers, air-conditioners, and ceiling fans. The 15 standard-category rooms are noisy and lack balconies. The best rooms for the money are the recently renovated deluxe-category rooms. ◆ Deluxe ◆ Kent Ave. 952.5510, 800/726.3257

26 **Sandals Royal** $$$ Here is an all-inclusive, 190-room resort that features a European atmosphere and an international crowd. It's quieter than sister resort Sandals Montego Bay but is likewise geared toward couples (singles and children are not allowed) looking for a low-key, sportive getaway. The genteel setting is lavish with well-tended gardens, a generous crescent of beach, and peacocks that stroll onto your terrace. The soft peach and aqua rooms feature king-sized beds, color TVs, air-conditioning, hair driers, safe-deposit boxes, telephones, and clock radios. The nicest and most sumptuous are the 60 oceanfront suites.

The meals served here are movable feasts. One night they're offered in the main dining room, another on the beach, and a third on an elegant patio beneath almond trees aglow with string lights. Buffets are held several times a week. And then there's the **Bali Hai** restaurant, for authentic Indonesian cuisine. Guests are also welcome to dine, for free, at any of the other Sandals resort restaurants; a minivan provides free transportation. (All sports, meals, drinks, taxes, tips, and airport transfers are included in the price.)

You can go scuba diving (lessons and the use of equipment are free), play tennis, burn calories in an aerobics class, or take a launch over to their private island for an afternoon of nude sunbathing. Golfers receive free green fees and transportation to the nearby 18-hole, par 72 **Ironshore Golf and Country Club.** ◆ Deluxe ◆ Mahoe Bay. 953.2231, 800/726.3257

27 **Holiday Inn** $$ If you shop by brand name, you won't be disappointed here. While this 516-room hotel isn't Jamaican in feel or atmosphere, it does make Americans feel right at

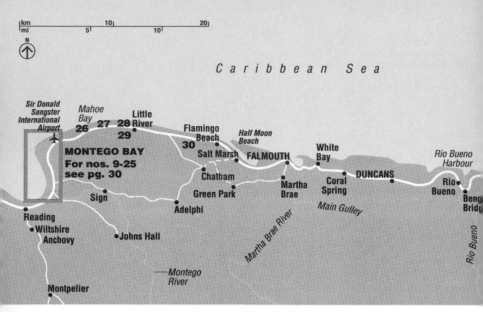

MONTEGO BAY
For nos. 9-25
see pg. 30

home. It's especially popular with singles and with corporate incentive or convention groups who want a lot to do and no surprises. The nonstop round of activities ranges from limbo contests to crab races. A video room keeps the kids happy while parents relax on the reconstructed beach that was destroyed by **Hurricane Gilbert** several years ago. Other amenities include four lighted tennis courts, nightly entertainment, a lagoon-style pool, and a complete watersports center. The on-premises restaurants provide something for everyone, and there's a shopping complex just across the street.
♦ 480 Rose Hall. 953.2485, 800/465.4329

28 Half Moon Golf, Tennis and Beach Club

$$$$ Classic elegance awaits guests of this sprawling country-clublike resort. The center is a colonial Great House with clusters of villas spread out on each side. The villas feature kitchens with stocked refrigerators, wide terraces, enormous bathrooms, and a tasteful mixture of Old World and modern decor. Facilities include a beautiful beach, two main pools, 17 semiprivate pools shared among the villas, four squash courts, a sauna, a comprehensive watersports center, and 13 tennis courts (seven of which are lighted for night play). Of special note is the 18-hole **Robert Trent Jones** championship golf course and clubhouse. And there are several good restaurants here, including the excellent **Sugar Mill.**

This hotel has been the vacation getaway of royalty, politicians, and celebrities. The vast amount of space ensures lots of privacy. Peace and quiet reign here, rather than action, loud music, or high-energy evening activities. The evenings are dressy, especially in the winter season. Everything here is à la carte, unless you purchase the all-inclusive package called the **Platinum Plan.**
♦ Deluxe ♦ Coastal Rd, 7 miles east of Montego Bay. 953.2211, 800/237.3237

29 Rose Hall

Reputedly haunted by its husband-murdering mistress, this restored Great House looms over sprawling grounds and looks out to the Caribbean Sea. According to the tale, **John Rose Palmer** inherited the mansion from his magnate uncle and in 1820 brought his wife, **Anne,** here to live. Anne purportedly dabbled in black magic, poisoned her husband, tortured and bedded her slaves, and became feared as the White Witch of Rose Hall. At the age of 29, she supposedly was strangled to death by a slave lover, and her ghost still inhabits the house. The tale of love, lust, and murder is, in itself, worth the price of admission. Afterward, sip a Witch's Brew in **Anne's Pub** (formerly the dungeons). ♦ Admission.

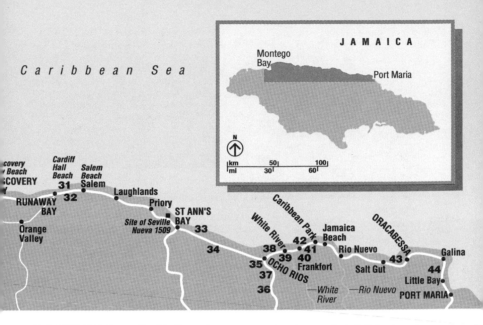

Daily 9AM-6PM. Queens Dr, 10 miles east of Montego Bay. 953.2323

30 Greenwood Great House and Antique Museum This plantation house once belonged to a cousin of the English poet **Elizabeth Barrett Browning. Sir Richard Barrett,** a wealthy sugar baron, built Greenwood in 1790, intending to entertain guests here (a testament to the elegance and extravagance of plantation life in the 19th century). The antique treasures include an inlaid rosewood piano and a mantrap used for catching runaway slaves. Some of the books in the Barrett family's original library date back to 1697. ◆ Admission. Daily 9AM-6PM. Coastal Rd, near Trelawny-St. James Parish line. 954.2470, ext. 183

31 Jamaica Jamaica $$$ This all-inclusive **SuperClubs** resort prides itself on offering guests an immersion into all things Jamaican. The emphasis here is on sports, entertainment, and social interaction—a plus, as this resort draws a good number of single guests. The 234 rooms and four suites—none of which have TVs—are basic and clean, but nothing to write home about. The beach, however, is wide and inviting; heaven for sports enthusiasts. A section of it is designated for nude sunbathing.

Jamaica Jamaica's **Golf Academy** is an intensive program with professional instruction, video presentations, swing analysis, lectures, daily play at the nearby 72 par **Runaway Bay Golf Club,** and on-premises putting and driving ranges. Tennis buffs receive equal attention, with one-on-one instruction, video analysis, and four lighted courts for night play. Beach cricket, soccer, reggae dancing, and patois lessons are likewise on the agenda. Other activities include relaxing horse-and-buggy rides, shuttles to Ocho Rios and Dunn's River Falls, and horseback riding. The meals tend to emphasize Jamaican cuisine, and everything you can think of is included. Children under the age of 16 are not allowed as guests. ◆ Runaway Bay. 973.2436/8, 800/858.8009 (US), 516/868.6924 (NY), 800/553.4320 (Canada)

32 FDR Resort $$ Also known as **Franklyn D. Resort,** this new all-inclusive resort is one of the top places on the island for families with children. It's geared toward an upscale market, with all-suite accommodations ranging from one to three bedrooms. The spacious suites offer a master bedroom, kitchen, and living room (with a pull-out sofa bed). Best of all, each suite comes with a "Girl Friday" (always a woman) who arrives at 9AM, leaves at 4:30PM, and is at your service as a nanny, cook, housekeeper, and kitchen stocker. For a slight charge, she'll even babysit in the evenings.

The daily activities program for children and teens runs the gamut from arts and crafts to volleyball, a petting zoo, a playground, and a miniclub with video games. Other amenities include an alfresco restaurant and beach grill, several bars, a lighted tennis court, a pool, a fitness center, an evening piano bar, and a discotheque.

There's no beach at this Mediterranean villa-style hotel, but it's only a short walk to the nearby public sands. To get there, however, you have to pass by the **Jamaica Jamaica** resort's nude beach, which, depending on your point of view and the age of your kids, may offend your sensibilities.

Jamaica

The rates include a Girl Friday, all meals, airport transfers, a glass-bottom boat tour, a shopping trip to nearby **Ocho Rios,** land and water sports (including scuba diving), nightly entertainment, and courtesy rounds of golf at **Runaway Bay Golf Club.** Children under 16 stay free in their parents' suite. ♦ Runaway Bay. 973.3067, 800/654.1337

33 Sandals Dunn's River $$$ Sandals Resorts poured a lot of money into renovating this property, which used to be Eden II. The overall effect is Italian Renaissance, with an open-air lobby that flows onto a piazza shaded by almond trees. The accommodations are all stylish, comfortable, and aesthetic; the decor is a pleasing melange of turquoise, emerald, peach, and mauve. One highlight is their ultramodern spa/fitness center, open to the sea breezes, with massage rooms upstairs, sauna and steam rooms built for two, and a Roman-style hot tub and cold plunge pool. A high-energy activities schedule with everything from power walking to body sculpting and yoga is offered daily.

The resort is located on the beach, but guests tend to loll around the huge free-form pool, currently the largest in Jamaica. Like its sister resorts, this is an all-inclusive property for couples only, with a complimentary massage and a tour of **Dunn's River Falls** thrown in for good measure. Facilities include a water-sports center (with scuba diving, snorkeling, waterskiing, kayaking, glass-bottom boats, and windsurfing), tennis courts, a pitch-and-putt golf course, and four restaurants (Oriental, Continental, Jamaican, and Italian). This is the newest and priciest of the Sandals resorts. The focus is on healthy vacationing with lots of hedonistic trimmings. ♦ Dunn's River, a few miles west of Ocho Rios. 972.1610, 800/726.3257

A small bird called the Jamaica tody makes its nest in a hole in the ground. Also known as the robin redbreast (not to be confused with the robin redbreast of England), this particular tody is found only in Jamaica.

34 Dunn's River Falls These famous falls are featured in virtually all the Jamaican ads and brochures. They're a must-see attraction, for where else can you literally climb up a 600-foot-high waterfall and return with photographs to prove it? This get-wet experience (there's no escaping the water) calls for old sneakers or scuba boots. First you walk from the top of the falls (where there are lockers for rent) down the stairs to the bottom, where the cascades meet with the sea. From here, the falls look like a tiered wedding cake.

Guides lead groups of people safely back up the water falls. If you're not with a group, just latch on to one by giving the last person in line your hand. The guides are glad to hang your camera around their necks, take your picture under the falls, and show you the placid pools and sliding rapids. Just be sure to give them an American dollar or two per person as a tip (and they do accept wet money). ♦ Admission. Daily 9AM-5PM. Dunn's River. No phone

35 Shaw Park Botanical Gardens Tranquillity—and usually not many tourists—can be found in these tropical gardens, located on a ridge in the hills overlooking Ocho Rios Bay. Roam past a tumbling waterfall, whispering streams, giant banyan trees, and ponds covered with water lilies to gardens filled with flamboyant chenille plants, bougainvillea trees, and hibiscus. Exotic flowers such as the bird of paradise and torch ginger also can be seen on the 25-acre grounds. ♦ Admission. Daily 9AM-5PM. Milford Rd, south of Ocho Rios, on the road to Fern Gully. 974.2723

36 Fern Gully Nature has turned this old river bed into a tunnel with a roof made of the interlocking leaves and branches of the tall trees and more than 550 varieties of ferns. The river bed is now part of the road leading from Ocho Rios to Kingston, so if you're going to the capital, your car will be encompassed in a cool verdant world for three miles. ♦ Rte A3, on the road to Kingston

37 The Enchanted Garden $$$ As Jamaica's prime minister, **Edward Seaga** developed the grounds of his family estate—a 20-acre botanical paradise filled with orchids, ferns, palm trees, and more than a dozen waterfalls—and opened it to the public. The estate (then known as the Gardens of Carinosa) is once again private, having been turned into the new all-inclusive hillside retreat named, appropriately enough, The Enchanted Garden.

The resort gets a fair mix of both singles and couples (children under the age of 16 are not allowed). The all-suite accommodations are modern oases of comfort; 40 of them even have their own plunge pools. Of special note is their spa, which offers guests a complimentary massage, facial, manicure, and pedicure.

Nature blends with the exotic here, with Jacuzzis built next to waterfalls and afternoon tea served under an Indian tent. Five restaurants offer specialties ranging from French to Lebanese to Thai. The one-price-covers-all policy includes meals, wine, bar drinks, nightly entertainment, tennis, green fees (and transportation to the golf course), horseback riding, taxes, tips, and airport transfers—ideal for nature-loving landlubbers. You can even get married in the garden for free. ◆ Deluxe ◆ Eden Bower Rd. 974.5346, 800/654.1337 (US), 516/223.1786 (NY)

37 Evita's ★★★$$ Northern Italian cuisine is served with a generous helping of spectacular view from the terrace of this authentic 1860 gingerbread house nestled on the hillside overlooking Ocho Rios Bay.

Brochures and waiters brag that this is the best little pasta house in Jamaica. It's certainly in the Top 10 for good service, consistent quality, and creative dishes, as well as longtime favorites. Try the snapper stuffed with crabmeat, fettuccine Carib-Alfredo or rigatoni *ai fruitti di mare*. Children under 12 eat for half price. Be sure to say hello to **Eva,** for whom the restaurant is named. She's from Venice and can converse with diners in English, Italian, French, German, and Spanish. ◆ Italian/Seafood ◆ Daily 11AM until the last guest leaves. Mantalent Inn, Eden Bower Rd (just below The Enchanted Gardens resort). Dinner reservations recommended. 974.2333

38 Jamaica Grande, A Ramada Renaissance Resort $$$ By November 1992, this resort—actually a combination of the old Mallard Beach Hotel and its next-door neighbor, the Americana Beach Resort—should be in full swing. A $20 million renovation is underway to turn the new megalith into Jamaica's largest resort, with 720 rooms and suites, as well as the most extensive convention and meeting facilities on the island. When completed, the resort will boast a plethora of fitness and entertainment facilities, five restaurants, seven nightclubs and lounges, and a fantasy pool with cascading waterfalls, a suspension bridge, and a rock grotto. There are already plenty of activities for every member of the family, with a supervised program for the kids, plus a water-sports center, health club, tennis courts, nightly entertainment, and on-premises shops. ◆ Main St. 974.2201, 800/228.9898

38 The Acropolis The locals outnumber the tourists at one of Ocho's hottest discotheques. The ambience is mellow, everyone dances, and you don't need a partner to get on the dance floor. Sunday is Reggae Night, Thursday is Ladies Night (free admission for women), and weekends the place rocks until the wee hours. ◆ Admission. W-Su 9PM-closing. 70 Main St, top floor of Mutual Security Mall. 974.2633

38 Double V ★★$ Step around the side of this roadside diner to see how the seasoned meat is cooked upon racks of allspice wood. The portions are hefty in size, easy on the wallet, and come with roasted yams and a sweet roll. This is, without a doubt, some of the best jerk pork and jerk chicken in Ocho Rios. ◆ Jamaican ◆ Daily 11AM-11PM. 109 Main St. 974.5998

Ciboney

38 Ciboney, a Radisson Villa, Spa and Beach Resort $$$$ Nestled in the hills overlooking the sea, the 264 villas and Great House of this ambitious new all-inclusive resort provide a blend of privacy and pampering in an upscale atmosphere where guests are treated like royalty. Each villa comes with a female attendant who will unpack your bags, iron your clothes, prepare and serve your breakfast, stock your bar and refrigerator, and even have cold drinks and a fruit platter waiting after your afternoon set of tennis. All you have to do is let her know what you'd prefer and, like a personal genie, she'll do her best to please.

The modern villas were designed with comfort in mind—spacious bathrooms, living rooms with remote-controlled TVs and VCRs (movies can be borrowed at the concierge desk), private balconies or patios, and private swimming pools. Open-air jitneys shuttle guests between their villas, the Great House (where all the action is), and the beach. All guests receive a complimentary Swedish massage, foot reflexology, back and neck

Jamaica

rub, manicure, and pedicure in the ultra-modern, Grecian-style spa and health club.

One of the four excellent restaurants on the premises even serves a spa menu, but with the free-flowing piña coladas and wicked dessert trays there's no way you will lose an ounce unless you sweat it off in the steam room or on the air-conditioned squash and racquetball courts.

Tennis aficionados will find six courts, plus free daily clinics, while golfers can play at two nearby courses (green fees and transportation are included in the rate). There's also a watersports center, but it's not up to the standards of the rest of the resort and the scuba operation is far from top-notch. Both pools have swim-up bars, and joggers will enjoy the well-maintained track. Overall, this is a good choice for couples, families traveling with children over the age of 16, and singles who want the plush atmosphere of an elegant resort with the activities and nightlife of an all-inclusive. ♦ Main St. 974.1027/5600, 800/333.3333

38 Sandals Ocho Rios $$$ Babbling brooks and manicured gardens interlace the grounds of this 237-room Italian masterpiece, where seashell-pink buildings are linked by lighted and landscaped walkways. Hammocks strung between the palm trees await duos in search of a little R&R. Mood music flows over the massive courtyard from ground speakers, and somehow the whole resort seems to flow to this romantic and serene orchestration.

The accommodations are spread among two-story garden villas and a five-story waterfront high rise. There are three restaurants, plus a beach bar and grill that transforms into an outdoor disco by the sea each night. Drinks are available at the piano bar, the swim-up bar, or at the other regular bars. There's a new show every night, plus several theme evenings such as Toga Night and Pirates Night, with guests encouraged to wear fun costumes.

As with her sister resorts, all meals, snacks, wine, bar drinks, water sports

(of which there are plenty, including sailing and scuba diving), tennis, land activities, entertainment, taxes, tips, and airport transfers are included in the price. Still new, beautiful, and run with excellent service, this remains a great choice for young-at-heart couples of all ages. ♦ Deluxe ♦ Main St. 972.1610, 800/726.3257

39 Calypso Rafting Venice has gondolas and Ocho Rios has bamboo rafts that drift down the **White River** (see "River Rafting" on page 25). River rafting is a relaxing way to fritter away an hour or so and a good way to experience a slice of Jamaica. ♦ Admission. Daily 9AM-5PM. Coastal Rd, east of Ocho Rios (turn right at the Flynn Texaco gas station and follow the billboards). 974.2527

40 Prospect Plantation See how Jamaica's crops are grown on this working agricultural property and learn how they are important to the economy. You'll get a closeup view of the banana, sugarcane, pineapple, and coffee fields from the seat of a motor jitney while a tour guide regales you with a slew of interesting farm anecdotes. Guests who are comfortable in the saddle can tour the plantation by horseback. There are three different guided trails to explore, with saddle time ranging from one to two-and-a-half hours.

For those who just want a diversion, stop in for a game of miniature golf—it's Jamaica's first (and so far only) putt-putt course. ♦ Admission. Jitney tours: M-Sa 10:30AM, 2PM, 3:30PM (children under 12 free). Horseback riding: M-Sa by appointment; call one hour ahead. Miniature golf: 9AM-3:30PM. 974.2058

Pirates Anne Bonny and Mary Read plundered and pillaged their way through the Caribbean before they were captured in 1720. On trial in Jamaica, they both avoided execution by telling the judge they were pregnant (English courts did not have the power to kill an unborn child, no matter how guilty the mother).

41 Harmony Hall A gingerbread-trimmed Victorian mansion turned art gallery features the work of some of Jamaica's top artists and artisans. The second room holds regular exhibits. Thanks to liberal customs laws, you can buy all the Jamaican art you want without having to pay a duty tax on it. The famous Annabella boxes made out of wood and crafted to hold all sorts of trinkets; hand-embroidered cushions; brightly painted ceramics; jewelry made from shells, leather, and beads; and small steel drums are among the temptations. Watercolors, drawings, and oil paintings cover the walls and shelves of Jamaican herbs, spices, and marmalades sit near the cash register. ◆ Free. Daily 10AM-6PM. Main St, 4 miles east of Ocho Rios (on road to Oracabessa). 974.4222

Within Harmony Hall:

Harmony Hall Restaurant ★★$ Dine alfresco beneath a white-lattice overhang in a garden-alcove setting. The Jamaican lunch special, a delicious sampler of red-snapper escovitch, ackee and codfish, rice and peas, and assorted vegetables is filling, well made, and reasonably priced. They also offer curried shrimp piquant and a memorable Appleton rum cake. A *mento* band entertains nightly after 7PM. Free transportation is provided to and from area hotels. ◆ West Indian ◆ Daily 11AM-10PM. Dinner reservations recommended. 975.4478

42 Couples $$$ The original all-inclusive, couples-only resort allows no singles or children. Much needed renovations have brought this property back up to par with its competition. Pluses include a private island for nude sunbathing (no bathing suits or cameras allowed), a new ultramodern fitness facility, horseback riding, and three new restaurants.

Part of the **SuperClubs** chain, this resort is ideal for young sportive couples who want round-the-clock activity. You can sail, scuba dive (or learn with their resort course), play golf (green fees and transportation are included), play racquetball or squash, or participate in the high-energy activities rang-

ing from hat weaving to aquacise and beach volleyball.

The service is not as efficient as at Sandals, but when you're so busy it may not matter. The energy continues at night, with a different show each evening followed by dancing, and then singing around the piano bar. There's a choice of restaurants, but all of them seat two or three couples at the same table to encourage socializing. Couples who want to marry can do so for free here. ◆ Tower Isle. 974.4271, 800/858.8009 (US), 516/868.6924 (NY), 800/553.4320 (Canada)

43 Boscobel Beach $$$ Another all-inclusive **SuperClubs** resort, this one is ideal for families traveling with children. The accent is on fun for everyone, with lots of extras for both tots and adults. Most of the property is child-proof, with sturdy furniture the order of the day. There's an extensive, supervised mini-club for infants and young children, and another for preteens and teens. Sports, computer games, picnics, donkey rides, movies, arts and crafts, and a separate disco keep the kids happily entertained.

Adults enjoy scuba diving, golf, tennis, the beach, and an activities program designed just for them. There are three restaurants, two pools, a fitness center, several bars, and a piano lounge. Up to two children under the age of 14 stay free in their parents' room. ◆ Coastal Rd, 10 miles east of Ocho Rios. 974.3330, 800/858.8009 (US), 516/868.6924 (NY), 800/553.4320 (Canada)

44 FireFly Writer **Noel Coward's** former home is still tended with loving care by his former housekeeper turned tour guide, **Immogene Fraser.** The house sits atop a hill a thousand feet above **Blue Harbour,** commanding a spectacular view of the mountains, hills, and sea. It is purported to have been the lookout spot of **Sir Henry Morgan,** the pirate who later become governor of Jamaica. Coward wrote his only novel, *Pomp and Circumstance* here. He entertained often, and his guest list reads like a *Who's Who* of Hollywood. Errol Flynn came, as did Laurence Olivier, Vivien Leigh, Mary Martin, Katharine Hepburn, and David Niven. He is buried on the grounds just above the view he loved. ◆ Admission. Daily 9AM-4PM. Port Maria, 3 miles west of Oracabessa. No phone

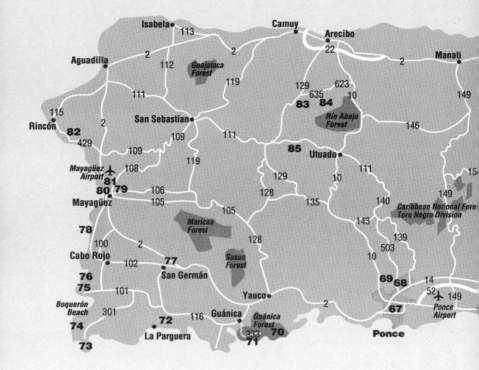

Atlantic Ocean

Isabela • 113   Camuy   Arecibo

Aguadilla   2   112   Guajataca   2   22   Manati
                          Forest
                    119   2

111   129   623
                          635   10   149
Rincón   115   San Sebastián   83   84
82   2   Río Abajo
429   109   109   111   Forest
Mayagüez   108   119   85   Utuado   146
Airport   81
80 79   106   129   10   111   15
Mayagüez   105   128   140   149
                          135   Caribbean National Fore
78   105   Toro Negro Division
100   2   Maricao   143
Cabo Rojo   102   Forest   128   139
76   77   Susua   503   10
75   101   San Germán   Forest   69 68   14
Boquerón   301   Yauco   52   149
Beach   72   116   Guánica   67   Ponce
74   La Parguera   Guánica   333   Airport
73   Forest   70
                    71   Ponce

Caribbean   Sea

N
↑

km   20   40
mi   10   20

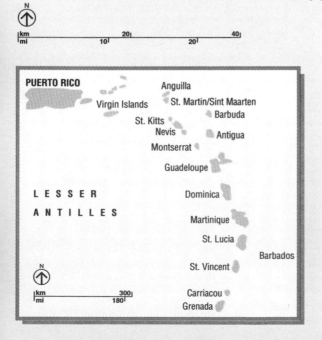

PUERTO RICO   Anguilla
        Virgin Islands   St. Martin/Sint Maarten
            St. Kitts •   Barbuda
            Nevis   Antigua
        Montserrat •
            Guadeloupe

L E S S E R   Dominica
A N T I L L E S
                Martinique
                St. Lucia
                        Barbados
        N   St. Vincent
        ↑
        km   300   Carriacou •
        mi   180   Grenada

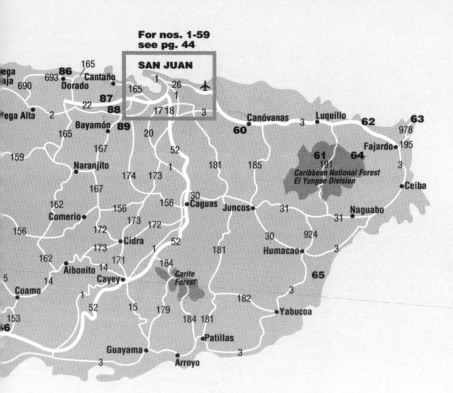

For nos. 1-59
see pg. 44

Puerto Rico

Wherever Puerto Ricans are gathered, expect to hear some political debates, as they're very serious about local politics. More than 80 percent of the voters go to the polls every year, an unusually high amount for any country or state. Puerto Rico is a commonwealth of the United States and is made up of a proud population of people whose interests in politics stem from a 1950s government program that made the standard of living on the island higher than in any of its Latin American neighbors.

The island was deeded to the states after the **Spanish-American War** in 1898, and Puerto Ricans were granted American citizenship in 1916. Up until 1950, island governors were appointed by the United States government. In 1951 Puerto Rico elected its first native-born governor, **Luis Muñoz Marín**, whose innovative **Operation Bootstrap** program brought industrialization and wealth to the island. His party, the **PDP** (Popular Party), has remained in power almost exclusively since then, and Muñoz Marín is still revered as a national hero.

41

Located at the eastern end of the **Greater Antilles,** the island measures roughly one hundred miles east to west and 35 miles north to south. The **Cordillera Central** mountain range, which reaches heights of more than 4,000 feet above sea level, dominates the middle of the island. Miles of pristine beaches grace the coastline, facing the Atlantic Ocean in the north and the Caribbean Sea in the south. The mountain towns depend on agriculture (coffee and some tobacco) for income while the low-lying areas support the manufacturing (rum, textiles, and sugar) industry.

Puerto Ricans regard the Spanish language as a part of their culture, and it's the country's official language. However, both the government and large segments of the general population fear the loss of the language through the increased use of English.

Climate is Puerto Rico's crowning jewel. It's warm year-round, with an average temperature of 77°F. Daytime temperatures are generally in the 80s; nighttime temperatures hover around the 70s. The seasons are subtle, with rainy weather from May through November and low humidity throughout the rest of the year.

Puerto Rico

For the past quarter of a century, tourism has helped shape the development of the island. The **San Juan** area, mainly the **Condado** and **Isla Verde** strips of beaches, hotels, and casinos, is the most popular destination. **Old San Juan,** a preserved section of the city harking back to the Spanish conquistadores, draws millions of tourists yearly. The *paradores/puertorriqueños,* a chain of government-owned-and-operated country inns, offer clean and efficient lodging at moderate prices in the mountains or by the sea.

Puerto Rico was originally called **Borinquen** by the Tainos, the South American tribe that first settled on the islands, and it became known as San Juan after **Christopher Columbus** landed here in 1493 on his second trip to the New World. **Ponce de León,** who led the Spanish settlers to the island, saw the *puerto rico* (rich harbor) in the San Juan Bay and, hence, the city's name was born. Later the settlement became known as San Juan, and the island inherited the name Puerto Rico.

Area code 809 unless otherwise noted.

Getting to the Island

Airlines

Aeropostal	721.2166
American Airlines	800/433.7300
British Airways	800/247.9297
Canadian Airlines International	800/426.7000
Delta	800/221.1212
Iberia	800/221.9741
Lacsa Airlines	724.3330
Lufthansa	800/645.3880
Mexicana Airlines	800/531.7921
Trans World Airlines	800/892.4141

Airports

Isla Grande Airport The airport located on Isla Grande (Large Island), a strip of land jutting out in San Juan Bay between Puerta de Tierra and Santurce, was once part of the United States Navy base. Today it's used for general aircraft and privately owned planes, although a few small commuter airlines make their headquarters here. The 5,000-foot-long runway and air-traffic control tower accommodate large aircraft, but no jets. Call 724.3376 for additional information.

Luis Muñoz Marín International Airport Located in the San Juan metropolitan area, this is the island's primary airport, servicing all major airlines. Call 791.4564 for more information.

Inter-Island Carriers

Air Jamaica	800/523.5585
Airport Aviation Service	791.0969
BWIA International	800/327.7401
Dominicana	724.7100
Isla Grande Flying School	722.1160
Ponce Air Charter	791.8370
Sunaire Express	800/595.9501

Getting around the Island

Car Rentals

Avis	791.2500
Budget	791.3685
Dollar	791.1870
Hertz	791.0840

Charter Buses

Angelo Tours	784.4375
Borinquen Tours	725.4990
Gray Line Sight-Seeing	727.8080

Ferry Service

Ferries leave daily every half hour from 6AM to 9PM from Old San Juan to Hato Rey and Cataño.

Ferries depart from Fajardo to Vieques and Culebra daily. The fare is $2 for adults and $1 for children.

Limousines

Airport Limousine Service	791.4745
Bracero Limousines	740.0444
Cordero Limousine Services	799.6002
Dorado Transport Corporation	796.1214

Taxis

Major Taxi Cabs	723.2460
Rochdale Radio Taxi	724.3232

FYI

Hospitals

Ashford Memorial Community Hospital	721.2160
Carolina Health Center	750.8000
Children's Hospital Guaynabo	783.2226
Hato Rey Community Hospital	754.0909
Medical Center	754.3535
Metropolitan Hospital	793.6200
San Juan Health Center	725.0202
San Pablo Hospital Bayamón	740.4747
Teachers' Hospital	758.8383

Phone Book

Civil Defense	724.0124
Coast Guard	729.6770
FBI	754.6000
Fire	343.2330

Poison Control	754.8536
Police	343.2020
Red Cross	759.7979
United States Marshal	729.6780
Unites States Secret Service	766.5339

Publications

The English-language *San Juan Star,* a Scripps-Howard daily, commands a large readership, while the Spanish-language *El Nuevo Día* and *El Vocero* are the two most popular dailies. *Caribbean Business,* an English-language weekly, is widely read within the business sector. *Claridad,* the "voice of independence," is published monthly. Tourist publications include *Qué Pasa,* a government monthly, and *Sunspots. Imagen* and *Caras* are monthly magazines devoted to fashion.

San Juan

San Juan is really composed of two cities. The popular Old City, a seven-square-block area that has preserved the flavor of Old Spain, is steeped in more than five centuries of Spanish history and architecture, whereas metropolitan San Juan is a growing amalgam of old and new sections: **Puerta de Tierra, Miramar, Santurce, Condado,** and **Isla Verde.**

Puerta de Tierra serves as an entryway to Old San Juan. History envelops the massive limestone and sandstone **City Wall** that belts the ancient city. **La Fortaleza,** the home of the governor, was originally built as a fortress in 1540 to protect against marauders (a purpose it failed to fulfill). The **San Juan Gate,** north of La Fortaleza, stands as a unique opening in the City Wall. Autos seem out of place going through this great wooden portal wrought in 17th-century Mediterranean style. From its narrow cobblestoned streets, Spanish architecture, ancient churches, and artsy shops and galleries to its harbor views, Old San Juan is a living museum.

1 San Felipe del Morro Fortress In its heyday more than 300 years ago, this fort that rises 140 feet above the sea protected the city. Today it's protected by the National Park Service. El Morro's (*morro* means "headland") 16-foot-thick walls overlook the Atlantic, providing one of the great views on the island. The cannons, sentry boxes, and tunnels hark back to the 16th century. The vast field, once used as a small golf course, is traversed by all kinds of people out for a walk in the park. The land actually covers a system of mining tunnels that was constructed in the 1500s.

Attacks on San Juan were commonplace during the 16th and 17th centuries, the most famous antagonist being English navigator **Sir Francis Drake.** El Morro and San Cristobal were instrumental in keeping the island under the Spanish flag. El Morro was last under siege in 1898, when the Americans pounded it with shells. The orientation and slide programs are available in Spanish and English. ♦ Free. Daily 9:15AM-6PM. Calle Norzagaray. 729.6960

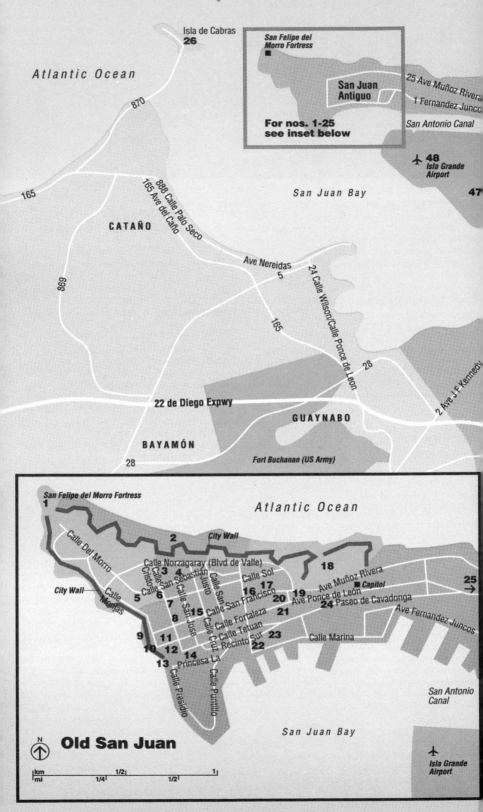

Isla de Cabras
26

Atlantic Ocean

870

San Felipe del
Morro Fortress ■

San Juan
Antiguo

25 Ave Muñoz Rivera
1 Fernandez Junco

San Antonio Canal

**For nos. 1-25
see inset below**

✈ **48**
Isla Grande
Airport

47

165

888 Calle Palo Seco
165 Ave del Caño

CATAÑO

San Juan Bay

Ave Nereidas
5

24 Calle Wilson/Calle Ponce de León

28

869

165

2 Ave J.F.Kennedy

22 de Diego Expwy

GUAYNABO

BAYAMÓN

28

Fort Buchanan (US Army)

San Felipe del Morro Fortress
1

Atlantic Ocean

2   City Wall

18

Calle Del Morro

Calle Norzagaray (Blvd de Valle)

Calle Cristo

3   4
Calle San Sebastián

Calle Sol

Calle Justo

Ave Muñoz Rivera
■ Capitol

25
→

City Wall

Calle Monjas

5   6

7

16   17

Calle San Francisco   19

20

Ave Ponce de León

24 Paseo de Cavadonga

Calle San Jose

8   15

Calle Cruz

Calle Fortaleza

21

Ave Fernandez Juncos

9   11

Calle Tetuan
23

10 12   14

Recinto Sur
22

Calle Marina

13

Princesa La

Calle Presidio

Calle Puntilla

San Juan Bay

San Antonio
Canal

✈
Isla Grande
Airport

Ⓝ
↑
Old San Juan

km
mi   1/2   1
       1/4   1/2

44

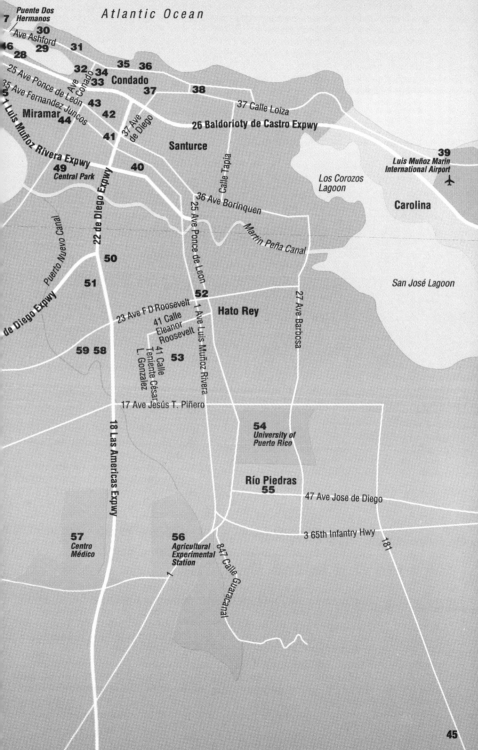

km 1 2
mi 1/2 1

N

Atlantic Ocean

7 Puente Dos
Hermanos

30
Ave Ashford
46 29
28 31

32 34 35 36
33 Condado
25 Ave Ponce de León 37
35 Ave Fernandez Juncos 43 37 Calle Loiza
5 42 38
Miramar 44 41 26 Baldorioty de Castro Expwy
1 Luis Muñoz Rivera Expwy
Santurce
Ave Condado
37 Ave de Diego
Calle Tapia

49 40
Central Park

Los Corozos
Lagoon

Luis Muñoz Marin
International Airport 39

Carolina

36 Ave Borinquen

25 Ave Ponce de León

Martín Peña Canal

Puerto Nuevo Canal

22 de Diego Expwy

San José Lagoon

50

de Diego Expwy

51

52

23 Ave F D Roosevelt Hato Rey

41 Calle
Eleanor
Roosevelt

27 Ave Barbosa

59 58 53

41 Calle
Teniente César
L. González

17 Ave Jesús T. Piñero

54
University of
Puerto Rico

18 Las Americas Expwy

Río Piedras
55

47 Ave Jose de Diego

3 65th Infantry Hwy

57
Centro
Médico

56
Agricultural
Experimental
Station

847 Calle Guadacanal

181

45

2 La Perla On a slope between Calle Norzagaray and the sea, just outside the northern City Wall, you'll see the homes of one segment of San Juan's poorest people. The shacklike houses, most topped with green roofs and TV aerials, are so closely grouped that you can reach from one window to the house next door on some passageways. As the drug culture grew more prevalent on the island, La Perla became known for its "shooting galleries," places where addicts shoot up with heroin and other drugs. The best-selling novel *La Vida*, written by **Oscar Lewis** in the late sixties, portrays the degrading conditions in this classic slum. ◆ North coast, Old San Juan

3 San José Church This is the second oldest church (illustrated above) in the western hemisphere. Vaulted ceilings supported by coral-rock walls and Romanesque arches highlight the ancient Dominican chapel. The coat of arms of **Ponce de León's** son-in-law is on display. ◆ M-Sa 8:30AM-3:30PM; Su Mass 12:15PM. Calle Cristo (Calle San Sebastián). 725.7501

3 Dominican Convent This huge sanctuary is the headquarters of the **Institute of Puerto Rican Culture.** The versatile building has survived for centuries, serving first as a shelter from hostile **Caribs** and much later as headquarters for the **US Army.** Oftused galleries grace two floors. There are a chapel museum and a large interior patio that's sometimes used for cultural activities. The library contains works of the Dominican order. ◆ Museum W-Su 9AMnoon, 1-4:30PM. 98 Calle Norzagaray (Plaza San Jose). 724.0700

4 Plaza San José The statue of **Juan Ponce de León** that stands in this popular plaza was made from a cannon captured during the British attack on San Juan in 1797. It had been believed that the blue stones used in the streets were really ballast from Spanish galleons, but recent studies have identified the stones as *adoquines* (paving stones), cast from 19th-century European iron foundries. ◆ Calle San Sebastián (Calle Cristo)

4 Pablo Casals Museum One of Puerto Rico's truly great musical sons has been immortalized in a museum (illustrated above) next to the San José Church. The two-story building displays memorabilia of the cellistconductor **Don Pablo Casals,** who was born in Spain but settled in his mother's birthplace, Puerto Rico, late in his life. Besides manuscripts, photographs, recordings, and videotapes, you can see the master's wellworn cellos. ◆ Tu-Sa 9:30AM-5:30PM; Su 1-5PM. 101 Calle San Sebastián (Calle San Jose). 723.9185

4 Casa de los Contrafuertes Historians believe the **House of Buttresses** is the oldest private residence in San Juan, dating back to the early 18th century. The **Pharmacy Museum** features a 19th-century drugstore complete with old bottles, scales, and historical documents. The **Museum of Latin American Prints** is on the second floor. ◆ W-Su 9AM-4:30PM. 101 Calle San Sebastián (Calle San Jose). 724.5949

Restaurants/Clubs: Red   **Hotels:** Blue
Shops/ 🌳 Outdoors: Green   **Sights/Culture:** Black

Take Me Out to the Ball Game

Some of baseball's all-time great players have graced Puerto Rico's baseball fields: **Roberto Clemente, Johnny Bench, Gary Carter, Wally Joyner, Mike Schmidt, Reggie Jackson,** and **Orlando Cepeda,** among others. And while American fans await the spring season in the states, Puerto Ricans get an early start on the grand old game. The six professional clubs in the island's Winter League throw the first pitch in November and wrap up the season at the end of January. The champion goes on to compete in the **Caribbean Series,** which usually features teams from the Dominican Republic, Mexico, Venezuela, and Puerto Rico.

Whether you're rooting for the San Juan Metros, Santurce Crabbers, Bayamón Cowboys, Arecibo Wolves, Mayagüez Indians, or the Ponce Lions, you can usually find a seat at their games in the San Juan and Ponce ballparks, although the play-offs always draw large crowds. And, best of all, tickets are inexpensive—about $5, depending on the seating area.

5 Casa Blanca Home to the family of **Juan Ponce de León** during the 16th century and part of the 17th century, Casa Blanca (pictured above) now houses the **Museum of Family Life,** which concentrates on that period in its exhibits. (Ponce de León never lived in the house; he died in Cuba when it was being built.) In 1779 the family sold it to the Spanish government, who in turn lost it to US forces in 1898. It is the oldest continuously inhabited residence in the hemisphere. ♦ Free. W-Su 9AM-4PM. 1 Calle San Sebastián. 724.4102

6 El Convento Hotel $$$ A 17th-century Dominican convent has been transformed into a 100-room hotel in the heart of the Old City. The hotel retains much of the Old World charm, complete with a large interior patio that's been converted into a restaurant. ♦ 100 Calle Cristo, (Calle San Juan). 723.9020

Within El Convento Hotel:

Frailes ★★$$$ Seafood, lamb, and beef are prepared in typical Spanish style. Try the sangria (wine mixed with fruit juice). ♦ Spanish ♦ Daily noon-10PM. 723.9020

Patio del Convento ★$$ The interior patio restaurant features light fare such as sandwiches and Spanish specialties. ♦ International ♦ Daily 7AM-10PM. 723.9020

6 Step Streets An inspiration for many artists, the two *escalinatas* (step streets) in the Old City are **Caleta de Las Monjas** near El Convento Hotel and **Caleta de San Juan** to the northwest. ♦ Calle Christo, NW side of San Juan Cathedral

7 San Juan Cathedral The remains of Spanish explorer **Juan Ponce de León** are entombed in marble here. The original cathedral, built of wood and thatch, was knocked down by strong winds and rebuilt in 1540. The cathedral standing here today was built in the 19th century. ♦ Daily 8:30AM-4PM. 153 Calle Cristo (Caleta de San Juan). 722.0861

8 Calle Cristo One of the most exciting streets in the Old City runs north-south, with a few small museums, interesting shops, and novel eating places along the way. **Il Perugino** (★★★$$$), for example, is an authentic Italian restaurant hidden away in an interior patio surrounded by shops. ♦ Calle San Sebastián-Cristo Chapel

9 San Juan Gate One of the sights in the Old City almost guaranteed to draw oohs and aahs is this gate, where the street ducks down and through the massive City Wall. The huge wooden door was once used to enter the city from boats docked in the bay. The memorable drive leads through the gate, then runs along the shore to Puerta de Tierra. ♦ Calle San Francisco (Calle Recinto Oeste)

10 La Fortaleza The home of the governor of Puerto Rico was occupied by the British and Dutch during the 16th and 17th centuries. Erected in 1540 and redone in 1846, the building is the oldest executive mansion still used in the western hemisphere. ♦ M-F 9AM-4PM, except holidays. Tours in English every hour on the hour, in Spanish on the

half hour. Calle Fortaleza (San Juan Harbor). 721.7000 ext. 2211

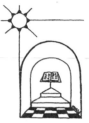

11 La Casa del Libro This small museum in a restored 18th-century house reveres its rare volumes. The unique library contains masterpieces of bookmaking, some of which go back centuries. Special exhibitions are held periodically. Each month, the museum schedules musical concerts. ♦ Tu 11AM-4:30PM, 7:30-10PM; W-Sa 11AM-4:30PM. 255 Calle Cristo (Calle Fortaleza). 723.0354

12 Calle Fortaleza The shops and restaurants along the street include the **Butterfly People** (★$$), for sandwiches and a light lunch; **Siglo XX** (★★$$), for Spanish fare and snacks; and **Beijing Palace** (★★★$$), a better-than-average Chinese garden of delight. Chef/owner **Tommy Kuo** introduced Szechuan-style cooking to Puerto Rico 15 years ago. Down the street, **Albanese** deals in first-rate professional culinary equipment. The store carries a wide range of items, from Italian coffeemakers to Puerto Rican orange peelers. Galleries and souvenir shops are plentiful, although jewelry stores dominate the busy street. ♦ San Juan Gate-Plaza Colón

12 **Pigeon Park** Not only is **Parque de las Palomas** (Pigeon Park) for the birds, but people enjoy it, too. The pocket park is located at the top of the City Wall, overlooking **La Puntilla,** a flat area recently developed for residential homes and parking. It commands a magnificent view of the harbor and a wide perspective of the island. Enjoy a rest from the rush of the city on a tree-shaded bench. ♦ Calle Fortaleza (Calle Cristo)

13 City Wall The Spanish began to erect the fortification in 1630 to protect San Juan from pirates and European invaders. The two 40-foot-high parallel walls are held together by limestone, mortar, and sandstone. Their width varies from 20 feet at the base to 12 feet at the top. ◆ Located around the perimeter of Old San Juan

14 Cristo Chapel History converges with tall tale at **La Capilla del Cristo** (Cristo Chapel; pictured above), which was restored 65 years ago. Legend has it that a young man jumped over the City Wall on horseback and landed here during a traditional race in homage to **Saint John the Baptist.** The chapel is open during Holy Week and during other church holidays. ◆ Calle Cristo (Calle Tetuan)

15 Plaza de Armas The recently redesigned plaza serves as a meeting place for residents and tourists alike. The design, a radical change from the original, continues to develop with age, as the trees grow and the pigeons gather. **City Hall,** the office of the mayor of San Juan, faces the plaza, with statues representing the four seasons and a Florentine fountain. ◆ Calle San Francisco (Calles San Jose-Cruz)

16 La Zaragozana Restaurant ★★$$$ This replica of an old Spanish dining hall specializes in dishes from Cuba, Spain, and Puerto Rico. The veteran staff of the 30-year-old restaurant takes pride in its black bean soup, a Cuban staple, served with rice and chopped onions and peppers. ◆ Spanish ◆ Daily 11AM-closing. 356 Calle San Francisco (Calle Tanca). 725.3262, 723.5103

17 Calle San Francisco Shoe stores, clothing boutiques, souvenir emporiums, and restaurants line the colorful street, where vacationers stroll into the garish tourist traps and glittering jewelry shops. **El Imperio** (209 Calle San Francisco) offers international designs on dresses, women's suits, and bridal accessories. A Franciscan church amid the dozens of shops hovers above the crowds. ◆ Calle O'Donnell-City Wall

18 Fort San Cristóbal It is said that some nights the spirit of a lone sentry walks his post at San Cristóbal. The conquistadores built the strategic masterpiece in the 18th century, when El Morro needed help at its eastern flank. The 27-acre fort is made up of five bastions that reach as high as 150 feet above the sea. The ground floor features a museum. The orientation is available in English and Spanish. ◆ Daily 9:15AM-6PM. Calle Norzagaray. 729.6960

19 Old Casino Just off the Plaza Colón, you'll find the Old Casino, built 75 years ago in Louis XIV style. Puerto Rico's elite once gathered here for parties, large and small. During WWII, the US Army took over the building for use by the USO. The **Free School of Music** and the **Institute of Puerto Rican Culture** moved in until it was restored in 1984. Now the government holds social activities within its rococo walls. ◆ Tours W-Su 2-4PM. Avenida Ponce de Leon (at the Plaza Colón). 722.2121 ext. 230

What the Natives Now Nibble

Traditional Puerto Rican food has been influenced by the ancient Taino Indians, Spanish, and Africans, and more recently by the Cubans, Dominicans, Argentinians, Mexicans, and Americans. Here are some of the island favorites:

Tubers, rice, beans, and plantains are the staples for most native dishes, even though rice and beans are not grown on the island, except for gandules, a lentil-type bean that grows in the hills and is usually prepared for celebrations.

Yautia, a starchy root, is a primary ingredient of many dishes, although the *papa* (potato) has made deep inroads in recent years, especially in the growing number of fast-food restaurants.

Plantains are featured in a variety of Puerto Rican specialties. The ripe *amarillo* (plantain) resembles a large banana and is usually fried or baked and served as a side dish; unripe green plantains that have been peeled, pounded into flat cakes, then deep fried and served like potatoes are called *tostones;* and mashed plantains mixed with garlic and pork rinds are known as *mofongo.*

Bacalaitos (codfish fritters) and *alcapurrias* (yautia and banana fritters filled with beef or crabmeat) are favorite snack foods.

Arroz con pollo (rice and chicken) is probably the most commonly eaten main dish, followed by *asapao,* a rice stew with seafood or meat.

Pasteles, a holiday favorite, are plantains and yautia that have been seasoned and wrapped in banana leaves and boiled.

20 Plaza Colón A stately, towering statue of **Christopher Columbus** greets all who enter the Old City at Plaza Colón, a small park on the east side of the city. The plaza also serves as a meeting place for residents, some of whom may engage in a heated game of dominoes, a pastime second only to political discussions. Columbus, who looks to the horizon, landed on the western side of the island in 1493 during his second trip to the New World. Ironically, the statue and record of his voyages replaced the original statue of **Juan Ponce de León** in 1848, even though Columbus never actually visited the city of San Juan.

The plaza usually bustles during the day. Bus passengers queue up at the terminal as visitors and residents check out the surrounding shops before wending their way through the city. ♦ Calle O'Donnell (Calle Fortaleza)

21 Tapia Theater Drama, dance, music, and poetry are part of Puerto Rico's soul, and many local artists have bared their souls on this stage. The Tapia (illustrated above), the oldest proscenium theater in the western hemisphere, lifted its first curtain in 1832 as the Municipal Theater. The building was renovated in 1878, renamed in 1937 for **Alejandro Tapia,** Puerto Rico's first playwright, then renovated again in 1949 and in 1976. While its boards have been trod by international performers over the years, it takes a back seat to the modern **Performing Arts Center** in Santurce. ♦ Avenida Ponce de Leon. 722.0407

22 Yukiyu Sushi Bar and Restaurant
★★★$$ This fine Japanese restaurant is known for its artistic and delicious sushi and sashimi. ♦ Japanese ♦ M, Sa-Su noon-2:30PM; Tu-F noon-2:30PM, 5-11PM. 311 Recinto Sur (Calle Tanca). 721.0653

23 Pikayo ★★★$$$ Cajun-style cuisine is prepared in gourmet fashion at this hole-in-the-wall, Art Deco "in" spot. Some of San Juan's most discriminating diners (and visiting celebrities) come here. ♦ Cajun ♦ M-Th 6-10PM; F-Sa 6-11PM. 315 Recinto Sur (Calle Tanca). 721.6194

24 Ateneo Puertorriqueño A private society provides for this library, small museum, and theater, where plays have been presented by Spanish and English acting groups. Courses for would-be dramatists are given here. ♦ M-F 9AM-5PM. Avenida Ponce de Leon, just east of Plaza Colón. 722.4839

24 Carnegie Library There's a limited collection of books for public use at this library donated by **Andrew Carnegie** in the early 20th

century. The library is closed to the public, but may reopen in 1992. ♦ Avenida Ponce de Leon, east of Plaza Colón. 724.1046

25 Archives and General Library The Institute of Puerto Rican Culture has set up a library and historical archives in this former cigar factory. Afterward, **Bacardi** produced rum here, and then it became a storehouse for old theater sets. ♦ M-F 8AM-4:30PM. 500 Avenida Ponce de Leon. 725.7405

Cave Country

Spelunking opportunities are numerous in Puerto Rico, which is the home of the famous **Camuy Cave,** a government-controlled site south of Camuy where a path descends into a sinkhole directly to the mouth of the cave. Guides lead tours of the cave in a rubber-tire trolley and then on foot, and focus on the stalactites and stalagmites.

For the very adventurous, there are dozens of caves that have been explored only by a handful of individuals over the years. One such cave is called **Los Angeles,** which is south of Camuy Cave and is part of the undeveloped Río Camuy system. (The Camuy is the third largest underground river in the world.) The descent into the 500-foot-deep sinkhole must be journeyed on foot. A fall is not uncommon on the steep, slippery path that leads to the mouth of the cave; just dust yourself off and keep walking.

Hiring a guide is highly recommended for the exploration of a major cave system (some individual spelunkers have never returned). If you prefer to explore on your own, however, follow the river into the bowels of the cave. And before you embark, acquire a good map, a helmet, a backpack with a change of clothes (in case you get wet), food, water, rope, and a life jacket (for managing the underground river at various points).

Aventuras Tierra a Dentro, the only spelunking tour group on the island, offers visits to the Los Angeles cave, which is located on Route III in the northwest part of the island. For more information, call Rossano Boscarino at 788.5461.

26 Isla de Cabras This elongated isle strung with palm trees has a beach, a picnic area, and **El Canuelo Fort.** The military installation began in the early 17th century to help fortify the El Morro system. ♦ San Juan Bay

Condado

The narrow peninsula between **San Juan Island** and **Santurce** flourished as the exclusive playground for Puerto Rico's well-heeled masses. The Condado's two miles of immaculate beaches and its blue lagoon attracted the carriage set in the early part of the 19th century. And when **Cornelius Vanderbilt** built the **Vanderbilt Condado Beach Hotel** in 1919, visitors came from around the world, setting the

groundwork for a construction boom 30 years later.

In the fifties and sixties, rows upon rows of condos took root on Condado, thanks in part to the Department of Tourism's convincing pitch: Build it, and the tourists will come. As promised, vacationers came in droves via prop airplanes and cruise liners.

The tourist explosion mushroomed in the seventies, bringing all sorts of business establishments, notably the fast-food restaurants, snack stands, and pizza parlors that give the section its carnival look. A concerned citizenry has tried to hold the garishness to a minimum, but, as you will see, progress marches on.

27 Caribe Hilton $$$ Since it was built in 1949 as part of Operation Bootstrap, a government program geared to encourage industry, the Caribe (as it's called by locals) has been dear to the hearts of islanders. Puerto Rico's showplace hotel grew along with the island's burgeoning economy (Bootstrap brought in thousands of factories and millions of people). Heads of state, superstar performers, and great athletes are common sights in the lobby. Although the 707-room luxury hotel has undergone major changes over the years, it still enjoys a strong local following and an international reputation. The 18th-century Spanish fort **San Geronimo** stands in water behind the hotel. Besides holding a military museum, the fort is occasionally used for grand banquets, complete with waiters dressed as conquistadores. ♦ Deluxe ♦ Calle Los Rosales (San Geronimo grounds). 721.0303, 800/932.3322

Within the Caribe Hilton:

El Batey ★★★$$$ This is one of the best seafood restaurants on the island. The lavish, expensive shellfish buffet (more than $40 a person) leaves little to be desired. ♦ Seafood ♦ Daily noon-midnight. 721.0303

Peacock Paradise ★★$$ The colorful, grand restaurant features specialties from various regions of China. ♦ Chinese ♦ Daily noon-11PM. 721.0303

Rotisserie II Giardino ★★★$$$ The fine fare served here ranges from osso buco to paella marinara and duck l'orange—the best in town. ♦ Italian/Spanish ♦ Daily noon-midnight. 721.0303

28 Condado Lagoon Puente Dos Hermanos (Two Brothers Bridge) spans a portion of the lagoon where Puerta de Tierra meets Condado. Fishers drop their lines over the side, while the teenage crowd congregates on weekends. Sailboats and jet-skis keep the inlet's azure waters churning at the end of the bridge. A small beach borders the property of the Condado Plaza Hotel. ♦ Separates Avenida Ashford from Baldorioty de Castro (Puente Dos Hermanos-Calle Joffre)

29 Avenida Ashford The main drag is named after **Dr. Bailey Ashford,** a pioneer in tropical medicine. It begins over the bridge past the Condado Lagoon, hugging the ocean until it reaches **Calle San Jorge,** almost two miles away. The avenue runs two ways until it meets **Parque Las Nereidas,** where it turns into one-way traffic at the Ashford Medical Center. Along the richly landscaped avenue are the palms that sway beside hotels, restaurants, boutiques, and even the house where the doctor lived until his death in 1934. Now the Gonzalez family lives in the glorious pink house, one of Condado's most historic sites. ♦ Puente Dos Hermanos-San Jorge

30 Condado Plaza Hotel and Casino $$$ This hotel spreads out on both sides of Avenida Ashford. A clear Plexiglas-enclosed bridge connects the two buildings that include one of the largest casinos on the island, five restaurants, and 587 rooms. Before the bridge was built, wire-walker **Karl Wallenda** fell to his death while attempting to cross the avenue on a wire stretched from building to building six floors up. The great aerialist did not take the heavy breezes into account. ♦ Deluxe ♦ 999 Avenida Ashford. 721.1000, 800/468.8588; fax 721.4613

Within Condado Plaza Hotel and Casino:

L.K. Sweeney and Son Ltd. ★★★$$$ Enjoy seafood in an elegant, London club atmosphere further enhanced by the attentive service. **Larry Sweeney,** one of the island's premier restaurateurs, runs a tight ship. The lobster and shrimp dishes are classic. ♦ Seafood ♦ Daily noon-11PM. 721.1000

The Caribbean Sea may be rich in coral and colorful fish, but it's poor in nutrients, which is why the water is pale rather than dark blue.

Akee, a tropical fruit featured in many Caribbean dishes, is highly poisonous before its red body completely ripens and opens to reveal its bright yellow flesh.

31 Condado Beach Hotel $$ This Spanish-style hotel caters to both the conservative traveler and Puerto Rico's old guard. Built in 1919 by **Cornelius Vanderbilt**, it still retains **The Vanderbilt Club,** a private floor for executive services. The hotel adjoins **El Centro** (the Puerto Rico Convention Center), which offers three levels of huge facilities for meetings, seminars, and conventions. With 18 rooms, El Centro totals 79,500 square feet, making it the largest convention center in the Caribbean. The 234-room **La Concha Hotel** ($$) is also part of the convention center. ◆ 1071 Avenida Ashford. 721.6090, 800/468.2822; fax 722.3200

Within the Condado Beach Hotel:

El Gobernador ★★$$$ This restaurant is where the elite meet to eat, lending even more elegance to the hotel. Steaks, seafood, and Spanish specialties are served here in grand style. ◆ Continental ◆ Daily noon-11PM. 721.6090

32 Ramiro's ★★★★$$$ Owner/chef **Jesús Ramiro** offers highly unusual dishes with a Spanish flavor. The presentation is the most imaginative on the island. The haute cuisine includes sweet red pepper stuffed with salmon and, for dessert, sliced, caramelized mango on a bed of strawberry sauce designed in the shape of a strawberry. With a large wine loft, this is a restaurant to remember. ◆ Continental ◆ Daily noon-10PM. 1106 Avenida Magdalena. 721.904

33 Avenida Condado This four-block-long avenue in Santurce has some pleasant surprises amid the condos. There's the **Don Pepe** restaurant (★★★$$$), which serves fine paella, and **Molino Italiano** (★$), for spaghetti. The **Dutch Inn** ($$) finds favor with residents, especially for its small intimate casino. And the popular **Green House Coffee Shop** (★$) prepares some of the juiciest hamburgers in town. ◆ Avenidas Ashford-Fernandez Juncos

34 Martino ★★★$$ Chef/owner **Martin Acosta** serves excellent Italian fare in the inviting roof garden. Try the veal and spinach-stuffed gnocchi covered in a pesto sauce. ◆ Italian ◆ Daily 6-11PM. 55 Avenida Condado. 722.5256

35 Dupont Plaza Hotel A monument to catastrophe, the hotel has been closed since an arson fire in 1986 that killed 97 people and injured 140, most of them in the casino. ◆ Avenida Ashford (Avenida Condado-Calle Cervantes)

36 Ambassador Plaza $$ A busy, noisy casino and an equally trafficked **Howard Johnson**

restaurant on the ground floor welcome visitors to one of Condado's most recently renovated hotels. Before it was given its grand look, this was a typical HoJo inn. ◆ 1369 Avenida Ashford. 721.7300, 800/468.8512

Within the Ambassador Plaza:

Jade Beach ★★$$$ Pearl shrimp and whole red snapper are done to an elegant turn here. The smartly furnished, air-conditioned dining room overlooks Condado Beach. ◆ Chinese ◆ Daily noon-3PM, 5:30-11:30PM. 721.7300

Giuseppe's ★★★$$$ Veal, seafood, steaks, and pasta are prepared in regal fashion. Try the buffalo mozzarella-tomato appetizer (the cheese is made from buffalo milk) and the classic zuppa Inglese for dessert. The in-between main courses are treats, as well. ◆ Italian ◆ Daily noon-11PM. 721.7300

37 Avenida de Diego The principal avenue leading from commercial Santurce to resort-packed Condado was once a street of nightclubs and restaurants. Now there's the **Pueblo** supermarket, **Departamento de Hacienda** (Motor Vehicle and Licenses Bureau), and assorted stores, offices, and residences. Avenida de Diego leads to the **Performing Arts Center** in Santurce. ◆ Avenidas Ashford-Ponce de Leon

Trolleys Make Tracks through Old San Juan

After a few hours of walking along the cobble-stoned streets of Old San Juan, climb aboard one of the five trolleys that runs through the historic city and give your feet a rest and your eyes a treat—all for free. The open-air buses resemble San Francisco cable cars, except they run on rubber tires, sans rails, and the drivers provide colorful anecdotes as they point out the various 16th-century landmarks. You can hop aboard the cars at any trolley stop or at the Covadonga and La Puntilla parking lots at the end of the pier area near the Customs House. Trolleys operate daily from 6:30AM to 6:30PM.

Restaurants/Clubs: Red   Hotels: Blue
Shops/ 🌴 Outdoors: Green   Sights/Culture: Black

38 Shannon's Pub This hangout attracts the under-20 crowd on most evenings, although older clients tend to congregate during happy hour. The local beer Medalla and popular standbys such as Budweiser and Heineken flow freely. ♦ Daily 11:30AM-3:30AM. 1503 Calle Loiza (Avenida de Diego). 728.6103

39 El San Juan Hotel $$$ This hotel's international atmosphere and marble and wood-paneled lobby, complete with a harpist, hark back to turn-of-the-century Europe. The large bar in the center of the lobby is generally crowded, and tables are spread about the grand room, where guests enjoy cocktails, conversation, and people-watching. The 392-room resort hotel offers beach and water facilities, a health club, a huge glitzy casino,

and five restaurants, all near the Muñoz Marín Airport. ♦ 187 Avenida Isla Verde. 791.1000, 800/468.2818

Within El San Juan Hotel:

Dar Tiffany ★★★$$$ Fine steaks and seafood head the menu at this top-of-the-line restaurant. Dark woods and leather provide a rich contrast to the select foliage in the dining room. The impeccable service affords a fine dining experience. ♦ American ♦ Daily 6-11PM. 791.7272

Back Street Hong Kong ★★$$$ This is one of the most imaginatively designed restaurants on the island. The entrance is a replica of a street in Hong Kong that was originally displayed at the 1964 World's Fair in New York. A huge aquarium lights up the dining room, which is constructed of fine woods reminiscent of Old China. ♦ Chinese ♦ M-Th 6PM-midnight; F-Sa 6PM-12:30AM; Su noon-midnight. 791.2035

Santurce

This is the real San Juan, home to close to one million people who go about their daily lives in just about every conceivable occupation. Santurce is made up of myriad pastel-colored, small-frame houses and scores of high-rise condominiums. Unfortunately, one of the fastest growing enterprises is the multimillion-dollar grillwork business. The iron bars were once used as ornamentation, especially in the Spanish-style architecture, but now they're needed mostly for security reasons.

40 La Casona ★★$$$ Garlic soup, rack of lamb, and vanilla flan provide a touch of class amid the Santurce foliage. ♦ Spanish ♦ M-Sa noon-11PM. 609 Calle San Jorge (Avenida Fernandez Juncos). 727.2717

41 La Borincana ★$$ The fare usually features roast chicken, steak, and rice and beans. Aesthetics are not a strong suit; the decor, with oil-cloth table covers, is merely functional. ♦ Puerto Rican ♦ Daily 6PM-2AM. 1401 Avenida Fernandez Juncos (Calle Hipodromo). 725.8815

42 Bellas Artes The big show in town is usually here at the **Performing Arts Center.** The complex, built in the seventies, provides for dramas, symphonies, operas, and films, but is probably best known for the annual **Pablo Casals Festival** held here every year. ♦ Avenida Ponce de Leon (Avenida Jose de Diego). 725.7334

43 Avenida Ponce de Leon Shopping along the avenue is mainly a pastime for the locals. You can buy anything from a fancy dress at **Gonzalez Padin** to a basketball at **Rocafort** or a computer at **Puerto Rico Computer. New York Department Stores,** as in other locales, is an old-time establishment that carries large stocks of merchandise. The avenue has been getting a new look as old edifices have been replaced with buildings reminiscent of the thirties and forties. ♦ Avenidas Miramar-Barbosa

44 Peggy Sue This nightclub for the Yuppie crowd features music from the fifties. ♦ Daily 6PM-midnight. 1 Avenida Roberto H. Todd (Avenida Baldorioty de Castro). 722.4750

45 Windows of the Caribbean ★★$$$ The view through the large picture windows of this penthouse restaurant at the **Clarion Hotel** takes in all of San Juan. Rack of lamb, paella Valenciana, and prime rib top the menu of this ritzy establishment. ♦ Continental ♦ Tu-Th 5PM-midnight; F-Sa 5PM-1AM. 600 Avenida Fernandez Juncos. 721.4100

Miramar

Once the most fashionable neighborhood on the island, Miramar has lost some of its sheen but still commands a high real estate value. The stately homes on the old tree-shaded streets used to house the island's wealthy. Today, a mix of rich and middle classes calls Miramar home. Many of its former residents moved to the nearby municipality of Guaynabo into such silk-stocking neighborhoods as Garden Hills, Santa María, and San Francisco.

46 Club Náutico Some of the classiest yachts drop anchor in this marina. Deep-sea fishing trips may be arranged through **Mike Benitez,** who owns a fleet of fishing and pleasure boats. ♦ 1/2 Avenida Fernandez Juncos. 723.2292

47 Old Naval Base Battleships, destroyers, and cargo ships once docked at this former headquarters for the US Navy. Now the base houses local government offices where driver's licenses and car registrations may be obtained. ♦ Miramar

Restaurants/Clubs: Red   **Hotels:** Blue
Shops/ 🌳 Outdoors: Green   **Sights/Culture:** Black

48 Isla Grande Airport San Juan's alternate airport is mainly used for general aircraft. Cessna, Piper, and Beechcraft airplanes make their way back and forth from points on the island, as well as to destinations within the Caribbean. The first major commercial flights landed at this airport in the fifties, when Pan American World Airways scheduled runs of prop planes to and from Miami, Florida. The **Isla Grande Flying School** has turned out thousands of pilots.

Hato Rey

Driving through the Martin Peña area, where swamp squatters once thrived, you reach Hato Rey, the island's business center. Its **Golden Mile,** along avenidas Ponce de Leon and Muñoz Rivera, is lined with corporate offices and banks. The **University of Puerto Rico's** clock tower gives Avenida Ponce de Leon a metropolitan look. And large pockets of small homes, condos, schools, parks, businesses, and shopping centers can be found off the main avenues.

49 Central Park The park was built for the 1979 Pan American Games, so the sports facilities are top-notch. It's usually filled with hundreds of joggers and walkers. The heavily trafficked park has facilities for baseball and tennis. ♦ Daily 8AM-8PM. Hato Rey. 722.1646

50 Plaza Aquatica This water-park complex also features a dinosaur park, a playground area, and miniature golf. On weekends, children line up to go down the long slide into the pool. ♦ Admission. Sa-Su 10AM-closing. Federico Costa and Chardon in Hato Rey. 754.9500

51 Plaza Las Américas This three-level shopping center is the largest in the West Indies. **JCPenney, Sears,** and **Gonzalez Padin** are the large department stores. A multitude of smaller stores stocked with everything from jeans to television consoles fills in the spaces between the anchor stores. **El Kiosko** carries carvings, sculptures, paintings, shadow boxes, and jewelry created by local artisans. "Plaza," as it's called by locals, has an air-conditioning system that keeps the building comfortable even though temperatures may reach the 90s outside. The center also features a complete floor of fast-food restaurants, where throngs of shoppers queue up at the **Burger King, Orange Julius,** and **The Cookie Bus,** among others. ♦ M-Th, Sa-Su 9AM-6PM; F 9AM-9PM. Las Americas Expressway, exit Avenida Roosevelt. No phone

52 Metropol Restaurant ★★$ This no-nonsense restaurant in the Golden Mile area is busy most times of the day. Feast on some of the island's tastiest black bean soup, smoked stuffed chicken, rice and beans, and sangria. ♦ Cuban ♦ 124 Avenida Roosevelt. 751.4022

53 Muñoz Marín Park Families gather here mostly on weekends and school groups congregate during the week. A cable car runs right through the center of the park. The paths for walking, jogging, and bicycling get plenty of traffic. The gazebos host picnickers, while a toy-boat racing lake and a futuristic playground keep the kiddies busy. ♦ Tu-Su 9AM-5:30PM. Avenida Jesus T. Pinero (off of Las Americas Expressway). 763.0568

Puerto Rico

54 University of Puerto Rico The campus sprawls out over a single square mile that includes student and faculty living quarters. The university's museum generally offers a worthwhile exhibition in addition to its regular collection. The extensive library contains a Puerto Rican room that is invaluable to students of island history and customs. The university's tower (pictured above) is a well-known landmark. ♦ Avenida Ponce de Leon (Calle Gandara). 764.0000

55 Río Piedras Market The local market near the University of Puerto Rico goes back to the good old days, when food shopping meant going from the tomato stall to the spice dealer to the butcher. There's always an abundance of mangoes, passion fruit, limes, yams, onions, garlic, poultry, meat, clothing, toys, auto parts, radios, and people, people, people. The indoor public market will never pass a hygiene test, but the merchandise is usually in good order. And the best buys in town are found here. ♦ M-Sa 8AM-5PM. Avenida Jose de Diego (Avenidas Ponce de Leon-Barbosa)

56 Agricultural Experimental Station The acres of botanical gardens emphasize local plants such as orchids, succulents, and night bloomers. The station coordinates with the University of Puerto Rico in research programs. ♦ Tu-Su 9AM-5PM. 65th Infantry Hwy (Calle Guaracanal). 763.4408

57 Centro Médico The huge medical complex provides treatment free of charge to the public. ♦ Off of Las Americas Expressway, exit Rte 21 (Barrio Monacillo). 754.3535

58 Hiram Bithorn Stadium Winter League baseball teams play in this ballpark from November through January (see "Take Me Out to the Ball Game" on page 46). The stadium is also used for a multitude of activities, from car races to religious meetings. It was named for **Hiram "Hi" Bithorn,** a Puerto Rican major leaguer who pitched for the Chicago Cubs in the forties. ◆ Off of Avenida Roosevelt. 765.5000

59 Roberto Clemente Coliseum Basketball games, boxing and wrestling matches, rock concerts, trade shows, circuses, and college graduations are all held at the coliseum, named after Puerto Rico's superstar athlete who was killed in an airplane crash while attempting to bring food and medicine to victims of

an earthquake in Nicaragua. ◆ Avenida Roosevelt. 752.6410

Canóvanas

This municipality's main attractions are its basketball team (the **Canóvanas Indians**) and the **El Comandante Race Track,** where horse races are held three days a week. Canóvanas is in the northeast, a few miles south of Loizas.

60 El Comandante Race Track Pari-mutuel horse racing is held three days a week at this modern track in Canóvanas. Eight races feature the best horses in the Caribbean. Agencies around the island take off-track betting. There's a glass-enclosed restaurant overlooking the track, and TV sets are scattered around the room. ◆ Admission. W, F, Su 9AM-5PM. Rte 3, km 15.3. 724.6000

61 El Yunque This 28,000-acre rain forest (also known as The Anvil) is considered the crown jewel of the island. Just 30 miles east of San Juan you can see more than 200 tree species native to the area, as well as wild orchids. Also a bird sanctuary, El Yunque is home to the rare Puerto Rican parrot—the *Amazona vittata*. The two mountains—El Yunque and El Toro—peak at 3,493 feet and 3,532 feet, respectively. Dozens of trails lead to four forest types of vegetation, along which you may see tree snails as wide as a small child's forearm. And expect rain on your hike; more than one hundred billion gallons of rain falls here every year. From the observation tower, where the air is thin at more than 3,000 feet above sea level, listen to the sounds of silence within the low-lying clouds. ◆ Free. Daily 9:30AM-5PM. Rte 191, km 11.6

Luquillo

Made famous by Luquillo Beach, this town has become the home of a large group of "snowbirds" (people who live in Puerto Rico during the winter months, when it's cold in the states but warm on the island). The low-key area was transformed by the building of high-rise condominiums on the beach and a nearby shopping center.

62 Luquillo Beach Located 30 miles east of San Juan, bask in the sun on this world-renowned tropical beach surrounded by coconut palms. Snack bars and small restaurants specializing in seafood fritters and a wide assortment of alcoholic beverages are sold at this very popular stop-off point for day-trippers. ◆ Admission. Daily 9AM-5PM. Rte 3, west of Fajardo

Casino Codes

Puerto Rico's pit bosses and croupiers dress formally in the almost Monte Carlo-like settings of this island's gambling houses, although the gamblers' dress codes have changed over the years. Shirts and trousers are now acceptable (black-tie attire used to be required), but swimsuits are still banned (and at some gambling establishments, porters even check whether or not you're wearing socks).

Casino gambling has been legal in Puerto Rico for more than 40 years, and government inspectors make sure the action goes according to the Hoyle rules (each casino provides a book on the rules and methods of play).

Most of the gambling takes place in the hotels in San Juan, Dorado, and Mayagüez.

You can order a sandwich or soft drink while you're gambling, but alcoholic beverages are not served in any casinos on the island. The doors open at noon and the house stays busy until at least four in the morning.

CHRIS MIDDOUR

Fajardo

This boating-and-sailing town features **Seven Seas,** a public beach that's popular with sunbathers. An adventurous half-hour hike takes you to **Red Beach,** an unspoiled slice of paradise where few visitors stray. Large marinas in the area have led to an increase in boating-related businesses.

63 Puerto del Rey All sorts of boats (with pilots, too) may be rented or chartered from one of Puerto Rico's newest marinas. Nearby islands can be viewed or visited from here. ♦ Daily 9AM-5PM. Rte 3, km 51.4. 860.1000

64 Las Pailas Kids and adults have slipped down the rocks of this natural water slide for years. Getting here means parking your auto on the road, then descending a winding trail to the falls. ♦ Rte 983, south of Luquillo

Humacao

A sleepy eastern town that faces the Caribbean Sea and serves as a gateway to Puerto Rico's well-known **Palmas del Mar** resort.

65 Palmas del Mar $$$ The 2,750-acre layout includes a former coconut plantation, an 18-hole championship golf course, horseback riding, a pristine beach, and a marina. Guests can stay in either a villa next to the marina or one of the two hotels. ♦ Rte 906, south of Humacao. 852.6111, 800/468.3331

Within Palmas del Mar:

Palmas Inn $$$ This intimate, family run hideaway has almost two dozen junior suites and five luxury suites, as well as a private swimming pool. ♦ 852.6111

Candelero Hotel $$$ Cathedral ceilings and king-sized beds exemplify the ample proportions here. ♦ 852.6111

Coamo

The drive through Puerto Rico's southern coastal plain reveals a truly panoramic view. The town of Coamo, one of the oldest on the island, is famous for its baths, emanating from a warm natural spring that some claim has healing powers.

66 Parador Baños de Coamo $ This government-sponsored guest house girdles the natural springs where bath enthusiasts take to the warm waters daily. ♦ Rte 546, south of Coamo. 825.2239

Ponce

Puerto Rico's second largest city is often called the Pearl of the South. The pace in this sleepy southern town (pronounced *pont-say*) is slower than in San Juan. Ponceños are proud of their brilliant white town square, **Plaza Las Delicias.** The **Hotel Melia,** a landmark hostelry, faces the plaza as well as the legendary red-and-black wood firehouse, often perceived as the symbol of Ponce.

67 Ponce Museum This charming town's claim to fame is its art museum, designed by **Edward Durell Stone.** The museum exhibits international works, not world renowned, but significant in their own right. One is **Lord Frederick Leighton's** *Flaming June,* a large 19th-century painting of a young woman asleep on a sofa. The museum, former **Governor Luís Ferré's** gift to the people, has gained a fine reputation for its impressive collection of local art. ♦ Admission. M-F 9AM-4PM; Sa 10AM-4PM; Su 10AM-5PM. Avenida Las Americas, across from Catholic University. 848.0511

67 Catholic University The major institution of higher learning offers four-year programs in liberal arts and science as well as a graduate and a law school. ♦ Avenida Las Americas (Calles Muñoz-Hostos). 841.2000

68 Tibes Indian Ceremonial Center The grounds of this ancient cemetery and religious center feature seven courts built by pre-Columbian tribes presumably for ball-type games. The Amerindian site was discovered in 1974; since then, an Arawak village of thatched huts has been re-created. Archaeologists have also uncovered two dancing grounds. ♦ Admission. Tu-Su 9AM-4:30PM. Rte 503, km 2.7. 840.2255

69 Hacienda Buena Vista A restored coffee-and-corn farm from the 19th century contains a farmhouse, slave quarters, coffee mills, and agricultural machinery. Watch the original machinery pulp, ferment, rinse, dry, and husk the coffee berries. An intricate network of waterways drives the operation. ♦ Admission. W-Su 8:30AM, 10:30AM, 1:30PM, 3:30PM; Groups W-Th; in English W-Su 1:30PM. Rte 10, km 168.8, about 7 miles north of Ponce. Reservations required. 722.5882, 848.7020

Guánica

American troops landed here in 1898 without so much as a shot being fired. And a plaque in the town describes the Spanish-American War that ended with Puerto Rico surrendering to the United States.

70 Ballena Bay Club Med unsuccessfully tried to set up shop here a few years ago. Its tropical splendor is complete, with mangroves, swaying palm trees, and a small, white sand beach. That's the good news. The bad news is that the property is privately owned, so it's more of a "look but don't touch" arrangement, although locals often find their way onto the sandy beach. ♦ Guánica

71 Mary Lee's by the Sea $$ The completely furnished whimsical houses and apartments look out on the water. The houses are colorfully decorated and feature fully equipped kitchens. An available boat goes around the bay or heads out to nearby **Gilligan's Island**, where you just may have the isle to yourself on a slow day (but never on the weekend). ♦ Barrio San Jacinto. 821.3600

71 San Jacinto Restaurant and Boats $ This rickety establishment takes care of all your needs. It's a motel, restaurant, bar, and boat rental. You can take a ride around the bay on a colorful launch. If you want to be deposited on **Gilligan's Island** (just offshore) and be picked up at your appointed time, you may—for $3 per passenger. ♦ Barrio San Jacinto. 821.4941

Puerto Rico

Putters Prefer Puerto Rico

This island was destined to be a golfer's mecca, thanks to its rolling foothills and warm year-round climate. Numerous scenic championship courses on Puerto Rico, most of which are located at the larger resorts on the northern shore, were designed by prominent architects.

The **Hyatt Dorado** and **Cerromar** resorts boast two 18-hole courses apiece, adding up to a top-of-the-line golf complex designed by **Robert Trent Jones**. The popular S-shaped, 540-yard 13th hole on the Dorado's East Course and the L-shaped, five par 14th hole on the West Course will challenge even the most accomplished pro. As you tee off the West Course's eighth hole, take careful aim. **Juan "Chi Chi" Rodriguez** lives just off the fairway (you wouldn't want to break any of the great golf pro's windows). You may even see Chi Chi, who takes lessons from his brother, **Jesus,** practicing his drives here.

Green fees start at $10 and go as high as $30. Golf carts are mandatory at practically every course on the island and cost $20 to $40 to rent. (If the fees are too steep, try the lower-priced **Dorado del Mar,** just east of the Hyatt resorts, featuring some of the longest holes on the island.)

East of the Dorado, there's **Bahía Beach Plantation, Bervini Country Club,** and **Río Mar**. Designed by **George Fazio** and Chi Chi Rodriguez, the 18-hole Río Mar features water hazards on two-thirds of its holes. The mountains provide a spectacular backdrop and a private beach serves as its northern boundary. There's also a challenging course at **Palmas del Mar.** Gary Player lined this 6,660-yard course with palm trees and mangroves. A small river cuts through the fairway on the 18th hole. **Fort Buchanan's** nine-hole course in San Juan and **Punta Borinquen** in Aguadilla offer two layouts that are ideal for beginners.

Restaurants/Clubs: Red   Hotels: Blue
Shops/ 🌳 Outdoors: Green   Sights/Culture: Black

Cabo Rojo

Some historians claim that Columbus made his landing at this remote district in the southwest end of the island in 1493. Today, islanders flock to the area for quiet weekends at the popular beaches.

72 Phosphorescent Bay The quiet fishing town of **La Parguera** is famous for this bay, where millions of dinoflagellates (microscopic, luminescent organisms that live in the ocean) light up when the water is disturbed. There are two *paradores* (government-run country inns) and a bevy of seafood restaurants nearby.

72 Parador Villa Parguera $ Simple, clean rooms and wholesome local fare characterize this inn. ♦ Rte 304, south of San Germán. 899.3975

73 El Faro The Cabo Rojo lighthouse draws visitors who like to stroll about the grounds taking in the majestic beauty of the rugged coast. The doors and windows of the dramatic landmark are sealed off (the revolving light goes on at the flip of a switch in the Department of Natural Resources building nearby). A crescent-shaped beach with pelicans beckons from the foot of the lighthouse. ♦ Rte 301, south of Boquerón Beach

74 El Combate Beach A variety of boats bob about on the calm water at this large beach, a hangout for young people, many on motorcycles. The long wooden pier draws lots of fishing enthusiasts. ♦ Rte 301, end of Rte 301R

75 Boquerón Beach Islanders consider this white sand paradise the best that Puerto Rico has to offer. The government provides Spartan-like, inexpensive accommodations that must be reserved in advance (for reservations, you should contact the **Department of Recreation and Sports** by calling 722.1551). Seafood lovers will find plenty of small restaurants and snack stands to choose from nearby. And vendors on the street even shuck oysters and clams while you eat. ♦ Rte 101, west of San Germán

76 Buyé Beach Vast crowds congregate on this jewel-like family beach during the weekends and holidays. ♦ Rte 101, north of Boquerón Beach

San Germán

Puerto Rico's second oldest settlement was founded by the Spaniards more than 400 years ago in the rolling hills at the foot of the Cordillera. The streets that originally ran through the center of town remain intact, and are lined with white colonial buildings and town houses from the coffee era. Now this area is a university town, the home of **Inter-American University's** first campus.

77 Porto Coeli Church Built in 1606 by several Dominican friars, the church now serves as a museum of religious art, mostly with works from Mexico and 18th- and 19th-century wood statuary. *Porto Coeli* translates as "Heaven's Gate." ♦ Free. W-Su 9AM-noon, 1-4PM. 892.5845

78 Joyuda Beach More than 20 small seafood restaurants are crammed into this beach area. Broiled red snapper, Caribbean lobster, shrimp, and grouper make up most of the menus. ♦ North of Cabo Rojo

Mayagüez

This city (pronounced *ma-ja-wez*) is Puerto Rico's third largest and was rebuilt after an earthquake devastated it in 1917. It's supported primarily by its tuna fish canning industry. A statue of **Christopher Columbus** stands in the town plaza to greet all of Mayagüez's visitors.

79 Zoorico The island's only zoo offers the usual big cats, reptiles, monkeys, and elephants housed in cages and in natural habitat pits. There's an aviary with a large group of hawks. The zoo encompasses a full 90 acres. ♦ Admission. Tu-Su 9AM-4:30PM. Rte 108, behind the University of Puerto Rico's Mayagüez campus. 834.8110

80 University of Puerto Rico This campus offers agricultural and engineering courses. Besides providing for extensive research, the university's botanical gardens grow thousands of plants and trees. ♦ Rte 2, take the Avenida Post exit. 832.4040

81 Mayagüez Hilton $$$ A large group of locals comes to the hotel for long weekends or to the busy casino for a few hands of blackjack. The rooms are clean and well furnished. ♦ Rte 222, just off Rte 2. 831.7575

Within the Mayagüez Hilton:

Rotisserie Restaurant ★★★$$$ Motif buffets are featured nightly. The paella Valencia and the red snapper are particularly well-prepared specialties. ♦ Continental ♦ Daily 6-11PM. 831.7575

Rincón

The giant ocean waves draw surfers to this west coast town, and fine seafood restaurants lure many other visitors.

82 Horned Dorset Primavera $$$ The small Mediterranean-style hotel on the rocky west coast has a fine reputation for sophisticated elegance. It caters to those who seek privacy and luxury. The 24 suites are furnished with fine antiques, four-poster beds, and rattan furniture. Children under 12 years of age are not accepted as guests. ♦ Rte 429, km 3. 823.4030

Within the Horned Dorset Primavera:

Horned Dorset Primavera Restaurant ★★$$$ The restaurant's black-and-white marble floor and antique-style furniture set off by candlelight make this a leading candidate for top romantic spot on the island. The menu offers only two entrée choices, but they're both always good and often take advantage of the local produce. ♦ Continental ♦ Daily 6-11PM. 823.4030

Camuy

On the western side of the island, this small municipality has gained popularity through the Río Camuy Caves, which are quite a few miles south of town.

Puerto Rico

83 Río Camuy Caves After an orientation in the theater, visitors board a tram that winds down the sinkhole to the mouth of the cave. From there a footpath leads into the 170-foot-high cave, where the views extend all the way to the underground portion of the **Camuy River** (see "Cave Country" on page 49). Within **Clara Cave**, stalactites and stalagmites stand out dramatically in one of the most massive cave networks in the western hemisphere. A cafeteria and gift shop are on the premises. ♦ M-Sa 9AM-5PM; Su 9AM-8PM. Rte 129, south of Camuy. 756.5555

Arecibo

This coastal town serves mostly as a stop-off point to other places and is the home of the **Arecibo Wolves** baseball team. The road west (Route 2) heads to surfing country in Rincón and to Mayagüez. Heading east, there's Dorado Beach, Bayamón, and San Juan.

84 Arecibo Ionospheric Observatory This is where Cornell University scientists operate the world's largest radio telescope, a 20-acre dish constructed within a large sinkhole. The Arecibo Ionospheric Observatory is known for discovering pulsars and quasars. ♦ Free. Tu-F 2-3PM; Su 1-4PM. Rte 625, south of Arecibo. 878.2612

85 Caguana Indian Ceremonial Park Heading south to Utuado, there are Taino grounds that contain 10 playing courts. It is thought the inhabitants played some sort of ball game similar to soccer here more than 800 years ago. A small museum displays artifacts traced to the Tainos. ♦ Free. Daily 8:30AM-4:30PM. Rte 111, km 12.3, west of Utuado. 894.7325

Dorado

Route 693, lined with palms, sea grapes, and almond trees, leads to Dorado's beaches. Large rocks act as breakwaters to protect the trees, making this a lovely drive.

86 Dorado Beach Hotel $$$ This Hyatt hotel is paired with the **Cerromar Beach Hotel** for a total of four championship golf courses. **Juan "Chi Chi" Rodriguez,** the former director of golf here, plays the fairways throughout the year.

Before the hotel was built in the 1950s, the property belonged to **La Sardinera Plantation,** where grapefruits and coconuts were grown for export. The farm was owned by **Clara Livingston,** Puerto Rico's first woman pilot.

Puerto Rico

When the 50-year-old enterprise declined due to lower prices in the states, Livingston sold the 1,600 acres to **Laurance Rockefeller,** who in turn built the world-famous hotel. ◆ Rte 693, east of Dorado. 796.1234

Within Dorado Beach Hotel:

Su Casa ★★★$$$ One of the island's most charming restaurants is open only during the winter season. Kings and presidents have dined at the illustrious restaurant. The old plantation house is furnished in Spanish-style antiques. Some of the porticoed rooms on the veranda overlook La Sardinera Bay. The kitchen expertly prepares classic dishes such as oysters Rockefeller, beef Wellington, and filet mignon. ◆ Continental ◆ Daily 6-11PM; closed June-Oct. 796.1234

Bayamón

This metropolitan area is called the Sink of Puerto Rico because of the frequent rainfall in this part of the island.

87 Bacardi Rum Distillery Just outside of Bayamón is the popular Bacardi rum factory. Free guided tours are given at the plant, where 100,000 gallons of rum can be distilled in a day. ◆ M-Sa 9AM-4PM. Rte 22, west of San Juan. 788.1500

88 Luis A. Ferre Science Park US rockets loom next to the **Museum of Geology and Physical Sciences.** Taino artifacts are showcased within the **Museum of Archaeology,** antique cars in the **Museum of Transportation,** and mounted animals and a small zoo next to a lake with paddleboats. ◆ Admission. W-F 8AM-4PM; Sa-Su 10AM-6PM. Rte 167, south of the Jose De Diego Expressway. 740.6868

89 Central Park The grounds are highlighted by a 19th-century schoolhouse and a working sugarcane train from the 1930s. ◆ Hwy 2, across from City Hall

---

Restaurants/Clubs: Red
Shops/ Outdoors: Green

Hotels: Blue

Sights/Culture: Black

Almost Paradise: The Up-and-Coming Caribbean Islands

This book features the best tropical hideaways of the Caribbean and the Bahamas—those island destinations favored by folks who want to run away from the hustle and bustle of everyday life and retreat to a distant locale renowned for its deserted sandy shores, prime dive spots, fine dining, and first-rate fishing. And then there are the runners-up to these idyllic islands, those exotic places in the sun that make the preferred list of many a veteran traveler but don't quite get top billing—at least not yet. So if you can't get to the isle of your dreams, or you're just looking for a side trip to another tropical island, here are some not-so-publicized second-best choices to consider.

Grenada

White sand beaches ring the green, mountainous interior of this small volcanic island tucked away in the southern Grenadines. The essence of nutmeg, cinnamon, and cocoa permeates the air of this 12-by-21-mile tropical paradise, hinting at the tons of spices grown, cultivated, packed, and sold in all of the island's six parishes that have inspired Grenada's nickname, **Spice Island.**

The mountain roads wind through lush foliage that's thick with mace, nutmeg, bananas, and calabash. And at 1,700 feet above sea level, **Grand Etang** crater lake affords a clear view of the distant mountains.

St. Georges, the capital of Grenada, was built around a natural harbor and is dotted with its distinctive tile-roofed houses. Cruise liners and commercial freighters from around the world deposit their passengers along the capital's colorful esplanade, where a basket of spices may be purchased. **Fort George,** the site of former prime minister **Maurice Bishop's** execution in 1983, was built by the French in the early 18th century and provides a stunning view of the entire harbor. Another major attraction is the fort's underground passageways and dungeons.

In 1983 American paratroopers poured out of the sky to begin their famous six-day invasion of Grenada on **Grand Anse Beach** (*L'anse aux Pines* as it's known in French) on the southwest side of the island. Today the beach is known for its excellent hotels and restaurants.

Nevis

For the vacationer who's truly looking for a Caribbean retreat that's not on the tourist fast-track, Nevis (pronounced *nee-vis*) is an ideal locale.

This cross-shaped island measures only nine by seven miles, and it was once called *Nieve* (Spanish for snow) by Columbus because it reminded him of the Sierra Mountains of Spain.

Alexander Hamilton was born on the isle and **Lord Horatio Nelson** married **Fanny Nesbitt** here (St.

John's Church in **Fig Tree Village** has the records), but not much news has come out of the cloud-shrouded island in the last few centuries. In fact, in charming defiance of modern architecture, most of the hotels on Nevis are renovated plantations.

Nevis is integrally tied to its sister island, St. Kitts. A ferry runs daily between **Charlestown** (the capital of Nevis) and Basseterre on St. Kitts.

Saint-Barthélemy

Commonly referred to by its nickname, **St. Barts,** this very expensive island is populated primarily by Swedish and French expatriates. For the most part, Saint-Barthélemy (pronounced *san bar-tel-le-mee*), an eight-square-mile isle, has retained its French flavor. Some say it looks like an exotic Mediterranean village.

Gustavia, the capital, was named for the Swedish **King Gustav III,** who in 1784 acquired Saint-Barthélemy from the French in a trade. The village of **Corossol** on the northwest peninsula is home to descendents of French settlers who have created fine straw baskets, hats, and other straw goods for more than two centuries.

St. Barts has become a favorite nesting place for American and international celebrities searching for unique, out-of-the-way island homes. The hills above the island's countless coves and bays provide a completely private tropical setting.

St. Barts' beaches are all public and many allow nude sunbathing; some of the best are **Columbier, Flamands,** and **St. Jean.**

St. Kitts

On a clear day atop **Brimstone Hill** on the island of St. Kitts, you may not see forever, but you can see all the way to Montserrat, Saba, Nevis, St. Eustatius, St. Barts, and St. Martin/Sint Maarten—six islands in one fell swoop.

The fortress atop 800-foot-tall Brimstone Hill was built in the 17th century, when the British and French were pummeling each other for control of the 68-square-mile island and other islands in the area. The bastion (and the island) finally surrendered to the British in 1783.

Originally named **St. Christopher** after Columbus' patron saint, St. Kitts is an unassuming place. Tourism is still new to the island. The hotels are more like guest houses than upscale resorts, although the numerous hostelries gratify a wide range of tastes and pocketbooks, and there are only three major roads on the entire island. Best of all, the roads are virtually empty. The many stop-off points enable visitors to experience fabulous views and enjoy the exotic foliage.

A stroll through **Basseterre,** the major town on St. Kitts, reveals its quietude at **Independence Park,** the popular meeting place for residents and the site for African slave-trading during the 18th and 19th centuries. And out in the verdant center of the island, monkeys frolic in the shadow of St. Kitts' highest point, **Mount Misery,** a dormant volcano that sightseers can actually climb into.

Turks and Caicos Islands

Ever since the exclusive **Meridian Club** (Club Med) was founded on tiny **Pine Cay** in the Caicos chain, these islands at the southeastern tip of the Bahamas have seen a gradual increase in tourism. The sailors discovered them first, followed by divers, and, most recently, general travelers as well as guests of Club Med. **Provo** has exploded with new hotels, including the Ramada with its popular casino. A Sheraton has been scheduled to open for some time, but as of now is still an uncompleted skeleton. **Grand Turk,** the capital, has also seen some development, though not as extensively as Provo. The hot spot to watch in this chain is a speck of rock called **Parrot Cay,** where an upscale private resort will be completed soon.

Puerto Rico

Bests

Glenn D. Patron
Businessman, Puerto Rico

Picnicking and swimming in the clear mountain streams of **Puerto Rico.**

Sailing anywhere in the Caribbean with the stereo playing classical music.

Eating roast pig at Christmastime.

Dancing the merengue all night.

Watching the sunset in **San Juan, Puerto Rico,** with a good Caribbean drink.

Dr. German E. Malaper
Physician, San Juan, Puerto Rico

Old San Juan—rich in traditions and culture with the old castles and cobblestoned streets.

El Yunque, the rain forest near **Loiza,** for its trees, flora, and fauna.

The beautiful, interesting **Camuy Cave** near **Aguadilla.**

Jajome Terrace Restaurant—located high in the mountains, it has a beautiful view, good food, and reasonable prices.

Playa de Salinas Restaurants (there are several)—features beautiful views of the bay and excellent, fresh seafood at reasonable prices.

The various *paradores* (motels) around the island that are run by the Puerto Rican Tourism Company. They offer peace and quiet and good food.

Coral is made by tubular-shaped animals called polyps, which are about the size of a pencil eraser and are topped by a ring of tentacles that are similar in appearance to its relative, the sea anemone.

Speed bumps in the Caribbean islands are commonly called "sleeping policemen."

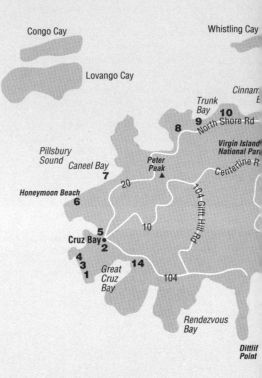

Congo Cay

Whistling Cay

Lovango Cay

Cinnam
E

Trunk
Bay   **10**

8 **9** North Shore Rd

Virgin Island
National Par

Pillsbury
Sound   Caneel Bay
7   Peter
Peak   Centerline R

Honeymoon Beach   20   ▲
6

5   10
Cruz Bay •
2
4 3   **14**
1   Great
Cruz
Bay   104

Rendezvous
Bay

Dittlif
Point

United States
Virgin Islands

Christopher Columbus named this cluster of more than 50 verdan islands and cays after the beautiful **Saint Ursula** and her 11,000 martyred virgins. The islands sit in the middle of the Caribbean archipelago, surrounded by crystalline, sapphire waters and cooled by trade winds blowing in from Portugal. The stunning scenery has inspired people from all walks of life—from explorers and infamous privateers to mainland dropouts seeking an unhurried lifestyle.

The residents of the three major islands—**St. Thomas, St. Croix,** and **St. John**—have more in common than just their surrounding sea and colorful past. As unincorporated territories of the United States, they also share the English language, US currency, and the all-American penchant for pleasurable pursuits. Amenities here match those of the mainland; the phone systems are as sophisticated as those in New York and cable comes in so clearly you won't have to miss even one episode of "Saturday Night Live."

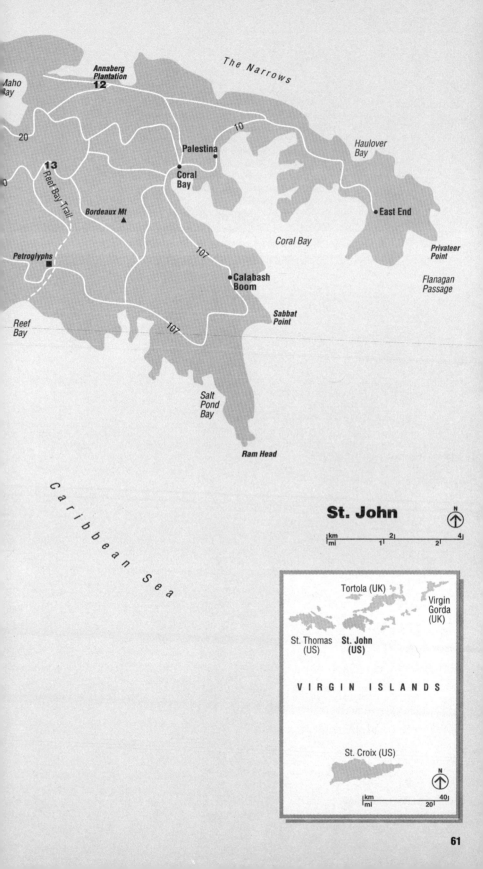

Maho
Bay

The Narrows

**Annaberg
Plantation**
12

20

13

0

Reef Bay Trail

Bordeaux Mt ▲

Palestina

**Coral
Bay**

10

*Haulover
Bay*

• **East End**

Coral Bay

Petroglyphs
■

107

• **Calabash
Boom**

*Privateer
Point*

*Flanagan
Passage*

*Reef
Bay*

107

*Sabbat
Point*

*Salt
Pond
Bay*

Ram Head

C a r i b b e a n   S e a

St. John

N
⬆

| km | | 2 | | 4 |
| mi | 1 | | 2 | |

Tortola (UK)

Virgin
Gorda
(UK)

St. Thomas
(US)

**St. John
(US)**

VIRGIN   ISLANDS

St. Croix (US)

N
⬆

| km | | 40 |
| mi | 20 | |

Getting to the Islands
Airlines

American Airlines................................800/433.7300

Braniff International...........................800/272.6433

British Airways 800/247.9297

Continental 800/525.0280

Delta...800/221.1212

Inter-Island Carriers

The following airlines fly between the US Virgin Islands, as well as from Puerto Rico and several other Caribbean islands.

Air BVI...800/468.2485

American Eagle.................................800/433.7300

LIAT..800/253.5011

US Virgin Islands

Sunaire Express...............................778.4852

Virgin Air 800/522.3084

VI Seaplane......................................773.1776

Airports

Alexander Hamilton Airport American Airlines and Braniff International provide the only nonstop flights from the states to **St. Croix.** Call 778.2773 for more information.

Cyril E. King Airport American Airlines, Braniff International, Continental, and Delta fly nonstop from the United States to the southcentral shore of **St. Thomas.** Call 774.5100 for more information.

St. John has no airport. Visitors must fly into Cyril E. King Airport on St. Thomas and take either a ferry or seaplane to the island.

Cruises

Day-trippers can hop around to various uninhabited isles to snorkel or scuba dive, picnic, or just explore. All types of boats are available, from sailboats to ferries, motor yachts, and party trimarans. The following list of companies allow you to choose your own itinerary.

On St. Croix:

Ruffian Enterprises 773.6011

On St. John:

Coral Bay Watersports................................776.6850

Ocean Diver...776.6922

On St. Thomas:

Naked Turtle..776.5506

Stormy Petrol...775.1851

Wet Pleasures 776.6922

For day, snorkel, sunset, half-day, and moonlit sails, contact one of the following boats.

On St. Croix:

Big Beard's Adventure Tours.......................773.4482

The Elinor...773.7171

Mile Mark Watersports........773.2628, 800/524.2012

Teroro II..773.4041

On St. John:

Calypso Queen (glass-bottom boat)............776.6922

Gratia (sloop)...776.6330

Jolly Mon (catamaran)................................776.6922

On St. Thomas:

Alexander Hamilton (schooner)...................775.6500

Daydreamer (trimaran)...............................775.2584

True Love (sailing vessel)............................775.6547

Getting around the Islands
Buses

On St. Thomas, there's service throughout Charlotte Amalie and connecting service between Charlotte Amalie and Red Hook Harbour, and Charlotte Amalie and Bordeaux; for more information, call 774.5678. St. Croix has taxi vans that run between Christiansted and Frederiksted; for more information, call 778.1088. St. John has no bus service.

Car Rentals

On St. Croix:

Avis 778.9355

Budget..778.4663

Caribbean Jeep...773.4399

Hertz...778.1402

On St. John:

Avis...776.6374

Budget..776.7575

St. John Car Rental 776.6103

On St. Thomas:

ABC Auto and Jeep Rental...776.1222, 800/524.2080

Budget.............................776.5774, 800/626.4516

Dependable.......................774.2253, 800/522.3076

National...777.8616

Driving

All three islands require driving on the left side of the road. On St. Thomas, rush-hour traffic is as congested as in any major American city. Parking in Charlotte Amalie is difficult, and if you park where you're not supposed to, chances are you'll get a $25 ticket. Avoid the problem by parking in the large pay lot beside Fort Christian.

Outside of the main towns, locals will sometimes stop in the middle of the road to chat for a moment with a passing a friend...be patient with them. Also, it's customary when going around a blind curve to give notice by beeping your horn a few times. The roads are paved and tend to be good on all three islands. However, beware the occasional mongoose, goat, or grazing donkey; they do not always give you the right of way. Most rental-car companies require drivers to be at least 25 years of age. After that, all you need is a valid American driver's license and a major credit card.

Ferry Service

The following ferries provide regular service from Charlotte Amalie and Red Hook Harbor on St. Thomas to St. John.

Interisland Boat Services 776.6597

Smiths Ferry 775.7292

Transportation Services of St. John 776.6282

Taxis

The cabs are not metered, but fares are regulated by the Virgin Islands Taxi Commission. Fees vary according to the number of passengers and suitcases. All cabs are required to carry a copy of the official rates and to show it to passengers when asked. Local tourist guides also print the fares between popular destinations. Always agree on the fee before you start. It's not unusual for a taxi to pick up additional passengers headed in the same direction.

Tours

To view the islands from the air or to be dropped off on an uninhabited isle for the day, consider booking a helicopter from one of these firms on St. Thomas.

Air Center Helicopter Tours 775.7335

Antilles Helicopter Tours 776.7880

Yacht Charters

The Virgin Islands have a reputation for some of the best sailing waters in the world, and the charter operations have grown to accommodate the increasing number of people who want to explore the area. You can charter a boat with a captain and crew (usually one person who acts as the first mate/cook/chief bottle washer), or bareback-style, which is without a captain or crew (or supplies unless you request them in advance).

The largest charter fleet in the Caribbean is based in the Virgins, so it's easy to rent a boat that meets your needs. Most charters are hired for a week or longer. For more information, contact one of the following charter organizations.

On St. John:
Proper Yachts 775.7335
Tropic Isles Yacht Charters 776.6863

On St. Thomas:
Caribbean Adventures Yacht Charters 776.7245
Club Nautico 779.2555
Leisure Enterprises 800/843.3566
Ocean Incentives 775.6406
VIP Yacht Charters 776.1510

FYI

Money

The American dollar is used here, just like at home. Banks are open M-Th 9AM-2:30PM; F 9AM-2PM, 3:30-5PM.

Personal Safety

Expect to live on island time, which means not on time (no one really ever rushes around here). Also, expect to encounter cultural gaps. While the islands are technically American, they are Caribbean in history, culture, and attitude. And remember, even on laid-back St. John, crime still exists. Lock the car doors and don't leave your valuables in sight. Never walk down deserted streets or alleys at night and always keep your wallet in your front pocket or a zippered pocketbook.

Phone Book

Ambulance...922

Diving Emergencies/Decompression Chambers:
On St. Thomas 776.2686
On St. Croix....................................778.6311 ext. 2664
Directory Assistance 913
Fire...921

National Park...776.6201
Operator Assistance......................................0
Police..915
St. Croix Hotel Association..................800/524.2026
United States Coast Guard Rescue:
On St. Thomas 774.7984
On St. Croix...773.2838
Visitor Information................................800/878.4636

Scuba Diving

The Virgin Islands are a diver's playground, with an abundance of reefs and sunken ships just waiting to be explored. The water is warm and the visibility averages close to one hundred feet.

Novices can take a three-hour scuba-diving course (commonly offered at resorts) that gets them in the water the same day, or combine their vacation with a five-day intensive certification course offered by the following dive operations.

On St. Croix:
In Christiansted:
Dive St. Croix......................773.3434, 800/523.3483
VI Divers 773.6045, 800/544.5911
In Frederiksted:
Cruzan Divers 772.3701, 800/247.8186

On St. John:
Cinnamon Bay Watersports........................776.6330
Cruz Bay Watersports.................................776.6234
Paradise Watersports.................................776.7618

On St. Thomas:
Aqua Action...775.6285
Chris Sawyer Diving Center 775.7320
St. Thomas Diving Club 776.2381
Underwater Safaris.....................................774.1350
Virgin Islands Diving School 774.8687

St. John

When Virgin Islanders want a vacation, they head over to St. John, which they've nicknamed **Love Island** because they say there's not much else to do on St. John except make love. But that's not *entirely* true. St. John's other lures include its soaring mountains, curving white beaches, underwater coral gardens, and slow pace of life. Furthermore, two-thirds of the island is a national park (donated to the United States in 1956 by multimillionaire **Laurance Rockefeller**) that provides numerous walking trails within a cover of jungle. There are no airports, neon signs, late-night discos, or traffic lights. Of course, there's also no traffic—unless you count the occasional stubborn donkey or darting mongoose. This one-village island caters to nature-loving escapists with either thick wallets or a yen for camping.

US Virgin Islands

Area code 809 unless otherwise noted.

1 Virgin Islands National Park Visitor's Center St. John is two-thirds national park, so you should make this your first stop. The center is full of information on the Park Service's numerous hiking trails, evening programs, and cultural demonstrations. Lots of activities are free for the whole family, including children's environmental programs, birdwatching hikes, and a series of hour-long evening lectures on subjects that range from endangered animals to medicinal plants and coral-reef ecology. There's a charge for their snorkel tours, hikes, and Monday historic bus tours to the east end of the island, but they're worth every penny, as the tours are led by park rangers who are chock-full of knowledge about the island's history, culture, and animal and marine life.

Programs are held year-round, but there are more during the peak tourist months of January through April. The programs change seasonally, so stop in for the latest trail maps, hiking advice, and list of activities. ♦ Daily 8AM-4:30PM. Cruz Bay. Evening programs: Free. M, W, Th 7:30-8:30PM. Cinnamon Bay campground amphitheater. 776.6201

2 Cruz Bay When St. Johnians say they're going into town, they mean this sleepy place. The small boutiques are filled with local handicrafts and the cafes with people who come to browse, chat, gossip, argue politics, and watch the boats cruise into the harbor. Everyone's friendly (everyone knows each other on an island this size), and it's rare to come across someone who's in a rush. While life in St. John is casual, there is one caveat: it's against the "Keep St. John Beautiful" law to walk around town in a bathing suit.

Restaurants/Clubs: Red
Shops/ 🌴 Outdoors: Green
Hotels: Blue
Sights/Culture: Black

3 Wharfside Village An unusual number of original-art emporiums resides in this three-story minimall where everything from prints to pottery, paintings, and clothing is sold. You'll also find smaller outlets of the trendy duty-free shops selling name-brand perfumes, watches, and jewelry in St. Thomas, including **Colombian Emeralds** and **Blue Carib Gems.** Stop in at **Third World Electronics** for the latest in reggae, calypso, and steel-band cassettes and CDs. ♦ Daily 9:30AM-9PM. Just south of Ferry Dock. 776.7658

4 Mongoose Junction This pleasant mix of shops and restaurants (illustrated above) built of native stone is the place to watch artisans at work and buy one-of-a-kind crafts, pottery, fine art, resortwear, and even antique West Indian furniture. Look for batik, silkscreened, and hand-painted wall hangings, beachwraps, and bolts of material at the **Fabric Mill.** Pottery and hand-blown glass reflecting the richness of color in the USVI can be found at the **Donald Schnell Studio,** while Caribbean crafts, folk art, and furniture are carried by **Bamboula.** For handcrafted silver and gold jewelry, stop by **R&I Patton Goldsmiths.** ♦ Daily 9:30AM-9PM. Three blocks north of Ferry Dock. 776.6267

Within Mongoose Junction:

Paradiso ★★$$ This restaurant is known for combining two favorite island activities: people-watching and eating. The setting is a veranda, the fare features pasta and veal, and the ambience tends toward crowded American. ♦ Northern Italian ♦ Tu-Sa 11:30AM-2:30PM, 6-10PM. Dinner reservations recommended. 776.8806

5 Elaine Ione Sprauve Museum Pottery and tools made by both the gentle Arawak and fiercer Carib Indians line the shelves of this former plantation house, once known as **Enighed.** There are also displays and old photographs from the island's past, a working windmill model, and a few colonial-era relics. Changing exhibits occasionally showcase the work of island artists and artisans. The small museum shares its home with the public library. ♦ Donation. M-F 9AM-5PM. Just southeast of Cruz Bay. 776.6359

6 Honeymoon Beach Just beyond the narrow crescent of white beach lies a unique experience: the tame manta rays in these shallow waters will eat out of your hand. Just wade out into the knee-deep water, swish some bread about to attract the rays, and wait. If the small rays are around, they'll be happy to swim over for the free handout. ♦ Daily 11AM-2PM (best times). 776.6111

 **CANEEL BAY**

7 Caneel Bay $$$$ Multimillionaire **Laurance Rockefeller** turned this sprawling wilderness into his dream resort, a place where privacy and peace prevail, crowds are unheard of, and the hassles of civilization are left outside the front gate.

There's a beach for every day of the week and an acre for every room (the 171 rooms are spread out along the sandy shore or overlooking the gardens and 11 tennis courts). The atmosphere is a cross between that of an exclusive country club and a genteel island plantation; the meticulously kept grounds overflow with more than 2,000 varieties of trees, plants, shrubs, and exotic flowers. The rooms are comfortable and basic—cooled by ceiling fans and tropical breezes flowing through louvered windows—and meant to provide no distractions. The idea is to relax on the beaches or among the gardens, or take advantage of the complimentary windsurfers, snorkel gear, and day-sailers. Guests also are invited to a weekly garden walk led by the grounds botanist, evening movies, exercise classes, and marine slide shows. For an extra fee, you can enjoy excellent scuba diving, an excursion to **Virgin Gorda,** and both day and sunset cruises. Three restaurants round out the picture. ◆ Deluxe ◆ Virgin Islands National Park. 776.6111, 800/223.7637

8 Peace Hill This peak is considered one of the top spots for viewing St. John. You'll share the view of the North Shore with St. John's famous 30-foot-high statue *Christ of the Caribbean.* ◆ 2.8 miles north of Cruz Bay (North Shore Rd)

9 Trunk Bay *National Geographic* singled out this slice of brilliant white coral sand as one of the world's most beautiful beaches. Sunbathers who can drag themselves off the shore will find an underwater trail marked by a series of floats. Snorkelers can peer down at the written displays to read about reef life and watch the fish in action. The Park Service maintains the entire bay, including the picnic areas, snack bar, changing rooms, and showers. Lifeguards are on duty and there's a shack that rents snorkel gear. ◆ Free. Daily 8AM-5PM

10 North Shore Road From Cruz Bay, head north on this winding, well-paved road that hugs the hills overlooking the shoreline. Driving is on the left, but then so are all the scenic overlooks. From different vantage points, you can even see the islands of **St. Thomas, Jost Van Dyke,** and **Tortola,** to name a few. Just drive carefully, as there are no traffic lights, and donkeys, goats, and mongooses sometimes forget the road was built for people. ◆ Cruz Bay-Coral Bay

11 Cinnamon Bay $ Its campsites, comprised of tiny wood cabins and tent platforms, hug a long scalloped beach. The locale is lovely, but the accommodations—which are perfect for a troop of Boy Scouts—are only for those who have eschewed all semblances of luxury save a snack bar, commissary, and showers. The Park Service runs snorkel tours here, and begins several of their hikes at a point just across the road. They'll also teach you to bake johnnycake and other native favorites in the campground's outdoor woodburning oven. Believe it or not, you need to make reservations almost a full year in advance. ◆ Cinnamon Bay. 776.6330, 800/223.7637

12 Annaberg Plantation The National Park Service has restored the stone ruins of this 18th-century Danish sugar mill. Pick up their guide at the entrance and wander through the ruins of slave quarters, the sugar mill, and

storage buildings. Three times a week, St. Johnians gear up for a morning of colonial crafts, cooking, and gardening to show visitors what life was once like here. ◆ Free. Tu,W, F 9AM-noon; Jan-April. Call for May-Dec schedule. 776.6201

13 Reef Bay Trail This is considered the most popular hiking trail in the USVI, probably because it's all downhill. The 2.6-mile trail is self-guiding, with signs that tell about the island's history and the hundred-plus species of birds and trees found along the path. Listen to the rattling pods of the tree known as the Mother-in-Law's Tongue, smell the foul Stinking Toe, and laugh at the red, peeling Tourist Tree.

The ruins of four sugar estates can be seen from the dirt path, echoing the hopes and dreams of the early Danish settlers. About midway, look for a trickling waterfall and follow it to its base. Here, primitive "graffiti," supposedly carved by either the Arawak or Carib Indians, can be seen on the rocks alongside the placid pools.

This trail is just one of 21 maintained by the National Park Service, which offers guided tours for a small fee on Monday and Wednesday. The benefit is they arrange a ride back to Cruz Bay from the bottom of the trail—which certainly beats walking back up. ◆ Daily dawn-dusk. Centerline Rd, 4.9 miles northeast of Cruz Bay. 776.6330

14 Hyatt Regency St. John $$$$ The main reason to choose this hotel over the Caneel Bay resort is air-conditioning—this hotel has it; Caneel Bay doesn't. The 285 guestrooms, suites, and town houses here also feature color TVs, telephones, marble bathrooms, and private terraces or balconies. Be aware, though, that what you gain in amenities, you lose in ambience. The island-feel is lost among the pink buildings and giant fan-shaped pool. Sure, there are lots of palm trees and the beach is a dream, but you can never forget you're in a top-notch American resort dropped into a Gilligan's Island setting.

That said, there's lots to do. Sign the kids up for **Camp Paradise,** then take advantage of the free snorkeling, windsurfing, kayaking, and tennis. There are three restaurants, nightly music, and a weekly comedy show. Children under the age of 18 stay free in their parents' room. The hotel provides complimentary rollaway beds. ♦ Deluxe ♦ Great Cruz Bay. 776.7171, 800/233.1234

St. Croix

A more tranquil Virgin Island, especially at night, St. Croix (pronounced *saint kroy*) is often referred to as "the other Virgin," as it's the least known. It was also the Caribbean

island hardest hit when **Hurricane Hugo** blew through in 1989. Almost $1 billion dollars of insurance money was spent repairing, renovating, and refurbishing the homes, hotels, restaurants, towns, and attractions on this largest of the United States Virgin Islands. Hugo stories still abound, but many believe the island looks better now than it did before. Certainly, a number of the hotels and restaurants do. Once an island of planters, the rolling hills and grassy valleys beckon with the ruins and restorations of more than one hundred sugar mills and Great Houses.

St. Croix has a drier climate than her siblings, but the lushness that's missing aboveground is found offshore in what the islanders call the gardens of the Caribbean—a vibrant underwater world filled with coral formations, giant sponges, and tropical fish. Hustling and bustling are virtually unheard of here, and what little action there is occurs in the island's two historic Danish towns, **Christiansted** and **Frederiksted.**

Christiansted, one of the Caribbean's most charming towns, offers a mixture of Danish and Caribbean architecture in a jewel box of pastel colors. Narrow, mostly one-way streets make driving difficult, so your best bet is to take a cab to town and start your walking tour at the **Old Scale House** by the wharf, where plantation owners once took their produce to be weighed. Boutiques filled with resortwear; crafts; and duty-free cameras, perfumes, watches, and jewelry can be found at the **Pan Am Pavilion, Market Square Mall,** and **King's Wharf.** Guides offer free walking tours of the town at the **Tourist Office.** "Take a Hike" historical tours of Christiansted are led by **Ms. Verne Fredericks** on Saturday mornings. Call 778.6997 for reservations and more information.

Restaurants/Clubs: Red   Hotels: Blue
Shops/ 🎋 Outdoors: Green   **Sights/Culture:** Black

1 Fort Christiansvaern This is the best preserved of the five remaining Danish forts in the Virgin Islands. Its color comes from the yellow bricks used in its construction—a prime example of 18th-century Danish colonial military architecture. An exhibit on local military history is displayed in the Commandant's Quarters on the second floor. ♦ Admission. M-F 8AM-5PM. Park at King's Wharf. 773.1460

1 Steeple Building Built by the Danes in 1735 to be a Lutheran church, this was subsequently used as a military bakery, hospital, and school. Today it houses the **National Park Museum,** with exhibits on island archaeology, black history, and Danish architecture. ♦ Admission. Tu-Sa 9-11AM, 1-3PM. Company St (Hospital St). 773.1460

1 Kendrick's ★★★$$
Consistently good food and top-notch service differentiates this Italian restaurant from the others in its crowd. It's located in the middle of Christiansted, on the second floor of an old town house. Like many Virgin Island restaurants, a little bit of everything has gone into creating the ambience. In this case, it's a mix of West Indian and French provincial decor. Diners can eat in either an air-conditioned or tropical-breeze setting. There's no view; just a pleasant atmosphere and memorable homemade pastas and grilled fish. ♦ Italian ♦ M-Sa 6-10PM. Queen Cross St (King-Strand Sts). Dinner reservations recommended. 773.9199

1 Elinor Almost a century old, this three-masted schooner sails from Christiansted to Frederiksted serving light snacks, drinks, sun, and fun. They also offer daily sunset cruises from 5-7:30PM and a monthly evening cruise in honor of the full moon. Call for a schedule, as it changes according to demand. ♦ Admission. King's Wharf, Christiansted Harbor. 773.7171

1 Top Hat Restaurant
★★★★$$$ The 20-year-old St. Croix institution serves true Danish food in a restored Danish town house. Come early for a drink and some gawking, as the walls and ceiling of

their bar are plastered with hundreds of photographs of famous and not-so-famous folks who've eaten here.

The menu features lots of meat dishes, several quasi-German entrées, and a number of Scandinavian specialties. The Danish dishes include roast duck with apples, prunes, and red cabbage, as well as homemade sausages and herring. ♦ Danish ♦ M-Sa 6-10PM; 1 Nov-1 May. 52 Company St. Reservations required. 773.2346

1 Cormorant Beach Club $$$$ Refurbishments after Hurricane Hugo included tasteful new furnishings for the 34 beachfront guestrooms and four penthouse suites, plus a new open-air lobby with an adjacent raised bar providing a bird's-eye view of the beach and swimming pool.

This small resort is geared toward adults, so you won't be tripping over many children here. You're encouraged to lounge in the hammocks or on the chaises that dot their pristine palm-shaded beach. Many businesspeople vacation at the Cormorant due to the excellent discount offered corporate employees.

You have a choice of two meal plans, but since the quality of the food is inconsistent, you may not want to lock yourself into eating only here. The thoughtful extras, such as the longtime staff quickly learning your name, cold beverages packed in a cooler by the tennis courts, and free afternoon tea and desserts served in the lobby, single out this hotel.

Snorkel equipment is provided and marine lovers will be pleased to find the reef starts right offshore. Wear booties, as the sea here is a bit rocky. Swimmers and splashers will fare better in the free-form pool with its massaging waterfall. There are no TVs in the rooms, but a big-screen TV can be found in the video/game room. Children must be older than five to stay here. ♦ 4126 LaGrande Princesse. 778.8920, 800/548.4460

Jumping Ship to Get Hitched

Many couples are skipping the expensive traditional weddings at home and eloping to the US Virgin Islands instead. Standard operating procedure is to contact a wedding planner service such as **Leisure Enterprises** (775.9203, 800/ 843.3566) on St. Thomas and leave the leg work up to them. They arrange all the paperwork, help the couple select a romantic site, schedule the officiant, order the flowers and the cake, hire a professional photographer or videographer, line up the limo, and chill the champagne. All the couple has to do is show up. In fact, the newest trend for getting hitched is to book a cruise, start the honeymoon, abandon ship in the US Virgin Islands to marry, and then reboard the ship to finish honeymooning.

2 Hilty House $$ This new addition to St. Croix's flourishing accommodations scene sits on top of a hill above Christiansted. Opened in 1991 by Brits **Hugh** and **Jacquie Hoare-Ward,** the family operated guest house is garnishing rave reviews as *the* bed-and-breakfast to reserve.

The property is part of an old sugar plantation (the current estate house used to be the rum factory). Hand-painted Florentine tiles adorn the floors of the five guestrooms, while crystal chandeliers hang in three of the six bathrooms. There are also three one-bedroom cottages on the grounds, available to reserve by the week or month.

Amenities are plentiful, but they're the kind that appeal to seekers of a gracious retreat: peace and quiet surrounded by wild mango, tamarind, lime, and papaya trees; a swimming pool; and a sundeck.

Everything is geared toward couples and singles, with no scheduled activities and nothing for children. Most guests who stay here rent a car, as breakfast is the only meal provided. ♦ Questa Verde Rd (Hermon Hill). 773.2594, 800/524.2026

3 The Buccaneer $$$ With Carambola Beach Resort and Golf Club closed and awaiting a new buyer, this full-service resort has moved into position as the island's flagship property. Extensive grounds and three beaches spread out over 240 acres provide the backdrop for a variety of accommodations ranging from basic rooms to tennis villas and superdeluxe oceanfront suites.

The golfers who gravitate here are lured by the Buccaneer's 18-hole, par 71 course. Parents play at ease while their children stay busy in a supervised program offering arts and crafts, sand-castle building, snorkel parties, and other fun activities.

A comprehensive water-sports program, including lessons, is offered by the **Beach Shack,** while pros offer tennis instruction on eight Laykold courts. There are two pools, three restaurants, an 18-station exercise path, day and evening cruises, a shopping arcade, and a health salon offering massages, seaweed wraps, and reflexology. And what the longtime staff lacks in service, it definitely makes up for in friendliness.

The property is owned and run by the Armstrong family, which has lived on St. Croix for nine generations. **Elizabeth Armstrong** leads free weekly nature walks, pointing out exotic flowers and plants while enchanting guests with stories of the resort's history. As with

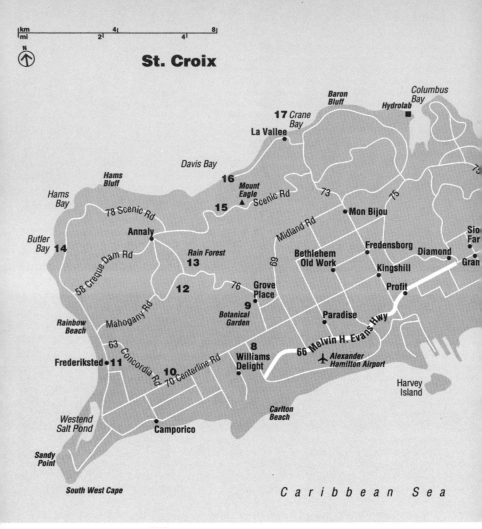

St. Croix

Baron Bluff
Columbus Bay
Hydrolab
17 *Crane Bay*
La Vallee
Davis Bay
Hams Bluff
16
Mount Eagle
Scenic Rd
73
75
Hams Bay
15
Mon Bijou
Sio Far
Butler Bay **14**
78 Scenic Rd
Annaly
Midland Rd
Fredensborg
Diamond
58 Creque Dam Rd
Rain Forest
13
Bethlehem Old Work
Kingshill
Gran
12
76
Grove Place
Profit
Rainbow Beach
Mahogany Rd
9
Botanical Garden
Paradise
63
Concordia Rd
Frederiksted **11**
70 Centerline Rd
10
8 Williams Delight
66 Melvin H. Evans Hwy
Alexander Hamilton Airport
Harvey Island
Westend Salt Pond
Camporico
Carlton Beach
Sandy Point
South West Cape
Caribbean Sea

room prices, the rates range from "room only" to the new **Treasures** program—a semi-inclusive package covering meals, water and land sports, several tours, and airport transfers. Children under 12 stay free. ♦ Deluxe ♦ Gallows Bay. 773.2100, 800/223.1108

bouillabaisse, and rack of lamb for two. Sunday brunch is an all-you-can-eat buffet complete with desserts. ♦ Continental ♦ Tu-Sa 4PM-10PM; Su 10AM-2PM, 4PM-10PM. Green Cay Marina, east of Christiansted. Dinner reservations required. 773.9949

4 The Galleon ★★★$$$ This local favorite serves traditional French and Northern Italian cuisine along with live music, courtesy of a wonderful pianist. Oneophiles will appreciate the large selection of fine wines available by the glass. Of special note is their foie gras,

5 Duggan's Reef ★★$$ Overlooking the beach and **Buck Island**, and popular with locals and tourists in the know, this informal restaurant serves the best conch fritters on St. Croix. Owner **Frank Duggan** keeps both the service and the smiles flowing. Try their fresh fish, served island style or blackened with a side

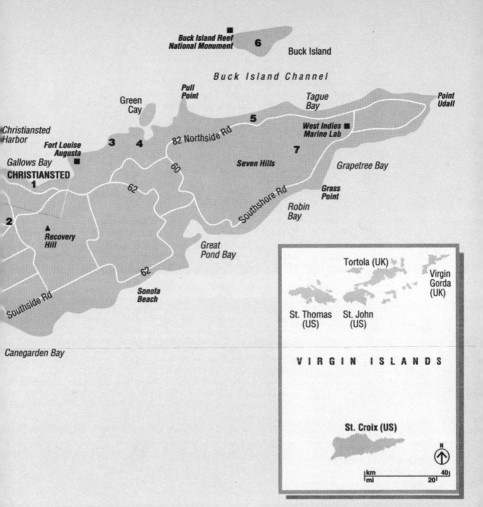

order of pasta. ♦ American/Seafood ♦ Daily noon-3PM, 6-9:15PM. Reef Beach, take Rte 82 to east end of island. Dinner reservations recommended. 773.9800

6 Buck Island This reef-encircled isle just six miles off Christiansted's shore is a snorkeler's paradise. The reef lies just beneath the water's surface, with an average depth of only 13 feet, making it as close to scuba diving as a snorkeler can get. The underwater trail is very clearly marked, with angelfish, parrotfish, and groupers feeding near the signs. As you swim along, schools of iridescent blue tangs part to let you pass.

The reef is alive with color and filled with tons of Elkhorn, Brain, and Finger coral in formations that would make a sculptor green with envy. Your best bet is to go during the week, as on weekends the island gets crowded with Crucians basking on the powder beaches and lolling in the aquamarine lagoon. The island is protected by the National Park Service; souvenir collecting will get you a severe fine. Trips to the island are offered by **Mile Mark Watersports** (King Christian Hotel, Christian-

sted. 773.2628, 800/524.2012), **Teroro II** (Green Cay Marina, Christiansted. 773.4041), and **Big Beard's Adventure Tours** (Pan Am Pavilion, Christiansted. 773.4482).

7 Villa Madeleine $$$$ Nestled in a ridge atop a large hill on the east end of the island lies this elegant gem with views of the sea from both sides.

In a format reminiscent of Acapulco's Las Brisas, 25 lemon-colored one- and two-bedroom villas are terraced along the hill below the main house. The designer-decorated villas have plush living rooms with color TVs and VCRs; oversized pink-marble showers; his and her closets; modern kitchens with microwave ovens, dishwashers, and refrigerators stocked

69

at your request; and bedrooms with center-piece four-poster beds. Sets of French doors open onto a private, patio-enclosed pool and sun terrace. The overall effect is a slice of Mediterranean luxury.

You are encouraged to borrow a book from the library, shoot pool in the billiards room, or play tennis on the two courts. The nine-hole **Reef Golf Course** is just down the hill. The Villa Madeleine is geared toward couples or families traveling with older children. ◆ Deluxe ◆ Estate Teague Bay. 773.8141, 800/548.4461

Within the Villa Madeleine:

Cafe Madeleine ★★★★$$$$ This fine restaurant is expensive and worth every penny—for both the incredible views from the terrace and the mouth-watering Italian cuisine. Cafe Madeleine is housed in the West Indian-style main building high above **Teague Bay,**

with a ceiling draped in a floral-print fabric picked out by former White House decorator **Carleton Varney.** Dinner can be enjoyed either alfresco on the canopied terrace overlooking the sea or in the air-conditioned dining room.

The creative menu changes frequently, but relies heavily on fresh pastas, fish, and meat. Leave room for the devastating **Chocolate Blackout** dessert. This is currently considered the best restaurant on the island, so make your reservations early. ◆ Italian ◆ Daily 6-9:30PM. Reservations recommended. 778.7377

8 Cruzan Rum Factory When you order a rum punch in these parts, this is what gives it the "punch." Before Hurricane Hugo ripped through the island, the factory used to offer free tours of their distillery followed by rum tastings. The factory is running again, but so far the tours haven't resumed. You may want to call and check when you get on island. ◆ Estate Diamond. 772.0280/03

9 Botanical Garden Ask for the guidebook to the tour that follows the brown-and-white signs throughout the property's 350-plus species of trees, flowers, vines, and shrubs. You'll see the Mother-in-Law tree, so named because the brown pods rattle when the wind blows, making a chattering noise. The signs also label the soaring kapok tree, the quarter-sized plumbago blossom, and the endangered Touch-Me-Not tree. Pull a nut off a tamarind tree, crush the shell, and lick the fruit inside. This sticky gel is used in jams and jellies. ◆ Admission. Daily 9AM-4PM. Centerline Rd, take Rte 70, just east of W. Airport Rd. 772.3874

10 Whim Plantation Estate The name has inspired lots of theories, including one contending that the man who bought the plantation in the mid-1700s was so rich he purchased it on a whim. Perhaps. Certainly the Great House is unlike any others found in the Caribbean (see the map below). It's oval-shaped, with an "air" moat surrounding it and limestone walls three feet thick.

Whoever designed the house was ahead of his or her time. The moat makes sense, allowing air to flow around and through the basement; cooler air means less spoilage of stored goods. The thick walls have withstood every storm and hurricane to hit the island.

Inside, the house has been restored to its French neoclassic designs and colonial

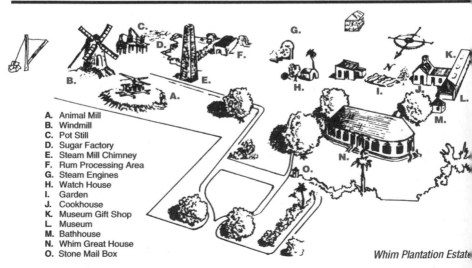

A. Animal Mill
B. Windmill
C. Pot Still
D. Sugar Factory
E. Steam Mill Chimney
F. Rum Processing Area
G. Steam Engines
H. Watch House
I. Garden
J. Cookhouse
K. Museum Gift Shop
L. Museum
M. Bathhouse
N. Whim Great House
O. Stone Mail Box

Whim Plantation Estate

furnishings. There's even a johnnycake lady who bakes the fried island specialty the old-fashioned way.

Sugar was once milled on the grounds, and if the wind didn't blow, the donkeys were harnessed to the churn. When steam became available, it too was used. Today, all three styles of sugar mill can be seen on the grounds. ♦ Admission. Tu-Sa 10AM-4PM. Centerline Rd, take Rte 70, just east of Frederiksted. 772.0598

11 Frederiksted Rich in history and anecdotes, but somewhat legendary in actual sights, this town is the reason Virgin Islanders refer to St. Croix as the "tale of two cities." Cruise ships dock here and walking about is a time-honored tradition. Stop in for a map at the **Tourist Board** (772.0357), which is located in the **Port Authority** building at the entrance to the pier.

Fort Frederik (located next to the pier) has been restored to the way it looked under Danish rule in 1760; you can browse through the parade grounds, the barracks, and the command building (M-F 8AM-5PM). Several of the town's churches were built in the early 1800s, while the **Market Place** dates back to 1751. Vendors still use the spot at Queen and Cross streets to sell fresh fruits and vegetables (M-Sa 6AM-3PM).

New to town and on the list of sights to see is the **St. Croix Aquarium** (F-Su 10AM-6PM), an educational marine center with hundreds of tropical fish. It's on Strand Street, across from the pier. Call 772.1345 for information.

During the winter months, turn toward the sea at sunset to look for the "green flash." When the atmospheric conditions are just right, a green streak can be seen on the horizon for a brief moment as the sun drops below the sea.

12 Leap Shop In this enormous workshop deep in the rain forest, local artisans produce magnificent furniture, carvings, and kitchen items from the wood of dead mahogany, saman, and tibet trees. A film of sawdust covers everything, including the satin-smooth coffee tables, free-form wall clocks, windchimes, bookends, and cutting boards sold here. Better yet, they take credit cards and will even ship your purchase to the US. ♦ Mahogany Rd, 2.5 miles northeast of Frederiksted. 772.0421

13 Rain Forest While not a true rain forest, it's called one because it's the wettest—and greenest—area on the island. The road that passes through this forest is canopied by tree boughs, including those of the saman, which looks like an enormous bonsai tree. White flowers grow atop the yaki yaki tree, while the flamboyant tree is awash in brilliant red blossoms. ♦ Mahogany Rd (paved) or unpaved Rain Forest Rd (Creque Dam)

Restaurants/Clubs: Red   Hotels: Blue
Shops/ 🌳 Outdoors: Green   Sights/Culture: Black

14 Jill's Equestrian Center Jill Hurd, born and raised on St. Croix, runs this show, entertaining visitors with a combination of stories and facts. Her trail rides cut through the rain forest, past streambeds and Danish ruins, and over the hills of the west end. Tour guides point out termite nests, grazing cattle, and the infamous mongooses, brought to the island in its sugarcane heyday to kill rats. (The strategy didn't work; mongooses are day-loving creatures, while rats prefer the dark of night.)

Hurd also offers sunset rides into the hills, and full-moon rides through the forest. Pants are a must, and you'll be disappointed if you forget your camera. No children under the age of eight are admitted. ♦ Admission. Daily 10AM, 3PM. Reservations recommended. Call in advance for sunset and moonlight

schedule. Sprat Hall Plantation, take Rte 63, 1.5 miles north of Frederiksted. 772.2880

15 The Scenic Road Partially paved and partially dirt, this one-lane road meanders through some of St. Croix's loveliest scenery, from **Ham's Bay** by Frederiksted through **Caledonia Valley** over the hills of Annaly to **Mount Eagle.** On the way, it passes through the rain forest. Your best bet is to go in a four-wheel-drive Jeep; watch out for darting mongooses! ♦ Hams Bay-Mount Eagle

16 Carambola Golf Course Laurance Rockefeller hired **Robert Trent Jones** to design this outstanding 18-hole course. Coconut markers used to line the fairways; today they are lined with palm trees. ♦ Admission. Daily 7AM-6PM. Carambola. 778.5638

17 St. Croix Wall/Cane Bay Experienced scuba divers will smile for weeks, for there are not many places in the world where you can wade into the surf off the beach, slip into your dive gear, and within 80 yards free-float over a coral wall that drops two miles straight down.

The reef starts at the beach and gently slopes down until you're in 30 feet of water. Below, purple sea fans undulate and iridescent fish dart past. A minute later, the reef has disappeared down the sheer ledge and you're surrounded by the bluest water imaginable. The wall stretches along four miles of St. Croix's north coast. **Dive St. Croix** (773.3434, 800/523.3483) and **V.I. Divers** (773.6045, 800/544.5911), both in Christiansted, offer wall and other dives, resort courses, certification courses, and equipment rentals. ♦ Salt River-Hams Bluff

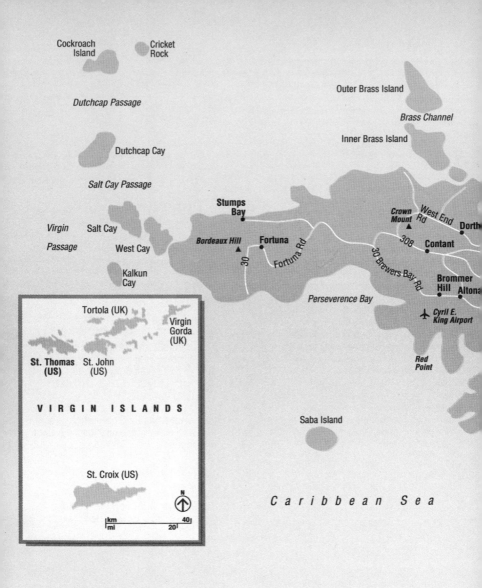

Cockroach Island

Cricket Rock

Dutchcap Passage

Outer Brass Island

Brass Channel

Dutchcap Cay

Inner Brass Island

Salt Cay Passage

Stumps Bay

Crown Mount ▲

West End Rd

Dorth

Virgin

Salt Cay

Bordeaux Hill ▲

Fortuna ●

Fortuna Rd

308

Contant ●

Passage

West Cay

30

30 Brewers Bay Rd

Brommer Hill ●

Altona

Kalkun Cay

Perseverence Bay

✈ Cyril E. King Airport

Tortola (UK)

Virgin Gorda (UK)

St. Thomas (US)

St. John (US)

Red Point

V I R G I N   I S L A N D S

St. Croix (US)

Saba Island

N ↑

km	40
mi	20

C a r i b b e a n   S e a

St. Thomas

The capital of the United States Virgin Islands is the most developed and the most commercialized, with a bustling port city and a deep harbor that's often filled with one or more cruise ships. Good roads wind through the green mountains of St. Thomas, leading visitors to the multitude of shimmering beaches, upscale resorts, and gourmet restaurants. Of the three sisters, this is the one to come to for action, nightlife, and shopping.

1 Frenchtown This town was originally settled by fishers who immigrated from **St. Barts,** a small French island in the Caribbean. Tiny wooden homes with gay-colored paint and red-tin roofs, and several excellent French restaurants characterize the colorful hamlet.

1 Chez Jacque ★★★★$$ Lawyers, doctors, and other professionals flock to this French brasserie at happy hour to unwind with friends and place an order at the wine bar, island-famous for serving more than 30 fine wines and champagnes by the glass. Most stay for dinner, ordering one or more of the 25 appetizers or traditional French entrées. Offerings include sweetbreads, lamb sausage, pâtés, escargot, or lobster bisque. The food is excellent, local art adorns the walls, and sometimes a live combo entertains on weekends. ◆ French ◆ M-Sa 5PM-midnight. Frenchtown. 776.5797

2 Sugar Reef Cafe ★$$ This is a popular hangout for locals, tourists in the know, and the yachting set. The food pales next to the lively atmosphere—this is definitely a place

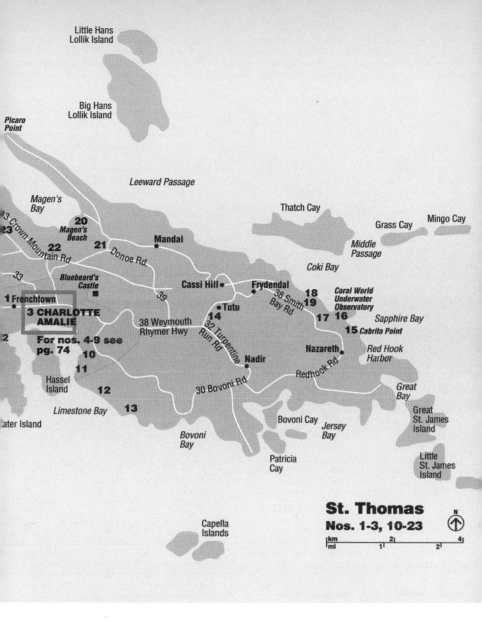

Little Hans
Lollik Island

Big Hans
Lollik Island

Picaro
Point

Leeward Passage

Thatch Cay

Grass Cay   Mingo Cay

Magen's
Bay

3 Crown Mountain Rd.
23

20   Magen's
         Beach
22   21   Donoe Rd.

Mandal

Middle
Passage

Coki Bay

33

Bluebeard's
Castle

Cassi Hill

Frydendal

Coral World
Underwater
Observatory

1 Frenchtown

39

Tutu

38 Smith
Bay Rd

18
19

17   16

Sapphire Bay

15 Cabrita Point

3 CHARLOTTE
AMALIE

14
38 Weymouth   32 Turpentine
Rhymer Hwy   Run Rd

Nazareth

Red Hook
Harbor

2

For nos. 4-9 see
pg. 74

10

Nadir

Redhook Rd.

11

Hassel
Island

12

30 Bovoni Rd.

Great
Bay

Limestone Bay

13

Great
St. James
Island

ater Island

Bovoni Cay

Jersey
Bay

Bovoni
Bay

Patricia
Cay

Little
St. James
Island

St. Thomas
Nos. 1-3, 10-23

km   2   4
mi   1   2

Capella
Islands

N

---

to see and be seen, especially at lunchtime. The alfresco setting overlooks the luxury yachts docked in **Gregerie Channel**. There's lots to look at, from the batik tablecloths and the soaring cormorant birds to the goings on at the bar. ♦ Seafood/American ♦ M-F 11:30AM-2:30PM, 6-10PM; Sa 6-10PM; Su 10:30AM-3PM. 17 Crown Bay, Gregerie East. 776.4466

3 Charlotte Amalie Pastel homes dot the hills surrounding this port city; and a city it is, with lots of traffic, honking cab drivers, and sidewalks busy with people. Main Street is lined with old-style Danish buildings and converted warehouses typical of early West Indian architecture—hipped roofs of corrugated metal, arcaded first floors with Moorish-arched doorways, heavy wood shutters,

and second-story verandas. The major shopping action takes place here.

Visitors from the US are allowed to take $1,200 worth of merchandise home duty free. Stop in at **Down Island Traders** for Caribbean spices and crafts, parrotfish earrings, West Indian dolls, and larimar jewelry (made of a turquoise stone found in Santo Domingo). Around the corner is **Little Switzerland,** with a 50 percent-off corner featuring china, crystal, and figurines by Wedgwood, Lalique, and Lladro. Try the **Linen House** for tablecloths from China, **A.H. Riise Caribbean Art Gallery** for framed and unframed prints by local artists, and **Animal Crackers** for a wide selection of children's gifts, toys, and mechanized stuffed animals—or just to play.

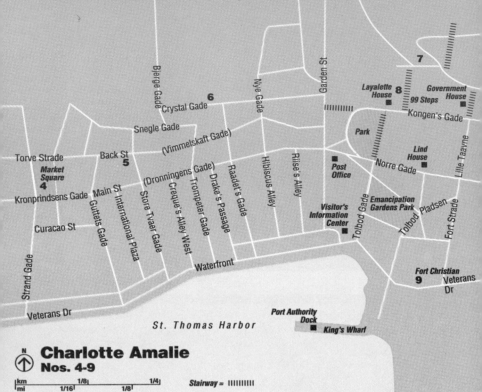

Charlotte Amalie
Nos. 4-9

| km | 1/8 | 1/4 |
| 1/16 | 1/8 | Stairway = ||||||||||| |

4 Market Square Produce and fruit vendors ply their wares in open-air stalls on the grounds of this former slave market. It's worth a stop for the color, bustle, and taste of island-grown fruit. You can also buy local crafts here. ♦ Strand Gade (Main St)

5 Virgilio's ★★★$$$ Walk through the Danish archways to enter the dining room where paintings by local artists decorate the walls and impressive stained-glass windows extend from the banquettes to the ceiling. Osso buco, a veal shank marinated in a delicious sauce and served with fettuccine, is the specialty of the house. Here you'll find fine dining in an intimate setting capped off with impeccable service. ♦ Northern Italian ♦ M-Sa 11:30AM-9:30PM. Back St (Store Tvaer Gade). Reservations recommended. 776.4920

6 Jewish Synagogue The second oldest temple in the western hemisphere (the oldest is in Curaçao), is also the oldest synagogue in continuous use. The sand on the floor commemorates the biblical exodus of the Jews from Egypt. About 150 tourists stop in each day to see the chair of Elijah, which is still used for circumcisions; the 900-year-old menorah from Cordoba, Spain; and two beautiful torahs dating back 140 years. Visitors are welcome to join Shabbat services held every Friday at 7:30PM and every Saturday at 11:15AM. ♦ Free. M-F 9AM-4PM; Sa 9AM-noon. Crystal Gade (Synagogue Hill). 774.4312

7 Blackbeard's Castle You can reach Blackbeard's Castle by climbing the **99 Steps** built by the Danes in the 1700s (trust us, there are more than 99 steps), or you can drive. The castle is actually a watchtower, purportedly built by pirate **Edward Teach**— the infamous **Blackbeard**—to scan the surrounding seas for ships to loot and plunder. There's not much to see except an unsurpassed view of Charlotte Amalie and its harbor (the reason: visitors are not allowed inside the watchtower, as it's part of the Blackbeard's Castle Hotel complex and has been turned into several guestrooms). ♦ Blackbeard's Hill, at the crest of Government Hill. 776.1234

8 Hotel 1829 ★★★$$$$ Old World elegance is still alive in this historic building overlooking both Charlotte Amalie and the harbor beyond. Ask for a table on the terrace in order to take in the view, then tread over the 200-year-old Moroccan floor tiles into the dining rooms to soak in the Moorish and Mediterranean decor.

With only 27 tables, the setting remains intimate, romantic, and hedonistic—perfect for a last-vacation-night splurge. Order the wilted spinach salad, a house specialty prepared tableside, along with an appetizer of smoked Scotch salmon tartar. For your main course, try the fresh Anguillian rock lobster or the rack of spring lamb, both of which are tender and perfectly prepared. ♦ Continental ♦ Tu-Su 6-10:30PM. Government Hill. Reservations required. 776.1829

Restaurants/Clubs: Red   **Hotels:** Blue
Shops/ 🌿 Outdoors: Green   **Sights/Culture:** Black

9 Fort Christian This national historic landmark was the first major building erected on St. Thomas (circa 1666). In the past, the brick-colored fort served as a jail. It then was turned into a police station, which is how it remained until 1982. Today it houses the historical museum, medicinal-plant exhibits, and a display of seashells. Graffiti engraved in the walls by prisoners can still be seen in the narrow jail cells. The museum boasts a fine collection of preserved turn-of-the-century furniture. ♦ Free. M-F 8:30AM-4:30PM; Sa 9:30AM-4:30PM. 1 Fort St. 776.4566

10 Ramada Yacht Haven Hotel and Marina $$ Lots of business travelers stay here, as this resort is convenient to Charlotte Amalie and the growing **Havensight** business district. It's also popular with people chartering upscale boats; a number of charter operations leave from their marina. A recent facelift has made this a pretty property both inside and out. There's no beach on the premises, but there are a complimentary beach shuttle and two pools on the grounds, one with a swim-up bar. ♦ 4 Long Bay Rd. 774.9700, 800/228.9898

11 Havensight Shopping Mall This low-key mall located in a booming business district is a great place to shop and avoid the crunch of the downtown mob. Most of the major stores in town have satellites here with the same prices. Beware the days when a cruise ship is in port, though, as the disembarking passengers are there to shop until they (or you) drop—literally. ♦ M-Sa 9AM-5PM; Su when a cruise ship is in town. Across from West Indian Dock. 774.7305

Within Havensight Shopping Mall:

Atlantis Submarines Next to scuba diving, this is as close as you can get to a deep natural reef without getting wet. Just board the air-conditioned submarine and relax while it dives up to 90 feet below the sea. Large portholes allow for easy viewing of the teeming reef as the 46-passenger submarine cruises past brilliant-hued fish, vibrant sea fans, and giant purple and orange sponges. Occasionally a shark swims by, chasing off the cloud of curious yellowtail snappers that have drifted over to investigate the sub. A guide narrates the hour-long journey. ♦ Admission. M-Sa 9AM-3PM (dives leave every hour on the hour). Building VI-L. Reservations: 776.5650. 24-hour information: 776.0288, 800/253.0493

12 Marriott's Frenchman's Reef Beach Resort $$$ There's a little bit of everything at this full-service resort spread out among two properties: Marriott's Frenchman's Reef high on the hill, and the more pricey and upscale **Marriott's Morning Star Beach Resort** ($$$$), with 96 luxury units right on the beach. Guests are welcome to use the facilities of both resorts, from the comprehensive water-sports center to the seven restaurants.

The action takes place up on the hill, accessible by elevator from the beach. Here 420 rooms overlook the four tennis courts, two free-form pools, and, depending on their view, either the harbor or the sea. Their free daily activities program is well attended, with workshops offered in rum tasting, water aerobics, and island cooking. Guests are also encouraged to attend the free tennis, windsurf, and snorkel clinics. Their **Calypso Carnival** show is an upbeat taste of the Caribbean and should be considered a "must-see." Also check out the wedding gazebo. Hundreds of couples have married here, and the resort even has a special wedding planner (call 800/FOR.LOVE) who arranges every detail, from the ceremony to the photos. Evenings, there's live entertainment in **La Terraza Lounge.**

As for the Marriott's Morning Star, the beach is the type vacationers dream about: soft,

clean white sand with lots of palm trees. If you want to shop in town, you can hop on the resort's free water taxi. While children's programs are offered during the holiday, this resort is geared more toward honeymooners, adults, and couples than families. The rate plans range from "room only" to an all-inclusive package. There are also three different "Weddings in Paradise" packages for couples tying the knot at the resort. ♦ Morning Star Beach. 776.8500, 800/524.2000

13 Bolongo Elysian Beach Resort $$$$ Sitting smack on **Cowpet Beach** is this ultramodern resort that seems to have been built with aging baby boomers in mind. The coral-colored, low-rise buildings scattered around the landscaped grounds contain rooms as nice as your rich uncle's super-deluxe condo. They're filled with four-poster beds, sleek bamboo and wicker furniture upholstered with thick cushions, remote-controlled color TVs, VCRs, limited-edition prints by up-and-coming artists, stocked minibars, and balconies with views of the water.

The room rates include breakfast, but their big draw is the all-inclusive package, the most upscale and deluxe on the island. Part of Bolongo's "Club Everything" program, it includes meals, wine, bar and soft drinks, land and most water sports (scuba diving is extra), an all-day yacht cruise to St. John, a half-day snorkel cruise, a sunset cruise, a one-day free car rental, admission to **Coral World,** nightly entertainment, and tips. It may seem expensive at first glance, but you won't be nickeled and dimed for everything you do, eat, or drink, and at least you know the bottom line up front.

The beach is lovely, though not very large, but the seaview is obstructed by anchored boats bobbing about in Cowpet Bay. The only other possible drawback is the food, which seems to be striving toward mediocrity. Otherwise, there's lots to do, with tennis courts, a complete water-sports center, and a state-of-the-art health club on premises. ◆ Cowpet Bay. 775.1800, 800/524.4746

14 Tillet Gardens Art Center Iguanas wander unhindered in this small artists colony where visitors can watch artisans silk-screening maps, hand-painting T-shirts, and goldsmithing custom wedding bands in their studios. You can buy a painting or print in one stall and have it framed in another. The **Caribbean Enameling Guild,** a cooperative studio and retail outlet, is also here. ◆ M-Sa 10AM-5PM. 126 Estate Anna's Retreat, take Rte 38, across from Four Winds Plaza. 775.1405

US Virgin Islands

SAPPHIRE BEACH

15 Sapphire Beach Resort and Marina $$$$
This resort is geared toward fun-loving families and beach buffs. It sits on the beach, where the island's hottest bodies strut their stuff and top-notch windsurfers make the sport look easy. A lively steel band plays at the beach bar on Sunday.

Parents can take advantage of the complimentary Sunfish, day-sailers, snorkel equipment, tennis courts, and windsurfers, while their young children are entertained in the **Little Gems Kids Klub,** which offers three hours a day of free, supervised activities to all youngsters under age 12. Babysitting services are available for the evening for an extra cost. Kids 12 and under also stay and eat for free. Accommodations are all suites or villas with complete kitchens. ◆ Sapphire Bay. 775.6100, 800/524.2090; fax 775.4024

16 Coral World Underwater Observatory and Marine Gardens The glass-enclosed marine observatory lies 20 feet below sea level. Think of it as a "reverse zoo": you're in the cage, watching to your heart's content the fascinating interactions of reef fish, coral, and sponges going about their business in the open sea. Bring your postcards; the "world's only underwater mailbox" is by the staircase.

One level up is the **Reef Tank** filled with moray eels, sharks, stingrays, and barracudas. Be sure to show up at 11AM, when scuba divers feed these predators by hand. The marine gardens and nature trail wind past the flamingo pond, sea-turtle pool, and touch pond, where you can pick up sea urchins, conch, and starfish. If you only have one day on the island, this is the number one must-see attraction. ◆ Admission. Daily 9AM-6PM. Fish feedings: 10AM, 11AM. Shark feeding: 2PM. Guided tour: 3PM. Coki Point (Rte 6). 775.1555

17 Eunice's Terrace ★★$$ Conch fritters, boiled fish, fried conch, peas and rice, and fungi are all served at this native diner. Some say the cafe's overrated, but it's still one of the more popular placesfor sampling local dishes. ◆ West Indian ◆ M-Sa 11:30AM-4PM, 6-10PM; Su 5:30-9PM. 67 Smith Bay Rd, east of the Coral World turnoff, Rte 38. 775.3975

18 Point Pleasant Resort $$$$
Honeymooners and families gravitate to this ideal combination of privacy, upscale amenities, and luxurious accommodations. This all-suite resort was designed to serve as a 15-acre sanctuary of beauty where people and nature could live in harmony.

The rooms are built in a tiered fashion into the green hills overlooking **Pineapple Beach** and **Water Bay,** with gallery-style terraces, vaulted ceilings, skylights, modern kitchens, and tiled floors covered with scatter rugs. The best ones are the superior-category suites in either the C or D units.

The grounds were landscaped to provide numerous nooks and crannies for seekers of solitude. A nature trail winds past a gazebo overlooking the sea, a quiet glade replete with a bench and shallow pond, and a hammock strung between two poles. When you're not taking advantage of their free half-day car rental to tour the island, you can windsurf, sail, snorkel, play tennis, or just laze around one of their three pools. Beach buffs can either climb down the steep stairs or take the free shuttle. In fact, the beach—shared with guests of the Stouffer Grand—and the stairs are the only drawbacks here. As for the stairs, there are lots of them, and you may end up walking up and down them more often than you'd like. If your legs are up to it, you'll find this 134-room resort idyllic, and just far enough away from the hustle and bustle of Charlotte Amalie to make you believe you're on another island. ◆ Deluxe ◆ Estate Smith Bay. 775.7200, 800/524.2300

Within Point Pleasant Resort:

The Agave Terrace ★★★$$$
This top island restaurant is situated on a breeze-cooled terrace overlooking the sea. The menu features shellfish, fresh fish, and prime cuts of beef prepared in delectably creative ways. The excellent choices include their crab Paradise appetizer served with an orange-marmalade dip, lobster Angelina on

angelhair pasta, and tuna or grouper with either a fresh dill or lobster cream sauce. Save room for their totally wicked peanut butter cheesecake.

To make this evening even more memorable book a table to correspond with the full moon, which rises above **Water Bay.** ♦ Continental/Caribbean ♦ M-Sa 7-10AM, 11:30AM-2PM, 6-10PM. 4 Smith Bay. Dinner reservations required. 775.4142/7200

19 Caribbean Mini Golf Hit your ball through miniature cruise ships, sugar-mill ruins, and a small-scale Fort Christian at this clever, 18-hole course designed to take you on a golf tour of all three US Virgin Islands. ♦ Admission. Daily 10AM-10PM. Smith Bay Rd, Rte 38, across from the entrance to Coki Beach. 779.2822

20 Magens Beach This heart-shaped beach is written about in every guide book and magazine article, yet the soft sands bordering the calm bay and backed by a thick fringe of palm trees are rarely crowded (probably because vacationers tend to veg-out on the beach nearest their hotel). Magens is worth seeing if only because it epitomizes everything you ever dreamed an island beach should be. ♦ Admission. Daily dawn-dusk. Magens Rd (Rte 35)

21 Drake's Seat Privateer **Sir Francis Drake** supposedly sat here, spyglass in hand, to watch for passing enemy ships to plunder. The seat is a stone bench built into the hillside above **Magens Bay.** When the weather conditions are right, you can see as far as

Jost Van Dyke and Tortola. It's a commercial spot, with several vendors selling souvenirs and trinkets. For a dollar, you can even have your photo taken alongside a donkey adorned with a crown of hibiscus around its ears. ♦ Free. Rte 40 (Magens Bay)

22 Fairchild Park Arthur Fairchild, a long-time resident of St. Thomas, donated this park to the island in 1951. It's seldom used, making it a perfect spot for an out-of-the-way picnic. Just bring everything you need, as there's only one bench in this tiny mountainside garden with views of both the Atlantic Ocean and Caribbean Sea. ♦ Free. Daily 8AM-4:30PM. St. Peter Mountain Rd. 774.2640

23 Mountain Top Banana daiquiris were invented here more than 20 years ago, when the hotel restaurant with the famous view was still in one piece. (Hurricane Hugo

demolished the building in 1989.) You can still enjoy the spectacular view from here—the highest point on St. Thomas.

On a clear day, you can see more than 20 islands and even part of St. Croix, 40 miles away. It's a tradition to sip a banana daiquiri while enjoying the view and, island entrepreneurialism being what it is, several vendors have set up shop here to sell the famous drink. Check to see if they're still selling the "Hugo Survivor," a boardgame put together with tongue-in-cheek humor. ♦ Rte 33 (St. Peter Mountain Rd)

Island Smorgasbord: From Bull's Feet to Goat Meat

Some of the most exotic dishes in the world come from the Caribbean, where fresh fruit and seafood abound. After whetting your appetite in the sun, consider trying some of the native dishes; they're unlike any you'll probably ever come across on the mainland. Here are a few US Virgin Islands favorites:

Bullfoot Soup As the name implies, these are cow's feet boiled with a medley of vegetables and dumplings.

Callaloo These spinachlike greens (at least insofar as texture is concerned) are served in a soup accompanied by pork or crabmeat.

Caribbean Lobster Unlike its North American cousin, this shellfish has no claws. Most of the meat is in the tail and it's served broiled or mixed with other seafoods in a variety of ways.

Conch This mollusk, which resides in the large shells sold at roadside stands (see the cover of this book), is high in protein and low in cholesterol and calories—the perfect diet food. Try yours pan-sautéed, breaded and broiled, curried,

or in a spicy soup called conch chowder. Or you can delve into some more caloric and delicious breaded and fried conch fritters.

Fungi Mildly spiced cornmeal mush that is usually served as a side dish but is sometimes added as a thickener for callaloo soup. Fungi is the island's equivalent of potatoes.

Goat Water Stew with (what else?) goat meat as its main ingredient.

Johnnycakes Unleavened, deep-fried bread that is fattening but tasty.

Pates Palm-sized turnovers stuffed with meat and vegetables or salted fish (or whatever's fresh that day). They're usually sold at the Caribbean equivalent of a hot-dog stand.

Roti An inexpensive and filling dish of curried meat or seafood stuffed into a tortilla-type shell. An island staple—akin to the Big Mac (for some folks, anyway) at home.

Souse This stew is made from leftover pig parts: the head, tail, and feet. Spices and fresh lime juice add flavor.

British Virgin Islands

Originally formed by volcanic activity about one million years ago, the British Virgin Islands (BVI) probably started out as one large island. Now they number from 40 to 60, depending on how many of the tiny islets and cays you include in your count of this 59-square-mile area. The green-sheathed mountains (dormant volcanos) descend from the islands' centers to water that's as clear as glass, creating a paradise for sailors and divers.

Although many travelers anchor themselves to the islands' hotels, which range from simple inns to some of the world's top luxury resorts, the most popular activity is boating around the islands. The steady trade winds and scores of sheltered harbors are ideal for sailing; in fact, more than half of the visitors to the British Virgin Islands stay aboard private or charter boats. And **Tortola** is frequently referred to as the yacht-charter capital of the world.

The first sailors to discover the Virgin Islands were the **Ciboney Indians** from Venezuela, followed later by the peaceful **Arawaks**, who were in turn destroyed by the cannibalistic **Caribs**. In 1493, about a century after the Caribs arrived, **Christopher Columbus** discovered and named **Tortola**, **Virgin Gorda**, and **Anegada**. Although these islands were claimed by the Spanish crown, the Spanish explorers preferred developing the richer neighborhoods of **Puerto Rico** and **Hispaniola** (known as Haiti and the

Dominican Republic today). British privateers such as **Sir Francis Drake** (for whom the channel is named) and several Dutch pirates hid on the islands ignored by the Spaniards, and smuggling became the local industry.

The Dutch, Spanish, and French frequently fought against the British over these islands during the 17th century, with England finally annexing Tortola in 1672. Gradually, English settlers took over most of the Virgin Islands, except St. Thomas and St. John.

Today the British Virgin Islands remain part of the British Commonwealth, with a governor appointed by **Queen Elizabeth**. The queen's portrait on stamps, the customary serving of afternoon tea, and cricket games are traditions that pay homage to Merry Old England.

Tourism developed here later than in other Caribbean nations, beginning in 1964 when **Laurance Rockefeller** opened Little Dix Bay resort on Virgin Gorda, and **Charlie** and **Ginny Cary** created a resort called The Moorings on Tortola in the 1970s. (Little Dix Bay is still owned and operated by Rock-resorts, but the Rockefellers are no longer involved.) Getting to these islands isn't easy; usually it requires a flight to San Juan or St. Thomas, then another short flight or ferry ride. But that very inaccessibility has helped keep the British Virgin Islands from being inundated by tourists the way other islands have. There's a serenity here that's often missing elsewhere.

British Virgin Islands

The most developed islands are Virgin Gorda and Tortola, but several others are worth exploring—usually by boat. Anegada, the British Virgin Islands' only coral island, has a population of 250, and lies about 20 miles northeast of Tortola. The landscape is flat (the highest point is a mere 28 feet); however, what's off its 20 miles of sandy beaches and under sea level draws plenty of divers. The extensive reefs, including the third largest barrier reef in the western hemisphere, and 300 shipwrecks are the prime attractions. **Norman Island**, believed to be the original site of **Robert Louis Stevenson's** *Treasure Island*, has three caves at Treasure Point. Visitors often poke around by rowboat or dive here, and rumors of buried pirate treasure still persist.

A former stop-off point for ships taking on salt to preserve food, **Salt Island** is best known for the sunken ship *The Rhone*, a Royal Mail Steam Packet Company ship that went down in an 1867 hurricane. The two sections lying in 80 feet of water provide great snorkel and scuba adventures (this was the site used to film *The Deep*). In fact, it's arguably the best dive site in the western hemisphere and its numerous boat moorings prevent anchor damage to the fragile coral beds. For an outstanding history and drawings of the ship (regardless of whether diving is in your plans), consult the *Cruising Guide to the Virgin Islands* (Cruising Guide Publications; 813/796.2469), which contains reams of good advice for the other islands as well.

Peter Island is home to Amway's Peter Island Resort and Yacht Harbour, and a lovely, palm-lined beach. Tiny **Beef Island** lures visitors with dinner and shows at The Last Resort in Trellis Bay, where owner Tony Snell regales yachters with off-color songs portraying the pitfalls of sailing. And the island of **Jost Van Dyke**, named for a Dutch pirate, has mountains and a few rustic inns. But don't expect hi-tech amenities—telephones only arrived on Jost Van Dyke in 1990. If you enjoy local cuisine and calypso music, you can kick off your sandals here at such spots as Foxy's Tamarind Bar at Great Harbour. At the other extreme, **Necker Island** boasts a 10-bedroom villa for up to 20 people (a staff of 19 takes care of your needs), with a pool, tennis courts, and lots of privacy. **Princess Di** vacationed on the island, and for $9,000 a day, you can, too.

Getting to the Islands

Airlines

All flights to Virgin Gorda and Tortola originate in Puerto Rico or on St. Thomas in the United States Virgin Islands.

American Eagle 800/433.7300

LIAT...800/253.5011

Sunaire..800/524.2094

Virgin Air...800/522.3084

Airports

Beef Island International Airport Inter-island flights land on Beef Island, which is connected to Tortola by a one-lane toll bridge.

Virgin Gorda Airport This light-aircraft landing strip is just south of the Virgin Gorda Yacht Harbour.

British Virgin Islands

Getting around the Islands

Car Rentals

Most of the rentals are four-wheel drives. You'll need a British Virgin Islands' driver's license, available at car-rental agencies for about $10.

On Virgin Gorda:

Mahogany Rentals.............................5.5469, 5.5542

Potter's Car Rental 5.5329, 5.5960

Speedy's Car Rental 5.5235, 5.5240

On Tortola:

Avis Rent-a-Car..........4.3322, 4.2193, 800/331.1084

Budget Rent-a-Car..................4.5150, 800/472.3325

Caribbean Car Rental......................................4.2595

International Car Rentals.............................4.2516/7

Island Suzuki Rentals 4.3666

National Car Rental..4.3197

Ferry Service

Many visitors arrive by ferry from other islands; it's more fun plowing along in a metal craft with local residents than flying in on a plane.

Inter-Island Boat Services...............................5.4166

Native Son..5.4617

North Sound Express 4.2746

Peter Island Boat...4.2561/2

Smith's Ferry Services.......................4.4430, 5.4495

Speedy's Fantasy...................................5.5240/5235

Taxis

On Virgin Gorda:

Andy's Taxi..5.5511

Mahogany Taxi Service...................................5.5469

On Tortola:

BVI Taxi Association..........................4.2322, 5.2378

Style's Taxi Service 4.2260

Tours

Since there is no scheduled bus service on the British Virgin Islands, tours are offered in taxis or in open-air canvas-topped safari buses, with drivers often providing the narrative.

On Virgin Gorda:

In the Valley:

Andy's Taxi..5.5511

Mahogany Taxi Service 5.5469

On Tortola:

In Wickhams Cay I:

BVI Taxi Association.......................................4.2322

Style's Taxi Service 4.2260

In Road Town:

Travel Plan Tours..4.2872

FYI

Medical Emergencies

On Virgin Gorda, call the **Virgin Gorda Clinic** in The Valley (5.5337); on Tortola, call **Pebbles Hospital** in Road Town (4.3497, 4.5268).

Money

American currency is used on the British Virgin Islands.

Reservations

A speedy way to plan your trip is through the **BVI Reservation Service,** which handles all hotels, cottages, campgrounds, car rentals, ground transportation, ferries, island tours, and diving and sailing needs. Write to them at 210 Fifth Avenue, New York, NY 10010; or call 800/223.4483. The fax number is 212/655.5671.

Taxes

A seven percent hotel tax is levied into the rates. The departure tax is $5 per person when leaving by air; when leaving by sea, a $3-per-person tax is included in the ferry price.

Telephones

To call from the United States to the British Virgin Islands, you must dial area code 809, followed by 49 and then the five digits offered in these listings. When on the islands, however, you only need to dial the last five digits.

Virgin Gorda

Named by **Christopher Columbus,** who thought the skyline resembled an overweight woman lying on her back, today the "Fat Virgin" appeals to tourists with fat purses. The southern part of the 10-mile-long island boasts **The Baths,** a spectacular site of huge granite boulders, with a bit of commercialism at **Spanish Town.** All land higher than one thousand feet in the mountainous midsection is designated a national park and is filled with hiking trails. The northeastern section, by contrast, looks like a geological afterthought of spits and islets harboring numerous sailing fleets.

In colonial times **Spanish Town** was the capital of the British Virgin Islands. Virgin Gorda's population peaked in 1812 at 8,000, but has declined since. Today it is the second largest of the British Virgins (Tortola is much more developed) with a population of more than 1,500. Although fewer hotels and marinas are located here, Virgin Gorda is the home of several luxurious, upscale resorts, yet even these are casual in style. The resorts spilling down the hills to the sparkling beaches are often only reachable by boat.

From the United States, dial the prefix 809/49 unless otherwise noted; dial only the last five digits when on the islands.

1 **Virgin Gorda Yacht Harbour** Developed by multimillionaire **Laurance Rockefeller** to accommodate his luxury resort at nearby Little Dix Bay, the harbor is still owned and operated by **Rockresorts.** Today 120 boats are docked at this boating and shopping nucleus, where many visitors go through customs. A commissary and ship's store are on the premises. ♦ Daily 8AM-6PM. The Valley (St. Thomas Bay). 5.5555 ext. 150

Within Virgin Gorda Yacht Harbour:

The Bath and Turtle
★★★$$ The meals are served both outdoors and indoors in a pub-type setting with a polished wood bar, beveled glass, and brass railings that were purchased from New York's Carnegie Hall. The fare ranges from hamburgers and pastas to lobster, with local dishes such as conch fritters and soup. Reservations are necessary only on Wednesday and Sunday, when crowds gather to hear local bands play calypso, reggae, and soul music. ♦ American/West Indian ♦ Daily 7AM-midnight. 5.5239

Euphoric Cruises If you want to try out your sea legs in something small, rent a Boston whaler here. You may graduate to one of the outfit's 50-foot yachts, which can certainly induce a state of euphoria. All may be chartered for half-day, full-day, and week-long sails. ♦ Daily 9AM-1PM, 2-6PM. 5.5542; fax 5.5818

Misty Isle Yacht Charters The 27- to 51-foot-long sailboats and powerboats are available for day and week cruises, with or without crews. Skipper **Cliff Couture,** who has been chartering in these waters since 1981, often takes guests to the beautiful beach at **Deadman Bay** on Cooper Island. You can sign up for a sunset sail for a special touch of romance. ♦ M-Su 9AM-5PM. 5.5643, 800/668.7727; fax 5.5300

Island Woman You don't have to be an island girl to want to bring the Caribbean home with you. Get a jump-start here with Haitian paintings, smart-looking Indonesian batik

British Virgin Islands

clothes by **Java Wraps,** plus colorful kites and jewelry. ♦ M-Sa 9:30AM-5:30PM; Su 9:30AM-1:30PM. 5.5237

Virgin Gorda Craft Shop Great native handiwork is carried here, including island paintings, Anegada pottery, straw items, and jewelry. ♦ M-F 9AM-12:30PM, 2-5PM; Sa 9AM-12:30PM. 5.5137

Dive BVI Ltd. Those who can't resist taking the plunge in a big way may buy or rent snorkel and dive equipment here. Men's and women's sportswear and other necessities, such as that requisite sun block, are also for sale. ♦ Daily 8:30AM-5PM. 5.5513

Pelican's Pouch Boutique Casualwear made of natural cotton, along with swimwear and plenty of cool, comfortable T-shirts, fills the racks of this small store. ♦ M-Sa 9AM-6PM, Su 9AM-1PM. 5.5477

2 **Little Dix Bay** $$$$ Want to vacation like a Rockefeller? This 102-room **Rockresort** was opened in 1964 after years of planning by **Laurance Rockefeller** as a wilderness beach that would provide privacy and solitude. Millionaires and celebrities (**Dick Cavett** has vacationed here for years), as well as lots of honeymooners still stay here—it ranked among the Top 20 tropical resorts in *Condé Nast Traveler* magazine.

Little Dix is the epitome of laid-back luxury, with beautiful rooms featuring native-stone walls and floral fabrics. Some are a few steps off the beach, while the octagonal rooms are perched like opulent tree houses on stilts above the trees. The magnificent beach covers a half-mile of white sand on an almost-heart-shaped cove that served as the major fishing harbor for locals before the hotel was built. The grounds throughout the 500 acres are lushly planted, and botanical tours are given.

Remember the philosophy, though: there's no air-conditioning; telephones and televisions don't mar the silence; and pesticides harmful to native fauna are not used. Ceiling fans and insect repellent are provided, however, along with outstanding service (there's a one-to-one staff-to-guest ratio) and excellent food. The rates include tennis on seven courts, waterskiing, water taxis to nearby beaches, aerobic exercises, Sunfish lessons, movies, and a guided snorkel tour. ◆ Deluxe ◆ Little Dix Bay. 5.5555, 800/223.7637; fax 5.5661

British Virgin Islands

Within Little Dix Bay:

The Pavilion ★★★★$$$$ The four connected, silver-shingled peaks of the Polynesian-style pavilion shield the open-air dining room. All of the tables, especially those on the terrace, provide unimpeded, stunning views. The cuisine is American with Caribbean influences, including entrées such as sautéed kingfish with spinach leaves and citrus sauce or grilled chicken breast with island fruits and spices. The chilled cantaloupe soup is particularly memorable. Monday nights feature a manager's buffet. ◆ American ◆ Daily 8-10AM, 12:30-2PM, 7-9PM. Reservations accepted only for parties of 8 or more. 5.5555

Sugar Mill ★★★$$$$ A more casual dining room and lounge are located within the remains of an early sugar mill. The house specialties include grilled swordfish, fresh lobster, and thick black Angus steaks. ◆ Seafood/steak ◆ Daily 12:30-3PM, 7-9PM. Reservations required. 5.5555

3 Gorda Peak National Park Standing here at 1,500 feet, the island's highest spot, you can see where Virgin Gorda narrows so severely at certain points that the Atlantic Ocean and Caribbean Sea practically meet. You may drive to the park's entrance on the road leading to North Sound; hikers will find trails, including a new one along an old dirt road on the northwest side of the island. Signs direct visitors to **Virgin Gorda Peak**, with its observation tower and picnic area. ◆ Daily 24 hours. Main Rd. 4.3904

4 Biras Creek Resort
$$$$
Perched atop a breezy hill on a narrow neck of land, this grouping of native-stone and wood-shingle buildings has been pampering those seeking privacy and gourmet cookery since 1973. There's more to do than just eat and drink, though; occupants of its 32 rooms and 16 suites will find a beach, a freshwater pool, two tennis courts, bicycling, and virtually every water sport available, including sportfishing. For many guests, the accent is on the outstanding food and wines available in the round dining room. Originally, all the chefs were Cordon Bleu-trained; current chefs hail from such prestigious kitchens as those at the Culinary Institute of America and The Ritz in London. ◆ Deluxe ◆ Biras Creek. 4.3555, 800/223.1108

5 The Bitter End Yacht Club $$$$ Once a rustic hangout for barefoot sailing types, this North Sound resort has upgraded and now offers a variety of accommodations in wooden buildings. They range from the simple, breezy, beachfront rooms with ceiling fans to the more luxurious air-conditioned chalets with marble baths—one hundred in all.

The focus here is still on the salty life, centered around a marina with one hundred yachts and watercrafts available for charter, including 10 live-aboard charter yachts. Rates include unlimited use of the fleet (including several dozen sailboats and 20 Boston whalers, plus Sunfish and sailboards) and introductory courses at the **Nick Trotter Sailing School** on the premises. A new program teaches sailing to kids from age seven.

Its location, combining a protected harbor with proximity to the open sea, makes it ideal for sailing, and fleets of boats moor here. (The area, incidentally, was called the Bitter End because it was the easternmost point in the Virgin Islands before ships struck out into the ocean.) The mile-long waterfront is enhanced by a pool; there's also a conference center. CNN is broadcast at the open-air video theater, along with nightly movies (the rooms have no TVs or phones). The rates include all meals. ◆ North Sound. 4.2746, 800/872.2392

Restaurants/Clubs: Red	**Hotels:** Blue
Shops/ 🌳 Outdoors: Green	**Sights/Culture:** Black

Within the Bitter End Yacht Club:

Clubhouse Steak and Seafood Grille
★★★$$$$ Indoor and outdoor dining at
the beach features seafood, steaks, and ribs,
plus the option of a buffet dinner. A steel-
drum band plays throughout dinner 7-9PM.
♦ American ♦ Daily 8AM-9:30PM. Bar: daily
8AM-11PM. 4.2746

English Carvery ★★★$$$$ This smaller
and more elegant, British-style restaurant
serves traditional carving-board fare: roast
beef, pork, chicken, and lamb. ♦ English
♦ Daily 6:30-9:30PM, Dec-May; Tu, Th
6:30-9:30PM, June-Nov. 4.2746

6 The Baths A spectacular natural sight awaits
at the southwestern end of Virgin Gorda. It
looks as if a giant has tossed smooth granite
blocks and marbles all around; some of the
boulders lying about are as high as a two-story
house. You may walk through and under some
of the grottos, where their tops come together
in an A-shaped peak like in a cathedral. The
sun's rays slant through some openings,
sparkling on the shallow pools of water as you
walk through; it's definitely an awe-inspiring
experience.

Many boaters drop their anchor nearby—the
snorkeling is excellent here—but the phenomenon may also be reached by taxi. Be sure
to arrange for your driver to pick you up later
at the gazebo where information and a map
are posted.

The excursion is via two trails leading down
a 250-yard descent, so wear sneakers or hiking shoes. A snack bar on the beach offers
cold drinks, bathrooms, and the ubiquitous
souvenir T-shirts. ♦ Daily 24 hours. The Baths.
4.3904 (National Parks Trust)

7 Copper Mine Ruins To the east of The
Baths, the ruins sitting on a bluff reveal chimney parts and stone walls from long-ago residences. The mines were modeled after those
in Cornwall, England. A trail leads to an information board. Warning: remain on the path-
ways; the open shafts are dangerous. The BVI
National Parks Trust plans to restore them by
late-1992. ♦ Daily 24 hours. Copper Mine Rd.
4.3904 (National Parks Trust)

Tortola

Home to **Road Town,** the capital of the British
Virgin Islands, Tortola is both the largest in size
as well as in population (more than 10,000) of
the crown colony's 50-or-so islands and islets.
The number of cruise ships that call on Road
Town will increase (up from a dozen) when the
new docks are completed on **Wickhams Cay I.**

Tortola's Quaker history is one element that
differs from many Caribbean islands. A Quaker
settlement was established in the early-18th
century by Friends who had left England and
then Barbados because they were persecuted

for their religious beliefs. Since they refused
to carry firearms and believed in freeing
slaves, the Quakers were uncomfortable in
the Caribbean and the movement died out by
the 1780s, with many of the Quakers moving
to Pennsylvania.

1 A.H. Riise Ltd. The same company that's
so predominant in St. Thomas carries a small
selection of liquor and beer here at prices
the management says are cheaper than in
the USVI because Tortola's taxes are lower.
♦ M-F 8:30AM-5PM; Sa 8:30AM-1PM. O'Neal
Complex, Port Purcell. 4.4483, 4.6615

2 The Moorings Even if you don't plan to
charter a yacht, you've got to see this operation. In 1969 **Charlie** and **Ginny Cary** began
their yacht-chartering business with six sailboats. Today the facility operates 140 yachts
that are 37 feet to 60 feet long, available with
crews or bareboat (meaning charterers operate the boat themselves). In addition to the
72-slip charter dock, there's a 70-slip visitors

dock. Just stroll along the docks and you're
bound to meet interesting people with colorful
sailing tales. ♦ Road Town Harbour, Wickhams Cay II. 4.2332, 800/535.7289

Within The Moorings:

Underwater Safaris Three boats answer
your scuba-diving needs. There are four-
day PADI certified diving courses and resort
courses, as well as two half-day completion
courses for those with previous training.
Guided half-day dive tours are available twice
weekly, and divers may rent equipment here,
including tanks, regulators, and wet suits.
♦ Wickhams Cay II. 4.3235, 800/537 7032;
fax 4.5322

The Mariner Inn $$$$ Primarily geared
to charterers for extending their stays, the
dockside hotel's 40 rooms are sometimes
available to landlubbers and offer a pool, two
tennis courts, and water sports. ♦ Wickhams
Cay II. 4.2332, 800/535.7289

Treasure Isle Hotel $$$$ Perched on a
hill above the harbor, the yellow and white
gingerbread buildings feature 40 air-conditioned rooms with ocean views. Some include
kitchenettes. A swimming pool, entertainment
on Friday and Saturday nights, and free use
of most water-sports equipment are included.
♦ Wickhams Cay II. 4.2501/4

Within the Treasure Isle Hotel:

The Veranda ★★★$$$ The casual open-
air restaurant beckons, serving local foods

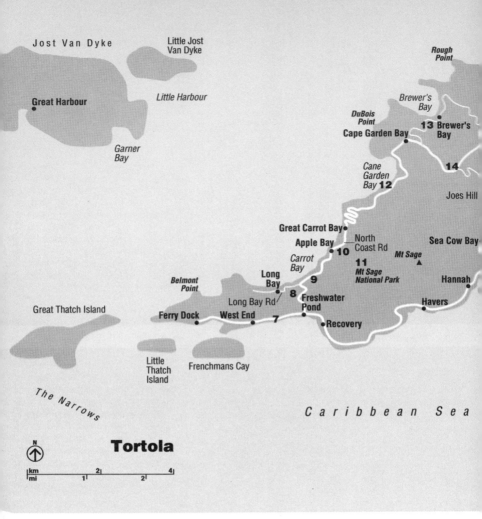

Tortola

N

km		2		4
mi	1		2	

with some Continental choices. Favorites include steamed Anegada lobster and grilled snapper. Top off your meal with their home-made strawberry cake. Wednesdays they grill outdoors; Fridays they serve a West Indian buffet; and Saturdays there's a barbecue with entertainment by a steel-drum band. ♦ Sea-food/Continental ♦ Daily 7:30AM-10PM, noon-9PM. Road Town. 4.2501

3 J.R. O'Neal Botanic Garden Curious about what the gorgeous tropical flowers are named or which exotic herbs grow locally? Visit the four-acre garden named after a BVI business-man; it features a fern house and a simulated rain forest with waterfalls. Horticulturists give guided tours for those who have trouble distinguishing between hibiscus and orchids. ♦ M-F 8:30AM-5PM; Sa-Su noon-5PM. Lower Estate. 4.4557

4 The Ample Hamper This is just the place to stock up on food and wine to take to that secluded beach or on your sailboat ride. Baked quiches and pâtés are among the goodies. ♦ M-F 8:30AM-6PM; Sa 8:30AM-3PM; Su 9AM-1PM. Wickhams Cay I. 5.4684

SEA URCHIN SHOPS

4 Sea Urchin In case you forgot to bring along a swimsuit—or you just feel like buying some new resort togs—this shop stocks them for men, women, and children. The brand names carried here include **Alegre** and **Catalina**. ♦ M-Sa 8:30AM-5PM. Abbot Building, Wickhams Cay I. 4.4108

4 Kids in de Sun Stylish duds for the little ones found here include **Java Wraps** for kids, plus items by **Jungle Rags** and **Pacific Coast Highway.** ♦ M-F 9AM-5:30PM; Sa 9AM-4PM; Su when cruise ships are in port. Abbot Building, Wickhams Cay I. 4.6268

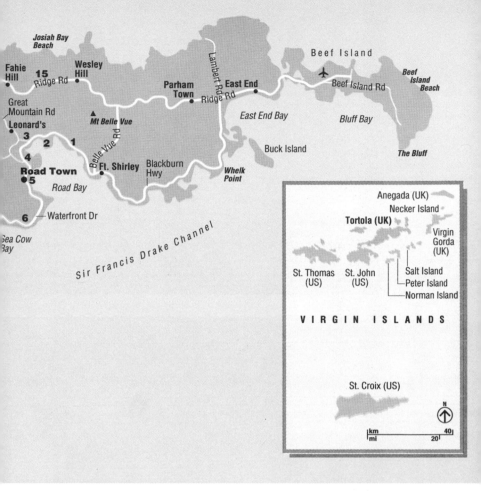

Road Town

Just a few years back, a street sign in Road Town read, "Warning. Livestock found trespassing on the cay are liable to be impounded or shot." The town is somewhat more businesslike now, even though most of the West Indian-style buildings are painted pink, green, or aqua with red-tin roofs. Even the newer concrete buildings display flamboyant colors. Road Town is primarily a place where boaters anchor and stock up on provisions, because the prices here are lower than on the other islands. If you're coming in off the boat, however, keep in mind that swimsuits without cover-ups are prohibited in town.

5 Tourist Board Stop by here to pick up maps, a copy of *Welcome* magazine for the latest happenings, and other helpful publications. ◆ M-F 8:30AM-4:30PM. Joseph Josiah Smith Social Security Building, Wickhams Cay I. 4.3134, 4.3489

5 Bonkers Gallery Trendy women's clothing (much of which is designed in St. Martin and manufactured in Indonesia), including **Samson** fashions, is carried here. ◆ M-F 9AM-5PM; Sa 9AM-1PM. Main St. 4.2535

5 Virgin Islands Folk Museum Items salvaged from *The Rhone,* the Royal Mail Steam Packet Company ship that sank in an 1867 hurricane, are displayed in this tiny white museum made of wood. There are also several photographs of early island homes. ◆ M-F 9AM-4:30PM; Sa 9AM-1PM. Main St. No phone

5 Pusser's Outpost ★★$$$ A smaller version of the original West End Pusser's features Victorian-style carved woodwork and faces the waterfront. Oceans of nautical memorabilia cover the walls. The more formal dining room upstairs serves Continental goodies such as beef Wellington and **Heart Smart** items for those watching their diets, along with Chinese specialties such as stir-fried meat and vegetables. The downstairs pub dishes up meat pies and sandwiches. The ground floor also offers

85

a deli and wood-paneled store. ◆ Continental/Chinese ◆ M-F, Su noon-2:30PM, 6-10PM; Sa 6-10PM. Main St. 4.4199

5 Sunny Caribbee Spice Company Spice up your stay with a visit to this West Indian-

style building where apothecary jars are filled with exotic seeds and powders. The company packages its own herbs, tea, coffee, spices, preserves, and herbal cosmetics. You might want to try their West Indian "Hangover Cure" tea, sold in an apothecary jar. Original hand-painted accessories, including pottery and papier-mâché items, are also on sale. The business was founded in 1982 by former Maine residents **Bob** and **Susan Gunter** and their son **Greg.** ◆ M-F 9AM-5:30PM; Sa 9AM-5PM; Su when cruise ships are in port. Main St. 4.2178

5 Little Denmark The store has a little bit of everything, but the Danish silver jewelry and cutlery and Royal Copenhagen china steal the show from the straw baskets and snorkel equipment. ◆ M-F 9AM-5PM; Sa 9AM-1PM. Main St. 4.2455

5 Antiquities and Presents Unlimited **Ermin Bonnet's** philosophy in her newly expanded shop is to present 18th- and 19th-century antiques from Africa, Asia, and South America that are functional as well as beautiful, along with modern crafts that meet the same standards. The items include a 1,000-year-old Chinese vase, copper pots, and wood trays. ◆ M-F 9AM-5PM. Waterfront Dr. 4.2439

5 J. R. O'Neal Ltd. Among the woven rugs and baskets, you'll spot hand-painted Italian dishes and hand-blown Mexican glassware at this home accessories store. ◆ M-Th 8:30AM-4PM; F 8:30AM-5PM; Sa 9AM-1PM. Main St. 4.2292

6 Fort Burt Hotel $$ A 300-year-old Dutch/English fort on the grounds adds a sense of history to this seven-room hotel. It's believed that the original fort was rebuilt in 1776 and named after **William Burt,** governor of the Leeward Islands. The remains

Tropical Texts

Find out more about the Caribbean islanders and their colorful culture by flipping through the pages of the following recommended titles.

Caribbean by James A. Michener (1989; Random House) Michener provides a fictional but informative and entertaining account of the settlement of the Caribbean region.

The Caribbean: Genesis of a Nationalism by Franklin W. Knight (1978; Oxford University Press) This book emphasizes cultural customs among islanders then and now.

The Caribbean: The Lands and Their Peoples by Eintou Pearl Springer (1988; Silver Burdett Press) Springer examines the customs, culture, and history of the Caribbean.

Democracies and Tyrannies of the Caribbean by William Krehm (1984; Lawrence Hill and Company) A history of the many injustices committed during the colonization of the islands.

Flying Fish and Sky Juice by Jessica Harris (1991; Simon and Schuster) Numerous traditional recipes

that have been handed down over the generations make up this excellent Caribbean cookbook.

The Modern Caribbean by Franklin W. Knight and Colin A. Palmer (1989; Chapel Hill University of North Carolina Press) A contemporary history of the Caribbean population.

On the Trail of the Arawaks by Irving Rouse (1974; University of Oklahoma Press) A fascinating look at Amerindian cultures throughout the Caribbean.

Paradise Island Story by Paul Albury (1984; Macmillan) The detailed and entertaining history of the popular vacation island just off Nassau.

The "Redlegs" of Barbados, Their Origins and History by Jill Sheppard (1976; KTO Press) Tales of the families brought to the island as indentured servants in 1627. "Redlegs" refers to their skin tone after exposure to the Bajan sun.

A Short History of the West Indies by J.H. Parry and P.M. Sherlock (1971; St. Martin's Press) One of the best-researched histories of the Caribbean.

include parts of the fort's foundation and a cannon. All of the rooms (none of which are in the fort) are air-conditioned, with televisions and ocean views. There are also a restaurant, a lounge, and a pool. ♦ Waterfront Dr. 4.2587; fax 4.2547

6 Prospect Reef Resort $$$$ Located on its own harbor (the center of many water activities), the resort's 131 accommodations—in buildings no higher than two stories—range from fan-cooled rooms to air-conditioned suites, some with kitchenettes. Vacationers who want more activity than lolling in a hammock or strolling among the lush gardens may choose from two fresh-water pools (one half-Olympic-size, the other circular), a saltwater pool, six tennis courts, and a nine-hole pitch-and-putt golf course; there's also a conference center. Kids, who stay free in deluxe rooms if they're under 12, will find plenty to do, especially in the two children's pools. ♦ West of Waterfront Dr. 4.3311, 800/356.8937; fax 4.5595

Sunscreen: The Great Cover-up

Many tourists, eager for a tan that will symbolize their Caribbean vacation to their friends and colleagues back home, burn and peel after overexposure to the powerful tropical rays. And nothing puts a damper on that long-awaited vacation faster than a bad burn.

Without using sunscreen, Caribbean sunbeams can penetrate your skin in only 15 minutes, causing serious inflammation, pain, and damage. Because the islands are so close to the equator, the ultraviolet rays are stronger than at the hottest spot in the sunbelt of the United States. If you're determined to leave with a bronze bod, however, start out slowly in the early morning or late afternoon (a quarter hour of sun the first day is probably enough) and always use sunscreen. The worst time of day to lay out is between 11AM and 2PM, when the sun's rays are most intense. The sun is also stronger when it's reflected off water, so be particularly cautious at the beach, pool, or on a boat.

The range of sunscreen products on the market today covers everyone's needs. Waterproof lotions are excellent but should be reapplied after swimming or physical exercise to ensure their effectiveness. A simple rule of thumb for selecting protection is to determine your skin type: The fairer your complexion, the higher the sun-protection factor (SPF) number you need.

Within the Prospect Reef Resort:

Upstairs Restaurant ★★★$$$$ Casual elegance characterizes the intimate areas, green with well-tended plants. You may dine *au deux* on duckling in cherry sauce, or fresh fish, grilled or sautéed, and perhaps covered with a Creole sauce or a lemon-and-garlic-butter sauce. ♦ Continental/West Indian ♦ M-F noon-2:30PM, 6-10PM; Sa-Su 6-10PM. Reservations required. 4.2228

The Harbour Cafe ★★$$$ Light, informal meals are served on a roofed harborfront

terrace, where you can relax and watch all the boating activity. Lunches are primarily hamburgers and salads, while the dinner menu offers small but juicy steaks and crispy fish and chips. ♦ American ♦ Daily 7AM-5PM, 6-10PM. 4.3311

7 Sopers Hole Marina This 18-slip marina on Frenchman's Cay harbors a few shops in pastel West Indian buildings. ♦ Sopers Hole Wharf, West End. 5.4553

Within the Sopers Hole Marina:

The Ample Hamper Pack a picnic lunch at this branch of the popular provisioner that features Fortnum & Mason jam, sliced meat, wine, liquor, and a variety of other treats. ♦ M-F 8:30AM-6PM; Sa 8:30AM-3PM; Su 9AM-1PM. 4.2494

Baskin in the Sun Alan Baskin and Eva Cope will help you resolve some of the mysteries of diving. Baskin started the business in 1969, with Cope joining in 1973. They offer PADI diving instruction with 10 certified instructors, scuba and snorkel trips on their three-boat fleet docked here at the tin-roofed headquarters or at **Prospect Reef**, and equipment sales. They'll also arrange dive packages with stays at the Long Bay Beach Resort, Prospect Reef Resort, Sebastian's on the Beach, and the Sugar Mill Hotel, including unlimited daytime dives. Baskin in the Sun offers two-tank dives every morning, a one-tank dive each afternoon except Wednesday, and an optional Wednesday night dive. ♦ Daily 8AM-5PM. 4.5854, 800/233.7938; fax 4.5853

Island Treasures West Indian oils, watercolors, and sculptures are showcased here, along with prints and books. ♦ Daily 9AM-5PM, 7PM-8:30PM. 5.4787

Pusser's Landing $$ The first of the Pusser's locations (now found throughout the Virgin Islands) was remodeled recently with lots of decorative wood and nautical doodads. If you fancy a steak-and-kidney pie, there's an air-conditioned deli on the ground floor next to the **Company Store,** which sells ship models and a variety of "adventure" clothing and jewelry. ♦ American/Seafood ♦ Daily 11AM-2:30PM, 6-10PM. 5.4554

Sea Lion This small store is owned by the same people and carries the same resortwear as the Sea Urchin in Wickhams Cay I. ♦ Daily 8:30AM-8PM. 5.4850

British Virgin Islands

Zenaida Tired of shell jewelry? This shop specializes in antique and modern jewelry from India, Africa, and Mexico, along with batik fabrics and **Java Wraps.** ♦ Daily 9AM-7:30PM. 5.4867

8 Long Bay Beach Resort $$$$ Snuggled between the verdant hills and a mile-long beach is this 50-acre resort with a full range of accommodations. Choose from 62 hillside rooms and studios, beachfront cabanas, or deluxe oceanfront rooms and villas—most of them air-conditioned. Should you tire of the ocean activities, there are a freshwater pool, a tennis court, and a nine-hole pitch-and-putt golf course. Children under 12 stay free. ♦ Long Bay. 5.4252, 800/729.9599; fax 5.4677

Within the Long Bay Beach Resort:

Beach Restaurant and Bar ★★$$ This West Indian restaurant is located in the stone sugar mill of a 200-year-old rum distillery. The à la carte menu emphasizes fresh fish and steaks. Live local bands provide entertainment most nights. ♦ West Indian ♦ Daily 7:30AM-10PM. 5.4252

The Garden Restaurant ★★★★$$$ Gentlemen are requested to wear slacks and shirts—but certainly not jackets and ties—at this somewhat formal restaurant set romantically among lighted gardens. Popular dishes on the set dinner menu include grilled wahoo, and the more ambitious filet of venison with port and cinnamon sauce. Vegetarian dishes such as curried tofu are also available, and the chef is happy to cater to any special diet requirements. A definite West Indian influence adds to the Continental flavor. And resident manager **Stephen Creese** is justly proud of his extensive wine list. ♦ Continental ♦ Daily 6:30-9:30PM. 5.4252

8 Sebastian's on the Beach $$$$ Begun as a beach bar, Sebastian's now has 26 rooms and lots of water sports. Rattan furnishings and angled wood ceilings add an island touch. Each fan-cooled room has a refrigerator. ♦ Little Apple Bay. 5.4212, 305/266.5256 (FL); fax 5.4466

Within Sebastian's on the Beach:

Sebastian's Restaurant ★★$$ The glass windows of this restaurant open to the breezes and ocean scenery. The dishes range from local specialties such as panfried fresh dolphin with Creole sauce to barbecued chicken and filet mignon. Sunday nights a band entertains diners with West Indian music. ♦ Seafood/Continental ♦ Daily 8AM-10PM. Bar: daily 3PM-midnight. 5.4212 ext. 1313

9 Mrs. Scatliffe's Bar and Restaurant ★★$$ For a special treat, try the West Indian cuisine prepared and served by **Una Scatliffe** and her family. It's served on the open-air second floor of her yellow and white residence. Everything is fresh, including the homegrown fruits and vegetables. Favorites include curried goat and chicken, a stew that's served in a coconut shell over rice. Lunch is served on weekdays noon-2:30PM by appointment only. Monday through Saturday nights, family members entertain with a live band that usually consists of someone playing a marimba box, a guitar, and a squash. ♦ West Indian ♦ Daily 7-8:30PM. Reservations required. Carrot Bay. 5.4556

10 Bomba's Surfside Shack ★★$ Local bands play on Wednesday nights, many Sunday afternoons, and for full-moon parties at this surfers hangout made of driftwood. ◆ Daily 11AM-10PM. Apple Bay. No phone

10 Sugar Mill Hotel $$$$ On the site of the 340-year-old **Appleby Plantation,** former California food writers **Jinx** and **Jeff Morgan** have created a resort with 20 rooms. The attractive decor is far from rustic. The circular pool is located where oxen once marched in circles to provide power for the mill. Children under age 10 stay free June through October but are not allowed November through May. ◆ Apple Bay. 5.4355, 800/462.8834; fax 5.4696

Within the Sugar Mill Hotel:

Sugar Mill Restaurant ★★★★$$$ Considered not just the best on the island, but superior to many throughout the Caribbean, this restaurant is set within the 17th-century stone boiling house. The Haitian paintings decorating the walls incorporate the cobblestones and slabs brought from Liverpool as ballast on ships carrying rum and sugar. Foodies love the skillfully created dishes such as scallops in puff pastry with roasted red-pepper sauce or pork medallions with peanut sate sauce. The tempting desserts include piña colada cake and Creole banana crepes. ◆ California/West Indian ◆ Daily 7-8:30PM (set seatings are scheduled on the half-hour). Reservations required. 5.4355

Islands Restaurant ★★★$$ Located on the beach, the less formal diner features island fare prepared with a decidedly gourmet touch. The *roti,* a Trinidadian dish, is East Indian flat bread filled with curried chicken; "jump up"—another house specialty—is grilled, marinated fresh fish with a salsa of chopped tomatoes, green onions, olives, and capers. ◆ West Indian ◆ Daily noon-2PM, 6:30-9PM. 5.4355

10 Apple Bay The waves are higher and the winds are stronger here than anywhere else on the island, especially between October and March. This bay is known as *the* surfing spot on Tortola. ◆ West of Road Town

Restaurants/Clubs: Red   **Hotels:** Blue
Shops/ 🌳 **Outdoors:** Green   **Sights/Culture:** Black

11 Mount Sage National Park Tortola's highest peak rises to 1,780 feet, providing spectacular views of Jost Van Dyke, Virgin Gorda, and St. John islands. The 92-acre preserve provides hikers with rain-forest and mahogany-forest trails. You can pick up a copy of a self-guided tour at the Tourist Board or BVI National Parks Trust Office (M-F 8:30AM-4:30PM. Fishlock Rd. 4.3904) to help identify the trees and plants as you traipse through the junglelike rain forest. Because of the steepness, this land was not cleared by the British in the 18th century when they created their cotton and sugarcane plantations. Today the towering trees still droop with vines as they did when the first European settlers arrived. ◆ Daily 24 hours. Ridge Rd

12 Cane Garden Bay Considered one of Tortola's loveliest beaches, Cane Garden Bay features a 1.5-mile white sand beach dotted with coconut palms and spots for snacks and

British Virgin Islands

changing. It's also regarded as one of the BVI's top anchorages, so you're bound to spot fleets of sailboats moored here. Several casual diners with bars dish up local goodies. ◆ Cane Garden Bay. No phone

13 Mount Healthy A stone windmill and a few other historical ruins that may date from the sugar plantation era are being restored here. But this area above Brewer's Bay is still a peaceful spot for an afternoon picnic. ◆ Brewer's Bay

14 Skyworld ★★★$$$ A quarter mile above Road Town, this restaurant with a view is furnished in rattan, with Haitian and local oil paintings and prints on the walls. Diners see both the Atlantic and the Caribbean through the glass windows. Favorite dishes include rack of lamb and grilled swordfish. Save room for the savory **Chocolate Suicide**—a rich concoction of dark and white chocolates. ◆ Continental ◆ Daily 11:30AM-9:30PM. Ridge Rd. 4.3567

15 The Cloud Room ★★★$$$ This is an experience not to be missed. Don't expect to get to this restaurant on your own; the ascent is so steep and precarious that guests are picked up and transported to the mountaintop aboard an open-sided, canvas-topped bus (included in the dinner price). At one point, the switchback road forces the driver to turn the vehicle around and back up. Once at the destination, enjoy cocktails on the veranda or inside the 10-table dining room, where a sliding roof rolls back in good weather. ◆ West Indian ◆ M-Sa 7:30PM-midnight. Reservations required. Ridge Rd. 4.2821

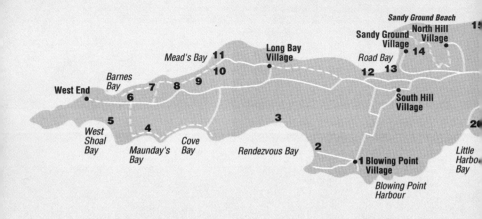

km ____1____2

mi ____1____2

N

Caribbean Sea

Crocus Bay

Sandy Ground Beach

Sandy Ground Village

North Hill Village

15

14

Road Bay

Mead's Bay 11

Long Bay Village

12 13

Barnes Bay

7 8 9 10

South Hill Village

West End

6

5

4

3

2

20

West Shoal Bay

Maunday's Bay

Cove Bay

Rendezvous Bay

1 Blowing Point Village

Little Harbour Bay

Blowing Point Harbour

Caribbean Sea

Puerto Rico

ANGUILLA

Virgin Islands

St. Martin/Sint Maarten

St. Kitts

Barbuda

Nevis

Antigua

Montserrat

Guadeloupe

LESSER

Dominica

ANTILLES

Martinique

St. Lucia

Barbados

St. Vincent

N

km ____300

mi ____180

Carriacou

Grenada

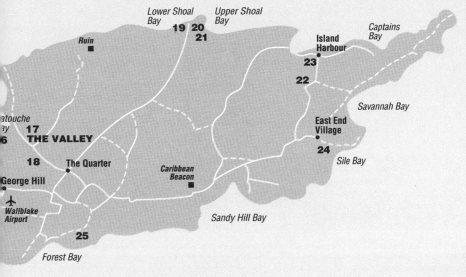

Anguilla

The tiny eel-shaped island of Anguilla (pronounced an-*gwee*-la) in the northernmost **British West Indies** is best known for its beaches. The sand resembles powdered sugar and the water is as clear as crystal. The island's serenity (there isn't much to do on Anguilla except enjoy the beaches) is another reason it has enjoyed a heightened popularity in recent years.

Celebrity actors **Michael J. Fox** and **Bruce Willis** have vacationed on the island, leading to featured spreads on the two "rich and famous" resorts they stayed in—**Malliouhana** and **Cap Juluca**—in a number of glossy magazines. And all this media hype has helped make Anguilla the resort island of the nineties.

Water sports are the top activity here. Whether you want to charter a boat for deep-sea fishing, snorkeling, or overnight or sunset cruising, this is the place to do it. If you simply want to relax on a white sand beach, Anguilla offers 30 of some of the prettiest in the world. There's **Shoal Bay** on the east side of the island, where day-trippers from **St. Martin/Sint Maarten** often take a dip before ferrying back; **Road Bay** at Sandy Ground; **Maunday's Bay**, **Barnes Bay**, and **Mead's Bay** on the west end; **Island Harbour Bay** to the north; and **Rendezvous Bay** (a historic beach where a French soldier from St. Martin once tried to invade the island), **Sandy Hill Bay**, and **Little Harbour Bay** on the southern coast.

Getting to the Island

Airlines

Air Anguilla, Air BVI, American Eagle, LIAT, Tyden Air Inc, and Winair serve the island via St. Martin/Sint Maarten, Antigua, and San Juan.

Airport

Wallblake Airport American Eagle flies between this small airport and San Juan on Puerto Rico, where passengers can connect with other flights. It's located just above Little Harbour. For information, call 497.2514.

Getting around the Island

Car Rentals

Apex Car Rental	497.2461
Budget Rent-a-Car	497.2217
Concept Cars	497.2671
Connors Car Rental	497.6433
High-Way Rent-a-Car	497.2183/2486

Anguilla

Island Car Rental	497.2723
Triple "K" Car Rental	497.2934/4233

Driving

Drive on the left side of the road, and limit your speed to 30 miles per hour. Roundabouts require granting the right-of-way. Anguilla's roads are fairly well paved and maintained, but they are not well marked. It's best to refer to a map before embarking on your trip.

FYI

Electricity

The voltage is 110 (60 cycles).

Money

Bank hours are generally M-Th 8AM-3PM; F 8AM-5PM. The currency is the Eastern Caribbean dollar, but American dollars are accepted island-wide.

Personal Safety

Crime isn't a big problem on Anguilla, but keep an eye on your belongings on the beaches. As elsewhere in the Caribbean, drugs may be offered for sale. The possession of drugs, other than pre-scription medications, is illegal on Anguilla.

Phone Book

Airport	497.2514
Cable and Wireless	497.2210
Chamber of Commerce	497.2701
Ferryboat Port	497.6853
Hospital	497.2551
Optometrist	497.3700
Pharmacy	497.2366/2738
Physicians	497.3792/3460/6522
Police	497.2333
Post Office (main office)	497.2528
Tourist Board	497.2759

Publications

The bi-weekly *Vantage* and the daily *Chronicle* are available in addition to the major American and London newspapers. *What We Do in Anguilla* and *Anguilla Life* are publications geared to tourists' informational needs.

Taxes and Tipping

Hotels charge 10 percent for service plus an 8 percent government tax is added to the room rate. Restaurants add a 15 percent service charge to food tabs. Ten to 15 percent tips are expected on taxi fares. Departure taxes are $6 if you leave by air, $2 if by ferry.

1 Ferry Boat Inn $$ The roomy kitchen apartments offer a view of St. Martin and the beautiful white sand beach. The restaurant features everything from burgers to steak. ♦ Blowing Point Harbour. 497.6613; fax 497.3309

2 Rendezvous Bay Resort $$ One of Anguilla's first tourist resorts, the Rendezvous Bay was recently redone to keep up with the island's building boom and upmarket tempo. There's a restaurant on the premises and a lovely white sand beach. ♦ Rendezvous Bay. 497.6549

3 Anguilla Great House $$$ Gracious West Indian-style buildings offer 25 rooms, each with a view of the ocean. The rooms can be expanded to form suites, making this an ideal choice for family vacations. There's a large swimming pool and various water sports are offered on the premises. The hotel restaurant serves West Indian, European, and American cuisine. ♦ Rendezvous Bay. 497.6061, 800/553.4939; fax 497.6019

4 Cap Juluca $$$$ With views of Maunday's and Cove bays that will knock your socks off, this elegant 78-room, 14-suite resort recently added an 1,800-square-foot swimming pool. (The pool area matches Cap Juluca's outstanding Moorish architecture and offers several private areas for sunbathing, each with a bell to ring for your personal attendant.) The luxurious hotel is named for the Arawak Indian rainbow god of Anguilla and took close to five years to complete.

Peter Shepherd, who worked at London's posh Savoy and the Hotel de Paris in Monte Carlo, is acting general manager. He should feel right at home, for the same elegance is obvious here, only this time it's of the casual sand-in-your-shoes variety. Completely outfitted in beige marble, the bathrooms are enormous and quite grand. Tennis and water sports are complimentary, and guests can tee off at the **Mullet Bay Golf Course** on nearby St. Martin. Door-to-door service, via a 15-minute boat ride, is available to hotel guests. The guest-to-staff ratio is two to one. ♦ Deluxe ♦ Closed Sep-Oct. Maunday's Bay. 497.6666, 800/235.3505

Within Cap Juluca:

Pimm's ★★★$$$ Fine food is served graciously alfresco overlooking Maunday's Bay at this romantic restaurant. ♦ Continental ♦ Daily noon-2:30PM, 7-9:30PM. 497.6666

Chatterton's ★★$$ Snacks, salads, and cold drinks served outdoors will tide you over until dinner. ♦ American ♦ Daily noon-7PM. 497.6666

5 Covecastles $$$$ The 12 posh villas and guest houses are brilliantly modern in design and attractively and elegantly furnished. ♦ Deluxe ♦ W. Shoal Bay. 497.6801; fax 497.6051

6 Mango's ★★$$$ Try the Caribbean pumpkin-shrimp bisque, the sesame swordfish, or the orange-pepper mahimahi. Mango's is one of the island's most popular restaurants. ♦ Caribbean/Seafood ♦ M, W-Su 6:30-10PM. Barnes Bay. Reservations recommended. 497.6479

7 Coccoloba $$$$ The West Indian fretwork on the charming yellow and green cottages makes this resort extremely attractive. Coccoloba has a program of ongoing renovations and the property always looks inviting. The rooms are just as pretty and the beach is pristine. A swimming pool and tennis courts will keep you busy if you've had enough beach time (on Anguilla, though, that doesn't seem to happen). The full American breakfasts are complimentary. ♦ Barnes Bay. 497.6871, 800/833.3559

8 La Sirena $$$ **Rolf Masshardt** of Switzerland manages the 20 hotel rooms, restaurant, and three delightful villas. Although the flat tropical island is eons away from an Alpine setting, many Swiss hotel touches are evident. La Sirena boasts two freshwater pools, shops, lush foliage, and a mile-long beach only minutes away. The popular restaurant provides a beautiful view. ♦ Mead's Bay. 497.6827; fax 497.6829

9 Carimar Beach Club $$ The 23 units are a mix of modern and fully equipped attractive one-, two-, and three-bedroom apartments. The Carimar shares a gorgeous beach with the Malliouhana Hotel; in fact, Mead's Bay has been named one of the best beaches in the Caribbean. Management will shop ahead to stock the refrigerator and arrange for a rental car if you give them advance notice. ♦ Mead's Bay. 497.6881, 800/235.8667; fax 497.6071

10 Malliouhana Hotel $$$$ Malliouhana is the original Indian name for Anguilla. Chic enough for a sheik and Moroccan in design, the hotel was created as a hideaway for those who want the very best. Malliouhana boasts 54 elegant rooms and suites, four tennis courts, two beaches, three swimming pools, and some of the most tastefully designed public areas in the Caribbean. The poolside bar, with its large white couches and brightly hued pillows, is a marvelous area for a late afternoon drink. The Malliouhana's rooms offer pedestal beds, white cotton spreads topped by at least a dozen pillows, and every imaginable amenity in the spacious bathrooms. The restaurant is supervised by **Jo Rostang** of La Bonne Auberge in Antibes, France, and La Regence at the Plaza-Athenee in New York. Shops include **La Romana,** where hotel guests only can purchase the designer goods in stock. ♦ Deluxe ♦ Closed Sep-Oct. Mead's Bay. 497.6111, 800/372.1232; fax 497.6011

Restaurants/Clubs: Red   **Hotels:** Blue

Shops/ 🌴 **Outdoors:** Green   **Sights/Culture:** Black

11 Arlo's Place ★★$$ Several fettuccine dishes, veal parmigiana, and spaghetti bolognese are all very good. ♦ Italian ♦ M-Sa 7-10:30PM. South Hill. Reservations recommended. 497.6810

12 The Mariners $$$ Varied single rooms, doubles, suites, and cottages—50 in all—dot the grounds of this beachfront hotel, a classic example of West Indian architecture. There's a pool, and tennis and water sports are available. ♦ Sandy Ground. 497.2671

13 Riviera ★★$$$ The Riviera promotes itself as a beach restaurant, bar, and boutique. The seafood and desserts would make a Parisian blush. ♦ French ♦ Daily noon-closing. Road Bay, Sandy Ground. 497.2833

14 Sydans Apartments $ The Spanish-styled self-contained units are located right off the beach, across from Tamarain Water Sports and several small restaurants. There are a boutique and a Mexican restaurant on the premises. ♦ Sandy Ground. 497.2214

15 Masara Resort $$ The villa-style resort with 11 one- and two-bedroom apartments has fulfilled the dream of owners **Mac** and **Sara Brooks.** Masara reflects a combination of their names— and their ideas. The rooms are spacious and simply furnished. ♦ Katouche Bay. 497.3200, 800/776.0110

16 Dorack's Paradise Cafe ★★$$ Caribbean specialties include sautéed snapper with citrus sauce; chicken breast with herb goat cheese; and curried chicken roti, a corn and flour crepe served with rice and beans. ♦ Seafood ♦ M-Sa noon-2PM, 6-9PM. Katouche Bay. Reservations recommended. 497.3210

17 Lloyd's Guest House $$ There are only 14 rooms here, set above Crocus Bay, five minutes away from the beach. ♦ The Valley. 497.2351

18 Koalkeel Restaurant ★★$$$$ One of Anguilla's best-known restaurants, the Koalkeel is housed in an 18th-century West Indian home. Enjoy the romantic and charming atmosphere. ♦ Caribbean/ Continental ♦ Daily noon-3PM, 7-10PM. The Valley. Reservations recommended. 497.2930

19 Fountain Beach Tennis Club $$$ The hotel's 10 studios and one-bedroom apartments feature a Mediterranean style and a sense of seclusion on the western end of Shoal Bay. Island antiques furnish each room. ♦ Lower Shoal Bay. 497.3491

Within the Fountain Beach Tennis Club:

Ristorante La Fontana ★★$$ Chef **Luca Voncini** is known for traditional menu items such as grilled fish and T-bone steaks but will prepare any special entrées if given advance notice. ♦ Italian ♦ Daily noon-2:30PM, 7-10:30PM. Reservations recommended. 497.3492

20 Shoal Bay Resort Hotel $$$ Apartments with kitchen facilities are located along two miles of one of Anguilla's prettiest beaches. Each unit is only a few steps from the water. ♦ Upper Shoal Bay. 497.2011; fax 497.3355

21 Shoal Bay Villas $$$ Management has created a "pick a package" program where guests can choose from 13 studios or one- or two-bedroom apartments with  fully equipped kitchens, and a variety of water sports programs. Each unit has a patio or balcony, and the beach is outstanding. ♦ Upper Shoal Bay. 497.2051, 800/722.7045

Within the Shoal Bay Villas:

Reefside Restaurant ★$$ Local seafood is served a variety of ways. The steaks are notable and the happy-go-lucky atmosphere makes dining here a pleasure. ♦ Seafood/ Steaks ♦ Daily 8AM-10PM. 497.2051

22 Le Fish Trap Restaurant ★★$$$ Fish and seafood are prepared with a gourmet touch. Appetizers include crab farci (local crabmeat mixed with sweet and hot peppers and baked with breadcrumbs) and tomato pie made of Swiss cheese, mustard, fresh tomatoes and garlic. Entrées include bouill-abaisse Caribe, a selection of fresh fish with conch, crayfish, and veggies. There's live entertainment on Wednesday night. ♦ Seafood/Caribbean ♦ Daily 7-9PM. Island Harbour. 497.5027

23 Hibernia ★★$$$ Overlooking the water, one loses sight of the island ambience. The service here is more French Riviera than Caribbean. ♦ French ♦ Tu-Su noon-2PM, 7-9PM. Reservations required. Island Harbour. 497.4290

24 Spindrift $$ Fully equipped apartments take advantage of Anguilla's eastern shore and the quiet, pretty surroundings. There are tennis courts, a pool, and water sports. ♦ Sile Bay. 497.4164; fax 497.2940

25 Smugglers Grill ★$$ Literally a few yards from the Wallblake Airport, the restaurant features traditional chophouse specialties. ♦ Steaks ♦ M-Sa 6PM-midnight. Forest Bay. 497.3728

26 Cinnamon Reef Beach Club $$$ Luxury and sophistication are the hallmarks at this impressive seaside hotel with 22 rooms, a quiet beach, and a huge freshwater pool. Water sports are available and there's an open-air restaurant. The resort's boutique sells delightful sportswear and jewelry. ♦ Little Harbour Bay. 497.2727; fax 497.3727

Where the Price Is Right

Some Caribbean islands claim to be duty free when, in fact, a small duty (tax on imports) is tacked onto the purchase price of various items; others are telling the truth. In many cases, the prices of imported goods are less expensive than those at home because it costs less to ship products from, say, France to a French island, such as St. Martin, just as it costs less to ship American products within the United States than it does to send them and sell them abroad.

Liquor, fragrances, crystal, china, woolens, cameras, fine jewelry, native art, and batik or hand-dyed island-made goods are considered the best values in the Caribbean, even on the islands that charge a small duty. Visitors typically purchase French perfume; British, French, or Swedish crystal; Italian designer leather goods; and the ubiquitous T-shirts bearing island logos or other messages. (Stores are more crowded when the cruise ships come in, so ask the staff at your hotel when they arrive so you can plan your shopping trips around their schedules.)

No taxes are paid on **St. Martin/Sint Maarten,** making it a truly duty-free island with some of the best liquor bargains in the region. Dutch cheeses are good buys on all the **Netherland Antilles** and **Aruba.** (Aruba has a low duty rate, so other things can be bargains as well.) In January 1992 the customs' duty on jewelry, perfume, crystal, liquor, china, linen, watches, and other goods was lifted in the **Bahamas.**

All of the former British islands—particularly **Bermuda** and **Anguilla**—offer discounted prices for china, crystal, and porcelain manufactured in the United Kingdom. The French islands—**St. Martin, Guadeloupe,** and **Martinique,** among others—are best bets for purchasing fragrances and cosmetics, especially the French brands.

St. Thomas, St. John, and **St. Croix** in the **US Virgin Islands** permit residents of the United States a $1,200 duty-free allowance, twice the limit of anywhere else in the world. For more information write to the **Virgin Islands Retailers Association,** Box 1275, St. Thomas, USVI 00804; or contact them by calling 809/774.7305.

Several stores have branches throughout the islands. **Little Switzerland,** which carries fine watches, jewelry, china, gifts, and perfume, can be found on all the major **Bahamian islands,** as well as on **St. Thomas, St. Croix, St. Martin/Sint Maarten, St. Barts, Antigua, Aruba,** and **Curaçao. Colombia Emeralds International** has jewelry stores in the **Bahamas, St. Thomas, St. John, St. Martin/Sint Maarten, Cartagena, Colombia, Grand Cayman,** and **Antigua. Benetton,** the international clothing store, and **Penha,** fragrance retailers, have shops on **Aruba, Curaçao,** and **St. Martin/Sint Maarten.**

Here's a sampling of price tags recently found on Aruba compared to those seen on the same items in New York:

Aruba's Price	New York's Price	
$75	$98	**Baccarat** crystal
$2,095	$2,850	**Cartier** sportswatch
$75	$125	**Gucci** handbag
$625	$910	**Lalique** figurine
$42	$60	**Valentino** perfume

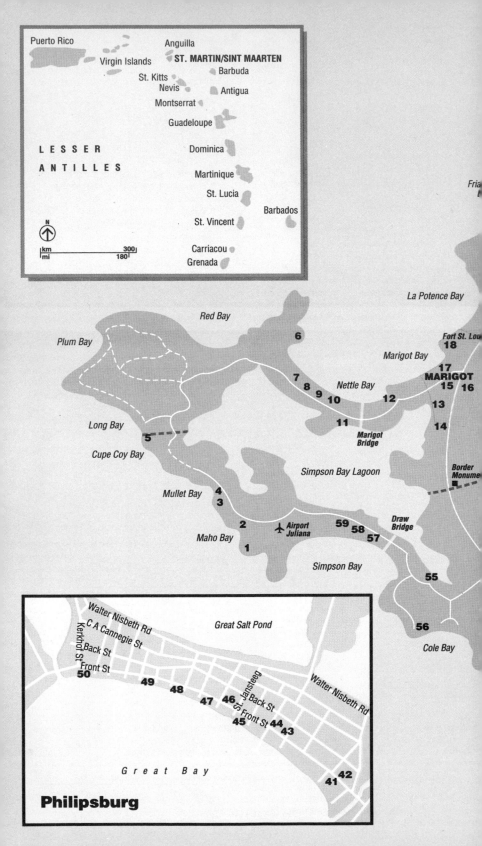

Puerto Rico

Anguilla

Virgin Islands   **ST. MARTIN/SINT MAARTEN**

St. Kitts   Barbuda

Nevis   Antigua

Montserrat

Guadeloupe

L E S S E R
A N T I L L E S   Dominica

Martinique

St. Lucia

Barbados

St. Vincent

km   300
mi   180

Carriacou

Grenada

La Potence Bay

Red Bay

Plum Bay

Fort St. Lou
18

Marigot Bay

6

7   Nettle Bay   17   MARIGOT
8 9   15   16
10   12   13
11   14
Marigot
Bridge

Long Bay
5

Cupe Coy Bay

Simpson Bay Lagoon

Border
Monume

Mullet Bay   4
3

Draw
Bridge

Maho Bay   2
1   59 58
Airport   57
Juliana

Simpson Bay

55

Cole Bay

56

Walter Nisbeth Rd

Great Salt Pond

C A Cannegie St

Back St

Kerkhof St

Front St
50

49   48   47   46   Jansteeg   Back St

45   St Front St   44 43

Walter Nisbeth Rd

G r e a t   B a y   41 42

Philipsburg

St. Martin/Sint Maarten

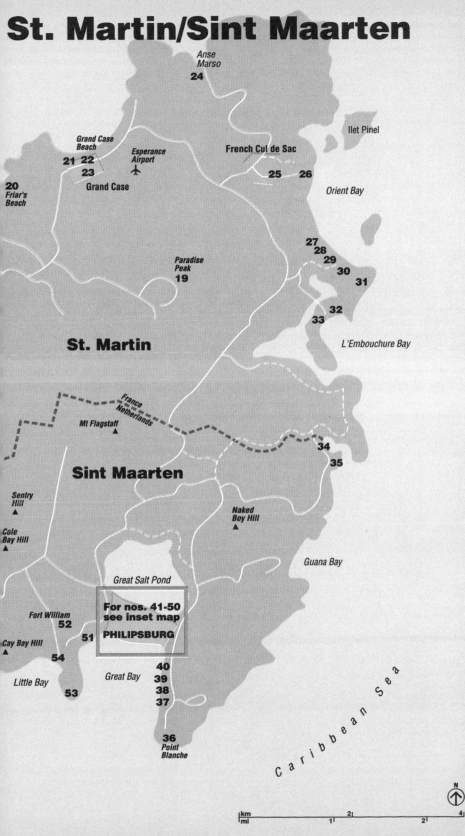

Anse Marso
24

Ilet Pinel

Grand Case Beach
21 22
23

Esperance Airport

French Cul de Sac

20 Friar's Beach

Grand Case

25 26

Orient Bay

Paradise Peak
19

27
28
29
30
31

32
33

L'Embouchure Bay

St. Martin

France
Netherlands

Mt Flagstaff ▲

34
35

Sint Maarten

Sentry Hill ▲

Naked Boy Hill ▲

Cole Bay Hill ▲

Guana Bay

Great Salt Pond

Fort William
52

51

For nos. 41-50 see inset map

PHILIPSBURG

Cay Bay Hill ▲

54

40
39
38
37

Little Bay

Great Bay

53

36
Point Blanche

Caribbean Sea

N ↑

km
mi   1   2   2   4

Christopher Columbus visited more Caribbean islands than today's most inveterate cruise-ship passenger. On his second trip to the New World he stopped at an island ringed with glorious white sand beaches. That island was St. Martin/ Sint Maarten, and today it's one of the most popular vacation destinations in the Caribbean.

This island is a wonderful mix of Dutch and French accents blended in a 37-square mile piece of land. It's approximately half Dutch and half French, and embodies the best of both worlds. Residents and tourists alike travel freely from one side to the other (the northern portion of the island is French; the southern Dutch). One can, for example, spend the day shopping in **Philipsburg**, the tiny Dutch capital; drive nine miles to have dinner in **Marigot**, the French capital; and return to the Dutch side for an evening of gambling.

The island is the smallest land mass in the world to be shared by two governments. This phenomenon dates back to the **Eighty Years' War** between Spain and the Dutch Republic. As the war drew to a close in early 1648, Spain closed its fort. According to local legend, a handful of French and Dutch crew members hid on the island until the Spanish fleet departed, then decided to divvy it up and live together in harmony. An agreement between the two nations was signed on 23 March 1648 dividing St. Martin in half. And the peaceful co-existence of the people here has continued for more than 300 years.

Just as the French and Dutch governments have continued to work independently of one another, each of their cultures has remained intact. The Dutch side is characterized by pastel "gingerbread" houses covered with fretwork and surrounded by flowers, while the fine restaurants, bistros

St. Martin/Sint Maarten

and tiny boutiques on the French side feature charming wrought-iron balconies. The oldest French settlement on the island is **Orleans**, also known as the French Quarter. The "big" towns—Philipsburg and Marigot—are small enough to explore on foot; and in a car, the entire island can be toured in less than four hours (although you should probably set aside a full day).

St. Martin/Sint Maarten, occasionally referred to as one of the Dutch Windwards, the Netherlands Antilles, or the French West Indies, is an idyllic place with widely varied landscapes. Salt flats characterize the south side, majestic mountains dominate the north (the highest is **Paradise Peak** at 1,278 feet), and gentle hills are interspersed in between. Powdery white sand beaches (the island boasts 37—averaging one per mile) and hidden coves line the perimeter. And it's the island's excellent beaches, wide range of water sports, and outstanding shopping bargains (no taxes are charged on imported goods) that draw more than 600,000 tourists a year. If you're looking for foreign culture in the midst of paradise, St. Martin/Sint Maarten may be the place for you.

Dial 011/599.5 from the United States to Sint Maarten, and 011/590 to St. Martin; when on the island, dial only the last five digits within Sint Maarten and the last six digits within St. Martin.

Getting to the Island
Airlines

Carriers serving St. Martin/Sint Maarten include American Airlines, which flies from New York, Dallas, Raleigh/Durham, and San Juan; Continental Airlines from Newark; and BWIA from Toronto and New York via Antigua. Air St. Barthelemy and WINAIR fly to and from St. Barts; Air Martinique, ALM, LIAT, and WINAIR offer inter-island flights. All of these service the **Princess Juliana International Airport.**

Esperance Airport on the French side is fine for island-hopping, and international flights may be scheduled soon. Expect a $10 departure tax from Princess Juliana and a 15 French franc tax from Esperance airports.

Getting around the Island
Car Rentals

Rental cars are available on St. Martin at Marigot's waterfront. On Sint Maarten, cars must be delivered to your hotel. In other words, take a taxi from the airport to your hotel, where you can rent a car (there should be an information desk in the lobby); the agency will deliver the car to you, however, the car should be returned to Princess Juliana International Airport unless other arrangements have been made.

Rental Agencies in St. Martin (French side):

A.F. Car Rental 87.59.79

Caribbean Auto Rentals................................87.51.22

Express Rent-a-Car 87.70.98

Hertz..87.33.33
St. Martin Auto..............................87.50.86

Rental Agencies in Sint Maarten (Dutch side):

Avis/Mercury 45322
Budget 54274
Dollar Car Rental 22698
Hertz..45294
Holiday Car Rental 52801

Driving

Drive on the right side of the road, as in the United States. Although speed limits are few and far between, 50 miles per hour is considered the maximum speed.

FYI

Drinking

The drinking age on both sides of the island is 18.

Gambling

Casinos are located on the Dutch side of the island. There's **Casino Royale** at the Maho Beach Hotel; **Grand Casino** at Mullet Bay Resort; **Rouge & Noir Casino** at the Seaview Hotel on Front Street, Philipsburg; **Golden Casino** at the Great Bay Beach Hotel; **Kaliste Casino** at the Belair Beach Hotel; and the **Pelican Resort and Casino.**

Money

Although the American dollar is accepted everywhere, the florin is the legal tender on the Dutch side and the franc the legal currency in French territory. Banks on the French side are open M-F 8:30AM-1:30PM. Bank hours on the Dutch side are M-Th 8:30AM-3:30PM; F 8:30AM-1PM.

Personal Safety

There are pockets of poverty on St. Martin/Sint Maarten and the crime that always comes hand-in-hand with them. Stay away from areas you're uncomfortable with and avoid walking alone in deserted areas. The highways on the Dutch side are busier and better lighted than those on the French side, where it is wise to avoid the lonely roads. Know where you're going at all times and be alert to your surroundings; don't hesitate to ask if you're unsure what areas are safe to visit, the staff at the hotel information desks will steer you in the right direction. Although drug dealing isn't as open or aggressive on St. Martin/Sint Maarten as it is, for example, on Jamaica, avoid them because local authorities are not friendly to tourists who abuse their laws.

Phone Book

Emergencies

St. Martin (French side):

Ambulance..87.74.14
Drugstore (Crespin) 87.51.68
Drugstore (Rita Choisy) 87.54.09
Fire 87.50.08
Hospital 87.50.07
Police..87.50.04
Telephone Company 87.53.14

Sint Maarten (Dutch side):

Ambulance..22111
Drugstore (Cole Bay) 44299
Drugstore (Philipsburg) 25576
Fire/Police..22222
Hospital 22300
Taxis...22359
Taxis (Airport)................................44317
Telephone Company 22211

Publications

For news and local information on the Dutch side, choose from three dailies: *The Chronicle, Newsday,* and *The Guardian.* Also look at the tourist-oriented *St. Maarten Holiday, Discover St. Maarten, St. Maarten Events, Focus,* and *St. Maarten Nights,* a guide to after-dark fun and games. On the French side of the island, *St. Martin's Week* and *The News* are the weeklies.

Telephone

From the United States, dial 011, then the area code (599.5 on the Dutch side and 590 on the French side), followed by the local number. If you're calling the Dutch side from the French side, dial 3 plus the five digits of the Dutch number. From the Dutch side to the French, dial 06, then the six digits.

Tipping and Taxes

Most hotels and restaurants on St. Martin/Sint Maarten include tax and service in the room rates and the restaurant bills. If in doubt, ask. A five percent government tax is always added to the 10 to 15 percent service tax.

Dial 011/599.5 from the United States to Sint Maarten, and 011/590 to St. Martin; when on the island, dial only the last five digits within Sint Maarten and the last six digits within St. Martin.

1 The Caravanserai $$ On the beach at beautiful Maho Bay, the Caravanserai represents the ultimate "do-nothing" resort, with 85 rooms and two swimming pools. You won't find activity counselors drumming up tour business or steel bands initiating limbo contests. Caravanserai is defined by *Webster's Dictionary* as "an inn surrounding a court, where caravans rest at night in eastern countries." The hotel is set on a rambling site, eastern in feeling and geared to a laid-back lifestyle. Tea is served daily in the **Palm Court Lounge.** This is strictly a retreat for visitors who want peace and quiet—and gorgeous beaches—all in sight of the Juliana Airport. Children under 15 are not allowed. ♦ Airport Rd (Maho Bay). 57510,800/223.6510

2 Maho Beach Hotel and Casino $$$ The Maho boasts 247 rooms and seemingly as many activities spread along a half mile of white sand beach. The lobby is filled with huge terra-cotta pots and bright pink cushions that spell out tropical resort loud and clear. This is an activities-oriented resort with four tennis courts, water sports galore, badminton, volleyball, and more. There's also a shopping arcade complete with the ubiquitous **Benetton** and pricey **Escada** boutiques. **Casino Royale,** with 17 blackjack tables, six roulette wheels, 206 slot machines, and three craps tables, is just across from the hotel. ◆ Maho Bay. 52115. 800/223.0757

At Maho Beach Hotel and Casino:

Ristorante Roma ★★$$ Substantial traditional food, nothing extraordinary, is prepared

St. Martin/Sint Maarten

quite nicely. There's the usual gamut of pasta and veal dishes, with equal attention given to local seafood. The attractive decor and gracious personnel are important plusses. ◆ Italian ◆ Daily 7-10PM. 42025

The Comedy Club Circuit-touring comics who play similar clubs throughout the region can be heard here. American travelers are a big topic for humor, ditto honeymooners and retirees (but don't take it personally). ◆ Admission. 10PM-4AM. 42115

Cheri's Cafe ★$$ Burgers, omelets, salads, and pasta specials make this a nice spot for a snack or light meal. There's live entertainment 8PM-midnight. ◆ American ◆ Daily 11AM-midnight. 53361

3 La Plage at Royal Islander Club $$$ The 25 attractively decorated one- and two-bedroom apartments in this beachfront hotel are fully equipped and guests have access to all the facilities at neighboring Maho Beach Hotel. ◆ Maho Bay. 42505, 800/223.0757

Restaurants/Clubs: Red   **Hotels:** Blue

Shops/ ◆ Outdoors: Green   **Sights/Culture:** Black

4 Mullet Bay Resort and Casino $$$ This is the flip side of the Caravanserai, a sister property. With 602 rooms spread over 172 acres and the only 18-hole golf course on the island, Mullet Bay is one of the island's biggies and it is go-go-go all day long. The resort has seven restaurants, 14 tennis courts, and a large water-sports center. The **Grand Casino** is one of the largest gambling houses in the Caribbean. A bank, a medical center, and the brand new **Towers** luxury apartments—the first of three to be built— team with the resort's own shopping center to make for a self-contained vacation site. ◆ Mullet Bay. 52801, 800/468.5538

Within the Mullet Bay Resort and Casino:

Mullet Bay Golf Course Until Port de Plaisance opened its golf course, Mullet Bay's 18 holes was the only game in town. In fact, guests at the posh Cap Juluca on nearby Anguilla recently gained golf privileges (by boat) at this venerable course. ◆ Daily dawn-dusk. 52801

Bamboo Garden $$$ Gourmet Chinese cuisine is served in absolutely elegant surroundings. The crisp whole sea bass is superb and the shark-fin soup packs a bite. ◆ Chinese ◆ Daily 3-10PM. 52801

La Romana The upscale shop carries sinfully elegant **Fendi** goods practically given away on a duty-free basis. ◆ M-Sa 9AM-6PM. 22181. Also at: Front St, Philipsburg; Rue de la Republique, Marigot

5 La Samanna $$$$ This super-posh resort has long had a reputation as a luxury hideaway. With its reputation still intact, the 85-room hotel was refurbished recently, retaining an air of exclusivity. A mirrored activity room offers state-of-the-art fitness equipment and water sports. Rather pricey for what's actually offered, the resort appeals to repeat visitors. ◆ Closed Sep-Oct. Long Bay. 87.51.22

6 La Belle Creole $$$$ Built around a cobblestoned courtyard, the resort was created to resemble a French fishing village on the Mediterranean. It took two decades to complete and the only thing missing is a backdrop of the Maritime Alps. The resort's 156 rooms—including 18 suites—on 25 acres along the bay all differ in shape and design. Amenities are excellent and include a new fitness-and-beauty center and a huge water-sports area. The pretty pool and romantic decor make the resort a favorite with honeymooners, who find the sculpted fountains and marble archways great for photos. This is a prestigious Conrad Hilton hotel. ◆ Nettle Bay. 87.58.66, 800/445.8667; fax 87.58.66

Within La Belle Creole:

La Provence ★★★$$$ The open-air terraced restaurant specializes in truly fine dining. Chef **Christopher Micy** prepares outstanding meal after outstanding meal. Veal medallions with mushrooms in truffle juice or baked shrimp stuffed with crabmeat are two of his specialty dishes. ◆ Creole/Continental ◆ Daily 7-10:30AM, 7-10:30PM. 87.58.66

7 Royal Beach Hotel $ This 113-room **Pullman** hotel is located right on the beach. Each room has a terrace and some are equipped with kitchenettes. ◆ Nettle Bay. 87.89.89

8 Anse Margot Resort Hotel $$ Tropical gardens surround 95 rooms, including 35 attractive one-bedroom suites and two swimming pools. ◆ Nettle Bay. 87.92.01; fax 87.92.13

9 Nettle Bay Beach Club $$ A complex of 123 rooms in the beachfront inn, plus 35 garden units, 139 duplex studios, and apartments called the Villas, this property can meet most family and group resort needs. ◆ Nettle Bay. 87.97.04, 800/223.9815

10 Radisson La Flamboyant Resort $$ Situated on 1,200 feet of beach, the resort offers 271 elegant hotel rooms, as well as one- and two-bedroom suites. The pleasant tropical decor is right on target, with two open-air bars, two freshwater swimming pools, and a complete water-sports center. A 400-slip marina is on the drawing board. ◆ Nettle Bay. 87.60.00, 800/333.3333; fax 87.99.57

11 Laguna Beach Hotel $ This small—64 rooms—hotel offers the traditional resort goodies with extras such as hair driers, videos, and private safe-deposit boxes. Water sports, three tennis courts, and a swimming pool are available for guests. ◆ Nettle Bay. 87.89.97

12 Le Jardin Créole ★★$$ **Isabelle** and **Alain Volpei,** natives of France, ran restaurants in Paris and Marseilles and in the French West Indies before settling on St. Martin two years ago. Gracious hospitality and quality food served with commitment to the diner are the hallmarks of their new restaurant. The menu changes seasonally, but conch stew, curry stew with fresh lobster, and crayfish fried in olive oil and flavored with basil are some popular entrées. ◆ Creole/Seafood ◆ Daily 7-11PM. 60 Eagle Rd (Sandy Ground) Marigot. Reservations recommended. 87.99.56

13 Marina Port la Royale The port offers some of Marigot's finest boutiques, boat rentals, and excellent restaurants in a postcard-perfect setting. The marina has 46 berths. ◆ Daily dawn-dusk. Marigot. 87.20.43

Within the Marina Port la Royale:

Hotel Marina Royale $$ Tourists may think they're in St. Tropez when they visit this hotel. Huge ocean-going sailboats in the harbor add to the area's pleasing ambience. Each of the 70 studios and suites has a private terrace or patio. ◆ 87.52.46

Jean Dupont ★★$$$ Bearing its owner's name (Dupont also operates the chic **Le Santal**), this restaurant (pictured above) has become one of the *in* places at the port. Crabmeat pâté is a house specialty and the off-the-water breezes are refreshing. The portions are huge. ◆ French ◆ M-Sa noon-3PM, 6:30-11PM; Su 6:30-11PM. 87.71.13

Le Café de Paris ★$$$ This terraced restaurant offers a view of the water and *très bon* cuisine. The gazpacho with basil and salad Niçoise are notable. ◆ French ◆ M-Sa noon-3PM, 6:30-11PM; Su 6:30-11PM. 87.99.36

Gingerbread Gallery Haitian art and handicrafts are gracefully displayed—the primitive figures are oh-so colorful. ◆ Daily 10AM-6PM. 87.73.21

Dalila This boutique carries women's and men's casual clothing with an "ooh-la-la" French flair. ◆ M-Sa 9AM-7PM. 87.77.42

Paris Art Gallery Owner **Christine Pelletier** features local artists' work in a variety of media ranging from delicate watercolors to vivid oils depicting typical Caribbean themes. ◆ M-Sa 9:30AM-7:30PM. 87.85.03. Also at: La Belle Creole, 87.58.66; Paris 8, Les Acacias, Anse Marcel, 87.34.87

Le Bistingo $ Pizza, snacks, and sandwiches offer a change of pace from the surfeit of French food found all over this part of the island. ◆ American ◆ Daily 11AM-11PM. No phone

Brasserie de la Gare $ The Brasserie is a great location for people-watching while eating ice cream or a quick snack. The harbor is always humming with activity. ◆ Snacks ◆ Daily 11AM-11PM. No phone

La Casa del Cigarro This shop carries Santo Domingan cigars made with age-old techniques. And to think that it all eventually goes up in smoke. ◆ M-Sa 10AM-noon, 2-8PM. No phone

Deviation Exciting avant-garde women's clothing from shoes to streetwear is available here. Try a French swimsuit, if you dare. Deviation also carries the unconventional **Naf-Naf** line. ♦ M-Sa 9AM-7PM; Su 9AM-1PM. No phone

14 Le Poisson D'Or ★$$$ Chef **Sylvain Boulais** has the golden touch with fish and seafood. Try the chilled cream of cucumber and crabmeat soup, red snapper in puff pastry with red wine sauce, or the smoked lobster in a salmon egg and dill sauce. ♦ Seafood ♦ Daily noon-3PM, 6-10PM. Rue de l'Anguille, Marigot. 87.72.45

15 Cafe Terrasse de Mastedana ★★$ The sidewalk cafe and bakery is named for **Oliver** and **Nicole Drouin's** four children: **Mark, Steve, Dany,** and **Nancy.** The family moved

St. Martin/Sint Maarten

to St. Martin from Montreal nine years ago. After 13 years with an international bottling company and another 13 as vice president of a Canadian ad agency, Oliver responded to a newspaper ad for a "Caribbean Bakery" and within four months moved his family to St. Martin. Steve is the baker now, turning out delightfully light croissants and brioche on the outer perimeter of Marina Port La Royale. The lunch menu includes pizza and pasta, bowing to France with a great quiche Lorraine. ♦ French/Italian ♦ M-Sa 7AM-6:30PM; Su 7AM-noon. Liberty St, Marigot. No phone

16 Gucci The typical array of Italian leather goods, watches, and clothing is sold here. The selection is good, with prices far below American costs. ♦ Daily 9AM-7PM. Rue de General de Gaulle, Marigot. 87.84.24

16 Beauty and Scents Select from an excellent range of French cosmetics and fragrances at prices to match. **Lancôme, Clarins, Yves Saint Laurent, Dior,** and **Chanel** are all carried here. ♦ Daily 9AM-6PM. Rue de General de Gaulle, Marigot. 87.58.77

16 Primavera Choose from a potpourri of outstanding glass, crystal, and porcelain objets d'art to bring back to the folks back home. ♦ Daily 9AM-6PM. Rue de General de Gaulle, Marigot. 87.74.20

Le Bar de la Mer

17 Le Bar de la Mer ★★$$ Colorful tiles set into the wooden bar and pastel-hued walls provide a cozy setting for a leisurely drink or light snack in the authentic French brasserie overlooking the harbor. ♦ French ♦ Daily 8AM-2AM. Blvd de France, Marigot. 87.81.79

17 La Calanque ★★$$$$ This fine restaurant has been an institution for more than two decades. Duck in banana sauce is a favorite menu item and the fish soup is not to be believed. ♦ French ♦ M-Sa noon-3PM, 6:30-10PM; Su 6:30-10PM. Blvd de France, Marigot. 87.50.82

17 Printemps The gift and liquor shop is convenient to the ferry port to Anguilla and faces the bustling Saturday market at the harbor. ♦ M-Sa 9AM-5:45PM. Blvd de France, Marigot. No phone

17 Oro de Sol Gifts, including **Pratesi** linens; fragrances; jewelry; and **Ebel, Piaget, Patek Phillipe,** and **Cartier** watches are sold here. ♦ M-Sa 9AM-6PM. Blvd de France, Marigot. 87.56.51. Also at: Rue de la Republique, Marigot; and Front St, Marigot

17 Messalina ★★$$$ A trattoria menu in the heart of French fare is most welcome. Although created by **Roger Petit** of Le Poisson d'Or and La Vie en Rose, the view of the harbor can sometimes be better than the food at this specific restaurant. ♦ Italian ♦ Daily 11:30AM-2PM, 6:30-10PM. Blvd de France, Marigot. 87.80.39

17 La Vie en Rose ★★★$$$$ Many consider this the premiere French restaurant on the island. One specialty is smoked salmon with salmon roe and pear tomatoes. Try the apple tart with crème *anglaise*. The earlier you eat the better chance you have of getting a much-desired balcony table. ♦ Daily 6:30-10PM. Blvd de France, Marigot. Reservations required. 87.54.42

18 Fort St. Louis Climb to the top for an out-standing panoramic view of the French capital, Marigot Harbor, and (on a clear day) over to Anguilla. Built in 1786 and since restored, the 20-minute trek is well worth the effort. ♦ Marigot

19 Paradise Peak St. Martin's highest peak, at just under 1,500 feet, is considered by photographers to be the best spot to shoot the French or Dutch capitals on surrounding islands. ♦ Southwest of Orleans

20 Friar's Beach The lovely, intimate beach and cove are popular with the fins-and-masks crowd. ♦ South of Grand Case

21 Fish Pot Restaurant ★★★$$$ Overlooking **Grand Case Bay,** fine food is served on charming gray-and-apricot china. The smooth and creamy lobster bisque is excellent, as is the fresh lobster prepared with a ginger-and-lemon sauce. Fresh vegetables and scalloped potatoes accompany each meal. The restaurant isn't air-conditioned, but there's always a breeze so try for a terrace table. ♦ French/Seafood ♦ Daily noon-3PM, 6:30-10PM. Grand Case. Reservations required. 87.50.88

21 Le Tastevin ★★$$$ This restaurant is operated by **Daniel** and **Martine Passeri** of L'Auberge Gourmande, which is just across the street in a two-room island house. Le Tastevin's pretty decor is complemented by fine service and an excellent wine list. The name means wine taster. ♦ French ♦ M-Tu, Th-Su noon-3PM, 6:30-10PM Jan-May, Aug-Dec; W 6:30-10PM Jan-May, Aug-Dec. Grand Case. Reservations recommended. 87.55.45

21 Hevea ★★$$$ The restaurant is actually the intimate dining room of the eight-room Hotel Hevea operated by **Jacqueline** and **Jean-Claude Dalbera** from Nice. The charming French-innlike decor is enhanced by elegant personalized service. ♦ French ♦ Daily 6:30-10PM Jan-Aug, Oct-Dec. Grand Case. Reservations required. 87.75.04

21 Chez Martine ★★$$$ The charming terrace of this eight-room guest house on the bay side of restaurant row specializes in Lyonnaise cuisine, including frog legs in champagne sauce and lobster tail in a puff pastry. ♦ French ♦ Daily noon-3PM, 6:30-10PM. Grand Case. 87.51.59

21 Rainbow ★★$$$ The chef is **Ken Pulomena** from John Clancy's in New York's Greenwich Village. The light menu features grilled meat and fish, as well as crispy roast duck and sautéed sweetbreads Dijonnaise. ♦ French ♦ M-Sa noon-3PM, 6:30-10PM January-May, December. Grand Case. Reservations required. 87.55.80

21 Sebastiano ★$$$ This is an oasis of Northern Italian cuisine in a sea of French cooking. The menu is varied, but any pasta with seafood item is bound to be good. ♦ Italian/Seafood ♦ Su noon-3PM, 7-9PM. Grand Case. 87.58.86

22 Grand Case Beach Club $$ Located on the ocean just outside the village of Grand Case, the club offers a wonderful view of the nearby island of Anguilla. Studios and one- and two-bedroom units, all fully equipped, are available complemented by a full water-sports program. ♦ Grand Case Beach. 87.51.87, 800/223.1588

23 Flamboyant Beach Villas $ The beautiful royal poinciana trees that lend their name to the property are ablaze in summer. The modest air-conditioned villas have one or two bedrooms. ♦ Grand Case. 87.50.98

St. Martin/Sint Maarten

24 Le Meridien L'Habitation $$$$ Presidents **George Bush** and **François Mitterand** picked this pricey traditional resort with a 1,600-foot-long white sand beach, a 100-slip marina, and charming decor for their 1990 soiree. Newly redone, the pool area now sports vibrant pinks, greens, and yellows. Bright Caribbean pastels have added to the new luxury wing, **Le Domaine,** with 125 rooms and 20 suites, a pool, and an open-air restaurant. The rooms in the $45 million addition all feature a large, round bathtub. The landscape bills alone came to $1 million when the Meridien folks took over. Many guests have been coming here for years. ♦ Deluxe ♦ Anse Marse. 83.33.33, 800/543.4300

25 Mark's Place $ This informal bistro along the road to Orient Beach is popular with tourists and locals alike. Daily specials are posted on a blackboard. ♦ Creole/Seafood ♦ Tu-Su noon-3PM, 6-10PM. French Cul de Sac. No phone

26 Golden Tulip St. Martin Hotel $$$ This low-rise hotel has 96 rooms and various water sports, as well as day and night tennis for guests. There's also a shuttle bus to casinos. ♦ French Cul de Sac. 87.89.98, 800/333.1212

27 Orient Bay Hotel $ Across the road from Les Jardins and also quite new, the 31 studios and apartments are set among lush foliage on the hillside. ♦ Mt Vernon. 87.31.10, 800/724.2609; fax 87.31.10

28 Les Jardins de Chevrise $$ This apartment hotel features 29 studios and duplexes overlooking **Orient Bay.** The traditional Caribbean architecture is attractive and serene. ◆ Mt Vernon. 87.37.79

29 Mont Vernon $$ This hillside hotel recently added 157 rooms, making it the largest hotel on the French side. Suites are available and all of the rooms offer an outstanding view of the ocean. ◆ Mt Vernon. 87.62.00, 800/223.0888; fax 87.37.27

30 Club Oriënt $$ Rooms at this clothing-optional beach resort (pictured above) are also sans air-conditioning, telephones, radios, or TVs. Delightful breezes cool the rustic, red-pine chalets imported from Finland. Amenities include a market, water sports, tennis, volley-

ball, and Swedish or Shiatsu massages. ◆ Orient Bay. 87.33.85; fax 87.33.76

31 Orient Beach Naturalists as well as swimsuit-clad sun worshipers enjoy one of St. Martin's finest beaches, more than a mile long and clothing is optional. The sand, as white as confectioner's sugar, and the amazingly turquoise waters are part of the attraction. T-shirt and souvenir shops and refreshments are available. ◆ Orient Bay

32 Pedro's Restaurant ★★$ Some of the best ribs in the Caribbean are served in this rustic beachfront shack. Hamburgers, chicken, french fries, and salad round out the menu. ◆ American ◆ M-Sa 9AM-5:30PM; Su 9:30AM-6PM. Orient Beach. No phone

33 Kon Tiki ★$ Having grilled chicken for lunch after you've been grilled on the beach isn't a bad idea. The Kon Tiki does a nice job of serving snacks and salads. China and silverware are an elegant touch even though the people at the next table may have left their clothes at home. ◆ American ◆ M-Sa 9AM-6PM. Orient Beach. No phone

34 Oyster Pond Yacht Club $$$ The villas are quite new and lovely at this posh resort with a saltwater pool overlooking the ocean. Scuba diving and horseback riding are among the activities available. In keeping with the ocean motif, the elegant accommodations—20

rooms, 20 suites—are named after sea vessels. Children under 10 are not allowed. ◆ Deluxe ◆ Oyster Pond Beach. 22206, 800/372.1323

35 Dawn Beach Hotel $$ Set on a secluded beach, the hotel's 155 rooms are decorated in soothing pastel shades. Each unit has a living room/bedroom, a kitchen, a private terrace, and some of the most magnificent views of the ocean. It's no surprise that this is a favorite honeymoon destination. ◆ Dawn Beach, just south of Oyster Pond. 22929, 800/351.5656; fax 24421

Within the Dawn Beach Hotel:

Dawn Beach Dining Room ★$$ The open-air terraced room features an outstanding view and freshly prepared island specialties. ◆ Seafood/Caribbean ◆ Daily 8-10:30AM, noon-2:30PM, 7-10PM. 22929

36 Monte Vista $$$$ Two- and three-bedroom condominiums are guarded by a 24-hour attended gatehouse entrance. Residential architects Kaufman Meeks Inc. of the US teamed with Caribbean-based design firm Onions Bouchard and McCulloch and the construction firm of Balfour Beatty NV to create a Mediterranean-like community of opulence and beauty. High atop **Point Blanche,** Monte Vista is minutes away from the casinos, restaurants, and shops that make a vacation so pleasant. ◆ Deluxe ◆ Point Blanche. 25831, 800/325.9768

37 Chesterfields ★★$$ Popular with boaters, this restaurant is adjacent to the Great Bay Marina. The decor is decidedly nautical. Shrimp salad is a specialty, made with shrimp that may have been swimming only a few hours earlier. If you're tired of seafood, this is also the place to have a cheeseburger. ◆ Seafood/American ◆ M-Sa 7AM-10PM; Su 11AM-3PM. Great Bay, Philipsburg. Reservations required. 23484

38 Bobby's Marina From here you can rent a boat to go sailing to **St. Barts,** where you can snorkel and picnic for half a day. ◆ Daily 9AM-5PM. Great Bay, Philipsburg. 23170

39 Great Bay Marina Fishers in their large boats and vendors peddling boat rentals vie for your dollars at this large marina. Many boat rentals include lunch, wine, and use of an underwater camera and snorkel equipment. ◆ Daily 9AM-5PM. Great Bay, Philipsburg. 22167

According to popular legend, St. Martin/Sint Maarten's boundaries were set in a walking contest in 1648. A Frenchman paced off 21 square miles and a less speedy Dutchman wound up with only 16 square miles (not exactly a Dutch treat).

St. Martin's Front Street Shopping Map

SCHRIJNWERKER SCHUINE

Il Pescatore
restaurant

POMPS WEDUWEN

Le Bec Fin
restaurant
Sea Palace Hotel
Zhaveri
jewelry

SCHEPPHOUWSTEEG SMIDSTEEG

La Romana	Gucci
leather goods	*leather goods*
Cafe Royale	
restaurant	
Cards & Such	
cards, stationery	
Ashoka	
electronics	

FRONT STREET

SPEELSTEEG SCHOOLSTEEG

	Ramchands
	electronics
Little Europe	Seaview Casino
jewelry, gifts	The Windmill
Taj Mahal	*porcelain*
linens, cameras	Rams
	electronics
	La Romana/Fendi
	leather goods

LOODSSTEEG HOTELSTEEG

Boolchand's	The Jewel Box
linens, cameras	*jewelry*
H. Stern	Colombian Emeralds
jewelry	*jewelry*
New Amsterdam Store	
linens, clothing	

ALOOPSTEEG ST. JAN

Artiste
jewelry

**APOTHEEK VAN ROMOND DAMSTEEG
WATHEY SQUARE**

Wathey	
travel agency	
Treasure Cove	
jewelry	
Little Switzerland	Penha
jewelry	*fragrances*
Kohinoor	
electronics	
Benetton	
clothing	
Batik Caribe	
batiks	

KERKSTEEG PASTORIESTEEG

Deviation	Roy's Jewelry
clothing	*jewelry*
Shipwreck	Holland House
souvenirs	*hotel*
The Gold Mine	Optique Caribe
jewelry	*eyewear*
Old Street Mall	
boutiques	

40 Holland House Beach Hotel $$ Set on a pretty beach, each of the 54 rooms has a kitchenette, balcony, and a nice view. The hotel is also in walking distance to shops, casinos, restaurants, and the port. ♦ Great Bay, Philipsburg. 22572, 800/223.9815

41 Pasanggrahan Royal Inn $$ Formerly a governor's home and now a guest house, the Pasanggrahan offers a white sandy beach and access to some of the best shopping in the Caribbean. The colonial-style building is Sint Maarten's oldest inn. Its **Sidney Greenstreet Bar** could be straight out of a 1940s movie. The name, *pasanggrahan,* is Indonesian for "guest house." ♦ Front St, Philipsburg. 23588, 800/365.8484

42 Scent Maarten Perfume Shop Local and traditional fragrance sources are used to create exotic scents such as Carnival Jump-Up, Carib Lime, and Reggae Rose for men and women. ♦ Daily 9AM-6PM. Front St, Philipsburg. 22965

42 Guavaberry Shop and Free-Tasting House This legendary aged liquor is made by islanders from rum and rare local berries. Most tourists take home at least one bottle. ♦ Daily 9AM-6PM. Front St, Philipsburg. 22965

43 Old Street Just east of the old courthouse (now the post office), Old Street features more than 20 fine boutiques and restaurants. Designed to resemble a street in Old Amsterdam, the brightly colored buildings house a variety of shops selling everything from fine Dutch cheeses to crystal (**Venetian Glass**), children's wear (**Naughty Nippers**), and fine leather (**La Maison du**

Cuir). ♦ M-Sa 8AM-noon, 2-6PM; Su 8AM-noon. Old St (Front St)

43 Philipsburg Grill and Ribs Company $ This is a fairly new addition to Front Street's dining establishments. Baby-back ribs, grilled chicken, and johnnycake (a fried biscuit of sorts) meld a little Caribbeana with Americana. ♦ American ♦ Daily 11AM-11PM. Front St (Old St), Philipsburg. 24723

44 Little Switzerland The Caribbean's best-known purveyor of jewelry, watches, crystal, and china has shelves of goodies such as **Lladro**, **Hummel**, **Aynsley**, **Baccarat**, **Lalique**, **Waterford**, **Audemars**, **Piguet**, **Vacheron & Constantin**, and **Girard-Perregaux**. ♦ M-Sa 9:30AM-6PM. Front St, Philipsburg. 22787

44 Callaloo $ Named for an island plant that looks something like spinach, the restaurant features regional and American foods amid the hustle and bustle of Front Street activities. ♦ Caribbean/American ♦ M-Sa noon-3PM, 7-11PM. Front St (Promenade Arcade). No phone

44 Shipwreck Shop Imagine a treasure trove of Caribbean merchandise and it's a safe bet you'll find it at the Shipwreck Shop. Batiks, baskets, books, hammocks, handmade jewelry, wood carvings, woven mats, and rugs are among the goods. Most visitors walk away with something. ♦ Daily 9:30AM-6PM. Front St, Philipsburg. 22962

45 Seaview Hotel $$ Sint Maarten's oldest hotel opened its doors in 1947, before the government of the Netherlands Antilles was reorganized. It has 45 rooms on Great Bay Beach, and it's close to a number of restaurants and shops. ◆ 67 Front St, Philipsburg. 22323, 800/223.9815

46 Coliseum Casino One of the newest casinos on the island, the Coliseum offers no lions, but six blackjack tables, 182 slot machines, poker, and two roulette wheels in a Romanesque sitting. ◆ 11AM-3AM. Front St, Philipsburg. 31213

47 L'Escargot ★★$$$ Since 1970 L'Escargot has been a prime French restaurant on the Dutch side of St. Martin/Sint Maarten. The site is a 250-year-old Antillian house. Snails—but, of course—and crisp duck in banana sauce are some of the reasons why the restaurant is always so busy. ◆ French ◆ Daily 11:30AM-2:30PM, 6:30-closing. 84 Front St, Philipsburg. Reservations recommended. 22483

48 Sint Maarten Museum The restored 18th-century West Indian house highlights the island's forts, military history, artifacts, and many contributions of the Arawak and Carib Indians. ◆ Admission. M-Sa 10AM-6PM; Su 9:30AM-noon. 119 Front St, Philipsburg. No phone

St. Martin/Sint Maarten

Within the Sint Maarten Museum:

Museum Cafe $ Crepes, croissants, sandwiches, and snacks are served in a West Indian arcade. ◆ Snacks ◆ Daily 8AM-6PM. No phone

48 Le Bec Fin ★★$$$ Actor **Omar Sharif** filmed a scene for "Lifestyles of the Rich and Famous" and **Queen Beatrix** of the Netherlands dined here—classic celebs seeking classic fare. Civic-minded owner **Christian Cartayrade** provided space for the Sint Maarten Museum. ◆ French ◆ Daily 11:30AM-2:30PM, 6:30-10PM. 119 Front St, Philipsburg. 22976

49 The Wajang Doll ★★$$$ Dine on authentic Indonesian food, a concept brought back from the East Indies by Dutch settlers. Try the *rijsttafel,* an Indonesian rice table that incorporates more than a dozen dishes in a complete dinner. ◆ Indonesian ◆ M-Sa 6:45-10PM. 125 Front St, Philipsburg. Reservations recommended. 22687

50 Sint Maarten Sea Palace $$ Its Front Street location is ideal for shopping enthusiasts. The rooms are adequate; suites have fully equipped kitchens and balconies. ◆ Front St (Great Bay Beach). 22700

51 Great Bay Beach Hotel $$ The convenient location, close to Philipsburg's shopping center and the port, is one of the hotel's greatest features, along with the mile-long Great Bay Beach. Completely renovated at a cost of more than $10 million, the hotel (a sister to Maho Bay and La Plage) has two swimming pools,

and every room has a marble bath. The Great Bay Casino features live entertainment each evening. ◆ West end of Great Bay Beach. 22446, 800/223.9815

52 Fort William The drive to Fort William, located on the western edge of Philipsburg, is treacherous, so plan to walk. Try early morning or late afternoon, starting from the dirt road just opposite the **Great Bay Beach Hotel.** It takes just an hour to reach the top. A television transmitter tower makes it easy to find. The fort offers an outstanding view of the entire island and area. The English began to build Fort Trigge in 1801 on the hill. The Dutch renamed it Fort Willem in 1816. Both countries had financial problems, prompting them to build walls without cement. Consequently, the fort quickly fell to ruin. ◆ Salt Pond, west of Philipsburg.

53 Fort Amsterdam Established at Great Bay Harbour in 1631, Fort Amsterdam was the first Dutch port in the Caribbean. Two years later Spain captured the fort, making it their most important bastion east of Puerto Rico. Spain demolished much of the structure before leaving it to the Dutch in 1648. ◆ Great Bay Harbour

54 Divi Little Bay Beach Resort $$ Every room has a private patio or balcony, and guests can enjoy two pools and three tennis courts. The casino has just been renovated. ◆ Little Bay. 22333

55 Plaza del Lago Shopping Center The open-air shopping center has a strong Spanish theme, with whitewashed walls and a terracotta tile roof. Beautiful tile murals depict life in a typical Spanish fishing village. ◆ Simpson Bay. 43378

Within the Plaza del Lago Shopping Center:

Nativa This boutique carries gift items, jewelry, and handmade clothing from India, Africa, and throughout Latin America. ◆ M-Sa 10AM-6PM. No phone

Gallery International Art from throughout the region is showcased here. ◆ M-Th 10AM-1PM, 2-6PM; F 10AM-1PM, 3-6PM, 7-9PM; Sa 10AM-5PM, 7-9PM. No phone

Saratoga ★$$ Chefs **John** and **Daniel Jackson,** graduates of the Culinary Institute of America, feature local seafood on an innovative menu. Consider the grilled kingfish with spicy cherry-tomato salsa and batter-dipped soft-shell crabs with parmesan and herbs. The menu changes daily. ◆ American ◆ M-Sa 6:30PM-closing. 42421

56 **Pelican Resort and Casino** $$$ More than 660 rooms and one- and two-bedroom suites sprawl up and down a hillside just seven minutes from Juliana Airport. **Richard Dreyfuss** and **Holly Hunter** filmed portions of *Once Around* at this resort. The rooms are comfortable and outfitted with safe-deposit boxes and refrigerators. A minimarket makes light housekeeping convenient. **L'Aqualine Health Spa Massages** offers state-of-the-art techniques in beauty and health care. Other amenities include a Las Vegas-style casino, six pools, and three beaches. Among the available water sports are two 60-foot cata-marans that sail to Anguilla and St. Barts from Pelican's own docks. ♦ Pelican Keys, Simpson Bay. 42503, 800/223.9815

Within the Pelican Resort and Casino:

Crocodile Express Cafe $$ Breakfast and snacks are served on the Great House balcony overlooking the gigantic property. ♦ American ♦ Daily 8AM-midnight. 42503

57 **Mary's Boon** $$ A dozen efficiencies are right on the beach near Juliana Airport. Each of the rooms has its own patio overlooking Simpson Bay. ♦ Airport Rd (Simpson Bay). 54235, 800/365.8484

Within Mary's Boon:

Mary's Boon Restaurant ★$$ This popular dinner restaurant doesn't have air-conditioning and it's located next to the runway, so it gets a bit noisy, but the food is good. The menu is set every night, so call ahead to find out what's being served. ♦ French/American ♦ Daily 8PM-closing. Reservations required. 54235

58 **The Horny Toad Guest House** $$ At one time this lovely corner of the island was the home of the governor of St. Martin/Sint Maarten. Now containing eight roomy apartments on Simpson Bay Beach less than five minutes from Princess Juliana International Airport, the Horny Toad Guest House is a warm, homey place convenient to restaurants and casinos. ♦ Simpson Bay Beach. 54323, 800/365.8484

59 **Pizza Hut** $ This is one of the best island bargains and it's similar enough to the US version to keep tourists happy. Ask for gouda cheese atop your pizza for a Dutch/American twist. It just might be a habit you take back home. ♦ Pizza ♦ 11AM-11PM. Airport Rd (Simpson Bay). 43210

Togs for the Tropics

Your best bet for Caribbean resortwear is anything made of cool cotton. The tropics can get pretty muggy, so keep in mind that synthetic fabrics and dark colors absorb heat, while whites and pastel shades are cooler.

On a number of Caribbean islands, vacationers virtually live in their swimsuits. But if you plan to go out on the town, the basic evening attire is lightweight cotton sportshirts and slacks for men, and cotton sundresses or dressy blouses and pants for women. The dress codes are fairly relaxed, although a few hotels—most notably the newly remodeled Sandy Lane on Barbados—require men to wear jackets in the evenings. Some hotels or restaurants in the region require ties, however. Many tourist publications recommend that you wear "elegantly casual" attire, which can mean a dress or a stylish T-shirt and pants for women, and a long-sleeve sportshirt for men.

Cruise lines offer the exception to the casual-wear rule. After dusk, when there are formal events scheduled (and on week-long cruises there are usually one or two formal occasions), a tuxedo or a dark suit may be required, whereas women tend to wear very glitzy evening dresses.

St. Martin/Sint Maarten

Pop Quiz on Paradise

Take this Caribbean test to determine your island IQ.

1. What are the ABC islands?

2. Where is the oldest church in the western hemisphere and whose tomb is housed there?

3. What island is known as the Isle of Spice?

4. Which British Virgin Island inspired Robert Louis Stevenson's novel *Treasure Island?*

5. Which islands were named for the crocodiles that inhabit the mangrove swamps?

6. What is the southernmost island in the Caribbean?

7. Which island has no beaches?

8. What island is named for its eel-like shape?

Answers: 1. Aruba, Bonaire, and Curaçao **2.** Santo Domingo, Dominican Republic; Christopher Columbus **3.** Grenada **4.** Norman Island **5.** Cayman Islands **6.** Trinidad **7.** Saba **8.** Anguilla

IQ Score:

Seven or more correct answers: Consider yourself an island savant.

Four to six: You're no slouch, but a little more Caribbean culture wouldn't hurt.

Three or fewer: Do you even know where the Caribbean is?

Courtesy of *Tradewind Magazine*

Antigua

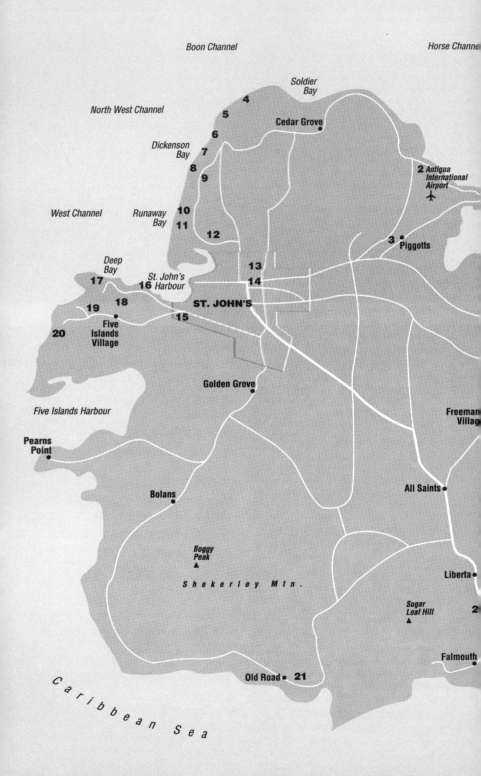

Boon Channel

Horse Channel

Soldier
Bay

4

5

Cedar Grove

North West Channel

6

Dickenson
Bay

7

8

9

2 Antigua
International
Airport

West Channel

10

Runaway
Bay

11

12

3 • Piggotts

Deep
Bay

13

14

17

St. John's
Harbour

16

ST. JOHN'S

19

18

15

20

Five
Islands
Village

Golden Grove

Five Islands Harbour

Freeman
Village

Pearns
Point

Bolans

All Saints •

Boggy
Peak
▲

S h e k e r l e y   M t n.

Liberta •

Sugar
Loaf Hill
▲

2

Falmouth

Old Road • 21

C a r i b b e a n   S e a

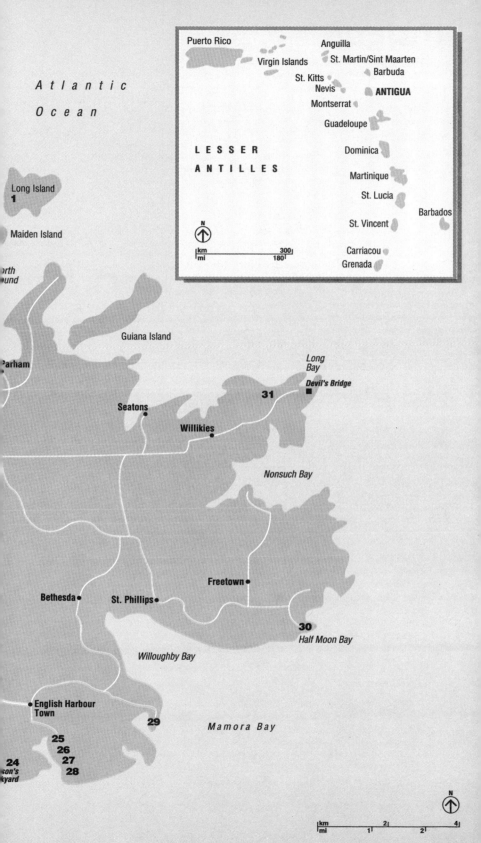

Atlantic

Ocean

Puerto Rico
Virgin Islands
Anguilla
St. Martin/Sint Maarten
St. Kitts
Barbuda
Nevis
ANTIGUA
Montserrat
Guadeloupe

LESSER
ANTILLES

Dominica

Martinique

St. Lucia
Barbados

St. Vincent

Carriacou
Grenada

N

km 300
mi 180

Long Island
1

Maiden Island

North
Sound

Guiana Island

Parham

Long
Bay
Devil's Bridge

31

Seatons

Willikies

Nonsuch Bay

Freetown

Bethesda

St. Phillips

30
Half Moon Bay

Willoughby Bay

English Harbour
Town

29
Mamora Bay

25
26
27
28

24
son's
kyard

N

km
mi 1 2 2 4

Pronounced "an-*tee*-ga" (with a hard *g*), this island's 365 beaches, cooling trade winds, and exotic trees and plants will entice the most persistent mainlander. **Antigua,** the largest of the **British Leeward Islands** (almost 80,000 people live on its one-hundred-plus square miles), and **Barbuda,** her little sister island, are gems of beauty and serenity in the Eastern Caribbean.

Each inlet and bay around this roughly circular island has its own white sand beach, most of them fronted by a hotel or resort. The beaches provide a striking contrast to the lush rain forests and pineapple groves that flourish in the center of the island.

St. John's, the capital city on the northwest coast, and **English Harbour,** a restored 18th-century port on the south shore, are the focal points of Antigua, with shopping, restaurants, hotels, and plenty of historical points of interest, including a fortress that was built to defend against a French invasion.

The French weren't the only ones interested in the rolling hills and graceful contours of this island. Ever since **Christopher Columbus**, on his second trip to the New World, named Antigua for **Santa María della Antigua** (the miracle-working saint at the Seville Cathedral), Antigua had been the focus of a territorial tug-of-war between Spain, France, Holland, and Great Britain. It wasn't until the 1630s that colonists from the nearby island of St. Kitts successfully claimed Antigua for the English crown.

Slave labor enabled the Brits to grow tobacco and sugarcane on the island until 1834, when the abolishment of slavery dealt the economy a blow and increased pressure for a free-trade market. Prices plummeted throughout the region and hard times followed as Antigua's sugar estates collapsed.

Antigua

Then, in 1981, Antigua gained independence and tourism became the island's major industry, followed closely by agriculture. One reason for Antigua's increased popularity is its central location, with easy access to dozens of other Caribbean islands.

Barbuda, for instance, is readily accessible from Antigua's north shore. Many tourists make the 26-mile trip by plane (an easy 15-minute flight) or a relaxing four-hour boat ride. A day trip to the quiet island may include such diverse activities as cave climbing, bird-watching, and hunting, not to mention lounging on the pink beaches.

Area code 809 unless otherwise noted.

Getting to the Island

Airlines
Service to the island is provided by American Airlines, Lufthansa, British Airways, Air Canada, BWIA, LIAT, and various charters from London, New York, Miami, Puerto Rico, Toronto, Frankfurt, Guadeloupe, Baltimore, St. Martin/Sint Maarten, and Atlanta. Chicago-Antigua flights make stopovers in San Juan, and Paris-Antigua flights change in Guadeloupe.

Airports
V.C. Bird International Airport The main port of entry to the island is on the northeast shore. A small snack bar and a duty-free shop are in the building. For more information, call 462.1469.

Getting around the Island

Car Rentals
Avis Rent-a-Car	462.2840
Budget Rent-a-Car	462.3009
Cages Car Rental	461.1071
Capital Rental and Tours	462.0863
Carib Car Rentals	462.2082
Charles Apartment & Car Rentals	461.0424
Dollar Rent-a-Car	462.0362
Huntley Car Rental	462.1575
Jones Rent-a-Car	462.3760
National Car Rental	462.2113
Prince's Rent-a-Car	462.0766
Ramco Car Rentals	462.3997
Rent-a-Car Association	462.4600
Richard's Rent-a-Car	462.0978
St. John's Car Rental	461.0449
Silston's Car Rental	462.2113
Sunshine Rental	462.2426
Trinity Car Rentals	462.0100
United Rent-a-Car	462.3021
Village Car Rental	462.3751

Driving

A valid driver's license enables you to obtain a temporary Antiguan license at no cost. Unlike American driving laws, traffic moves on the left side of the road. Antigua's roads are coarse and rugged and many are unmarked. Parking is almost impossible, especially in St. John's. Think twice before deciding to rent a car to visit the capital; it's better to stick to the taxis, although they are not metered. Make sure the fare you are quoted is in US$ not EC$. Hotels can provide a list of taxi fares to and from major points on the island.

FYI

Annual Events

Tennis Week (January) is an event that celebrates the fact that Antigua has more tennis courts per hotel room than any other island in the Caribbean.

Sailing Week (April/May) consists of five short yacht races.

Carnival (July/August) is a 10-day celebration, with parties, parades, and various competitions.

Independence Day (1 November) commemorates the island's independence from Britain.

Electricity

The wattage serviced on the island is either 220 or 110 volts. For more information, check with your hotel service desk or carry current adaptors.

Money

The Eastern Caribbean dollar is the Antiguan currency, but major credit cards are accepted. Bank hours are typically M-Th 8AM-1PM; F 8AM-noon, 3-5PM.

Personal Safety

Drugs are a very common currency on the islands so avoid suspect areas.

Phone Book

Air/Sea Rescue	462.3062
Department of Tourism	462.0480
Emergency	999/911
Fire	462.0044
Medical/Ambulance	462.0251
Office of Disaster Preparedness	462.4402
Police	462.0125

Publications

Worker's Voice, Outlet, The Nation, and *Sentinel* are weeklies published in St. John's. *What's Happening* is published four times a year. *Trinidad Guardian, Jamaican Gleaner, E.C. News*, and *The New York Times, USA Today*, and other American and London papers are available.

Taxes and Tipping

A seven percent government tax is added to all hotel bills and some restaurant checks. Most restaurants add a 10 percent service charge to the tab. Other tipping is discretionary. Plan on a $10 departure tax.

Area code 809 unless otherwise noted.

1 Jumby Bay Resort $$$$ This "ultraposh" getaway is one of the most exclusive resorts in the Caribbean, and is set on its own 300-acre private island less than two miles off the northeast coast of Antigua (access is by ferry). The 38 rooms are superbly decorated. Activities include tennis and water sports. Free laundry service is available, too. ◆ Deluxe ◆ Closed Sep-Oct. Long Island. 462.6000; fax 462.6144

2 Antigua Beachcomber Hotel $ This budget hotel offers 36 rooms near the airport. There's also a pool. ◆ Airport Rd, 1 mile north of the airport. 462.3100; fax 462.2110

3 Antigua Sugar Mill Hotel $$ The 30-room airport hotel is located one mile from the beach in a structure that was a sugar mill 250 years ago. You can relax by the pool. ◆ Coolidge Rd, 3 miles southwest of the airport. 462.3044; fax 462.1500

4 Blue Waters Hotel $$$$ Oh, are they ever—the Caribbean never looked so good. Lush tropical gardens surround 46 elegant rooms and eight grand villas on the beach. Free activities include day and night tennis and myriad water sports. Golf is available nearby. ◆ Deluxe ◆ Soldier Bay. 462.0292

Within Blue Waters Hotel:

Cacubi Room ★★$$$ The à la carte menu at this prize-winning restaurant features seafood, steaks, and flambé dishes with a local touch. ◆ Caribbean ◆ Daily 7:30-11PM. 462.0292

5 Halcyon Cove Beach Resort and Casino $$$ Water sports, tennis, volleyball, and shuffleboard are among the activities here, and golf is available nearby. If all you want is to relax, there's a wonderful beach area and all 129 rooms and suites feature either a balcony or patio. ◆ Dickenson Bay. 462.0256/7; fax 462.0271

Within Halcyon Cove Beach Resort and Casino:

Warri Pier $$ Snacks, salads, complete meals, and drinks are served at this peaceful and breezy waterfront restaurant. ◆ American ◆ Daily 7AM-11PM. 462.0256

Clouds $$$ The exquisite hilltop restaurant has a magnificent view of the island and Dickenson Bay, especially at sunset. (Many guests drive up to the restaurant early to watch it.) The menu features gourmet seafood specialties. ◆ French/Creole ◆ M-Sa 7PM-closing. Reservations required. 462.3751

6 Sandals at the Anchorage $$$ **Butch Stewart**, the genius behind the couples-only Sandals resorts on Jamaica, created this 150-room beauty on the site of the former **Anchorage Hotel.** Beautiful landscaping surrounds four freshwater pools—including the Sandals hallmark swim-up bar—Italian marble, hot and cold whirlpools, and four Jacuzzis. There are also a superb beach and various restaurants, including a Japanese establishment and a deli for bagels on the beach. Water sports, a spa, and activities are offered all day long. ♦ Dickenson Bay. 462.0267

7 Antigua Village $$$ All of the studios and one- and two-bedroom apartments in the villa setting are on the beach and have kitchen facilities. Water sports, the casino, and a minimarket are among the amenities, and golf and tennis are available nearby. ♦ Dickenson Bay. 462.2930/4299; fax 462.0375

Antigua

Within Antigua Village:

Spinnakers ★★$$ This restaurant is the home of the **Vivian Richards Cricketeer Club. Vivian Richards** is the former captain of the West Indies Cricket Club and an island hero. He's the draw, but the salads, snacks, and cheeseburgers can stand on their own. ♦ American ♦ Daily 7:30AM-11PM. 462.4158

8 Siboney Beach Club $$$ The intimate suites hotel was named for the early Indian residents (*siboney* means "stone people" in Arawak) and stone artifacts, relics of those days can be found in the Antigua and Barbuda Museum just a few miles away in St. John's. There are water sports and a pool on the premises and golf and tennis nearby. ♦ Dickenson Bay. 462.0806, 800/533.0234

Once former hostage Terry Anderson was released to the United States, he moved his family to Antigua because he wanted to live in a quiet, uncrowded environment.

9 The Island Inn $ Owner/manager **Doreen Barnard** has created a delightful two-story hotel with 10 modern one-bedroom studios. She calls it a "friendly family resort" and it is just that. A swimming pool is under construction. ♦ Anchorage Rd, less than 2 miles north of St. John's. 462.4065; fax 462.4066

10 Barrymore Beach Club $$ The fairly dramatic beach- and garden-view rooms are convenient to restaurants, shops, and casinos in a combination of 36 hotel rooms and one- and two-bedroom apartments. ♦ Runaway Bay. 462.4101

11 The Lobster Pot ★★$$ This Runaway Beach Club restaurant stresses lobster and seafood dishes, but the steaks are good enough to sink your teeth into. ♦ Seafood ♦ Daily 7:30AM-midnight. Runaway Bay. 462.2855

12 Le Gourmet ★★$$$ Chef and owner **Jochen Mathe** operates a Swiss-style restaurant in an 85-year-old colonial house. Mathe who hails from Zurich, specializes in live lobsters, sliced veal, stuffed fish, and delectable homemade ice cream. He's a veteran restaurateur who has worked in Zurich, Malta, Calcutta, and throughout the Caribbean. ♦ Continental/Swiss ♦ Tu-Su 6:30PM-closing. Fort Rd, St. John's. Reservations recommended. 462.2977

13 Heritage Quay From T-shirts to designer luggage and pricey diamond watches, you can find it among the dozens of shops—many with international names such as **Little Switzerland, Gucci, Benetton,** and **Colombian Emeralds**—in the brightly decorated open-air mall. ♦ Thames St (St. John's Harbour). No phone

Within Heritage Quay:

West Indies Ice Company Here you'll find fine jewelry, with interesting work in gold and precious and semiprecious stones, and a large collection of watches. ♦ M-Sa 9AM-5PM. 462.3463

The Body Shop You might find the ultimate treat here for the gang back home. The Brighton, England-based company creates hair and skin products that are not tested on animals and are sold in biodegradable packaging. ♦ M-Sa 8:30AM-5:30PM. 462.2810

Restaurants/Clubs: Red   **Hotels:** Blue
Shops/ ♥ Outdoors: Green   **Sights/Culture:** Black

La Parfumerie Fine names in fragrance and cosmetics from around the world, including Chanel, Nina Ricci, Van Cleef & Arpels, Clarins, Dior, Estée Lauder, and Jean Patou, fill the counters. ◆ M-Sa 9AM-5PM. 462.2601

Naf Naf Oo-la-la! These French fashions are so up-to-date you'll be the talk of the office.◆ M-Sa 9AM-5PM. 462.2608

Whispers and Rumours The magnificent imported lingerie features French-accented designs. ◆ M-Sa 9AM-5PM. 462.2811

13 Heritage Hotel $ This hotel caters to the business traveler, and yet it's close to casinos, restaurants, shops, the beach and tennis courts. ◆ Thames St, St. John's. 462.1247

14 Redcliffe Quay Architect **William Fraser** kept the traditional Redcliffe-style facades of the original dockside warehouses and shops. Those early shops tempted British sailors with a variety of wares. Today's shops are attractive, eclectic, and filled with wonderful goods from around the islands and the world. ◆ Lower Redcliffe St, St. John's. No phone

Within Redcliffe Quay:

Karibbean Kids of Antigua Owner **Barbara H. Bauer** creates hand-painted clothes for youngsters from cradle to high school. They're attractive and unique—the perfect memento of an island vacation. ◆ M-F 9:30AM-4:30PM; Sa 9:30AM-3PM. 462.4566

A Thousand Flowers Batik sundresses and sportswear you won't find back home are sold in this unusual women's boutique. ◆ M-F 9:30AM-4:30PM; Sa 9:30AM-2PM. 462.4262

Dalila Boutiques Fashions *avec* a Parisian attitude are sold by the same folks operating shops on the island of St. Martin/Sint Maarten. ◆ M-Sa 9AM-5PM. 462.3625

The Lady Hamilton The gift items sold here sport a British flair. There are crystal, pottery, and jewelry specialties. ◆ M-Sa 9AM-5PM. 462.1423

The Toy Shop Wonderful and unique toys, British goods, and fireworks can be found in this store, a reminder of the way Christmas shopping may have been done in the last century. ◆ M-Sa 9:30AM-4PM. 462.1041

14 Big Banana Holding Company Ltd. This firm operates three restaurants—a sort of conglomerate of good times. ◆ Daily 10:30AM-2:30PM. Redcliffe Quay, St. John's. 462.2621

Thrillers Filmed in the Tropics

The predictably clear weather and naturally exotic settings have drawn Hollywood producers and celebrities to the islands for years, both to vacation and to make films. Here's a list of some of those famous flicks they've filmed in the Caribbean.

Cocoon (1985) A group of old geezers discover the secret to eternal youth. Don Ameche and Brian Dennehy star in this film directed by Ron Howard. Much of it takes place in the Bahamas.

The Day of the Dolphin (1973) In this spy thriller, research scientist George C. Scott teaches dolphins to talk and operate against the bad guys. The film is set in the Bahamas.

The Deep (1977) Two lovers searching for a shipwreck run into unexpected trouble in this adventure film. Produced in the Bahamas, and stars Jacqueline Bisset, Nick Nolte, and Robert Shaw.

Island in the Sun (1957) Social tensions tear Harry Belafonte and Joan Fontaine apart. Filmed in the fishing village of Woburn on Grenada.

Jaws: The Revenge (1987) The third sequel of the vengeful great white shark and its pursuit of people in the Bahamas.

Once Around (1991) Richard Dreyfuss, Holly Hunter, and Danny Aiello star in this love story about how opposites attract. Features stunning scenery of St. Martin.

Shoot to Kill (1988) A city cop and a mountain guide track a killer. Sidney Poitier, Tom Berenger, and Kirstie Alley are the big names in this film, which was made in the Bahamas.

Splash (1984) A mermaid (Daryl Hannah) tries to swim against the tide of New York City and instead falls in love with a man (Tom Hanks). Many of the scenes were shot in the Bahamas.

The Spy Who Loved Me (1977) James Bond (Roger Moore) and a female Russian agent change a villain's plans to destroy the world. The locale is Paradise Island and Nassau in the Bahamas.

The Tamarind Seed (1974) A widowed English secretary (Julie Andrews) and a KGB agent (Omar Sharif) fall in love, only to stumble onto several Cold War spy escapades that lie in the way of romance. Sections of the movie were filmed in St. Peter's Farley Park on Barbados.

Thunderball (1965) This film was remade as *Never Say Never Again* in 1983 and both times, Agent 007 saves Miami from the atomic bomb (although the action is really taking place on Paradise Island and in Nassau in the Bahamas).

Within the Big Banana Holding Company Ltd:

Pizzas on the Quay ★★$$ Pizza, salads, and baked potatoes with the works are complimented by music on the weekends. ♦ American/Caribbean ♦ Daily 8AM-closing. 462.2621

Tropix Disco and Nightclub There's a late-night piano bar and noisy (but that doesn't mean bad) international and Caribbean music in the disco. ♦ Admission. Tu-Su 10PM-closing. 462.2621

Ginger House ★★$$ This establishment completes the trio of two restaurants and a nightclub in the Big Banana complex. The soups served here include pumpkin, cucumber, and mint. The Creole meatballs, curried tuna, and pineapple salad platter are also popular. ♦ Antiguan/Creole ♦ Daily 2-4PM, 6-11PM. 462.2317

Antigua

14 Kennedy's Liquor World Ltd. Antiguan rum is the best buy. ♦ M-Sa 8:30AM-9PM; Su 10AM-5PM. Lower Market St (Nellie Robinson St). 462.0715

15 Joe-Mikes Downtown Hotel $ Owned and operated by **Anthony Michael,** this clean 12-room downtown hotel is the modest centerpiece in a complex that features a beauty salon (operated by Anthony's wife, **Bernadette**), **Speedy Joe's** fast-food restaurant, **Smugglers Den** cocktail lounge, and an ice-cream bar. ♦ Corn Alley (Nevis St). 462.1142

15 The Antigua and Barbuda Museum Housed in a former courthouse built in 1750, the museum is funded by the **Canadian International Development Agency, UNESCO,** and private donors. The museum exhibits the highlights of archaeological digs on the islands dating back to about 2000 BC. There's a collection of ancient utensils, naval history, and a large Arawak Indian house. ♦ Admission. M-Th 8:30AM-4PM; F 8:30-3PM; Sa 10AM-2PM. Long St (Market St). 462.1469

15 The Pot Hole ★$ Take the green stairs to a spot where locals and tourist relish the food—not the atmosphere. Snacks and sandwiches make up the menu. ♦ Caribbean/British ♦ M-F 11AM-11PM; Sa 3-11PM. Newgate St, St. John's. 462.0136

15 18 Carat Restaurant and Bar ★$ The garden setting is the perfect backdrop for snacks and meals featuring island fare. ♦ Caribbean ♦ M-Sa 10AM-10PM. Lower Church St, St. John's. 462.0016

15 Brother B's ★$ This downtown restaurant and bar has an 18-year history of serving hearty local cuisine, as well as traditional snacks, sandwiches, and salads. Shoppers find it particularly convenient. ♦ Antiguan/Seafood ♦ Daily 7:30AM-10PM. Long St, St. John's. 462.0616

16 Pillar Rock Hotel $$$ Set atop a hillside, the 60 villas, suites, and studios all have views of the sea. There's a pool, water sports, parasailing, tennis, and horseback riding. Dine at the popular **Pavilion Restaurant.** ♦ Deep Bay. 462.2326; fax 462.2327

17 Ramada Renaissance, Royal Antiguan Resort $$$ Once lovely, now in need of serious renovation, this 266-room hotel boasts three restaurants, a casino, tennis courts, a swimming pool, and a superb beach. The location is ideal if you just want rest and relaxation. ♦ Deep Bay. 462.3733; fax 462.3732

Within the Ramada Renaissance, Royal Antiguan Resort:

The Andes ★$$$ On the beach overlooking Deep Bay and named for the ship that sank here in 1907, the restaurant offers local dishes and seafood. ♦ Caribbean ♦ Daily 7-10:30PM. 462.3733

The Lagoon Cafe $$ Salads and sandwiches are served here, but the tiny gnats that fly around while you eat may ruin your appetite. Spray first. ♦ Daily 7AM-11PM. 462.3733

18 Jaws ★★$$ Both the food and the hilltop view of Deep Bay are outstanding. Pasta, seafood, steaks, and local specialties make up the menu. The sunsets are great, too. ♦ Continental ♦ Daily 5:30PM-closing. Deep Bay. 462.2428

19 Yepton Beach Resort $$ Beachfront studios and one-bedroom apartments with fully equipped kitchens occupy a quarter mile of private white sand beaches. There are balconies or patios in each unit. ♦ Deep Bay. 462.2520, 800/361.4621

20 Hawksbill Beach Resort $$$$ Set on almost 40 acres along the beach, the resort boasts 84 rooms, a Great House and a deluxe villa where families may want to stay, two restaurants (one award-winning), two bars, water sports, and tennis. ♦ Deluxe ♦ Five Islands. 462.1515/0301

21 Falmouth Harbour Beach Apartments $$ The fully equipped studio apartments—28 in all—are on a beautiful white sand beach and on the hillside across from St. John's. The complex is owned and operated by **The Admiral's Inn** in Nelson's Dockyard. ♦ Falmouth Harbour. 460.1027; fax 460.1534

Restaurants/Clubs: Red   Hotels: Blue

Shops/ ♦ Outdoors: Green   Sights/Culture: Black

21 Curtain Bluff Resort $$$$ An elegant resort with 61 rooms on the island's southwest coast, Curtain Bluff actually offers two beaches, one for surfing, another with calm seas. ♦ Old Rd, St. John's. 462.8400; fax 462.5409

22 Dolphin Restaurant and Bar ★★$$ Canadian **Natalie Murphy** and her Antiguan husband **Peter** have owned and operated the attractive little restaurant for more than six years. They specialize in Antiguan-style saltfish, Creole chicken, and shrimp sautéed in black pineapple sauce. "Local flavors are served at local prices," as the Murphys say, and the taste and the price are all right. The couple has also filled the open-air roadside restaurant with their collection of beer bottles from around the world. ♦ Caribbean ♦ M-F noon-3PM; Sa-Su noon-3PM, 7-11PM. All Saints Rd, St. John's. 462.1183

23 Harbour View Apartments $$ The six split-level, two-bedroom apartments offer a great view of the water. Harbour View is set near Antigua's only national park, **Nelson's Dockyard.** ♦ All Saints Rd, St. John's. 460.1762

24 Nelson's Dockyard Restoration of this national park began in 1951; today, the shops, inns, and restaurants are functioning businesses built in keeping with the original style of architecture. The re-created buildings provide a great historical backdrop. **Lord Horatio Nelson** and the **Royal Navy** used the dockyard during many Caribbean wars with the French, Spanish, and Dutch in the late 18th century. Nelson first arrived at English Harbour in 1784, when he was 26 and in command of the **Boreas,** a 28-gun frigate. Look for **Fort Charlotte** and **Fort Berkeley,** standing guard over the harbor entrance. A 15-minute walk from the dockyard up to Fort Berkeley is an ideal way to see the area. ♦ South end of English Harbour

Within Nelson's Dockyard:

The Admiral's House This museum features artifacts of the dockyard's 200-year history. (Factually speaking, the house was not Lord Nelson's; it was built in 1855 and Nelson died in 1805.) ♦ Daily dawn-dusk. No phone

The Copper and Lumber Store Hotel $$$ The former warehouse is now a delightfully charming hideaway richly furnished in attractive Georgian elegance. The hotel boasts 14 suites, each named after one of Lord Nelson's ships engaged in the Battle of Trafalgar. There's fine dining in the **Wardroom** daily from 6-9:30PM, and meals are also served in the courtyard. ♦ 460.1058/1529

The Art Centre Lou Cottage, an American who has spent more than 10 years on the island, originally came to Antigua as a member of the Peace Corps. These days he operates a lovely gallery filled with island art in various mediums, featuring works by many local artists. ♦ M-F 9AM-5PM; Sa 9AM-noon; Su 1-4PM. 460.1380

The Admiral's Inn $$ The charming waterfront inn has 14 twin-bedded rooms, all unique. The 17 pillars outside were brought over from England as ballast. The royal palms were planted in the 1960s by **Queen Elizabeth II.** ♦ 460.1027/1153; fax 460.1534

Within the Admiral's Inn:

The Terrace Restaurant ★★$$ A slice of history is served with every course. Dine outdoors in this beautiful setting at the water's edge. ♦ Caribbean ♦ Daily noon-2:30PM, 7:30-9PM. 460.1027

Antigua

25 Clarence House Built in 1786 for **King William IV** (he commanded the *Pegasus* and was Prince William when the house was built), the house is filled with British-style furniture, including a coromandel chest, a Victorian buffet, and an unusual lead-lined octagonal wine cooler. Maintained by the Antiguan government, the four-bedroom house was used by **Winston Churchill** for a nap during one of his visits and by **Princess Margaret** and **Lord Snowdon** on their Caribbean honeymoon in 1962. During state visits in 1966, 1975, and 1985, **Queen Elizabeth II** used one of the bedrooms to freshen up. Catch a view out back of English Harbour that will take your breath away. ♦ Donation. Daily dawn-dusk. On the hillside facing Nelson's Dockyard. No phone

Nelson's Dockyard

26 The Inn at English Harbour $$$$ Brits **Peter** and **Ann Deeth** operate 22 rooms on the beach and six more up on the hillside (their inn provides a shuttle to take guests back and forth)—a little bit of the UK in the bright Antiguan sun. The inn was built more than 30 years ago when Peter Deeth stopped flying for British Airways (formerly BOAC) and the couple moved their family to the island. The restaurant on the terrace offers a stupendous view of English Harbour.
♦ English Harbour. 463.1014; fax 460.1603

27 Galleon Beach Club $$$ On the island's south coast, below Shirley Heights, the Galleon's 35 cottages with full kitchens and private sundecks overlook Freeman's Bay, the entry to English Harbour. This is one of the prettiest settings on Antigua. Not only are there shops on the premises, but water sports, fishing, boating, and tennis are available through the Galleon. ♦ Freeman's Bay, English Harbour. 463.1024; fax 463.1450

Within the Galleon Beach Club:

Colombo's Italian Restaurant ★★$$$ The first Italian restaurant on Antigua, the restaurant has enjoyed great popularity with tourists and locals alike. Original chef **Salvatore Piras**, from Sardinia, still prepares the pasta, seafood, and veal specialties.

Antigua

♦ Italian ♦ Daily noon-2:30PM, 6:30-11PM. 463.1452

28 Shirley Heights Lookout Drive to the top for an eagle's-eye view of English Harbour, Falmouth Harbour, and Nelson's Dockyard. For snacks and gifts, there's a shop open daily from 9AM-10PM. A Sunday barbecue at the lookout features steel-band music from 3-6PM and a reggae band from 6-9PM.
♦ All Saints Rd, St. John's. 463.1785

29 St. James's Club $$$$ The decidedly upscale resort set on one hundred acres has 73 two-bedroom villas, 20 suites, and 85 rooms—all facing the brilliant blue ocean. Activities include tennis (**Martina Navratilova** is the resident pro), water sports, fishing, and croquet. There are also a private yacht club and marina. ♦ Deluxe ♦ Mamora Bay. 463.1430; fax 463.1113

30 Half Moon Bay Hotel $$$$ Another elegant and luxurious vacation spot, the hotel has 98 rooms, two suites, and the requisite water sports set on a gorgeous pinkish-white sand beach. Professional tennis tournies are held here in January, April, and October. There's also a nine-hole golf course. ♦ Deluxe ♦ Half Moon Bay. 460.4300; fax 460.4306

31 Pineapple Beach Club $$$ The spa, nature trails, tennis courts, water sports, freshwater pool, and shopping trips to the city keep guests busy at this 125-room secluded resort on the island's east coast.
♦ Long Bay. 463.2006; fax 463.2452

Shipshape Luxury Liners

The Caribbean is the world's premier cruise destination. Each year, hundreds of thousands of passengers board the dozens of floating resorts that sail into Caribbean ports. They disembark in search of beaches, bargains, and natural beauty, then reboard for more food, fun, and relaxation.

The development of ports in the Bahamas, Puerto Rico, Jamaica, the British Virgin Islands, St. Martin/Sint Maarten, Aruba, Martinique, and Guadeloupe attest to the region's allure. Three- and four-day sailings to the Bahamas from Florida have always been popular, but longer trips, ranging from seven to 10 days, are becoming the preferred route. Passengers can visit three to four islands during a week's cruise, sampling a variety of cultures, from African, British, and Dutch to French, Spanish, and Creole.

The adventure begins the minute you board the ship. The immaculately clad crew member who leads you to your cabin is typical of the friendly staff that will try to meet your every need. Not only does the crew serve up to half-a-dozen meals a day, it also entertains and amuses, provides information about island ports and shopping, and does everything in its power to pamper and please.

Most passengers will venture off the ship at least a few times (separate fees are charged for land tours, but round-trip transportation is usually provided by the cruise line). A typical week-long cruise itinerary includes stops at the ports of Nassau, San Juan, and St. Thomas in the Eastern Caribbean, with a day's outing to a Bahamian island. Week-long Western Caribbean itineraries call at the Cayman Islands and at Plaza del Carmen, near Cozumel, Mexico. The cruise lines offer an array of sight-seeing packages, which may include a tour of the **San Felipe del Morro** fortress in Puerto Rico, a ride in an Atlantis submarine and a trip to the underwater observatory at **Coral World Bahamas** in Nassau.

Just as the itineraries vary, however, so do the cruise lines. **Carnival Cruise Line,** for instance, offers trips year-round with a fleet that sails out of the Port of Miami, Port Everglades, and Port Canaveral. Carnival introduced the megaship *Fantasy* in 1990 and her sister vessel, the *Ecstasy,* in mid-1991. Other cruise ships, such as **Cunard's** *Queen Elizabeth 2* and *Vista-fjord,* only visit the area during the winter months.

Cruise-ship travel has grown steadily since 1984, when **Cruise Lines International Association (CLIA)** ships carried 800,000 passengers. The number of people traveling on a cruise line jumped 175 percent at the beginning of the nineties, when bigger and better ships came on line.

While some cruise companies have inaugurated new services, others have added additional ships ranging in capacity from 100 to 2,500 passengers. And then there are companies that have elected to renovate their existing fleets. For example, **Norwegian Caribbean Line's,** 1,035-foot *SS Norway,* the longest passenger ship ever built, has been refurbished with two glass decks housing 135 luxury cabins, a 6,000-square-foot spa, and a supper club.

Here are some of the most prominent lines offering Caribbean cruises (followed by the season they're in operation):

Admiral Cruises (year-round)
1220 Biscayne Boulevard
Miami, FL 33132
305/374.1611

Carnival Cruise Lines (year-round)
3655 NW 87th Avenue
Miami, FL 33178
For more information, contact your travel agent

Chandris Cruises (year-round)
5200 Lagoon Drive
Miami, FL 33126
305/262.5411, 800/423.2100

Clipper Cruise Line (winter)
Windsor Building
7711 Bonhomme Avenue
St. Louis, MO 63105-1965
314/727.2929

Commodore Cruise Line (year-round)
800 Douglas Entrance
Coral Gables, FL 33134
305/529.3000

Costa Cruises (year-round)
World Trade Center Building
80 SW Eighth Street
Miami, FL 33130
305/358.7325

Crystal Cruises (winter)
2121 Avenue of the Stars
Los Angeles, CA 90067
213/785.9300

Cunard Line (winter)
555 Fifth Avenue
New York, NY 10017
212/880.7500

Dolphin Cruise Line (year-round)
1007 N. America Way
Miami, FL 33132
305/358.5122, 800/222.1003

Epirotiki Lines (winter)
551 Fifth Avenue
New York, NY 10176
212/599.1750

Holland America Line (winter)
300 Elliott Avenue West
Seattle, WA 98119
206/281.3535

Majesty Cruise Lines (year-round)
1007 N. America Way
Miami, FL 33132
305/358.5122, 800/532.7788

Norwegian Cruise Line (year-round)
95 Merrick Way

Coral Gables, FL 33134
305/445.0866

Paquet French Cruises (winter)
1510 SE 17th Street
Ft. Lauderdale, FL 33136
305/764.3500

Premier Cruise Lines (year-round)
400 Challenger Road
Cape Canaveral, FL 32920
407/783.5061

Princess Cruises (year-round)
10100 Santa Monica Boulevard
Los Angeles, CA 90067
213/553.1770

Regency Cruises (winter)
260 Madison Avenue
New York, NY 10016
212/972.4499

Renaissance Cruises (winter)
1800 Eller Drive, Suite 300
Ft. Lauderdale, FL 33316
305/463.0982

Royal Caribbean Cruise Line (year-round)
903 S. America Way
Miami, FL 33132
305/379.2601

Royal Cruise Line (winter)
1 Maritime Plaza, Suite 1400
San Francisco, CA 94111
415/956.7200

Royal Viking Line (winter)
95 Merrick Way

Antigua

Coral Gables, FL 33134
305/447.9660

Seabourn Cruise Line (winter)
55 Francisco Street
San Francisco, CA 94133
415/391.7444

Sun Line Cruises (winter)
One Rockefeller Plaza, Suite 315
New York, NY 10020
212/397.6400, 800/468.6400

Windstar Cruises (winter)
300 Elliott Avenue West
Seattle, WA 98119
206/281.3535

Day or evening party cruises to the Bahamas or "cruises to nowhere" from Florida ports are a popular way to get a taste of the cruise experience. The following three companies arrange short cruises:

Discovery (Port Everglades)
305/525.7800; 800/226.7800

MV Tropic Star (Port of Miami)
305/539.3500; 800/354.5005

SeaEscape (Port of Miami, Port Everglades)
305/476.4300

If you have a great deal of time and a sense of adventure, you might consider traveling via freighter. **Ivaran Lines'** *Americana* is an 88-passenger vessel set on a modern working container ship with upscale amenities for travelers. Itineraries include 46-day trips from New York to South America, with a stop at San Juan, Puerto Rico. Shorter excursions are also available. For more information, contact **Ivaran Lines,** 111 Pavonia Avenue, Jersey City, NJ 07310-1755; 800/451.1639.

Puerto Rico

Anguilla

Virgin Islands

St. Martin/Sint Maarten

Barbuda

St. Kitts

Nevis

Antigua

Montserrat

Guadeloupe

L E S S E R
A N T I L L E S

Dominica

Martinique

St. Lucia

St. Vincent

BARBADOS

N

km
mi

300
180

Carriacou

Grenada

North
Point

St. Lucy

A t l a n t i c   O c e a n

2

31
Farley Hill
National Park

30

29 Speightstown

28

27

St. Peter

St. Andrew

32

Alleynes
Bay

26

25

Mt. Hillaby ▲

35

Bathsheba

1

St. James

24

23

22 Holetown

21

20

19

18

17

16

2

3

36 37

34

St. Joseph

33

St. Thomas

St. John

3

38

St. George

St. Philip

4

Sam Lord's
Castle

13

14

St. Michael

40

39

41

15

5

5

BRIDGETOWN

Carlisle Bay

■ Barbados Museum

12 9

11

10
Hastings

8

Christ Church

43

42

6

5

St. Lawrence

7 6

7

5

4   3

2

1 Grantley Adams
International Airport

Oistins Bay

South
Point

N

km
mi

4
2

8
4

118

Barbados

Portuguese explorers and traders who arrived on the easternmost Caribbean island in the early 1600s decided the lush tropical trees that covered this spot of land looked a lot like bearded men (*barbados* is Portuguese for "bearded men"), and so Barbados was christened. The name stuck, lasting through British colonization, African and American cultural influences, and more than a quarter century of independence. Now, Barbados enjoys one of the highest standards of living in the Caribbean, capitalizing on the tourism industry with dozens of posh resorts and grand estates.

Barbados, one hundred miles east of the other Caribbean islands, was colonized solely by Britain. Fourteen feet wide and 21 miles long, the island has been called more English than England herself for the islanders' fondness for afternoon tea, cricket, British-style police uniforms, and driving on the left side of the road, among other things. The **Scotland District**, in the northern part of Barbados, looks much like its namesake, with rolling green hills—or "bonnie braes"—and a mist that Scottish poet Robert Burns would have rhapsodized over. By contrast, the east coast is somewhat severe, with spectacular rocky shores. The flat west coast, shielded from the Atlantic trade winds, is filled with powdery coral beaches. Driving across the island, you'll pass thick tropical forests and fields of sugarcane. Barbados is somewhat tricky to tour by car, as its roads are narrow (though fairly well maintained), and on the east coast they're unpaved.

More than 350 years under British rule (until 1966) left the island with a **Trafalgar Square** in downtown **Bridgetown**, the capital, where a statue of **Lord Nelson** predates the London version by 27 years. Like England, the "Bajans" (used interchangeably with Barbadians to denote residents) have a tradition of drinking, only it's rum, not ale, the island is known for. Barbados was the first country to export rum; in fact, the word "rum" was coined on the island, possibly a derivation of the original Bajan word for the liquor, *rumbullion,* or of the Dutch and German word *roemer,* a large drinking glass. And even the towns here bear English names such as **Hastings, St. James, Vauxhall,** and **Brighton.**

Barbados

A 98 percent literacy rate and a high standard of living have made Barbados a role model for the rest of the Caribbean. Many island governments actually send their police forces here to be trained. But Barbados has had its low points in history, some of which left their marks on the landscape. For instance, the chattel houses (*chattel* means "movable property") scattered up and down the island are a leftover from the 18th and 19th centuries, when slaves brought over to work in the sugarcane fields were housed in these structures. The brightly painted clapboard houses have since been converted into shopping malls (the best shopping is on **Broad Street** in Bridgetown) and private residences.

Area code 809 unless otherwise noted.

Getting to the Island

Airports

Grantley Adams International Airport

International air service to Barbados is offered by Air Canada, American Airlines, British Airways, BWIA, Canadian Holidays, and Trump Airlines. Regional airlines include Aeropostal, Air Martinique, and LIAT. The airport is located at the south end of Christ Church Parish. For more information, call 428.7101.

Getting around the Island

Car Rentals

Auto Rentals Ltd.	428.9085
Corbins Car Rentals Inc.	427.9531
Courtesy Car Rentals	426.5219
L.E. Williams Tour Co.	427.6006
National Car Rentals	426.6003
P&S Car Rentals	424.2052
Sunny Isle Motors	428.8009
Sunset Crest Rent-a-Car	432.1482

Driving

Driver's licenses are available for visitors (with a current license) from many of the car-rental agencies at Grantley Adams International Airport and at police stations in the larger towns (Oistins, Hastings, Worthing, and Speightstown). The roads in Barbados are well paved and marked, but be prepared to drive on the left side in the British fashion. The maximum speed limit is 37 miles per hour in the country and 21 miles per hour in town, but no one adheres to it.

Taxis

Cab fares between major attractions on the island and to the Grantley Adams International Airport are fixed and posted in the airport or on a list available at the front desk of your hotel or from the cab driver. Taxis are readily accessible at most tourist points. Before you hop into a cab ask the driver for a predetermined fare to your destination, especially if you're unfamiliar with the island.

Touring

Visitors who choose not to rent a car can take public transportation to tour the island. The Transport Board's public buses or smaller, privately operated minibuses cost $1 (Bd). Helicopter tours provide a bird's-eye view of the island (one company is **Bajan Helicopters** at The Wharf in Bridgetown. Call 431.0069 for more information). An 80-mile bus tour of the coast is offered by **L.E. Williams Tour Co. Ltd.**, and this trip includes lunch, drinks, and entrance fees (they can be reached by calling 427.1042/6006, or by fax 427.6007). Day tours are available to the Grenadines (a chain of small islands extending from St. Vincent to Petit Martinique) from various Barbados hotels (call **Grenadine Tours** at 435.8451). Day or evening party cruises provide an opportunity to snorkel and swim in the lovely turquoise waters offshore. For more information, call **Bajan Queen** (436.2149/50) and **Jolly Roger** (436.6424).

FYI

Accommodations

Guest houses, resorts, cottages, hotels, and villas can be found throughout the island. Overall, Barbados tallies close to 15,000 guest beds. Many of the upmarket resorts are located on the scenic St. James coast, but don't expect a series of high rises. Even the larger buildings are designed to complement the island's natural beauty. Most of the resorts offer a variety of water sports, including jet-skiing, scuba diving, waterskiing, windsurfing, snorkeling, parasailing, surfing, and fishing.

Drinking

Barbados has no minimum drinking age, therefore drinks are served at the bartender's discretion. A general rule of thumb seems to be that those who look younger than 18 won't be served alcoholic beverages.

Electricity

The island uses 110 volts/50 cycles. Hotels generally have adaptors for personal appliances and transistor radios, but bring your own to play it safe.

Festivals

Barbados hosts many festivals throughout the year, including the following:

Holetown Festival (February) commemorates the first settlers' landing in 1627.

Oistins Fish Festival (Easter Week) honors the signing of the charter of Barbados and the contributions made by generations of fishers in this historic village in the town of Christ Church.

Crop Over Festival (July/August) celebrates the sugar cane harvest, which is the biggest festival here and it lasts the longest (one month).

National Independence Festival of Creative Arts (November) celebrates Barbadian independence.

For more information on Barbados festivals, contact the **National Cultural Foundation** at 424.0907.

Money

Banks in Bridgetown are open M-Th 9AM-3PM, and F 9AM-1PM, 3-5PM. Barclay's Bank and the Royal Bank of Canada open one hour earlier. On Friday the Royal Bank is open 8AM-5PM. The Barbados National Bank runs an exchange bureau at the airport daily 8AM-midnight. The Barbados dollar ($Bd) is the currency here, although American money and traveler's checks are accepted in most places.

Personal Safety

Barbados is a relatively safe island, but excercise common sense at all times and don't venture into areas that you don't feel comfortable in. Use hotel safe-deposit boxes to store your valuables; don't take anything extraneous to the beach that could easily be stolen.

Phone Book

Ambulance	426.1113, 436.6450
Coast Guard	427.8829
Fire	113
Police	112
The Samaritans	429.9999
United States Consular Section	426.3574

Publications

The two daily papers are the *Advocate* and the *Nation.* On weekends, the latter appears as the *Sunday Sun* and includes *Pelican Magazine.* British and American papers are also available throughout the island. Local magazines include *The Bajan,* published monthly, and *The Visitor,* a weekly. Other tourist publications include *What's On*, published monthly, and the bi-monthly *Sun Seeker.*

Taxes and Tipping

A 10 percent service charge and a five percent government sales tax are added to most hotel bills. If it's not tacked onto the bill and you feel the service merited it, a 10 percent gratuity is the accepted rate.

Area code 809 unless otherwise noted.

1 Grantley Adams International Airport
Built in the late 1970s, this airport was named for the first and only prime minister of the short-lived West Indies Federation. **Sir Grantley Adams** was also premier of Barbados before independence, and his son, **Tom Adams,** was prime minister. ◆ South end of Christ Church Parish. 428.7101

2 Fairholme Hotel $ Just five miles west of the airport and four miles from the beach, the Fairholme is very basic, but its 20 Spanish-style studios and 11 rooms in the converted **Maxwell Plantation House** offer a sense of what plantation living must have been like during the 18th century. ◆ Maxwell, Christ Church. 428.9425

3 Divi Southwinds Beach Resort $$ Towering cathedral ceilings in the lobby herald a gracious facility where you can kick back and enjoy yourself without the onus of dressing for dinner. The dress code, such as it is, is relaxed. The 166 air-conditioned rooms feature tropical decor, and there are lighted tennis courts, three freshwater pools, and a beautiful white sand beach. The suites feature fully equipped kitchens—ideal for vacationing families. ◆ St. Lawrence Gap, Christ Church. 428.7181; fax 428.4674

Within the Divi Southwinds Beach Resort:

Aquarius Restaurant ★$$ Overlooking the pool, this open-air restaurant offers Bajan fare, including flying fish and pumpkin fritters. ◆ Caribbean ◆ Daily 7:30-10:30AM, noon-2:30PM, 6-10:30PM. 428.7181

4 Pisces Restaurant ★$$ The menu may focus on Caribbean seafood specialties, but there's nothing fishy about the superlative view of the ocean. Dolphin diablo with mustard-yogurt sauce is a must. There are also meat and chicken dishes. ◆ Seafood ◆ M-Sa 11:30AM-2:30PM, 6:30-10PM; Su 6:30-10PM. St. Lawrence Gap, Christ Church. Reservations required. 435.6564

4 Witch Doctor ★★ $$ Shrimp in garlic sauce, lobster Thermidor, and spicy chicken Piri Piri are among the house specialties. The latter is a recipe from Mozambique—chicken marinated in lime and cooked with garlic and chili. ◆ African/Caribbean ◆ Daily 6:30-10PM. St. Lawrence Gap, Christ Church. Reservations recommended. 435.6581

4 Church of St. Lawrence This beautiful old Anglican church is located right on the beach. You can catch a wedding almost every weekend. ◆ Daily 9AM-5PM. St. Lawrence Gap, Christ Church. No phone

4 After Dark The American-style jazz and disco club is geared to Yuppie tastes. Weekends are wild here. Call ahead for a schedule. ◆ St. Lawrence Gap, Christ Church. 435.6547

4 Josef's Restaurant ★★★$$$ **Charlene Paterson** is the director of this romantic and popular upscale establishment. The fish and steak dishes are tops. ◆ Continental ◆ M-F noon-2:30PM, 6-9PM; Sa 6-9PM. St. Lawrence Gap, Christ Church. Reservations required. 435.6541

4 The Steak House ★$$ With a more than 20-year history of serving fine US beef and fresh-off-the-boat seafood, the restaurant has built a long tradition of good eating. The house specialties include steak St. Lawrence and filet Karen, named for the manager's daughter. The American-style steaks are choice meat and cooked to your request. ◆ Steaks ◆ Daily 6-10PM. St. Lawrence Gap, Christ Church. 428.7128

4 Chattel House Shopping Village A collection of tourist boutiques and souvenir shops are set up in brightly painted historic recreations of slave homes. The attractions include **Fat Willy's Ice Cream Shoppe, Beach Bum, Best 'n the Bunch, Perfections, Fine Crafts, Lazy Day, Bits 'n Bob's, and Biddy's Visitor Information.** ◆ M-Sa 9AM-7PM. St. Lawrence Gap, Christ Church. 428.2472

4 Black Renaissance Art Gallery The shop is filled with a fine collection of art in various media depicting the island's history. ◆ M-Sa 10AM-6PM. St. Lawrence Gap, Christ Church. 428.6333

4 Dover Cricket Club Bajans take the game of cricket very seriously (remember that British influence). There's always a match going on weekends at the field across from pretty Dover Beach. ◆ Daily dawn-dusk. St. Lawrence Gap, Christ Church. No phone

4 Dover Beach Vendors Mall The kiosks here sell batiks, T-shirts, and beautiful colored scarves. ◆ Daily dawn-dusk. St. Lawrence Gap, Christ Church. No phone

4 TGI Boomer's $ Snacks and sandwiches are served in a family run establishment with the typical restaurant/bar atmosphere. You can,

however, catch up with CNN headline news. ◆ Caribbean/American ◆ Daily 8AM-9:45PM. St. Lawrence Gap, Christ Church. 428.8439

4 The Appliqué Boutique T-shirts and beachwear covered with—you guessed it—appliqués. It's a little kitschy but still a step up from the usual T-shirt shop. ◆ M-F 9AM-6PM. St. Lawrence Gap, Christ Church. 420.8580

4 Luigi's ★$$$ This Italian restaurant has a delightful ambience. Try the shrimp in garlic butter and the stuffed pepper and manicotti specialties. ◆ Italian ◆ Daily 6-9:45PM. St. Lawrence Gap, Christ Church. 428.9218

4 David's Place ★★$$ Bajan food is prepared with a flair. Choose from memorable pumpkin fritters; pepper pot, a meaty stew; and coconut cream pie—three typical and delicious island favorites. ◆ Caribbean ◆ Tu-Su 6:30-10PM. St. Lawrence Main Rd, Christ Church. 435.6550

5 Star Discount Ltd. A variety of goods is sold in a discount-store format. There's a little of everything. Star Discount is kind of a K-Mart on the Caribbean. ◆ M-F 9AM-5PM; Sa 9AM-4PM. Main Rd, Rockley. 435.7431. Also at: Plantation City Centre Mall, Chapel St. 431.6575; Goddards Complex, Kensington, Fontabelle. 436.9830

Restaurants/Clubs: Red	**Hotels:** Blue
Shops/ 🌴 Outdoors: Green	**Sights/Culture:** Black

Barbados Museum

6 Ile de France Restaurant ★$$$ Grilled seafood is prepared with a French accent. Try the escargots de Bourgogne and the onion soup gratinée. The desserts include banana flambé, nougat glacé, and lemon tart. ♦ French ♦ Daily 6PM-closing. Hastings, Christ Church. 435.6869

7 Caribbee Beach Hotel $ With 55 rooms, the hotel is modest but at least it's air-conditioned and on the beach. Some rooms offer kitchen facilities. ♦ Hastings, Christ Church. 436.6232

7 Coconut Court Beach Hotel $ Charlie Blades and his family have owned and operated the beachfront hotel for the last 16 years. Just outside of the capital, the 90 rooms and suites are within walking distance of restaurants, nightclubs, banks, and shops. ♦ Hastings, Christ Church. 427.1655

8 Barbados Museum and Historical Society Housed in an old military prison at

St. Ann's Garrison, the exhibitions display the Arawak and Carib Indians contributions to the island, as well as input from Africans and Europeans. Dolls, household items, and clothing are displayed. The oldest part of the prison dates back to 1820. Don't miss the collection of fine maps and prints dealing with Caribbean history in the **Cunard Gallery.** There are also a cafe, a library with current and historical publications, and a gift shop on the premises. ♦ Admission. M-Sa 10AM-6PM. Library: M-F 9AM-1PM and by appt. Gift shop: M-Sa 10AM-6PM. Garrison, St. Michael. 427.0201, 436.1956

8 1627 and All That Sort of Thing A toe-tapping, exciting musical presentation of the island's colorful history is performed by local youngsters in a garden theater. Dinner includes traditional foods: peas 'n' rice, sweet potatoes, pumpkin fritters, fried flying fish, calypso chicken, and various salads. The price includes a tour of the galleries and transportation to and from the Barbados Museum. ♦ Tour: Su, Th 6:30PM. Show time: 7:30PM. Fourth Ave, Rendezvous Gardens, Christ Church. 435.6900

9 Brown Sugar ★★$$ Bajan specialties are prepared according to custom. The portions are enormous and the ambience mellow, and dinner is served by candlelight. ♦ Caribbean ♦ M-F noon-3PM, 6-10PM; Sa-Su 6-10PM. Aquatic Gap, St. Michael. 426.7684

10 Barbados Hilton $$$ Although the lovely oceanfront hotel has worn the Hilton tag for 25 years, it is decidedly Bajan and the tropical decor in all 185 rooms provides a lovely island retreat. Three restaurants, a swimming pool, tennis courts, and a wide range of water sports are among the amenities. The only jarring note is the Mobil Refinery next door. ♦ Aquatic Gap, St. Michael. 426.0200, 800/HILTONS; fax 436.8946

Within the Barbados Hilton:

Veranda Restaurant ★★$$$ Bajan specialties are served in a delightful setting designed to resemble a street scene with chattel houses and island architecture. Dining is offered inside and outside. ♦ Caribbean ♦ Daily 7-10:30AM, noon-2:30PM, 6:30-11PM. 462.0200

11 Garrison Historic Area British military barracks dating back to the 18th and 19th centuries and gravestones to the mid-17th century are situated around a race course. The first British soldiers were stationed near here in 1695. The horse races take place on Saturday afternoons, but there's no definite schedule, so check with your hotel. ♦ Bridgetown, St. Michael. No phone

Within the Garrison Historic Area:

Bush Hill House At 19, **George Washington** and his brother Lawrence, 14 years older, came to Barbados so Lawrence could recuperate from tuberculosis in a warmer climate. Lawrence's father-in-law's third wife was the sister of a prominent Barbadian, **Gedney Clarke,** and that tie probably influenced the brothers' travel plans. It wasn't until 1983 that the Bush Hill House was identified as the house they stayed in. ♦ Daily 9AM-5PM. No phone

11 Grand Barbados Beach Resort $$$ This beautifully decorated and landscaped resort has everything you could possibly require. For starters, there are a swimming pool, horseback riding, and tennis nearby, plus two restaurants and a coffee shop on the premises. ♦ Bridgetown, St. Michael. 426.0890, 800/227.5475

Restaurants/Clubs: Red   **Hotels:** Blue
Shops/ 🌳 Outdoors: Green   **Sights/Culture:** Black

Within the Grand Barbados Beach Resort:

The Golden Shell ★★★$$$$ This is one of Barbados' fanciest restaurants. The beef and seafood entrées are superb, and the service is elegant. ♦ Continental ♦ Daily noon-2:30PM, 6:30-10:30PM. 426.0890

The Schooner ★★$$ The hotel renovated a wonderful old pier and created a restaurant with an ambience that fulfills what everyone dreams of on a romantic tropical island. ♦ Seafood ♦ M-F, Su noon-2:30PM, 6:30-10:30PM; Sa 6:30-10:30PM. 426.0890

The Holiday Store Caribbean-designed clothing, paintings and pottery, featuring island motifs such as shells, starfish, hibiscus, and flying fish, are sold here. ♦ Daily 9AM-6PM. 462.0890

12 Waterfront Cafe $$ Caribbean and American sandwiches and other snacks are served here, the perfect spot for a cold drink after strolling through Bridgetown. ♦ American ♦ Daily 10AM-closing. Cavans Ln, Bridgetown. 426.1048

13 Barbados Synagogue and Cemetery The restored synagogue managed by the Barbados National Trust was built in the 1830s; the cemetery is filled with gravestones dating back to the mid-17th century. ♦ M-F 9AM-5PM. Magazine Ln, Bridgetown. 426.5792

14 West Indian Rum Refinery A re-creation of the island's rum business is entitled "Where the Rum Come From" and provides a look at the history of rum and includes a tour of the refinery, lunch, and a complimentary rum tasting. The refinery has produced **Cockspur** for more than 100 years. ♦ Tours: W noon-2:15PM. Black Rock, St. Michael. Reservations required. 435.6900

14 Mount Gay Distillery Barbados' famous rum has been made here for more than one hundred years, despite English Archbishop **Thomas Tenison's** theory that rum is "destructive to nature, wasting its vitals and an enemy of propagation." ♦ M-F 8AM-4PM. Spring Garden Hwy, about 1 mile uphill from parish church in St. Lucy. 425.9066

15 Atlantis Submarines Visit the ocean depths to view the living world of coral reefs and an outstanding sampling of colorful sea life up close. The sub ride takes an hour and is a perfect opportunity for dedicated photo buffs. ♦ Admission. M-Sa 9AM-9PM. The Wharf, Bridgetown. Reservations required. 436.8929

16 Paradise Village and Beach Club $$$ This beachfront resort offers 172 rooms in 12 buildings sloping toward the magnificent white sand beach. All rooms have either a terrace or balcony. The resort, operated by the same folks who run **Cunard Lines,** the famed cruise line, sprawls over 13 acres, with tennis courts, two pools, water sports, and a fitness center. There are also a restaurant, a beach bar, and shops. ♦ Black Rock, St. Michael. 424.0888, 800/222.0939

17 Koko's ★★$$$ On a cliff overlooking the sea, this small restaurant has a loyal following. The menu features unusual and creative Bajan dishes, with an emphasis on seafood. ♦ Seafood ♦ Daily 6PM-closing. Prospect, St. James. Reservations recommended. 424.4557

18 Barbados Beach Village $$ Villas with private terraces—89 in all—create a relaxed atmosphere on one of the island's prettiest beaches. A pool, tennis courts, and water sports are all available. Many repeat visitors seek out this 20-year-old property. ♦ Prospect, St. James. 425.1440, 800/223.9815

18 Hippo Nightclub Male strippers are usually on tap at this popular hot spot. ♦ M-Tu, Th-Su 9PM-closing. Prospect, St. James. 425.1440

18 Coconut Creek Club Hotel $$ This cottage colony offers water sports on two beaches, plus 50 rooms (all with either a patio or balcony), a freshwater pool, and an English pub called **The Cricketers.** ♦ Prospect, St. James. 432.0804

19 La Cage Aux Folles ★★$$$ The teeny-tiny restaurant is currently one of the island's hottest dining spots. Owned by **Nick Hudson**

and **Suzie Blandford,** the restaurant features an intimate room for private parties of up to 16 people. The menu is à la carte, with an emphasis on French gourmet cuisine. Try the lobster or steak, they're exceptional. ♦ French ♦ Daily 6PM-closing. Paynes Bay, St. James. Reservations required. 424.2424

19 Fathoms Seafood and Bar ★★$$$ Shrimp and crab étouffée is a great starter and sautéed conch cutlets an ideal main course, but there's a wide selection of seafood and meat dishes, too. The beachfront setting is casually elegant. Fathoms and Koko's are owned by the same folks. ♦ Seafood ♦ Daily 11AM-3PM, 6:30-10PM. Paynes Bay, St. James. 432.2568

19 Shakey's Pizza Restaurant $$ Besides pizza, they also offer chicken, burgers, and sub sandwiches. ♦ American ♦ M-Th 11AM-11PM; F-Sa 11AM-12:30AM; Su 11AM-11PM. Main Rd, Hastings. 435.7777. Also at: Sunset Crest, Holetown. 432.7777

20 Tamarind Cove Hotel $$$$ Luxury is everywhere at this newly renovated (to the tune of $16 million) and expanded hotel with 117 rooms and 500 feet of beach. There are water sports, three pools, and an open-air lobby that's been decorated in soothing peach and gray marble with lots of lovely Spanish arches and fountains. This is one of the

St. James Beach Hotels—the others are the Coconut Creek Club and Colony Club hotels. ◆ Paynes Bay, St. James. 422.2741, 432.1332; fax 422.1726

Within the Tamarind Cove Hotel:

Harrisons This branch of the Bridgetown department store offers an elegant array of fine duty-free (mainly Italian) leather goods. ◆ M-F 9AM-5PM; Sa 9AM-1PM. 432.5338

Amazone Fashion-forward ladieswear for island days and tropical evenings is guaranteed to be the envy of the folks back home. ◆ M-F 9AM-5PM; Sa 9AM-1PM. 432.2358

Neptunes ★★$$$ This relatively new and stylish restaurant is considered one of the island's most unique. The saltwater aquarium is a great conversation piece. The shrimp, lobster, and swordfish specialties are the best choices. ◆ Seafood ◆ M-Sa 6-10PM. Reservations required. 432.1332

20 Smugglers Cove $ The small—21 rooms—hotel has a pool and a small restaurant with a small menu. Some of the rooms have kitchens. ◆ Paynes Bay, St. James. 432.1741

Barbados

20 The Coach House ★$$ Ever heard of an English pub with calypso music? It may sound strange, but this restaurant, which is just that, is one of the hot spots on the island. A posted dress code asks patrons to "please dress nicely." There's a British phone booth on the grounds, probably because the restaurant is next to a branch of the Barbados Phone Company. The eclectic menu ranges from chicken liver pâté to pan-fried flying fish. ◆ British/Caribbean ◆ M-F, Su noon-2:45PM, 6:30-10:30PM; Sa 6:30-10:30PM. Paynes Bay, St. James. 432.1163

21 Divi St. James $$ Casual and relaxed are the operative words at this elegant beachfront hotel with 131 rooms, two bars, and one restaurant. There's a health club, with sauna, tennis, and water sports. Transportation to the Divi Southwinds Beach Resort is provided for guests who purchase the all-inclusive package. ◆ Vauxhall, St. James. 432.7840, 800/367.DIVI

21 Frangipani Boutique This is a one-stop shop for T-shirts, souvenirs, snacks, and casual women's wear. ◆ Daily 9AM-6PM. Vauxhall, St. James. No phone

21 Sandy Lane $$$$ Possibly one of the best-known hotels in the Caribbean and certainly one of the most famous on Barbados, this 30-year-old ultraelegant hotel has undergone a $10 million face-lift. Founded by **Ronald Tree**, Sandy Lane has always appealed to the jet set. All of the bedrooms and baths have been enlarged and redesigned, the public areas refurbished, the restaurant renovated, and new marble and terrazzo floors have been added in the public areas. The oceanview rooms have been expanded by 50 percent and new plumbing, electricity, ceilings, and walls added. Work was also done on the tennis courts and the 18-hole championship golf course. ◆ Deluxe ◆ Sandy Lane Bay, St. James. 432.1311, 800/225.5843

Within Sandy Lane:

Sandy Bay Restaurant ★★★$$$ Fine cuisine is served in a luxurious setting. The restaurant features a large wine list. ◆ Continental ◆ M, W-Th, Sa-Su 6-10PM. Reservations recommended. 432.1311

Seashell Restaurant ★★★$$$ Smashing preparation and service go into the entrées, featuring local seafood and the finest ingredients. ◆ Italian/Seafood ◆ Daily 7-9PM. Reservations required. 432.1311

22 Sunset Crest Shopping Plaza The small strip center is anchored by a **Cave Shepherd** department store. There are also a bank and a supermarket. ◆ M-Sa 9AM-6PM. Holetown, St. James. No phone

Within the Sunset Crest Shopping Plaza:

The Brig ★$$ Standard shopping-center fare—sandwiches, salads, and snacks—is served here. ◆ American ◆ M-Sa 8:30AM-10PM. 432.1103

23 Golden Palm $$ Each of the 71 units in this refurbished apartment hotel has a fully equipped kitchen. There's also a swimming pool for guests. ◆ Golden Coast Beach, St. James. 432.6666; fax 432.1335

23 Monument to Holetown Settlers Captain **John Powell** landed the ship *Olive Blossom* here on 14 May 1625 and claimed the island for **King James**. This monument commemorates the event. ◆ Holetown, St. James

23 St. James Parish Church One of four surviving churches, St. James is more than 300 years old. **Ronald** and **Nancy Reagan** celebrated Easter services here during an island visit in 1982. ◆ Daily 9AM-5PM. Holetown, St. James.

23 Discovery Bay Hotel $$$ The lovely beach is topped off with casual but elegant appointments in 84 rooms and one villa. The property, more than 21 years old, features tennis courts and water sports. ◆ Holetown, St. James. 432.1301; fax 432.2553

Within the Discovery Bay Hotel:

Best of Barbados Shop Souvenirs and locally made goods are sold in this shop, one of several on the island. ◆ M-Sa 9AM-5PM. 422.3060

24 Sandpiper Inn $$$ Tennis, complimentary water sports, and access to the nearby Sandy Lane Hotel Golf Course make this 20-room hotel a perfect getaway. The restaurant has received gourmet awards and features such delicacies as Caribbean fish soup; and, for dessert, a wonderful walnut and coconut tart. ◆ Porters, St. James. 422.2372/2251

Within the Sandpiper Inn:

Sandpiper Inn Restaurant ★$$$ The local foods excellently prepared include potato pancakes sautéed and topped with smoked salmon, caviar, and sour cream, as well as stuffed eggplant. ◆ Caribbean ◆ Daily noon-2:30PM, 6:30-10PM. 422.2251

24 Settlers Beach Hotel $$$$ The hotel's cachet is that it is located near where the first British settlers set foot on Barbados. The 22-villa resort is popular with UK guests. There are water sports and a pool. ◆ Settlers Beach, St. James. 422.3052; fax 422.1937

24 Folkstone Underwater Park and Marine Museum The unique park encompasses both land and sea. There are a popular picnic area, a snorkeling trail on nearby Dottins reef, an aquarium, and exhibitions of marine antiques. ◆ M-Sa 10AM-5PM; Su 10AM-6PM. Porters, St. James. 422.2871

25 Coral Reef Club $$$ Privacy is a major factor at this sister resort to the Sandpiper Inn, and well-designed terraces, patios, and balconies provide intimate settings. With 75 accommodations that vary in size, the Coral Reef is beautifully decorated and comfortable. Cocktail cruises aboard the club's 30-foot catamaran are a favorite activity. ◆ St. James Beach, St. James. 422.2372; fax 422.1776

25 Colony Club Hotel $$$$ Casuarina trees shade the pretty beach at this 74-room island-elegant hotel. There's a swimming pool on the premises. ◆ St. James Beach, St. James. 422.2335

Within the Colony Club Hotel:

Colony Club Restaurant ★★$$$ An old private home built in the white coral that was popular in the 1930s, the restaurant is the ultimate mix of island elegance and European sophistication. The Monday buffet offers suckling pig, baked ham, and various local dishes; Wednesday features a steak

barbecue and a live band; and Sunday is known for the beach buffet. ◆ Continental ◆ Daily 12:30-2:30PM, 7:30-9:45PM. 422.2335

25 Chateau Creole ★★$$$ Seasonings and spices get great play here with shrimp remoulade, crab diablo, New Orleans pumpkin soup, and a variety of mouth-watering Cajun and island specialties. ◆ French/Creole ◆ M-Sa 6:30-11:30PM. Alleynes Bay, St. James. 422.4116

26 Glitter Bay $$$$ The name of this resort says it all. Lots of white marble sets off all that glitters (and it's a lot), but the lovely watercolor paintings take some of the sting out of the decor. The landscaping is spectacular. The property once belonged to **Sir Edward Cunard** of the shipping family. White Bermuda shorts and pith helmets are a nice touch on the doormen. The shops here carry more trendy designer items than anyone could ever hope to purchase. There are water sports, tennis, and afternoon tea. ◆ Deluxe ◆ Alleynes Bay, St. James. 422.5555; fax 422.3940

Within Glitter Bay:

Piperade ★★★$$$ The open-air restaurant features nightly entertainment and an eclectic menu. ◆ West Indian/Continental ◆ Daily 6:30-11PM. 422.4111

26 Royal Pavilion $$$$ The sister resort and next-door neighbor to Glitter Bay has a huge supply of its own glitz and glamour in 75 oceanfront accommodations. ◆ Deluxe ◆ Alleynes Bay, St. James. 422.5555; fax 422.3940

Within the Royal Pavilion:

Tabora's ★★$$$ Named after the landscape artist **Fernando Tabora,** who designed the hotel's gardens, the key to this restaurant is informal elegance. It is a fashionable spot that often attracts celebrities. ◆ Continental ◆ Daily 7:30-10:30AM, noon-3:30PM Apr-Nov. Daily 7:30-10:30AM, noon-3:30PM, 7:30-10:30PM Dec-Mar. Reservations recommended. 422.4444

27 The Legend ★★$$$ Veteran Bajan restaurateur **Andrew Gomes** formerly owned the Pig 'n' Whistle Pub on Barbados. His new venture, The Legend, made its debut in 1991 in a 180-year-old plantation house with beautiful gardens. Live lobster is served in season, and there's always seafood and steaks. ◆ French/Bajan ◆ Daily 6:30-10PM. Mullins Bay, St. Peter. Reservations required. 422.0631

27 Coco Banana ★$$ Snacks or dinner are served in a tropical setting. Choose from burgers, chicken, steaks, or seafood and enjoy live music every night but Wednesday. ♦ American ♦ Tu-Sa 7PM-1AM. Mullins Bay, St. Peter. Reservations recommended. 422.0640

28 Kings Beach Hotel $$$ This attractive beachfront hotel has 57 rooms, each boasting a terrace or patio. Water sports and a pool are also available at Kings Beach. ♦ Road View, St. Peter. 422.1690, 800/223.1588; fax 422.1691

29 Sandridge Beach Hotel $$ Popular with UK visitors, the 52-room hotel offers various accommodations from single rooms to deluxe one-bedroom suites. Amenities include a white sand beach, two swimming pools, and complimentary water sports. Tennis matches can also be arranged. ♦ Speightstown, St. Peter. 422.2361; fax 422.1965

29 Cobblers Cove $$$$ Owned by Brits **Hamish** and **Linda Watson,** the small 38-room hotel is

Barbados

a member of the upscale Relais and Chateaux group and reminiscent of a quaint hotel in the British countryside, complete with a charming lounge for tea or reading. The red-tiled pool and terraced dining room overlooking the sea are romantic enough to make this an ideal honeymoon destination. There are also a complete water-sports program and tennis courts. ♦ Speightstown, St. Peter. 422.2291

Within Cobblers Cove:

Cobblers Cove Restaurant ★★★$$$ Dine on *fritto misto* (dorado, shrimp, flying fish, and calamari, lightly breaded and served with a tangy tomato sauce) or sautéed leeks wrapped in puff pastry with a cordon of leek sauce. ♦ Continental ♦ Daily 8-10AM, 12:30-2:30PM, 7-9PM. 422.2291

30 Heywood's $$$ The Wyndham resort was once a sugar plantation owned by the Heywoods. They're no longer there, but the original mill remains. The 30-acre resort is made up of seven buildings that re-create a bit of history. Dinner is often served in **Caroline's Restaurant,** named for **Caroline Lee,** a 19th-century hotelier; Pringles, another building, is named for **Rachel Pringle,** the island's first hotelier. Heywood's has three pools and an extensive beachfront shopping arcade. ♦ Speightstown, St. Peter. 422.4900

31 The Barbados Wildlife Reserve Animals unique to Barbados and many from other Caribbean islands, among them monkeys, tortoises, and iguanas, roam free through the four acres of mahogany forest. A few animals are caged—parrots and pythons, for example—but visitors are cautioned to keep alert as they walk through the grounds. The reserve was founded in 1985 with seed money from the Canadian International Development Agency. ♦ Admission. Daily 10AM-5PM. Farley Hill, St. Peter. 422.8826

31 Farley Hill National Park Just across from the Barbados Wildlife Reserve, the park contains an old ruin where *Island in the Sun* was filmed. Don't forget to bring a camera—views from the park of the wild and rocky east coast and due north to the Scotland District are breathtaking. ♦ Admission. Daily 7AM-6PM. Farley Hill, St. Peter

32 Barclay's Park The British bank folks have created a charming and scenic picnic area right along the coast. The 50-acre park commemorates the island's independence in 1966. ♦ E. Coast Rd, north of Bathsheba, St. Joseph

Within Barclay's Park:

Barclay's Park Snackette $ Snacks and cold drinks are refreshing and the view is unbeatable. Casuarina trees bent almost in half by strong coastal winds form a dramatic setting for photographers. ♦ M-F 10AM-6PM; Sa 10AM-7PM; Su 10AM-9PM. 422.9976

33 Harrison's Cave Subterranean caverns are served by a tram (no twisted ankles in these caves, thank you). ♦ Admission. Daily 9AM-4PM; closed Sep. Reservations recommended. Welchman Hall Gully, St. Thomas. 438.6640

34 Flower Forest The flowers on this old sugar plantation provide a feast for the eyes as well as the soul. See more than one hundred species in the forest, including ginger lilies, puffball trees, and a variety of ferns, orchids, and palm trees. Follow the signs to Harrison's Cave, then followed by Flower Forest signs from there to where the St. Thomas, St. Joseph, and St. Andrew parishes meet. ♦ Admission. Daily 9AM-5PM. E. Coast Rd, north of Bathsheba, St. Joseph. 433.8152

35 Edgewater Hotel $ There's a very Spanish feel to this once private home with old wooden benches and furniture designed to re-create earlier times. The building is more than one hundred years old. Of the hotel's 20 rooms, No. 221 has the most remarkable view of the island's east coast. ♦ Bathsheba, St. Joseph. 433.9900; fax 432.9902

35 Bonito Bar and Diner ★★$ Owned by **Enid Worrell,** this second-floor establishment overlooking the beach and boulders offers a superb value. Flying fish, potato pie, rice and peas, and couscous (cornmeal with okra) are among the house specialties. ♦ Caribbean ♦ M-F, Su 10AM-6PM. Bathsheba, St. Joseph. 433.9034

36 Andromeda Gardens The gardens on a coral cliff were created in the mid-1950s by **Iris Bannochie** on land her family had owned for more than two centuries. Among the thousands of plants are tropical bougainvillea, hibiscus, heliconia, orchids, palms, cacti, and succulents. She created a wild and wonderful world of plants that anyone, especially those with green thumbs, can enjoy. You'll also discover great photo opportunities. ♦ Admission. Daily 8AM-5PM. Bathsheba, St. Joseph. 436.9033

37 Atlantis Hotel $$ Once a simple family guest house, this eight-room inn dates back to 1882. Some rooms have private balconies overlooking the flower gardens or the ocean. ♦ Bathsheba, St. Joseph. 433.9445

Within the Atlantis Hotel:

Atlantis Restaurant ★★$$ This seaside establishment is best known these days for its outstanding seafood buffet, including fried fish, okra, pumpkin fritters, fried plantains, and pickled bananas. ♦ Seafood/Bajan ♦ M-Sa 11:30AM-2PM. Reservations required. 433.9445

37 St. John's Parish Church The beautiful Bajan/Anglican architecture is complemented by a spectacular view of the east coast. The pulpit contains six kinds of wood: ebony, locust, mahogany, manchineel, oak, and pine. There's a souvenir and refreshment shop on the grounds. ♦ Daily 9AM-5PM. St. John. No phone

38 Barbados Zoo Park and Oughterson Plantation The only zoo and botanical garden in the Caribbean is in a sugar plantation setting. There are lots of monkeys, birds, and goats, plus a petting zoo for children. ♦ Admission. Daily 9:30AM-5PM. St. Philip. 423.6203

39 Sunbury Plantation House This 300-year-old plantation is now a lived-in estate house filled with antiques and wonderful relics of days past. See how sugar barons lived the sweet life amid their fine possessions. There are also an exhibition of carriages and a snack bar. ♦ Admission. M-Sa 10AM-4:30PM. St. Philip. 423.6270

40 Marriott's Sam Lord's Castle $$$ Look at Sam's home now. This full-service resort offers a lot of activities, 256 rooms, 18 suites, and 10 castle rooms, bars, restaurants, lighted tennis courts, swimming pools, and whirlpools. What do you think the old pirate would think of his old neighborhood? ♦ From Grantley Adams International Airport, go east on Hwy 7 for 6 miles, St. Philip. 423.7350; fax 423.5918

Within Marriott's Sam Lord's Castle:

The Wanderer ★★$$ Buffet breakfasts are served here, and Sam's Sunday Feast is an island favorite. There's music every night except Monday and Thursday. ♦ American ♦ Daily 7:30-10:30AM, noon-2:30PM, 6-10:30PM. 423.7350

The Sea Grille ★★$$$ Local fishers sell their catch to this large restaurant with fine service. Daily fresh catch includes grouper, snapper, local lobster, and more. ♦ Seafood ♦ Daily 6-10:30PM. 423.7350

40 Sam's Lantern ★$$ Hats off to **Thelma Taylor,** who has a collection of caps that customers have left behind. The place is popular with locals as well as tourists who come for the spicy fried chicken and the always popular Bajan flying fish. ♦ Caribbean ♦ Daily 8AM-11PM. Long Bay, St. Philip. 423.5674

41 Ginger Bay Beach Club $$$ There are signs here to remind you that you are a million miles from your home and 35 kilometers from the closest traffic jam. The hotel has 16 rooms, and is surrounded by delightful ocean breezes that cool things down even during the summer. The wonderful laid-back atmosphere centers around the pool and tennis courts. Much of the furniture is Barbadian mahogany. ♦ Crane Rd, St. Philip. 423.5810

Within the Ginger Bay Beach Club:

Ginger's Restaurant ★$$ Flying fish top the list of Bajan specialties on the menu at this pretty open-air restaurant. A Caribbean buffet is featured on Sunday. ♦ Caribbean ♦ Daily 7:30-10:30AM, noon-3PM, 6-10:30PM. 423.5810

42 Crane Beach Hotel $$$ Cruise-ship visitors love the hotel's gorgeous beach. The 18 rooms aren't air-conditioned, but they do boast a view and a breeze that all Caribbean properties desire to match. The sand is like sugar and the ocean is an indescribable blue. Crane Beach opened its doors in 1867, so guests can enjoy its history as well as beauty. Don't miss the fabled Roman pool without taking a picture. The entire setting, with its panoramic view of the ocean, is magnificent. ♦ Crane Beach, St. Philip. 423.6220; fax 423.5343

Within the Crane Beach Hotel:

The Panoramic Restaurant ★★★$$$ They say this is the most romantic location in the Caribbean (it's certainly one of the most beautiful). Set high above the water where fresh lobster and other seafood are caught daily for the hotel's chef, the restaurant also overlooks the world-famous floodlit Crane Beach. ♦ Seafood ♦ Daily noon-3PM, 6-10:30PM; Tea 3:30-5:30PM. Reservations required. 423.6220

43 Outskirts English Pub $$ Bajan and English menus include pairings such as peas and rice and steak-and-kidney pie. There are a swimming pool on the premises and entertainment at the adjacent **Rat Trap Night Club** on the weekends. ♦ Daily 11AM-11:30PM. Rices, St. Philip. 423.6552

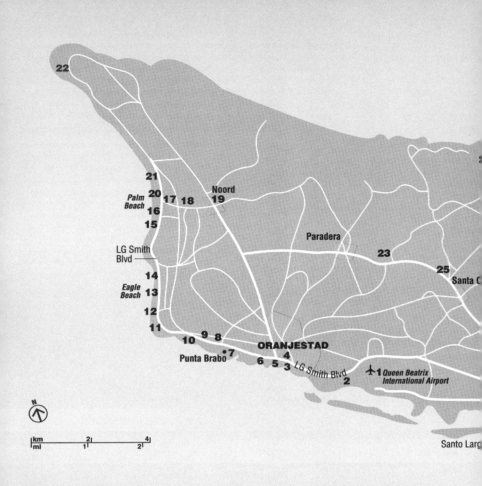

Aruba

Only 15 miles off the coast of Venezuela, Aruba is less than 20 miles long and barely six miles wide. The island's size makes it easy to explore in a day. When the Spanish discovered the island in 1499, they declared it an insignificant find, not particularly beautiful (vegetation is sparse), nor of any use. Little did the navigators realize, however, what a delightful spot they'd passed up. Tourists have changed the scene on this windswept island, which has become a hot spot for water sports. Scuba divers can explore the Caribbean's largest sunken wreck just off the northwest tip of Aruba, and there's an abundance of waterskiing, snorkeling, sailing, and swimming activities on this island.

While Aruba is outside the hurricane belt, the island enjoys strong breezes year-round, a feature that attracts hordes of windsurfers. Land-sailing, using three-wheeled carts with sails to propel riders across the ground, is also growing in popularity.

Tourism is the number one industry in Aruba, but earlier years (beginning in 1824) saw gold mining and (one hundred years later) oil refining as the leading businesses. In fact, **Lloyd G. Smith Boulevard** was named for one of the oil company's first managers. Now it's better known as "Resort Row."

The **Golden Tulip** opened on LG Smith Boulevard at Palm Beach in 1959, the first of the upscale resorts that quickly developed on Aruba's west coast. Dozens now line the boulevard, and it's no wonder—the

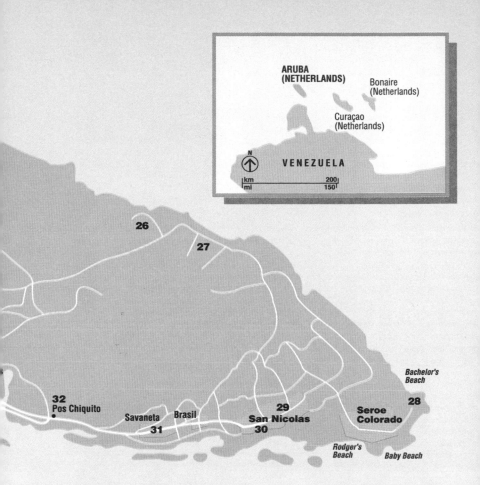

stretch between **Palm Beach** and **Eagle Beach** just west of **Oranjestad** (pronounced or-an-yeh-stat) is the prettiest in the vicinity.

Set aside a day or two for visiting Oranjestad, Aruba's Dutch-influenced picturesque capital. The main attraction is **Cayo Betico Croes,** a street lined with shops carrying the island's most fashionable designs. The lovely Dutch architecture is another reason to see the capital, which is best toured on foot. The island's oldest buildings are on the street **Wilhelminastraat.**

Aruba's European ties extend back to the early 17th century, when the Dutch took over the island. Now, with Holland and the Netherland Antilles, Aruba forms the Kingdom of the Netherlands. (The island has been an autonomous member of the kingdom since 1986.)

Indian culture likewise thrives on the island (the earliest settlers were **Arawak Indians**), and ancient Indian drawings can be seen on the walls of caves in **Arikok National Park** on the eastern coast.

From Indian to Dutch, more than 40 nationalities contribute to the local traditions. For instance, the language spoken here is Dutch and **Papiamento,** a mélange of Portuguese, Spanish, Dutch, African, English, and French. Spanish and English, however, are spoken and understood by most Arubans.

One way to sample the island's culture is at the weekly *bon boni* (which means "welcome"), a celebration of local folklore, crafts, music, and food. It's held every Tuesday in the courtyard of Aruba's Historical Museum at **Fort Zoutman.**

Dial the prefix 011/297.8 when calling from the United States; when on the island, dial only the last five digits.

Getting to the Island
Airlines

There are regular nonstop scheduled flights from JFK (New York), Newark, Atlanta, Miami, Amsterdam, Port of Spain, St. Martin/Sint Maarten, Curaçao, Bonaire, and Puerto Rico. Airlines serving Aruba are: Air Aruba, American Airlines, Aeropostal, ALM, Avianca, BWIA, Continental, KLM, VASP, VIASA, and Canada Air Connection.

Getting around the Island
Car Rentals

AC&E Car Rental	36373
Airways Car Rental	21845
Avis	28787
Budget	28600
Caribbean Car Rental	29118
Courtesy Car Rental	34000; fax 26757
Dollar	22783
Enterprise Rent-a-Car	23762
Five Star	27600
Hedwina Car Rental	26442
Hertz	24545
J/M Car Rental	23230
Marco's Car Rental	25889
National Car Rental	21967

Aruba

Optima Car Rental	35622
Ricardo's Car Rental	21161
Savings Car Rental	35959
Super Car Rental	38765

Thrifty Car Rental	3530
Toyota Rent-a-Car	3483

FYI
Money

The Aruban florin is a sound currency and American dollars are accepted everywhere. Bank hours are M-F 8AM-3:30PM.

Personal Safety

Crime is minimal on Aruba, but caution is advised when entering dark areas or neighborhoods away from populated sections. Know where you're going. Don't wear tempting jewelry or leave belongings unattended. In other words, use the same basic discriminating techniques you practice at home.

Phone Book

Aruba Tourism Authority	22777, 2377
Dr. Horacio Oduber Hospital	2430
Police	24555, 2400
Taxi	22116, 2160

Taxes and Tipping

A 10 to 11 percent hotel service charge and a five percent government room tax are added to your hotel bill (some hotels charge a higher service charge). A 10 to 15 percent tip is usually tacked onto restaurant checks. Additional tips may be offered at your own discretion. A $10 departure tax will be charged at the airport when you leave the island.

Telephone

To call Aruba from the United States, you must dial 011 (the international access code), then dial 297.8 (the area code for Aruba) followed by the local five-digit number. If you're unable to dial directly, dial 0 for the international operator and say you want to make a call to Aruba; your call will be transferred to the Aruba operator. To call within the island, just dial the five-digit number.

Dial the prefix 011/297.8 when calling from the United States. When on the island, dial only the last five digits.

1 Queen Beatrix International Airport
More than 500,000 visitors annually deplane at this modern airport located just east of Oranjestad. Aruba's first airfield, the small **Dakota Air Field,** opened in 1935, and as tourism has increased, the airport and its runways have expanded. All passengers are funneled into the air-conditioned building and into fairly quick-moving lines for immigration inspection. Baggage claim and customs clearance are generally handled with great ease. On average, more than 365 passengers are processed within 15 minutes.

Travelers who arrive during the day are often greeted with island music, the ubiquitous rum punch, and then Aruba's custom stamp that reads *bon bini* (welcome), which just

about says it all. The **Aruba Tourism Authority** has offices in the arrival hall. Transportation the island hotels, as well as to rental cars, can be found just outside the door. ♦ LG Smith Blvd. 24800

2 Talk of the Town $$ In 1964 Ike and Gret Cohen of Jacksonville, Fl, decided Aruba was great vacation spot and bought the **Strand Hotel,** which was built in 1942 and used as a office building in the sixties. The duo turned the property into a hotel called it the Coral Strand. The **Talk of the Town Restaurant** on the property became so popular that the Cohens renamed their hotel after it. In 1971 they bought the **Manchebo Beach Resort.** Today the hotel and the Manchebo and Bucu beach resorts are all part of the **Best Western** chain. The Talk of the Town has 63 rooms and is popular with business and leisure travelers alike. A courtyard surrounds the freshwater pool and there's a beach located just across the street. ♦ 2 LG Smith Blvd, Oranjestad. 23380, 800/223.1108

Within the Talk of the Town:

Talk of the Town Restaurant ★★★$$$ Famed for its prime rib, this elegant establishment is a **Chaine des Rotisseurs** member. Choose from the fine wine list. The crabmeat crepes and escargots are outstanding. ♦ Continental ♦ Daily 5:30PM-2AM. 23380

3 HarbourTown Located directly across from the Parliament building on LG Smith Blvd, this waterfront strip offers more than 50 shops and restaurants, a hotel, and a casino. ♦ Swain Wharf, Oranjestad. No phone

Within HarbourTown:

HarbourTown Hotel $$$ The 240 fully equipped suites were developed as timeshare apartments but are also available as rentals. All of the apartments are furnished in an elegant tropical decor and have ocean views. ♦ 35600, 800/223.9815

J&T Dynasty ★★$$ Traditional Japanese *teppanyaki* and Thai foods are served in elegant surroundings. ♦ Oriental ♦ Daily noon-2:30PM, 6-11:30PM. Reservations recommended. 36288, 37820

Ristorante Portobello/Pastagianni ★$$ The appetizers include calamari Fiorentina in garlic sauce with sweet peas, which are terrific, followed by the various seafood, veal, and chicken entrées, as well as pizza. The wine list is nice, but most people come here for ice cream and snacks. ♦ Italian ♦ Daily 11:30AM-11:30PM. 35966

The Waterfront ★★★$$$ This wonderful seafood restaurant has an ambience that could be Michigan Avenue, Beverly Hills, or Upper East Side. Owners and buddies **Roger Coster**, **Michael Jordan** (not the basketball star), and **Roy Leitch** have worked together at Divi hotels in the Caribbean for the last 20 years, and the trio reunited to open this popular establishment. The garlic crabs are great,

the escargot wonderful, and the lobster *fra diablo* is really hot stuff. Try the crusted shrimp baked with a light crust of fine herbs, bread crumbs, and Parmesan cheese, and served with a marmalade and horseradish sauce. The meal is worth the trip to Aruba. A return taxi to your hotel is provided courtesy of HarbourTown Casino with your dinner check. ♦ Seafood ♦ Daily 8-11AM, noon-3PM, 6-11PM. Reservations recommended. 35858

Eva's Boutique Shop here for a wide variety of women's swimwear in outstanding international designs. ♦ M-F 10AM-5:30PM; Sa 10AM-5PM. 38038

HarbourTown Casino This is the only waterfront casino in the Caribbean. ♦ Daily 10AM-5AM. 24222

4 Cayo Betico Croes It wasn't so long ago that Caribbean travelers dashed to **Nassaustraat** for the best bargains in the region. Shops line the busy street, and every day used to look like Christmas here. Now the street is named Cayo Betico Croes, after the late leader of Aruba's independence movement. The island's building boom brought shopping malls to downtown Oranjestad, where many of the trendier boutiques are now located. But good buys can still be had on Cayo Betico Croes, so don't miss it. ♦ Oranjestad

4 Ristorante Roma Mia ★$$ Traditional Italian specialties served here include risotto, calamari alla Veneziana, scallopine, and many seafood dishes. ♦ Italian ♦ Daily 6-11PM. 156 Caya Betico Croes, Oranjestad. 28639

4 Boonoonoonoos ★★$$ The "ooh" sound gets quite a workout here with a menu rich in island specialties such as Jamaican jerk ribs, pumpkin soup with cream and cheese, and *keshi yena* (an Aruban cheese casserole). ♦ Caribbean/Seafood ♦ Daily 6-11PM. 18A Wilhelminastraat, Oranjestad. Reservations recommended. 31888

4 Warung Djawa ★★$$ Try the *rijsttafel*, a "rice table" that presents a mix of exotic tastes and flavors blended with several Eastern spices. ♦ Indonesian ♦ M, W-F 12:30-2PM, 6-10:30PM; Tu 12:30-2PM; Sa-Su 6-10:30PM. 2 Wilhelminastraat, Oranjestad. 34888

4 Fort Zoutman Aruba's oldest building was completed in 1796 to protect the new capital from invasion. Since then it has functioned as the police headquarters, a prison, and a government building. The tower that marks the entrance was constructed in 1868 and bears the initials "WIII," for **William III**, the king of the Netherlands at the time. It has been a lighthouse as well as a public clock. The fort's **Historical Museum** features a number of cultural artifacts. ♦ Admission. M-F 9AM-4PM; Sa 9AM-noon. Zoutmanstraat, Oranjestad. No phone

4 Archaeology Museum Amerindian artifacts include utensils and relics of the early residents' agricultural techniques. Look at skeletons from the pre-Columbian period, burial urns, and various farming and cooking utensils. ◆ Free. M-F 8AM-noon, 1:30-4:30PM. 1 Zoutmanstraat, Oranjestad. 28979

4 The Grill House ★★$$ Steaks and fresh seafood are grilled to order here. ◆ Steaks ◆ Tu-Su noon-2:30PM, 6-11PM. 31 Zoutmanstraat, Oranjestad. Reservations recommended. 31611

5 Seaport Village Aruba's largest shopping mall features an eclectic collection of 85 high-fashion stores, fragrance shops, the terribly elegant second-floor European-style **Crystal Casino**, and a totally American **McDonald's**. A **Sonesta** hotel anchors one end of the mall. ◆ 82 LG Smith Blvd, Oranjestad. No phone

Within Seaport Village:

Limited Edition Men's casualwear with a European flair fills the racks. ◆ M-Sa 9AM-6PM. 23674

Little Holland Dutch-treat souvenirs place an emphasis on **Delft** blue tiles and linens. ◆ M-Sa 9:30AM-5:30PM. 36752

Deviation This is a one-stop shop for French-accented men's and women's clothing. ◆ M-Sa 9AM-6PM. 38917

Atlantis Submarines A narrative in Spanish and English describes the beauty of life in the depths of the sea and on a nearby natural reef. The sub passes within three feet of the reefs, which are like underwater hills or

mountains, then turns so that passengers on each side of the vessel can get up close to the fish of their choice. Before surfacing, the sub dives below to more than 120 feet. The Atlantis makes six to eight dives each day. ◆ Admission. Daily 8AM-5PM. 36090

5 Sonesta Hotel, Beach Club, and Casino Aruba $$$$ The 302-room hotel is the centerpiece of Seaport Village. A free shuttleboat leaves the lobby every 15 minutes for the 10-minute ride to the hotel's 40-acre private island with broad, white sand beaches. A separate "honeymoon island" offers privacy and tranquility, while another beach features various water sports. The pool at the hotel is large and attractive and overlooks the ocean. The Sonesta offers the best of both worlds—a resort hotel in a downtown location. ◆ 82 LG Smith Blvd, Oranjestad. 36000, 800/343.7170; fax 34389

Within the Sonesta Hotel, Beach Club, and Casino Aruba:

Les Accessoires This large and delightful shop run by New York fashion designer **Agatha Brown** and her husband, **Jerome Marder**, features Italian sweaters, elegant blouses from the Far East, beaded dresses by **Fabrice** and **Oleg Cassini**, plus magnificent leather goods created by Agatha herself. She gave up a career designing high-fashion separates on Seventh Avenue to retire to Aruba. "Retirement" means buying for their new shop around the world, and they're thriving on it. ◆ M-Sa 10AM-7PM. 37965

6 Port of Call Market Place This bustling waterfront center features duty-free shops for fragrance, liquor, jewelry, one-hour photo development, souvenirs, and more. There are plenty of fast-food restaurants, including a **Subway, Dunkin Donuts**, and **Domino's Pizza**. ◆ M-Sa 9:30AM-6PM. 17 LG Smith Blvd, Oranjestad. 37606

7 Bushiri Beach Resort $$$ The attractions at this resort include a health club, tennis courts, water sports, and 150 oceanview rooms. The lobby area is newly redone. You can hop on a shuttlebus to the casinos. ◆ 35 LG Smith Blvd, Punta Brabo Beach. 25216

8 Club Visage Disco The noisy entertainment center appeals to the young—or at least to the young at heart—with pizza, billiards, and plenty of music. ◆ Daily 9PM-6AM. 152 LG Smith Blvd, Punta Brabo Beach. 33541, 33418

9 Heidelberg ★★$$ *Ach du lieber!* Get your fill of wienerschnitzel, apple strudel, and "oompah-pa" jazz at the Heidelberg. ◆ German ◆ Tu, Th-Su 6-11PM. 136 LG Smith Blvd, Punta Brabo Beach. 25241

10 Divi Tamarijn $$$ These large rooms are made more attractive by the pool, tennis courts, and free transportation to the nearby Divi Divi Beach Hotel. There's a restaurant on the premises and services are exchanged with the Divi Divi. ◆ 64 LG Smith Blvd, Punta Brabo Beach. 24150, 800/367.3484

Restaurants/Clubs: Red	Hotels: Blue
Shops/ 🌳 Outdoors: Green	Sights/Culture: Black

11 Divi Divi Beach Hotel $$ Tennis courts, water sports, a poolside ice-cream bar, and 202 rooms face a 100-foot-long white sand beach. Services are exchanged with the Divi Tamarijn. ♦ 93 LG Smith Blvd, Punta Brabo Beach. 23300, 800/367.DIVI; fax 34002

11 Costa Linda Beach Resort $$$$ This brand new luxury resort on the ocean offers elegant two- and three-bedroom apartments built around beautiful atriums. The land-scaping is excellent. The resort is owned and operated by Sun Development Company, the same firm that operates Casa del Mar, the Aruba Beach Club, and Playa Linda which is currently constructing a golf course—**Tierra del Costa Linda**—on the northwestern edge of the island. ♦ 57 LG Smith Blvd. 38000; fax 37762

12 Manchebo-Bucuti Beach Resort $$ The informal, 70-room Manchebo hotel attracts an international clientele. Each of the large rooms has a balcony or terrace. Facilities are interchangeable with the Talk of the Town resort (in other words, you can eat there and charge it to your room here). The 63-room Bucuti hotel adjacent to the Manchebo offers some rooms with kitchenettes. The **Pirates' Nest** restaurant, a popular spot, is a replica of a shipwrecked Dutch galleon. ♦ 55 LG Smith Blvd, Manchebo Beach. 23444, 800/223.1108; fax 34646

13 La Quinta $$ This family oriented, 130-suite resort offers a pool, water sports, and a lovely beach just across the road. ♦ 228 LG Smith Blvd, Eagle Beach. 35010

13 Sandra's Restaurant ★$$ The salad bar, steaks, seafood, and ribs are the specialties of the house at this pretty oceanfront restaurant. ♦ American ♦ Daily 6-11PM. 224 LG Smith Blvd, Eagle Beach. 31517

13 Chalet Suisse Restaurant ★★$$ The scenic Alps are miles away but the Aruban-accented preparation of European foods is pretty darn dramatic. The fondue and veal dishes are excellent, and the US prime meats are flown in daily. ♦ Swiss ♦ M-Sa 6-11PM. 246 LG Smith Blvd, Eagle Beach. Reservations recommended. 35054

14 Amsterdam Manor $$ The luxurious resort is a Dutch treat, with a tropical setting along

Eagle Beach and 47 apartments with fully equipped kitchenettes. Every apartment faces the ocean. There are also a swimming pool and a minimarket on the premises. ♦ 252 LG Smith Blvd, Eagle Beach. 34376; fax 31463

14 La Cabana Beach and Racquet Club $$ The new, ultramodern, and very large resort is conveniently located near restaurants and along a bus route. The beach and huge pool area emphasize water sports, but racquetball, squash courts, and a fitness center also help guests keep in shape. Each apartment features a balcony and a Jacuzzi. There are restaurants, bars, and a casino on the premises, as well as a shopping arcade. ♦ 250 LG Smith Blvd, Eagle Beach. 39000; fax 35474

14 La Vie en Rose ★★$$$ This oasis of European-accented service is *trés bon*. The rack of lamb is also superb. ♦ French ♦ Daily 6-11PM. 521 LG Smith Blvd, Eagle Beach. Reservations recommended. 35955

15 Ramada Renaissance Resort $$$$ The hotel's 207 rooms and 91 suites on 10 levels surround a spectacular indoor atrium overlooking the Caribbean. The decor in the Ramada's elegant and informal restaurants and all its public areas is Italian. Neighboring **Aruba Royal Resort** is part of the same complex. Tennis and water sports galore are

offered and, if that isn't enough, there's a health-and-fitness center. ♦ 75 LG Smith Blvd, Palm Beach. 37000, 800/228.9898

15 Aruba Concorde Hotel and Casino $$ This is a biggie—there are 500 rooms and suites, each with a balcony view of the beach or tropical gardens and pool area. You'll also find entertainment, restaurants (one French, one international, and a coffee shop) and shops. There are also an Olympic-sized swimming pool and lighted tennis courts. ♦ 77 LG Smith Blvd, Palm Beach. 24466, 800/327.4150; fax 38217

The cassava plant that grows throughout the Caribbean is used in many island recipes. When ground up, the juice of the cassava's fleshy, edible rootstock becomes *cassareep*, a preservative and spice that's used in a traditional West Indian dish called "pepper pot." This spicy stew is made with meat and vegetables, and because cassareep is among the ingredients, pepper pot can literally cook for years without spoiling. In fact, the pepper pot on the menu of Grenada's Plantation House Morne Fendue has been cooking steadily since the early 1980s.

16 **Aruba Palm Beach Resort and Casino**
$$$ The informal, family oriented atmosphere in this renovated 173-room, high-rise hotel is complemented by tennis courts, water sports, three restaurants, and the **Palm Casino**. There are also a gorgeous pool area and beach. The colors pink and white dominate wherever you look. Shops include a beauty salon, a drugstore, a gift shop, and a fashion boutique. ♦ 79 LG Smith Blvd, Palm Beach. 23900, 800/345.2782

17 **Old Cunucu House Restaurant** ★$$$
Aruban fare is served in a 70-year-old house (*cunucu* means country cottage). Delicacies include coconut fried shrimp, fish soup, and various veal dishes. ♦ Aruban ♦ Tu-Su 5-10PM. 150 Palm Beach, Palm Beach. Reservations required. 31666

18 **Gasparito Restaurant and Art Gallery**
★$$ Much of the island art on display at Gasparito's (illustrated above) is for sale. Dine on local foods, including fish soup, oyster stew, and *keshi yena,* a cheese casserole that's an Aruban favorite. ♦ Aruban ♦ Daily 6-11PM. 3 Gasparito, Palm Beach. 37044

19 **La Paloma Restaurant** ★★$$ House specialties include veal Marsala and *pollo alla parmigiani* (chicken topped with eggplant and mozzarella), manicotti, and seafood. ♦ Italian/Seafood ♦ M, W-F 6-11PM. 39 Noord, Noord. Reservations recommended. 32770

19 **Le Chateau Restaurant** ★★$$ Owner **Alberto Bayona** offers an international menu including shrimp Hawaii (shrimp with pineapple) and seafood zarzuela (a stew filled with fish). ♦ French ♦ Daily 6-11PM. 82 Noord, Noord. Reservations recommended. 36699

19 **Santa Anna Church** Built by **Domingo Antonio Silvester** around 1772, the church's hand-carved oak altar by Dutch sculptor **Hendrik van der Geld** won an exhibition award in Rome in 1879. It is the second oldest church on Aruba. ♦ Noord (town center). No phone

20 **Golden Tulip Aruba Caribbean Resort and Casino** $$$ Cacti and boulders line the driveway, reflecting Aruba's dramatic terrain. Blue-and-white Delft tiles typify the Dutch influence in the lobby of this KLM airline-owned property with 378 rooms, including 23 suites with ocean and/or garden views. The trio of buildings is only a few steps from an outstanding beach. There are a health-and-fitness center, tennis courts, restaurants, and shops. This was Aruba's first luxury hotel, built in 1959. ♦ 81 LG Smith Blvd, Palm Beach. 33555, 800/344.1212

Within the Golden Tulip Aruba Caribbean Resort and Casino:

The French Room ★$$$ The design of this elegant dining room features classic touches adapted to the Caribbean. *Entre nous* it's veal and fish. ♦ French/Continental ♦ Daily 6-10:30PM. 33555

20 **Americana Aruba Beach Resort and Casino** $$$$ The 421-unit resort has continually been among the island's most popular. Opening in 1975, the resort was renovated to the tune of $16 million in 1989. Every room is air-conditioned, an advantage in Aruba. There are three restaurants in the twin eight-story towers and a wide range of beach activities, including snorkeling and windsurfing. Shops include **Little Switzerland** (for gifts), **Gandelman** and **Kenro** jewelers, and **Penha** fragrances. ♦ 83 LG Smith Blvd, Palm Beach. 24500, 800/223.1588

20 **The Steamboat Buffet and Deli** ★$$
The Hebrew National products available here include corned beef and pastrami as good as what you'd find in New York (it isn't kosher, however). ♦ Deli ♦ Daily 6AM-4AM. 370 LG Smith Blvd, Palm Beach. 36700

21 **Hyatt Regency Aruba Resort and Casino** $$$$ Brown-and-white striped oversized lounge chairs greet guests on the front terrace of the new and dramatic resort. The elegant lobby, decorated with stunning Oriental rugs and seven chandeliers, leads to the magnificently landscaped multilevel pool and lagoon area, complete with black swans. Below the pool is **Las Ruinas del Mar** restaurant. Steps lead out to the stunning beachfront on Aruba's northwest coast. The $52 million hotel has 360 luxurious rooms, plus exclusive **Regency Club** accommodations, the **Casino Copacabana**, a health spa, water sports, tennis courts, and six restaurants and lounges. Posh comfort are the operative words. The shops include **Gandelman Jewelers.** ♦ 85 LG Smith Blvd, Palm Beach. 31234, 800/233.1234; fax 21682

Within the Hyatt Regency Aruba Resort and Casino:

Las Ruinas del Mar ★★★$$$ Named in honor of Aruba's gold-mining history, the restaurant offers an incredible breakfast buffet including chicken-walnut salad, fresh shrimp, oysters, clams, calimari, smoked salmon, caviar, and more. Mediterranean specialties are offered at dinner. ♦ International ♦ Daily 7AM-noon, 6-10:30PM. Reservations required. 31234

Palms Grill and Bar ★$ The restaurant features sandwiches, fajitas, stir-fry chicken, and grilled snapper. A breakfast menu is also available. ♦ Seafood/Caribbean ♦ Daily 24 hours. 31234

21 Playa Linda $$$ Relax in the fully equipped luxurious studios or one- and two-bedroom apartments—194 units in all—with two restaurants, indoor and outdoor cocktail lounges, and various shops along a white sand beach. ♦ 87 LG Smith Blvd, Palm Beach. 31000; fax 25210

21 Holiday Inn $$$ Its 600 rooms make this the largest hotel on the island. Built along lovely Palm Beach, the Holiday Inn is 15 minutes from the airport and only 10 minutes from downtown Oranjestad. Facilities include four restaurants, three bars, the **Grande Holiday Casino**, a health spa, four lighted tennis courts, and great beaches. ♦ 230 LG Smith Blvd, Palm Beach. 23600, 800/465. 4329; fax 25165

Within the Holiday Inn:

Boutique Streda The glitzy and glittery resort clothes sold here will translate to summer partywear back home. ♦ M-Sa 10AM-6PM; Su 10AM-2PM. 21405

Little Switzerland Shop here for jewelry, watches, and porcelain and crystal gift items. ♦ M-Sa 10AM-1PM, 3-7PM. 23506. Other shop branches are located at **Americana Aruba, Golden Tulip, Aruba Palm Beach, Aruba Concorde,** and **Divi/Tamarijn** hotels

Restaurants/Clubs: Red   **Hotels:** Blue
Shops/ 🌿 Outdoors: Green   **Sights/Culture:** Black

Penha and Sons This fragrance store (pictured above) highlights French products, including **Chanel** cosmetics. ♦ M-Sa 10AM-6PM; Su 10AM-1PM. 26781

Empress of China Restaurant ★$$ Nicely served Oriental dishes offer a respite from the island or American foods that prevail on Aruba. ♦ Cantonese ♦ Daily 6:30-10:30PM. 23600

22 Alto Vista Chapel The chapel was built on the site of the island's first mission, where in the early 1700s prayer meetings took place under a tree or in a hut. The first chapel, built in 1750 by **Domingo Antonio Silvester,** fell to ruins within the next century. It was replaced in 1952 with this small church. ♦ LG Smith Blvd, on the far northwest end of the island

23 Casibari and Ayo Rocks The fascinating and beautiful collection of strange rock formations provides great photo opportunities (you can climb all the way to the top of Casibari and halfway up Ayo). Some geolo-

gists think these diorite rocks might be the result of earthquakes or volcanic eruptions, and they were originally part of the South American mainland. They're the size of buildings and weigh several tons. ♦ Turn east off LG Smith Blvd at the Pueblo Super Market opposite the Divi Tamarijn Hotel; just east of Hooiberg, turn north off the main road

24 Natural Bridge The bridge on the jagged northern edge of Aruba near **Noordkaap** has been carved over the years by the wind and sea. It stands more than 100 feet long and 25 feet above sea level. ♦ Turn east off LG Smith Blvd at Pueblo Super Market opposite Divi Tamarijn Hotel, and then off the main road and north to the ocean

25 Hooiberg Aruba's most visible natural landmark (*hooiberg* is Dutch for "haystack") has a staircase to the top—541 feet high—and a spectacular view. **Haystack Mountain,** as it's better known, is definitely worth the trek. ♦ Turn east off LG Smith Blvd at Pueblo Super Market opposite Divi Tamarijn Hotel; the Hooiberg is a few miles on the left

26 Boca Prins This small cove features magnificent white sand dunes. Dune sliding is an Aruban sport and best attempted wearing jeans and sturdy sneakers. ◆ Turn east off LG Smith Blvd at Pueblo Super Market opposite Divi Tamarijn Hotel; the dunes are past the Hooiberg, on Aruba's northeast edge

27 Arikok National Park The park has interesting nature trails and a restored *cunucu* (country cottage). Arikok is also home to the caves, a sight-seeing must. ◆ Follow directions to Boca Prins; then turn east and then south at the coast

Within the Arikok National Park:

Fontein Cave These caves feature thousand-year-old **Arawak Indian** paintings that are difficult to figure out but undeniably interesting. **Guadirikiri Cave** is named for the wife of an Indian chief: openings above allow the sunlight to enter and splash upon the paintings. **Huliva Cave,** one hundred steps down into a tunnel, is sometimes called the "Tunnel of Love."

28 Colorado Point A lighthouse marks the southeast point of the island. Access to **Seroe Colorado,** the residential area for refinery employees, is through private property belonging to ESSO Petroleum Company. Superb public beaches, including **Rodger's** and **Baby** beaches, are also located here. When the weather is clear you can see all the way to Venezuela, which is about 15 miles away. ◆ Located on the southeast corner of the islands

29 Mi Cushina ★★$$ Aruban fare is featured at this family run restaurant (pictured above) located on the site of an old supermarket. The owners have collected a group of antiques representing local history, specifically Aruba's role as an oil refinery island. The tools and cooking implements, musical instruments, and old photos collected here are as notable as the food, but you'll want to try some of the special Aruban dishes. There's *pan bati,* a local pancake, and *fungi,* a cornmeal bread served with fried fish. Turtle and stewed lamb are also popular entrées. ◆ Aruban ◆ M, W, F-Su noon-2PM, 6-10PM. Cura Cabai, on main road about 1 mile from San Nicolas. Reservations recommended. 48335

30 Charlie's Bar and Restaurant ★★$$ For more than 50 years Charlie's has been a popular site—tourists and Arubans alike enjoy the casual atmosphere. Holland-born **Charlie** and **Marie Brouns** opened the place for seafarers, contractors, and refinery and harbor workers in 1941. Their son, Charlie Jr., and his wife operate the place today. The **Queen of Holland** decorated Charlie Sr. in 1977 with the Orange Nassau medal. Lots of island memorabilia and artifacts of the oil-rush days are on display here. ◆ Aruban/Seafood ◆ M-Sa noon-9:30PM. 56 Zeppenfeldstraat, San Nicolas. 45086

31 Brisas del Mar ★★$$ This homey seafood restaurant near the police station is popular with the locals and tourists. The many Aruban specialties include conch, grouper, and shrimp dishes. Better yet, Brisas is located on the water. ◆ Seafood ◆ M 6:30-10:30PM; Tu-Su noon-2:30PM, 6:30-10:30PM. Bar: daily noon-midnight. 222-A Savaneta, Savaneta. 47718

32 Isla del Oro ★★$$ Walk through mangrove swamps to this restaurant featuring Spanish-accented seafood. Paella Valenciana is a house specialty. ◆ Seafood ◆ Daily noon-3PM, 6-11PM. Pos Chiquito. 45086

33 Balashi Gold Mine The ruins of the 19th-century mine are a living testimony to the island's gold rush. At **Spanish Lagoon,** formerly a pirates' hideaway, you can see Aruba's desalination and power plants. ◆ Between Oranjestad and Pos Chiquito

Papiamento Primer

The melodic language known as Papiamento is spoken on Aruba, Bonaire, Curaçao, and other Dutch islands. Dialects vary slightly from island to island, but this mix of French, Spanish, Dutch, Portuguese, English, and African languages is basically the same. While Dutch is the official language on Aruba, Papiamento is generally spoken in the home, although it is growing in popularity in schools and offices. Here are some popular Papiamento expressions:

English	Papiamento
Give me a hug	*Brasa mi*
Give me a kiss	*Duna mi un sunchi*
Good afternoon	*Bon tardi*
Good-bye	*Ayo*
Good evening	*Bon nochi*
Good morning	*Bon dia*
How are you?	*Con ta bai?*
How much?	*Cuanto?*
I am fine	*Mi ta bon*
I like you a lot	*Mi gusta bo hopi*
I love you	*Mi ta stima bo*
Let's dance	*Ban baila*
See you later	*Te aworo*
Thank you very much	*Masha danki*
Today	*Awe*
Tomorrow	*Majan*
Welcome	*Bon bini*

The Best of the Bahamas

Just 50 miles from southeast Florida's coast, the Bahamas offer the closest off-shore warm-weather resorts to the United States. Of the chain of 700 islands totaling more than 5,300 square miles, fewer than 30 islands are inhabited. These islands are visited annually by millions (three million toured the area in 1991) seeking fine beaches, outstanding fishing waters, and championship tennis and golf facilities. The other 670 islands are undeveloped.

Many vacationers also come to the Bahamas for the glitzy casinos, Las Vegas-type nightclub shows, and the gourmet restaurants nestled in **Nassau, Freeport,** and on **Paradise Island.** Others head to the magnificent and serene **Family Islands** (a name coined by the government to reflect the character of the islands' residents), which often resemble New England fishing villages as much as tropical islands. **New Providence** and **Grand Bahama** are the only Bahamian islands that are not in the Family chain.

The best of the Bahamas includes those islands preferred by tropical travel aficionados from around the world: **Bimini, Grand Bahama,** the **Abacos, New Providence, Paradise Island, Eleuthera,** and **San Salvador.** Tourism is the Bahamas' primary industry, and some of the islands even have ongoing training programs to keep hotel service up to par. These programs aren't always effective, but service is much better than it was 20 years ago, and the Bahamian government keeps a close eye on it to ensure visitors that not only will they experience a trip of a lifetime, but that they'll want to come back to this tropical paradise again and again.

Area code 809 unless otherwise noted.

Getting to the Islands

Airports

Abacos:

Treasure Cay Airport Airways International and American Eagle serve this small airport. There's no phone at the airport (they use cellular phones).

Marsh Harbour Airport Airways International, American Eagle, Bahamasair, Gulfstream International, TWA Express, and USAir Express fly into this airport. For information, call 367.2095.

Bimini:

North Bimini Airport This airport serves international flights from Florida and other Bahamian islands via Bahamasair and Chalks International Airways. There's no phone number to call for information.

South Bimini Airport Small private planes use this tiny airport. There's no phone number to call for information.

Eleuthera:

Governor's Harbour Airport Airways International, American Eagle, and TWA Express fly into this airport. Rental cars are available. Call 322.2016 for additional information.

North Eleuthera Airport This tiny airport just north of the Glass Window Bridge is served by Airways

International, Gulfstream International, and TWA Express. Cars can be rented here. For more information, call 333.0152.

Rock Sound Airport Airways International, Gulfstream International, and TWA Express serve this

small airport between Ocean Hole Park and Winding Bay. Taxis from here are costly; for example, from Rock Sound to the Cotton Bay Club, which is a distance of about 11 miles, is a $28 fare. Rental cars are available. Call 334.2124 for information.

Grand Bahama:

Grand Bahama Airport Bahamasair, American Eagle, Comair, and TWA Express fly into this airport. Taxis are plentiful and inexpensive. The fare from the airport to Lucaya Beach is about $8 per person. Call 352.6020 for more information.

New Providence:

Nassau International Airport The airport is undergoing a $55 million expansion that will create new airways and a state-of-the-art passenger terminal, complete with shops and restaurants. Air Canada, American Airlines, Bahamasair, Carnival Airlines, Comair, Delta Air Lines, TWA Express, and USAir all fly into Nassau. Rental cars are available at the airport and at hotels. For more information, call 327.7035.

Paradise Island:

Paradise Island Airport Paradise Island Airways serves this airport on the east end of the island. Call 363.2845 for additional information.

San Salvador:

San Salvador International Airport Bahamasair flies into this airport just north of Cockburn Town, on the island's western coast. All flights require a change of planes in Nassau. There's no phone number to call for information.

FYI

Drinking

The drinking age throughout the Bahamas is 18.

Driving

Bahamians drive on the left side of the road, so use caution when making turns. The speed limit throughout the islands is 45 miles per hour.

Money

The Bahamian dollar (B$) is the official currency, but American money is accepted, too. Currency transfers must be handled through banks. Traveler's checks are accepted by most large hotels and major department stores.

Banking hours on New Providence and in Freeport are M-Th 9:30AM-3PM; F 9:30AM-5PM. The hours on the other islands vary. Banks are closed Saturday and Sunday.

Personal Safety

Visitors are advised to use the same general precautions they observe at home. Keep your valuable belongings with you or in a hotel safe-deposit box. Car-rental companies and hotel information desks

The Best of the Bahamas

will provide additional maps and information about areas to avoid.

Drugs are occasionally offered for sale on the streets, especially in Nassau and Freeport, but don't buy them. Bail is prohibited for non-Bahamians.

Phone Book

Eleuthera Tourist Office 322.2142

Ministry of Tourism, Nassau......................322.7500

Ministry of Tourism, Freeport 352.8044

Emergencies

Abacos:

Fire Department...367.2000

Health Clinic 367.2510/2481

Police...919

Bimini:

Health Clinic...347.2210

Police/Fire..919

Eleuthera:

Health Clinic 332.2774

Police/Fire..919

Freeport:

Ambulance...352.2689

Health Clinic..346.6220

Nassau:

Aircraft Crash and Rescue..........................327.7077

Ambulance...322.2221

Fire Brigade..919

Princess Margaret Hospital........................322.3877

Telephone Directory Assistance 916

United States Embassy................................322.4753

San Salvador:

Health Clinic...207

Publications

The Guardian and *The Tribune* are the major Bahamian newspapers published every day but Sunday. *The Miami Herald* and *The New York Times* are available on most islands. *The Punch,* a gossip-oriented weekly, and the *Bahama Journal* are island publications.

Tipping and Taxes

Most hotels, resorts, and restaurants automatically add a service charge to cover gratuities. If you are uncertain whether or not the charge has been added, just ask. Tips are usually 15 percent of the bill, and the departure tax is $13 per person.

Gary L. Grimaud

Bimini

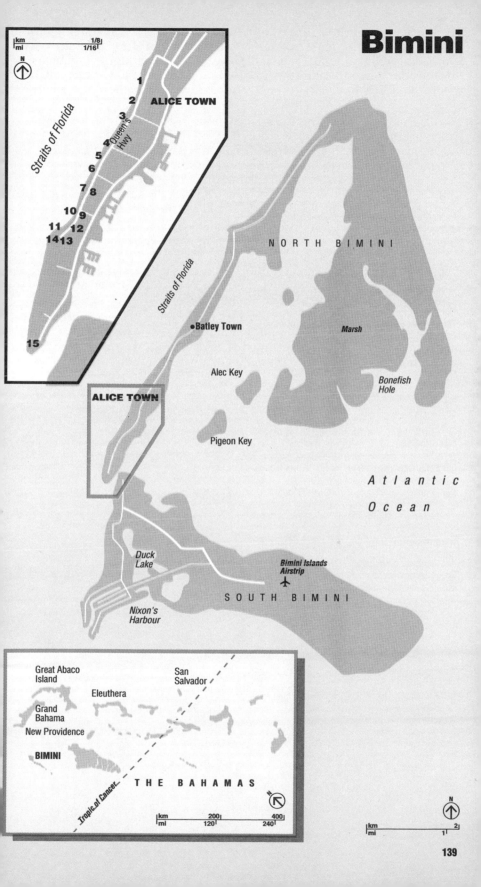

Inset (Alice Town detail):

km 1/8
mi 1/16

N

Straits of Florida

1
2
ALICE TOWN
3
4
Queen's Hwy
5
6
7
8
10 9
11 12
14 13

15

Main map:

NORTH BIMINI

Marsh

Straits of Florida

Batley Town

Alec Key

Bonefish Hole

Pigeon Key

ALICE TOWN

Atlantic

Ocean

Duck Lake

Bimini Islands Airstrip

SOUTH BIMINI

Nixon's Harbour

Bahamas locator inset:

Great Abaco Island

San Salvador

Eleuthera

Grand Bahama

New Providence

BIMINI

THE BAHAMAS

Tropic of Cancer

km 200 400
mi 120 240

N

km 2
mi 1

N

The **North and South Bimini islands** have gained renown as a premier fishing destination, and they're just 50 miles from the coast of Florida. Some even call South Bimini the game-fish capital of the world. Thousands of giant blue marlin, amberjack, bonito, tuna, tarpon, shark, and bonefish have been caught around Bimini. And the prized wahoo fish is found throughout the islands' offshore waters.

The Biminis encompass only eight square miles. South Bimini is popular with fishers, while North Bimini has enjoyed a variety of personas, but fishing and tourism remain its main industries. The Bimini islands are not the place for glamour, glitz, top-rated hotels, or restaurants; they attract those who want to fish and who love the sea. And their location has made them ideal for gun runners who smuggled weapons into the United States during the **American Revolution**, rum during **Prohibition**, and illegal drugs in recent years.

Ernest Hemingway, a Bimini aficionado, helped make the islands famous in the late 1930s. **Zane Grey**, another famous American novelist, also found the allure of fishing here too good to miss. Then **Captain Pappy Chalk's** sea-plane company began bringing great numbers of fishers to the islands, and their reputation grew even more. Soon boats from all over the United States and the Caribbean had discovered the tiny Biminis.

More fame came from the late New York Congressman **Adam Clayton Powell**, who not only fished in Bimini waters, but used the islands as a retreat from public life. And more recently, United States Senator **Gary Hart** headed toward the Biminis aboard the *Monkey Business* and not only found himself in "deep water," but out of the race for the presidential nomination.

Area code 809 unless otherwise noted.

1 End of the World Bar This is one of the oldest bars on Bimini, built during Prohibition. Very funky and with a sand floor, this bar could be a symbol of the single-mindedness of visitors to this isolated little island—the patrons come here to drink, not to admire the decor. The graffiti on the walls says many things, but note the island's credo: Let's catch

fish and have a cold one. Rustic is the operative word. ♦ Daily 11AM-closing. Queen's Hwy. No phone

2 Brown's Hotel and Dock $ **Harcourt Brown** began hosting guests in only four rooms here more than 40 years ago. Today he and his family operate 22 modest rooms and a popular marina at the same spot. Brown was a butler and bartender at **The Compleat Angler Hotel** in the 1930s, but when business slowed down during WWII, he decided to make a career as a fish-boat captain. The Browns own a lot of property on the island these days, but the sea is still their first love. ♦ Queen's Hwy. 347.2227

Within Brown's Hotel and Dock:

Brown's Restaurant and Bar $ Dine on Bahamian specialties and local fish dishes. The grouper, conch, and chowders are served with that wonderful thick-slabbed Bimini bread. ♦ Seafood ♦ M-Sa noon-10:30PM. 347.2227

3 Weech's Bay View Rooms $ Five rooms and one apartment, all with private baths, overlooking the scenic Bimini Harbour. Fishers from other islands can buy gas and wash their fresh catch at the same time at Weech's dock. ♦ Queen's Hwy (Bimini Dock). 347.2028

4 Straw Market This is one of many such markets found throughout the Caribbean. The merchandise includes tie-dyed T-shirts and a variety of straw goods—boxes, bags, hats—decorated with small shells and other island trinkets. ♦ Daily dawn-dusk. Queen's Hwy (Bimini Dock). No phone

5 The Perfume Bar Shop here for fragrances from around the world, as well as cosmetics and some souvenirs. ♦ M-Sa 9AM-5PM. Queen's Hwy, south of Bimini Dock. 347.2517

6 Butler and Sands This liquor chain has long been popular throughout the Bahamas for its selection of spirits. ♦ M-Sa 9AM-6PM. Queen's Hwy, south of Bimini Dock. 347.2202

7 The Marlin Cottage $$$ Ernest Hemingway purportedly completed the novel *To Have and Have Not* in this modest three-bedroom cottage. It was originally the guest house on an estate belonging to **Michael Lerner**, founder of Lerner Shops and a Hemingway cohort. Lerner shared the American writer's love of the sea and fishing and enjoyed the island for years. The cottage is now part of the **Blue Water Marina** complex. ♦ Queen's Hwy, south of Bimini Dock. 347.2166; fax 347.2293

8 Island House Bar Booze, island relics, and a sense of timelessness thrive here. The decor leaves something to be desired. ♦ Daily 11AM-3AM. Queen's Hwy, south of Bimini Dock. No phone

9 The Compleat Angler Hotel $$ Housing the **Ernest Hemingway Museum,** with hundreds of pictures and mementos of the great writer, the hotel has 12 rooms (Hemingway stayed in room No. 1). The *National Enquirer* took *the* picture of **Gary Hart** and **Donna Rice** here, the picture that may have done him in politically. The hotel bar is built atop rum barrels used during the island's infamous rum-running period. Bartender Morris Bowleg's **Goombay Smash** (pineapple juice, coconut rum, and grenadine) is one of the island's most popular drinks. The hotel was built in 1933 by **Helen** and **H.F. Duncombe**—he was a former commissioner of the district—with timber from an old liquor barge. The rooms are comfortable but funky—reminiscent of the thirties. ♦ Museum open daily 24 hrs. Queen's Hwy, south of Bimini Dock. 347.2122

9 Bimini Blue Water, Ltd. $$ One- and two-bedroom units are rented in **The Anchorage,** a Cape Cod-style house that's mentioned in **Ernest Hemingway's** *Islands in the Stream.* The view from here is outstanding. ♦ Queen's Hwy, south of Bimini Dock. 347.2166; fax 347.2293

10 Red Lion Pub $$ Legend has it that comics **Lucille Ball** and **Mickey Rooney** dined at the Red Lion, but the barbecued ribs and beef are no laughing matter. This is serious stuff and the Bahamian specialties— conch and grouper— aren't bad either. ♦ American/Bahamian ♦ M 11AM-2PM; Tu-Sa 11AM-2PM, 6-10:30PM. Queen's Hwy, south of Bimini Dock. 347.2259

11 Bimini Big Game Fishing Club and Hotel $$ Nassau-born **Neville Stuart** opened the club in 1945 and dozens of big names have stayed and fished here since. It was once so elegant that men not only had to wear a jacket to dinner, but a tuxedo was preferred. The contemporary celebrity list includes former **President Richard Nixon,** entertainers **Johnny Cash** and **Philip Michael Thomas,** and former US Senator **Gary Hart.** The impressive membership list boasts at least one **Rockefeller.** Owned by the **Bacardi Rum** folks, the hotel has 49 rooms, a freshwater pool, tennis courts, and a full-service marina on the premises. ♦ Queen's Hwy, south of Bimini Dock. 347.2391, 800/327.4149

Within the Bimini Big Game Fishing Club and Hotel:

Fisherman's Wharf Restaurant $$ Salads, grouper, conch, and Billy Bye's bisque—a creamy seafood soup—are the house specialties. ♦ Seafood ♦ Daily 7:30-10:30AM, 7-10PM. 347.2391

The Bahamian Kitchen $ Bahamian gumbo with conch, salt beef, and fresh veggies is a meal in itself, while traditional pepper pot takes beef stew to new island heights. ♦ Bahamian ♦ Daily noon-2:30PM, 7:30-10:30PM. 347.2391

12 Diandrea's Inn $ **Neville Stuart,** who founded the Big Game Fishing Club and Hotel across the street and brought electricity to Bimini, has been called the father of Bimini. This, his former home, is now a guest house with 14 rooms. Facilities at the Big Game Fishing Club or Blue Water are available to guests who stay here. ♦ Queen's Hwy, south of Bimini Dock. 347.2334

13 Manny's Grocery Store **Manny Rolle,** a member of the Big Game Fishing Hall of Fame who used to fish with Hemingway, now organizes a yearly wahoo tournament. His supermarket/deli/general store/sporting goods store is essentially the town center. Want to know what's happening or where the fish are biting? Ask Manny, he's an island legend. And don't miss his pickled eggs–they're a real treat. ♦ M-Sa 8AM-8PM; Su 7:30AM-noon, 2-6PM. Queen's Hwy, south of Bimini Dock. 347.2102

14 Bonefish Bill Bait, tackle, rain jackets, and plenty of fishing conversation can be found here. ♦ M-Sa 8AM-4PM. Queen's Hwy, south of Bimini Dock. No phone

14 Island Gems Jewelry, watches, and souvenirs are bought and sold under the watchful guidance of the Saunders family. **Captain Ansil Saunders** is one of many bonefish guides on the island. ♦ M-Sa 8AM-6PM. Queen's Hwy, south of Bimini Dock. 347.2098

15 Atlantis, The Lost Continent The strange formation of rocks just offshore has given many an archaeologist pause. Discovered in 1968, some think it may be the elusive lost continent, but whatever it really is, divers find the spot challenging. ♦ South end of the island

Restaurants/Clubs: Red   **Hotels:** Blue
Shops/ ♠ Outdoors: Green   **Sights/Culture:** Black

141

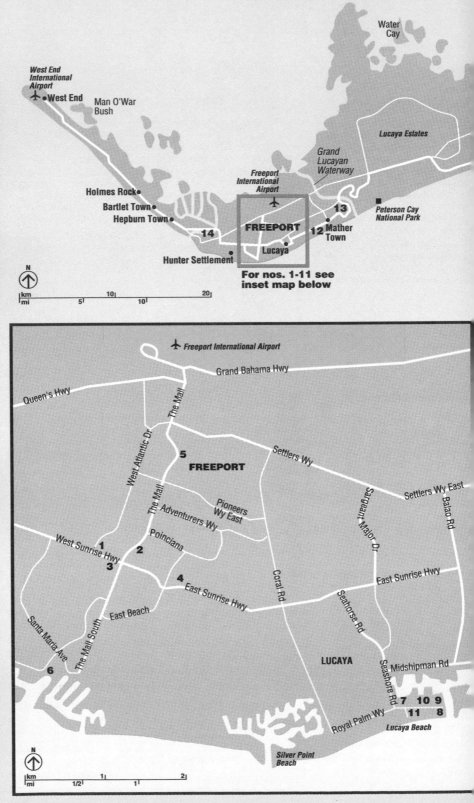

Water Cay

West End International Airport
✈ ●West End
Man O'War Bush

Lucaya Estates

Grand Lucayan Waterway

Freeport International Airport ✈

Holmes Rock●
Bartlet Town●
Hepburn Town●

14

FREEPORT

13

12 Mather Town

■ Peterson Cay National Park

●Lucaya

Hunter Settlement●

For nos. 1-11 see inset map below

N
km
mi
5   10   10   20

✈ *Freeport International Airport*

Grand Bahama Hwy

Queen's Hwy

The Mall

West Atlantic Dr.

5 **FREEPORT**

Settlers Wy

Settlers Wy East

Balao Rd

Sargeant Major Dr.

The Mall

Pioneers Wy East

Adventurers Wy

1
West Sunrise Hwy
2 Poinciana
3

East Sunrise Hwy

4 East Sunrise Hwy

Coral Rd

Seahorse Rd

East Beach

Santa Maria Ave

The Mall South

LUCAYA

Midshipman Rd

Seashore Rd

6

7 **10** **9**
11 **8**

Royal Palm Wy

Lucaya Beach

Silver Point Beach

N
km
mi
1/2   1   1   2

Grand Bahama

The island of Grand Bahama was developed as a holiday village in the early 1950s by British investor **Billy Butlin.** The project failed due to construction costs, but in the 1960s the island became a sports and beach destination. Now Grand Bahama is so popular that more than one million people visit every year.

The island has no significant history; however, to get a sense of how primitive life was on Grand Bahama before American financier **Wallace Groves** invested millions of dollars here, head out to the island's **West End.** Tiny fishing villages dot the thin strip of land between **Freeport** and the West End. For a trip back in time, pack a lunch and visit such spots as **Eight Mile Rock, Sea Grape, Holmes Rock,** and **Bottle Bay.** These wonderful old settlements maintain a Bahamian culture from days gone by that you can experience firsthand.

Grand Bahama is as flat as a pancake, but wonderful white sand beaches fringe the entire island. Most of the hotels and restaurants are located in the **Lucaya Beach** area and in Freeport on the island's southern coast. The tourist-oriented area is so spread out that most people refer to it as **Freeport/Lucaya.**

1 International Bazaar Designed originally by a Hollywood set designer as a potpourri of shops from around the world, this 10-acre complex now features dozens of T-shirt and souvenir shops. **The Midnight Sun** carries a good selection of Scandinavian glassware, and **Colombian Emeralds International** offers fine jewelry and gold watches. Choose from low-priced watches, table linens made in the Orient, and a selection of typical island items. ◆ M-Sa 9AM-6PM. W. Atlantic Dr (W. Sunrise Hwy). No phone

2 Baron's Hall Grill Room and Rotisserie ★$$ Although you drive on the left side of the road in the Bahamas, the palm trees, beaches, and heat tend to make you temporarily forget the British influence. Not here, where prime meats, fish, and fowl are prepared Brit-style. ◆ Steak/Seafood ◆ M-Sa 6-11:30PM. The Mall, across from the International Bazaar. 352.5109

3 Bahamas Princess Resort and Casino $$$ More Moorish than Moroccan, this huge Arabian fantasy is set on 2,500 acres featuring a high-rise hotel. Across the street, a country club-style hotel brings the room count to 965. Pastels and tropical prints are featured in the rooms. The Princess has 11 restaurants, ranging from casual coffee shops to gourmet establishments. The **Grete Waitz** jogging trail (named in honor of the 1984 Olympic medalist) stretches for 10 kilometers (6.2 miles) through residential neigh-

Grand Bahama

borhoods, two 18-hole golf courses, a dozen tennis courts, and two swimming pools. Service to the beach takes mere minutes. Play the slots, blackjack, roulette, and craps in the 20,000-square-foot **Princess Casino**. ◆ Casino: Daily 9AM-3:30AM. W. Sunrise Hwy (E. Mall Dr). 352.7811, 800/223.1834

Within the Bahamas Princess Resort and Casino:

Lemon Peel ★$$ Snacks and light meals, salads, burgers, and some Bahamian specialties are served at this coffee shop in the Princess Tower Hotel. ◆ American ◆ Daily 6:30AM-11PM. 352.9661

Crown Room ★★$$$ Choice meat and seafood entrées are prepared with a flair. ◆ Continental ◆ Tu-Sa 6AM-11PM. Reservations recommended. 352.7811

4 Kentucky Fried Chicken $ Try the franchised fried fowl with a Bahamian accent. Don't expect to pay what you pay at home—although it's not as pricey as hotel fare, even fast food is more costly outside of the US. ◆ Fast Food ◆ M-Th, Su 11AM-10PM; F-Sa 11AM-11PM. E. Sunrise Hwy (Somerville Dr). 373.4267. Also located at: East Mall Dr (Pioneer's Way). 352.2430

5 Freeport Inn $$ This economy motel offers 150 simply decorated rooms and a pool on the premises. Bus service to the beach is provided at the Radisson Xanadu Resort and the inn is close to shopping and restaurants. ◆ The Mall (Explorers Way). 352.6648

6 Radisson Xanadu Resort $$ The late recluse **Howard Hughes** spent time here in the mid-1970s hiding out in Penthouse C, one of four posh apartments with a view of some of the prettiest waters in the Caribbean. Only hand-selected employees served the late billionaire. At one point, when Hughes was dissatisfied with a seafood order, he decided to buy his own boats, hire a crew, and have them catch fresh seafood for him. There's not much Hughes memorabilia about, but if you ask staffers nicely you might hear tales about his ghost. Today the hotel has a new coat of paint in Art Deco colors that are sure to keep his and any other "ghosts" at bay. The color scheme clashes against this tropical setting, but the hotel's 175 rooms are all nicely done, the beach is super, and three in-house restaurants meet most culinary needs. ◆ Ocean Hill Blvd (Xanadu Beach). 352.6782, 800/333.3333

7 Port Lucaya This $10 million collection of shops and boutiques places a heavy emphasis on T-shirts and resortwear. **Gucci** and **Fendi** are the biggest designer names. ◆ M-Sa 9AM-6PM. Seahorse Rd (Royal Palm Wy). No phone

Within Port Lucaya :

Granville's Seafood Place ★$ Conch, shrimp, scallops, and chicken and ribs for landlubbers are served in this super-clean island version of a fast-food franchise. ◆ Bahamian ◆ Daily 8AM-11PM. 373.3945

China Cafe $ The self-serve specialties include a credible egg roll and other favorites. ◆ Chinese ◆ M-Sa 11:30AM-9:30PM. 373.2398

Luciano's ★★$$$ Elegant Italian and French dishes are the specialties at one of the island's most popular spots. The large dining room overlooks the water. The menu is very European. ♦ Continental ♦ M-Sa 6:30-11PM. Jacket required. Reservations required. 373.9100

Club Estee Want some music after a day on the beach? Jazz, disco, and contemporary music are on tap at Club Estee and you can hear it loud and clear. ♦ Daily 9PM-2:30AM. 373.2777

Body Talk Women's swimwear (as well as a few men's trunks) with world-famous labels such as **Gottex** from Israel, **Paul Klee** of Argentina, **Fiji for Men** of Italy, and **Lou Design** of Australia are carried here. You'll find dancewear and beach cover-ups, too. ♦ M-Sa 9AM-9PM. 373.2639

8 Lucayan Beach Resort and Casino $$$ Set along a two-mile pink sand beach, the 16-acre resort has 243 rooms with views of the water and an 18-hole golf course. After being closed for a dozen years, and several incarnations, the resort is now operated by the same people who run the Crystal Palace in Nassau. The 20,000-square-foot casino features a tropical theme. Choose from two freshwater pools and six restaurants. A family oriented musical production is performed nightly in the hotel's **Flamingo Showcase Theater.** ♦ Royal Palm Wy (Lucaya Beach). 373.7777, 800/772.1227

Within Lucayan Beach Resort and Casino:

Les Oursins ★★$$$ The name of this restaurant means sea urchins in French, and the shells are tastefully incorporated into the decor of the elegant dining room. The service is good, and the menu very French. Try the frog legs and the Bahamian lobster. ♦ French ♦ Daily 6PM-midnight. Jacket required. Reservations required. 373.7777

Hibiscus Brasserie $$ This coffee shop's broad menu offers something for everyone; unfortunately, the service is notoriously slow and the food is often served cold. ♦ Daily 11AM-4AM. 373.7777

9 Lucayan Marina Hotel $ There are 150 yacht slips and 142 hotel rooms right next to Port Lucaya and the UNEXSO scuba diving school. Water sports and access to Lucayan Beach Resort facilities are available to guests. There are also tennis courts, three PGA 18-hole golf courses, and one nine-hole course in the area. ♦ Midshipman Rd. 373.8888, 800/772.1227

10 Underwater Explorers Society (UNEXSO) This scuba-diving school trains more than 2,500 enthusiasts from around the world every year. Many tourists take the vacation opportunity to learn to scuba dive

and enjoy another great opportunity to swim with dolphins. **Treasure Reef,** where Spanish treasure was discovered in the sixties, is a popular UNEXSO dive site. ♦ M-F 9AM-6PM; Sa 9AM-5PM. Royal Palm Wy (Lucaya Beach). 373.1244, 800/992.3483

11 Radisson Holiday Beach Resort $$ The recently renovated 505-room oceanfront hotel across from Port Lucaya is ideal for family vacations. Participate in the water sports, tennis, and nearby golf. ♦ Lucaya Beach. 346.6432

12 Club Caribe ★$ Transplanted Americans **Phil** and **Bev Cave** operate the only Bahamian restaurant and bar with a Boston accent. The beachfront restaurant offers a variety of snacks and a view of Fortune Bay that fortunately doesn't bear a price tag. ♦ Bahamian ♦ Tu-Su 11AM-9PM. Midshipman Rd (Fortune Bay). 373.6866

13 Garden of the Groves Freeport's plant life is displayed for everyone to see on 11 acres with thousands of rare trees and flowers, all identified by markers. The hibiscus, crotons, and bright bougainvillea make this look like a colorful fairyland. The garden was created to honor pioneer developer **Wallace Grove** and his wife, **Georgette.** Guided tours are available. ♦ Admission. M-Sa 9AM-5PM. Midshipman Rd (E. Sunrise Hwy). 352.4045

Within the Garden of the Groves:

Grand Bahama Museum Learn more about the geography and history of the island by watching the slide shows and looking at the displays of pirates' treasures. ♦ Admission. M-F 9AM-5PM. 352.4045

14 Pier One ★★$$$ Tourists flock to Pier One (pictured above) to enjoy patio dining right on the harbor where the cruise ships come to call. Dine on oysters, mahimahi, king fish, snapper, shark, and tuna. In other words, go fish. ♦ Seafood ♦ M-Sa 11AM-10PM; Su 6-10PM. Freeport Harbour, west end of the island. Reservations required. 352.6674

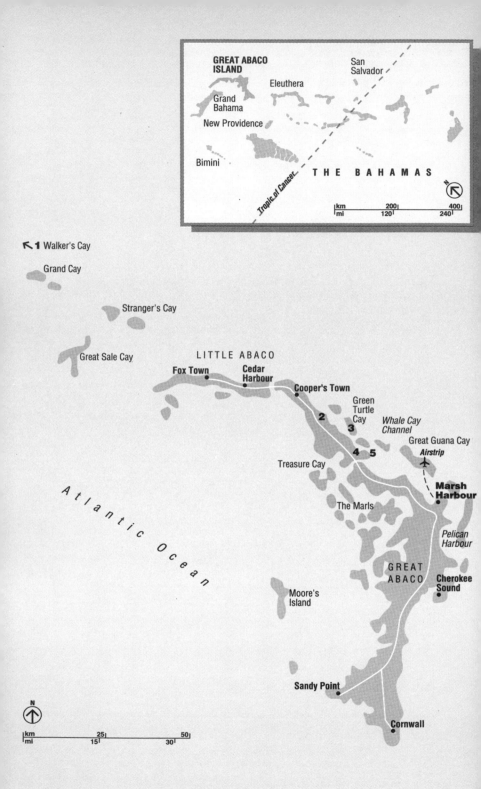

GREAT ABACO
ISLAND

San
Salvador

Eleuthera

Grand
Bahama

New Providence

Bimini

T H E   B A H A M A S

Tropic of Cancer

| km | | 200 | | 400 |
| mi | | 120 | | 240 |

↖**1** Walker's Cay

Grand Cay

Stranger's Cay

Great Sale Cay

LITTLE ABACO

Fox Town

Cedar
Harbour

Cooper's Town

Green
Turtle
Cay

2

3

*Whale Cay
Channel*

Great Guana Cay

Airstrip

4 5

Treasure Cay

**Marsh
Harbour**

A t l a n t i c   O c e a n

The Marls

*Pelican
Harbour*

**G R E A T
A B A C O**

**Cherokee
Sound**

Moore's
Island

N

| km | | 25 | | 50 |
| mi | | 15 | | 30 |

Sandy Point

Cornwall

The Abacos

The boomerang-shaped Abacos are a series of beautiful cays (pronounced *keys*) in the northern part of the Bahamas, about 160 miles north of **New Providence**. The islands' residents have been boat builders for hundreds of years. In the 19th century those who weren't building boats were generally pirates, rumrunners, and blockade runners who were hiding out in the cays. And in the 1930s, when only the wealthiest people visited these islands, the Abacos boat builders, despite their isolation, earned an international reputation for their skill in designing beautiful wooden crafts.

Even now in the 20th century the Abacos lend themselves to a solitary retreat. Many of the islands are undeveloped and uninhabited, and most don't even have electricity or running water. For the best of both worlds, tourists often stay in the resorts on **Walker's**, **Green Turtle**, and **Treasure** cays, and rent a boat to cruise around the more primitive areas.

Great Abaco and **Little Abaco** together form the main island, which stretches 130 miles north to south, and is scarcely more than five miles across. **Marsh Harbour** on Great Abaco is the third largest city in the Bahamas and the capital of the Abacos.

One of the most charming parts of these islands is along the north side of Green Turtle Cay, an area patterned after New England fishing villages. If you visit this part of the island, notice the speech patterns of the locals: Carolina colonists established plantations in the Abacos to escape British rule, and to this day the residents talk a lot like Carolinians.

Area code 809 unless otherwise noted.

1 Walker's Cay Hotel and Marina $$ The 62 rooms, white sand beaches, fine fishing waters, and full-service marina make this hotel a great catch for hundreds of fishers from all over the world. It's also the only hotel on Walker's Cay and a traditional "best" get-away. You can dine at the French-American restaurant on the premises. Water sports, tennis, volleyball, and shuffleboard are among the activities. ♦ Walker's Cay. 352.5252, 800/432.2092

2 Albert Lowe Museum and Sculpture Gardens Housed in an old private home, the museum is the focal point of the island's art community, which is growing steadily. ♦ Admission. M-Sa 9AM-4PM. Green Turtle Cay. 365.4094

2 New Plymouth Inn $$ This popular resort is in an old nine-room home filled with charm and grace and a sense of days gone by. ♦ Green Turtle Cay. 367.5211

★ ★ ★ ★ ★

3 Green Turtle Club $$ There are 30 charming rooms, some with their own docks, at this renovated inn where most of the guests are return visitors. Water sports range from snorkeling to deep-sea bone fishing, and a game of golf is available at nearby Treasure Cay. There are also plenty of tennis courts and a swimming pool if that isn't enough to keep you busy. ♦ Green Turtle Cay. 365.4272; fax 365.4272

4 Sandals Treasure Cay $$$ At one time this property—the former **Treasure Cay Resort and Marina**—was one of the most delightful in the Bahamas. It was neglected for a half dozen years until **Butch Stewart**, the Jamaican genius who created the all-inclusive couples-only Sandals Resort in Jamaica more than 10 years ago, took over

the property. Scheduled to open in 1993, the renovated Treasure Cay resort will include one hundred wonderful rooms with five tennis courts, squash and racquetball courts, three bars, three pools, and an extensive health club. ♦ Treasure Cay. 800/726.3257

5 Sandals Treasure Island $$$$ This is another **Butch Stewart** couples-only complex slated to open in 1993—a Robinson Crusoe-style, 50-suite upscale getaway. Guests are ferried across from Treasure Cay, less than six miles away. ♦ Deluxe ♦ Treasure Island. 800/726.3257

Restaurants/Clubs: Red · **Hotels:** Blue
Shops/ ♣ Outdoors: Green · **Sights/Culture:** Black

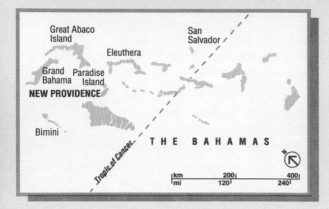

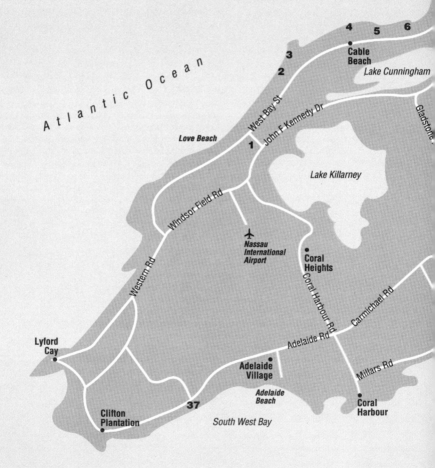

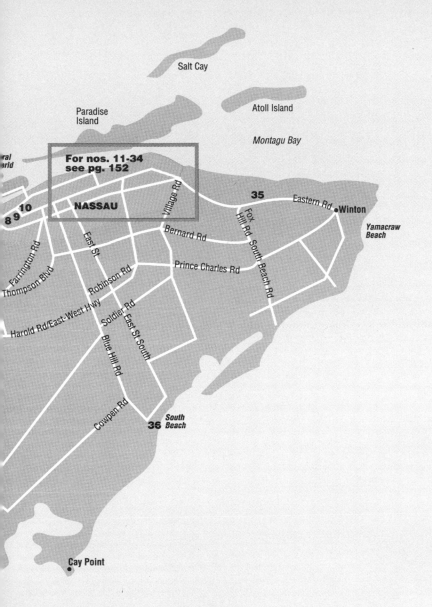

Salt Cay

Paradise
Island

Atoll Island

Montagu Bay

For nos. 11-34
see pg. 152

NASSAU

Village Rd

35

Eastern Rd •Winton

10
8 9

Farrington Rd

Thompson Blvd

East St

Bernard Rd

Fox Hill Rd

South Beach Rd

Yamacraw
Beach

Prince Charles Rd

Robinson Rd

Harold Rd/East-West Hwy

Soldier Rd

Blue Hill Rd

East St South

Cowpen Rd

36 South
Beach

Cay Point

New Providence

The historic city of **Nassau**, the capital of the Bahamas, sits on the northern side of New Providence, an island that measures only seven miles by 21 miles. Dense with palmetto and pine trees, New Providence is best known for **Cable Beach**, the luxury resort strip west of Nassau that has long been a destination for royalty and celebrities, including the Beatles at the peak of their fame.

From rock 'n' roll bands to kings and queens, the British have fostered an affinity for New Providence since 1666, when it was designated their second Caribbean colony. The first was **Charles Town** (in honor of **King Charles II**), which was later renamed Nassau. New Providence itself was originally known as Sayles Island, after **William Sayles**, the leader of the **Eleutherian Adventurers**, who settled the region.

Edward VIII of England, who became the Duke of Windsor after abdicating the throne in 1936, served as governor of Nassau in the early 1940s. His elitist cachet proved a boon to tourism, and celebrities from around the world immediately took to vacationing on the island, which is separated from **Paradise Island** by a 1,500-foot-long bridge. Now more than one million tourists visit the island annually. (A new $45 million harbor expansion program brings more than 20,000 tourists into the port each week.) A nice way to introduce yourself to the capital city is by taking a horse-and-carriage ride from **Rawson Square** north of Bay Street—opposite the statue of **Queen Victoria** in Parliament Square. The amiable guides are so well-informed, they may even recommend a new restaurant or two.

Area code 809 unless otherwise noted.

Getting around the Island
Car Rentals

Avis (International Airport)	327.7121/7182	National (British Colonial)	325.3716
Avis (Nassau)	326.6380	National (International Airport)	327.8300
Avis (Paradise Island)	363.2061	Wallace's U-Drive It	393.0650
Budget (International Airport)	327.7405	**Motorbikes, Motorcycles, Motor Scooters**	
Budget (Paradise Island)	363.3095	Bowe's Scooter Rentals	326.8329
Hertz (Ambassador Beach Hotel)	327.6866	B&S Scooter Rentals	322.2580
Hertz (International Airport)	327.6321	Cable Beach	327.6000 ext. 6374

---

1 **Conference Corner** The late President **John F. Kennedy,** British Prime Minister **Harold Macmillan,** and Canadian Prime Minister **John Diefenbaker** planted three trees at this street corner to mark their 1962 meeting in Nassau to discuss the future of Britain's independent nuclear force. ♦ Blake Rd (W. Bay St)

2 **Casuarina's Apartment Hotel** $$ Nassau businesswoman and civic leader **Nettie Symonette** operates the complex of 74 studio and two- and three-bedroom apartments. Afternoon tea is a must, a "veddy-British" tradition found in a few spots on the island. The resort has a pool and a small, pretty beach. ♦ W. Bay St (Delaporte Beach). 327.7921

New Providence

Within Casuarina's Apartment Hotel:

Round House Restaurant ★★$$ The **Fit for Life Diet** of various veggies and fruits highlights the menu. Owner **Nettie Symonette** is a devotee of diet authors Harvey and Marilyn Diamond, and she's created some inspired recipes designed to help guests lose weight. Entrées include broccoli or celery chicken and fresh fish with lots of protein and little fat. ♦ American ♦ M, W-Su 8AM-9:30PM. Reservations recommended. 327.7921

3 **Le Meridian Royal Bahamian** $$$$ This French-accented resort *avec* a full-service

spa was built in 1954. The former **Balmoral Beach Hotel's** 169 manor-house rooms and self-contained villas are all quite large. The **Meridian Company** is completely renovating the rooms, one floor at a time. It took $6 million to finish the sixth (top) floor and the money was well spent. Lovely green marble baths and island-inspired furniture are nice additions to the already commodious rooms. Ferry service from the hotel's dock takes guests to a nearby desert island for privacy and fine bathing beaches, although the resort is situated on one of the broadest stretches of sand in town. Water sports and aerobics classes are available, as well as two tennis courts. Guests can play golf at the three courses in Nassau. ♦ W. Bay St (Cable Beach). 327.6400, 800/543.4300; fax 327.6961

4 **Nassau's Crystal Palace Resort and Casino** $$$ With 1,550 rooms, the Crystal Palace is the largest hotel in the Bahamas—and possibly the largest purple hotel in the world. Owned by **Carnival Cruise Lines** and **Continental Company,** the resort is colorful to say the least. Architect **Joe Farcus**—who also designs Carnival cruise ships—used the color purple as the predominant hue in the hotel's interior and exterior design. Even the beach furniture is lavender and pink. The hotel, which consists of five towers, cost more than $250 million to build. It dominates Nassau's "Bahamian Riviera" area, right at Cable Beach (where, in 1907, underwater telephone cables first connected the island to

the US). Don't miss the **Yaacov Agam** kinetic sculpture in the lobby. In addition to a 35,000-square-foot casino, the Crystal Palace offers sailing, snorkeling, windsurfing, waterskiing, and a wacky water slide that can accommodate the whole family at the same time. Tennis courts are located across the street and golf is available at Crystal Palace's own course. Each of the hotel's suites is unique, ranging from subtle Japanese decor to a more outspoken Moroccan motif. There's even an outrageous Galactica Suite complete with Ursula, its own robot. Choose from the 19 dining establishments and bars on the premises. ♦ W. Bay St (Cable Beach). 327.6200, 800/222.7466

Within Nassau's Crystal Palace Resort and Casino:

Palace Theater $$$ See a Las Vegas-type nightclub review with topless dancers, comics, a magician, and more. Acts vary, so call for show times. ♦ 327.6200 (ask for the box office)

Sol e Mare ★★★$$ This beautifully decorated restaurant features a touch of Italy and specializes in Continental ambience. Traditional veal dishes are done well and their version of Caesar salad is above reproach. As if the fine cuisine wasn't enough, the restaurant overlooks the ocean; the sunsets are outstanding. ♦ Italian ♦ Daily 6-11PM. Reservations recommended. 327.6200

Oriental Palace ★★$$ Fairly excellent food is served in a beautiful atmosphere. The Peking shrimp appetizer is especially spicy, but delicious; the chicken dishes are quite good; and the *moo shu* pancakes are only so-so. The portions are large. ♦ Chinese ♦ Daily 6-11PM. Reservations recommended. 327.6200

Le Grille ★★$$$ Fish, seafood, and a fairly decent selection of steak and lamb are served in a quietly elegant dining room above the casino. High rollers and tourists alike enjoy the European-style ambience. ♦ Continental ♦ Daily 6-11PM. Reservations recommended. 327.6200

Bay Street Shopping Map

GEORGE STREET

Gold & Coral Factory *jewelry*	**Barry's** *clothing*
Colony Place Arts & Crafts Center *native art*	**Lightbourn's** *fragrances*
The Perfume Bar *fragrances*	**Treasure Traders** *crystal, china*
Beaumont Liquor Store	**Valentines** *fine jewelry*
Watch Out *watches*	**Tick-Tock** *clocks, watches*
Mademoiselle *clothing*	
Treasures *T-shirts*	
Straw Market *straw goods*	

(BAY STREET runs vertically between columns)

MARKET STREET

Cameo Parfums
fragrances
Johnson Bros.
jewelry, maps
The Island Shop
sweaters, cameras
The Beauty Spot
fragrances, cosmetics

FREDERICK STREET

The Linen Shop *fine linens*	**Nassau Shop** *clothing, jewelry,*
Fendi *leather goods*	*watches, gifts*
Little Switzerland *jewelry*	

CHARLOTTE STREET

Bernard's
china, crystal
Little Switzerland
fragrances, gifts
Guccini
jewelry
Alexandra's
jewelry
d'Orsy's
fragrances

PARLIAMENT STREET

BANK LANE

Gucci
leather goods

Goombay Mama ★★$$ Bahamian specialties prepared here include seafood gumbo, conch chowder, grouper fingers, and ribs. ♦ Bahamian ♦ W-Su noon-8PM. 327.6200

New Providence

5 Nassau Beach Resort Club $$$ When the worldwide **Forte** group took over the resort in 1990, a clublike atmosphere was created from the ever-popular Cable Beach destination. Each of the 411 rooms includes a balcony or patio. The attractive decor has a tropical theme. Other amenities include a pro shop, six tennis courts, two restaurants, two lounges, and a shopping arcade. Continental breakfast is offered daily in the Club Lounge. ♦ W. Bay St (Cable Beach). 327.7711, 800/225.5843

Restaurants/Clubs: Red   **Hotels:** Blue
Shops/ 🌳 **Outdoors:** Green   **Sights/Culture:** Black

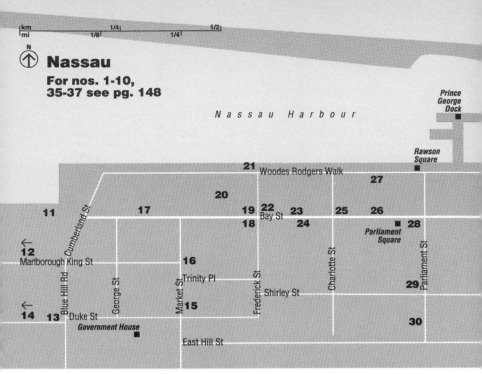

N a s s a u   H a r b o u r

Prince
George
Dock

Rawson
Square

21 Woodes Rodgers Walk

27

20

11   17   19 22 23   25   26
              18 Bay St   24

Cumberland St

12
Marlborough King St   16

Parliament
Square   28

Charlotte St

Parliament St

Trinity Pl

George St

Market St

Blue Hill Rd

Frederick St

Shirley St

29

14 13 Duke St   15
Government House

East Hill St

30

6 Wyndham Ambassador Beach Hotel $$$

The hotel's 400 rooms surround the lush tropical grounds like a horseshoe, and most rooms feature a view of the ocean. The rooms are on the large side, and those fronting the beach are rather grand. In addition to the pool area and beach, there are two restaurants, tennis courts, and guests have access to the Crystal Palace Golf Course. The usual water sports are also available. ♦ W. Bay St (Cable Beach). 327.8231, 800/822.4200; fax 327.6727

7 Coral World Bahamas

There's nothing "fishy" about this collection of sea life. The marine park features an underground observatory of sharks, moray eels, and hundreds of other creatures in all sizes and shapes. A snor-

New Providence

kel trail enables you to see the sea up close and personal. There are also a restaurant and gift shop on the grounds. ♦ Admission. Daily 9AM-6PM. Silver Cay, just off the main harbor entrance to Nassau. 328.1036

7 Coral World International $$$

Imagine 22 luxurious and tastefully decorated villas—each with its own private pool—facing the Atlantic. Got it? Then you've pictured this unique and impressive resort. The villas are the ultimate hideaways, complete with stocked refrigerator/freezers. Breakfast is delivered to your room—or left for you to pick up when you're ready. The view of the ocean from the bathtub is remarkable. ♦ Silver Cay. 328.1036, 800.221.0203

8 Ardastra Gardens and Zoo

Featuring the only zoo on the island, the gardens are set in almost five acres of lush, junglelike surroundings. Self-guided tours are clearly marked. See the daily parade of marching flamingos (the national bird of the Bahamas) daily at 11AM, 2PM, and 4PM. They nest and make their home around Lake Rosa on the Inagua islands, just southeast of Nassau. ♦ Admission. Daily 9AM-5PM. Chippingham Rd, 1 mile west of the British Colonial Beach Resort. 323.5806

9 Botanic Gardens

A potpourri of tropical plants, bushes, and flowering shrubs flourish in an 18-acre natural setting. Stroll along the garden's trails, past two lily ponds and a lovely grotto. ♦ M-F 8AM-4:30PM; Sa-Su 9AM-4PM. Chippingham Rd (W. Bay St). 323.5975

9 Fort Charlotte

The imposing late 18th-century fort has recently been restored. The **Earl of Dunmore,** also known as **Viscount Fincastle** and "His Excellency the Governor," built the fort of solid bedrock to guard Nassau Harbour. See **Queen Victoria's** monogram on the cannons. A guided tour includes the deep, dank dungeons. ♦ Admission. M-Sa 9AM-4PM. Chippingham Rd (W. Bay St). 325.9186

10 Tony Romas ★$$

The kind of portion-packed, mass-produced rib dinners designed to make Americans feel at home are served here. Try the cracked conch instead. ♦ American ♦ Daily 11AM-midnight. W. Bay St (Saunders Beach). 325.2020. Also located at: Paradise Island Bridge. 393.2077

Restaurants/Clubs: Red   Hotels: Blue
Shops/ 🌳 Outdoors: Green   **Sights/Culture:** Black

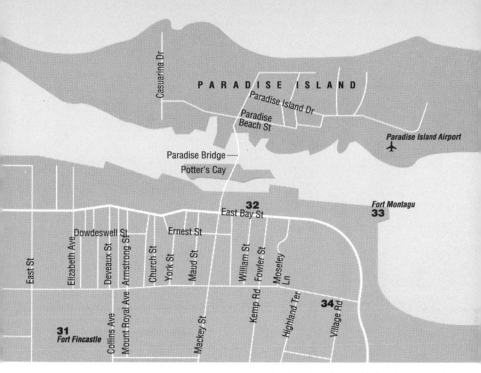

EL GRECO

10 **El Greco Hotel** $$ This family run Spanish-themed hotel is near Bay Street shopping. The rooms are nice, but fairly standard. ♦ W. Bay St (Saunders Beach). 325.1121

10 **Drumbeat Supper Club** $$$ This colorful evergreen night spot has developed a reputation for quality island entertainment. Limbo and calypso music are featured in two nightly dinner shows. ♦ Bahamian ♦ M, W-F 8:30-10:30PM; Tu, Sa 8-10PM. W. Bay St, 3 blocks west of the British Colonial Beach Resort. Reservations recommended. 322.4233

11 **British Colonial Beach Resort** $$ A 350-room landmark hotel heralds the start of Bay Street's renowned shopping area and has been a pink beacon of Nassau's tourist industry for more than 50 years. Built on the site of **Fort Nassau,** the oldest of Nassau's forts, the hotel is a veteran of several corporate entities (it was a Sheraton at one time and is now a Best Western property) and is the oldest continually operated hotel in the Bahamas. The "BC," as it has been called for generations, probably offers the best in-town location and is extremely popular with European vacationers. As the "Grand Dame of Nassau Tourism," she's been enlarged several times, so some rooms are smaller than others. The furnishings are standard throughout. The beach and harbour views are startling. ♦ Bay St (Marlborough St). 322.3301

Within the British Colonial Beach Resort:

Blackbeard's Forge ★★$$ Daily specials and three-course meals have been drawing

locals and tourists to this hotel restaurant for years. Try any of the conch dishes and save room for the memorable coconut cream layer cake, a Bahamian treat that's done especially well here. ♦ Steaks/Caribbean ♦ Daily 6-10PM. 322.3301

12 **Ambrosine** Discounted **Diane Freis** dresses and **Fila** sportswear are carried by this pleasantly designed boutique with an agreeable staff headed by owner **Rosemary Appleyard.** ♦ M-Sa 9AM-5PM. Marlborough St, across from the British Colonial Beach Resort. 322.4205. Also at: International Bazaar, Bay St. 322.2676

12 **Marlborough Antiques** **Brent Malone** and **June Knight,** a pair of transplanted Brits, operate the charming shop filled with antique maps, prints, books, and engravings. Malone has created some of his own interesting etchings of Lucayans (early Bahamians). **Crabtree &**

Evelyn products are also carried here. ♦ M-Sa 10AM-5:30PM. Bay St (Marlborough St). 328.0502

12 **Coco's Cafe** $ Snacks, burgers, and salads provide a nice balance to the usual cracked conch and steamed fish. ♦ American ♦ Daily 7:30AM-11PM. Marlborough St (Cumberland St). 323.8778

13 **Graycliff** ★$$$ For more than 250 years Graycliff has been a name to contend with in Nassau for those international travelers opting for the "lifestyles of the rich and famous." Years ago, when it was a private home owned by a British duke, Graycliff's guests included **Winston Churchill,** many European royals, and the late **Ari Onassis.** The menu tends to adapt Bahamian specialties to European cuisine. Expect dishes such as Bahamian crawfish in puff pastry with cream and saffron or grilled spiny lobster with two sauces. The food can be somewhat disappointing but the service remains elegant. Lace tablecloths and lace-trimmed napkins complement the fine china. There's no air-conditioning, so ask for a table near the window. If your expectations aren't too high, ambience and history may suffice. ◆ Continental ◆ Daily noon-2:30PM, 7-9PM. Reservations recommended. West Hill St (Bay St). 322.2796

14 Buena Vista ★★★$$$ This old island home features outstanding cuisine. Local grouper, done just about any way at all, is at its best here. Even better, the service and atmosphere are absolutely superb. ◆ Continental/Bahamian ◆ M-Sa 7-10:30PM. Delancy St, near Bay St. Reservations required. 322.2811

15 St. Michael's Merchandise marketed throughout the United Kingdom can be found in the popular **Marks & Spencer** stores. Select from toiletries, food items, lingerie, and men's and women's casualwear. ◆ M-Sa 9AM-5:30PM. Market St (Duke St). 322.4334

16 Choosy Foods ★$ **Ralph Wood** and **Derek Whyms** run Choosy Foods, a salads and snacks take-out deli, and Chatters, a formal restaurant. Choosy is a great place to pick up picnic items or what Bahamians call "walking-around food." ◆ Caribbean/Deli ◆ M-Sa 11:30AM-9:15PM. Market St (Trinity Place). 326.5232

16 Chatters ★★$$ The more formal of the Wood-Whyms dual restaurants offers an innovative and eclectic menu featuring conch Parmesan and seafood crepes. The pretty and exceptionally clean surroundings have an almost Californian feel, with lots of plants. ◆ American/Caribbean ◆ M-Sa 11:30AM-

New Providence

3PM, 7-10:30PM. Market St (Trinity Place). Reservations required. 326.6447

17 Gold and Coral Factory Interesting cameos and unusual jewelry are sold here at discounted prices. ◆ M-Sa 9AM-5PM. Bay St (Market St). 326.6668

17 Colony Place Arts and Crafts Center Local artists show their stuff, which ranges from batik work to hand-painted T-shirts and vivid paintings representing native art in all its brilliantly hued glory. ◆ M-Sa 9AM-5PM. Bay St (Market St). 326.6049

18 The Perfume Bar Fine fragrances from around the world are available for less than in the states. ◆ M-Sa 9AM-5:30PM. Bay St (Market St). 322.8913. Also at: Prince George Plaza, Savoy, International Bazaar, East St

19 Watch Out Every watch carried here has an interesting and different face. Gambling motifs are a big theme, and Bahamian stamp faces are popular. ◆ M-Sa 9:30AM-5:15PM. Bay St (Market St). 322.2102

19 Mademoiselle This chain store has been popular with tourists for several generations, featuring men's casualwear and clothing, including some trendy designer clothes for women. ◆ M-Sa 9AM-5PM. Bay St (Market St). 322.5132

20 Straw Market Rawson Square was the original site for this market, but the demand for hand-crafted hats, bags, dolls, and mats grew so large that it was moved two blocks west. Some say this is the largest straw market in the world. If you want to see some great—and also some perfectly ordinary—straw goodies, don't miss it. ◆ M-Sa 9AM-5PM. Bay St (Market St). No phone

21 Arcade Takeaway $ The snacks served here include typical Bahamian grouper cutlets, steamed fish, peas and rice, cole slaw, and macaroni. ◆ Bahamian ◆ Daily 7AM-4PM. Frederick St (Woodes Rogers Walk). No phone

22 The Linen Shop Since the mid-1940s this shop has featured outstanding linen goods. Most of the merchandise comes from the Orient, as well as Switzerland, Ireland, and the UK. The hand embroidery on much of the work is superb. Generations of Floridians have collected their trousseaus here. ◆ M-Sa 9AM-5PM. Bay St (Frederick St). 322.4266

23 Oriental Express ★$ The traditional Chinese menu is enhanced by the excellent speedy service. Try the chow mein. ◆ Chinese ◆ M, Th, Su 11:30AM-9PM; Tu-W, F-Sa 11:30AM-10PM. Bay St (Frederick St). 326.7110

24 Little Switzerland Throughout the major Caribbean islands Little Switzerland stores draw visitors to their imaginative displays of a wide array of merchandise. This branch carries only jewelry and fine watches. At the Little Switzerland store across the street, you can select from china, crystal, fragrances, and gifts. If you want a name-brand high-priced gift item, chances are Little Switzerland carries it. The selection includes **Rolex, Vacheron & Constantin, Rado, Lalique, Baccarat,** and **Hummel.** ◆ M-Sa 8:30AM-5:30PM. Bay St (Frederick St). 322.2201. Also at: Charlotte St, W. Bay St, major hotels

25 International Bazaar The unique shops featured here include **Las Tienda,** for leather goods and gift items from South America, and **Crystal Collection,** offering **Zawierce** hand-cut crystal from Poland. ◆ M-Sa 9:30AM-5PM. Bay St (Charlotte-Parliament Sts). No phone

Restaurants/Clubs: Red   **Hotels:** Blue
Shops/ 🌴 **Outdoors:** Green   **Sights/Culture:** Black

26 Prince George Plaza Walk down to **Prince George Dock,** where 30 or more Caribbean cruise ships are lined up alongside private yachts. The mall-like collection of boutiques includes **Athena,** with its gauzy Greek clothing and leather goods; the ubiquitous **Benetton; Le Bon,** for men's dress clothes; and **Purse String,** featuring accessories, handbags, and leather goods. ♦ M-Sa 9AM-5PM. Bay St (Charlotte-Parliament Sts). No phone

27 Prince George Dockside Restaurant ★★$$ Cruise-ship passengers tired out from shopping often stop here for a drink, salad, or sandwich. Fettuccine with salmon, spaghetti with conch, and chicken and ribs are popular orders. The Greek salad is a tasty lunch item. It's a great place to people-watch and keep an eye on your ship—or any other floating hotel in port. ♦ American/Bahamian ♦ M-Sa 11AM-11PM. Woodes Rodgers Walk (Charlotte St). 322.5854

28 Cole's of Nassau The mother-daughter team of **Marion** and **Diane Morley** operates one of downtown's most popular boutiques, with a great selection of trendy sportswear, shoes, silks, knits, and designer lines. ♦ Daily 9AM-5:30PM. Off Parliament St (Rawson Square). 322.8393. (Another branch of this shop is located at Marathon Mall)

29 Parliament St. Restaurant $$ Across the street from the government buildings, this is where Nassau's movers and shakers choose to dine on the "Bahamian Power Lunch." Expect meat-and-potatoes dishes. ♦ American/Bahamian ♦ M-F 10AM-4:30PM. Parliament St (Shirley St). 322.2837

29 The English Shop If it's a gift item from the United Kingdom—linens, knits, men's ties, **Aynsley** china—you'll probably find it here. ♦ M-Sa 9AM-5PM. Parliament St (Shirley St). 322.4420

30 Calypso Treasures The friendly shop is filled with T-shirts, jewelry, and kitschy limboland souvenirs. ♦ M-Sa 9AM-5PM. Parliament St (Shirley St). 357.6622

30 Pick-a-Dilly at the Parliament ★★$$ Famed for its banana daiquiris (but try the mango, soursop, guava, papaya, or pineapple versions, as well), this restaurant across from the govern-ment buildings gets big play from tourists, legislators, and locals. Cracked conch, coconut shrimp, and other island dishes share menu honors with stir fry and pasta specialties. ♦ American/Bahamian ♦ M-Sa 11:30AM-2:30PM, 5:30-10PM. 18 Parliament St (Shirley St). 322.2836

30 Pick-a-Dilly Bed & Breakfast $ With seven comfortable rooms, this small inn is centrally located and popular with business executives and government players. The guestrooms are attractive, but not luxurious. ♦ 18 Parliament St (Shirley St). 322.2836

31 Queen's Staircase Eighteenth-century slaves carved the 66 steps named for Queen Victoria out of solid limestone at the end of **Elizabeth Avenue.** Each step commemorates a year of her long reign (one step has since become part of the pavement). Atop the stair-case see **Blackbeard's Tower,** which stands 126 feet high and provides a perfect spot to photograph Nassau, the harbour, and nearby islands. The stairs also lead to **Fort Fincastle.** ♦ Elizabeth Ave

31 Fort Fincastle Lord Dunmore built the ship-shaped building in 1793 to protect his harbour. The fort has not been well-main-tained, but the old guns remain and the view is spectacular. ♦ Daily dawn-dusk. Elizabeth Ave (Queen's Staircase). No phone

32 Hartley's Undersea Walk Go beneath the ocean to view coral rock and magnificent tropical fish and to watch sponges breathe. **Christopher Hartley,** who has been diving since the day after his first birthday, shares the experience with visitors who board the yacht *Pied Piper.* ♦ Admission. Daily 9:30AM, 1:30PM. Nassau Yacht Haven, E. Bay St, 2 blocks east of Paradise Island Bridge. 393.8234

33 Fort Montagu Built in 1741, this is Nassau's smallest and oldest remaining fort. It played a role in the American Revolution when **George Washington** sent his navy to occupy His Maj-esty's fortification. ♦ Daily dawn-dusk. Bay St (Montagu Bay). No phone

34 Tamarind Hill Restaurant ★$$ Grouper in a nut crust will tempt even those who normally don't eat fish. Sandwiches are served all day. ♦ Seafood ♦ Daily 11AM-midnight. Village Rd (E. Bay St). 393.1306

35 Blackbeard's Tower One of the highest points on Nassau, these are the remains of a watch tower purportedly used by **Edward "Blackbeard" Teach,** the infamous pirate. He supposedly monitored passing ships from this point, deciding which ones he'd welcome—and then loot. A tiny footpath on the south side of the road can be climbed to the ruin for a panoramic view of the island. ♦ Daily dawn-dusk. Eastern Rd (an extension of E. Bay St)

New Providence

36 Makeba Beach Hotel and Lounge ★$ This tiny dining room features steamed turtle steak, steamed and cracked conch, and fried jack and snapper. Enjoy a cold Bahamian beer and an out-of-the-way view that most tourists miss. ♦ Bahamian ♦ Daily 8AM-midnight. South Shore (South Beach). 361.4596

37 Divi Bahamas Beach Resort Club $$$ Newer rooms feature Jacuzzis, but guests come to this 250-room property when they want to get away from the hustle and bustle of Nassau or Paradise Island. It's certainly away from it all. There's a golf course and water sports galore. ♦ S. Ocean Beach. 362.4391

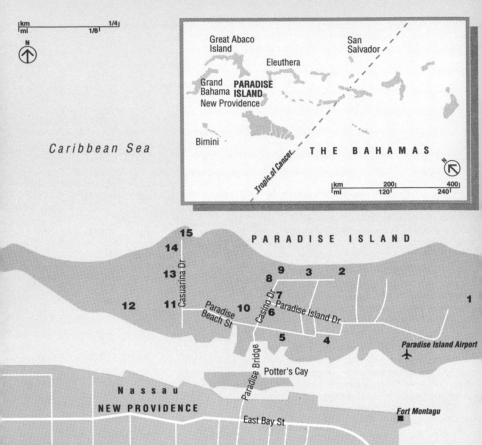

Paradise Island

This tiny strip of land located just off the northern tip of **New Providence** island was once called **Hog Island** (the first settlers on many of the Bahamian islands discovered wild hogs running around). The name was hardly appropriate for this beautiful tropical gateway, which measures only four-and-a-half miles by two miles.

Paradise Island was developed within the last 30 years to meet the demands of tourists. It offers white sand beaches, a golf course, tennis courts, shopping galore, and a variety of hotels and restaurants. A casino, the centerpiece of the **Resorts International** complex, is the focal point of the island.

Paradise's **Porcupine Club** was a fortress of wealthy Americans in the early 1900s The membership rosters read like a Who's Who of that era's financial circles, including the requisite **Vanderbilts, Cabot Lodges, Mellons, Morgans,** and **Astors.** (Club Med was built on the social club's exclusive property in 1977.)

Swedish industrialist **Dr. Axel Wenner-Gren** purchased this island in 1939 to develop a major international tourist resort. He then turned around and sold the island to A&P supermarkets heir **Huntington Hartford** for less than $10 million, and in 1962 Hartford convinced the government to change the island's name from Hog to Paradise.

Beginning in the late 1960s, Resorts International (now owned by **Merv Griffin**), began turning the island into a tourist mecca, building the **Paradise Island Hotel** adjacent to the Resorts casino. Twenty years later Griffin formed **Paradise Island Airways** and built a new airport at the island's east end, eliminating the long taxi ride to Paradise from the International Airport in Nassau. Now the island is truly an accessible tropical paradise.

1 Paradise Island Golf Course Two holes on the 18-hole course, home of the **Bahamas Golf Classic,** were redesigned to accommodate a runway of the Paradise Island Airport. With water on three sides, seemingly on a land spit jutting into the sea, some of the holes are quite beautiful. The PGA-sanctioned course was designed by golf pro **Dick Wilson.** ♦ Daily dawn-dusk. Far east end of the island. 363.3000

2 Ocean Club $$$$ Set across from the **Cloisters** (a re-created 14th-century French-Augustine cloister, complete with wonderful statues), the 70-unit Ocean Club features luxurious grounds with an elegant pond and a large pool. This was once an ultraposh private home and the grand style lives on. There's golf and tennis nearby. ♦ Deluxe ♦ Paradise Island Dr, east of Casino Dr. 363.3000, 800/321.3000

3 Sunrise Beach Club and Villas $$$ European-style one-, two-, and three-bedroom units are set in beautiful tropical gardens with two pools on a lovely three-mile-long beach. ♦ Paradise Island Dr, east of Casino Dr. 363.2234, 800/451.6078; fax 363.2252

4 Paradise Island Fun Club $$$ Honest, that's the name of this 250-room hotel on the edge of Nassau Harbour. Formerly the Flagler Inn, then the Harbour Cove, the hotel is building an enormous water park on the property. Myriad sports and games are geared to put the fun into a fundamentally enjoyable vacation. ♦ Paradise Island Dr, east of Casino Dr. 363.2561, 800/952.2426; fax 363.3803

5 Hurricane Hole Shopping Plaza Across from the marina at the foot of the Paradise Island Bridge, the new center offers a cross-section of typical island shops, plus a large airy supermarket with a drugstore and deli. ♦ M-Sa 9AM-6PM. Harbour Dr (Hurricane Hole Marina). 363.2245

Within Hurricane Hole Shopping Plaza:

Little Switzerland This shop carries the usual array of fragrances, jewels, watches, crystal, and china. **Ebel, Lladro,** and **Waterford** are part of the name game at this new branch of the Caribbean-wide chain. ♦ M-Sa 9:30AM-6PM. 363.3309

Cooper's Art Gallery Handmade jewelry and T-shirts, as well as paintings depicting island people, boats, and ocean scenes are showcased in this gallery. ♦ M-Sa 9AM-5PM. 363.2269

The Perfume Bar Like at its Nassau sister store, fragrances from Europe and the US are sold at discounted prices. ♦ M-Sa 9AM-6PM. 363.2397

Crown Jewelers Here you'll find the typical array of island memorabilia (shells and starfish) in gold, plus more traditional 14-karat jewelry, chains, watches, and more. ♦ M-Sa 9AM-9PM; Su 9AM-5:30PM. 363.2219

6 Paradise Cove Shopping Center Most of the tourist-oriented stores carry T-shirts and some reasonably priced sportswear. ♦ M-Sa 9AM-6PM. Casino Dr, across from the casino. No phone

Within Paradise Cove Shopping Center:

Paradise Island News Stand American newspapers, books, toiletries, and T-shirts are carried here. ♦ M-Sa 9AM-6PM; Su 9AM-5PM. 363.2792

Three Sisters Irish linens, as well as ladies sandals and silk eyeglass cases and lingerie bags, and other items from the Orient, are sold here. ♦ M-Sa 9AM-5:30PM. 363.3151

Pipe of Peace This is one of several island stores featuring tobacco products, jewelry, sportswear, and T-shirts. ♦ M-Sa 8:30AM-5:30PM. 363.2904

Paradise Island Wines and Spirits This is a good pit stop for ice-cold soda, mixers, and snacks, plus a complete line of liqueurs. ♦ M-Sa 9AM-9PM. 363.2272

7 Comfort Suites $$ This was the first hotel built on the island in the 1990s. **Bill Naughton,** who has a long history as general manager of the **British Colonial** in Nassau, has gathered a staff of veteran hotel personnel to run this pretty low-rise property. A shell motif is carried out in the furnishings, wall paper, carpeting, and even the tiles of the large swimming pool. Relax and enjoy the grand landscaping around the pool, equipped with a swim-up bar. There's a walkway to the beach and casino. Continental breakfast is served daily. ♦ Off Casino Dr (Paradise Island Dr). 363.3680, 800/228.5150

8 Paradise Island Resort and Casino $$$ The 30,000-square-foot casino is smack in the heart of the island. Guests meander through the hotel lobbies to the shops, restaurants, and the casino. Not only are there two pools, 1,200 rooms, a health club, and 21 tennis courts, there's also more than two miles of white sand beach. The rooms are lavish and the suites even more magnificent, but the standard rooms are standard. A concierge level offers very luxurious VIP treatment. ♦ Casino Dr (Paradise Island Dr). 363.3000

Paradise Island

Within Paradise Island Resort and Casino:

Cafe Casino $$ Deli-type snacks range from Reuben sandwiches to pizza and tuna salad. Conch fritters is the designated Bahamian menu item. ♦ American ♦ Daily 11AM-3AM. 363.3000

Villa d'Este ★★$$$ Pasta, veal, and seafood dishes are prepared with gusto. Shrimps sautéed in garlic and herbs served over a bed of fettuccine is a house specialty. The elegant decor adds to the pleasing ambience. ♦ Italian ♦ M-Tu, Th-Su 6:30-11PM. Reservations recommended. 363.3000

Bahamian Club ★★★$$$$ Many years ago this restaurant was part of a casino housed in the elegant Georgian building on Bay Street. Now a popular and elegant establishment, the classic British and Caribbean specialties continue to attract return visitors. Rack of lamb and broiled lobster are notable dishes. ♦ English/Bahamian ♦ M, W-Su 6:30-11PM. Jacket required. Reservations required. 363.3000

Le Cabaret Theatre The Las Vegas-type review features scantily clad women, singers, magicians, and more in a usually excellent production. ♦ Showtimes vary. 363.3000

The Grill Room ★$$$ Service is sometimes slow, but the food—fish, seafood, grilled meat, and poultry—is generally quite good and worth the wait. ♦ American ♦ M-Tu, Th-Su 6:30-11PM. Reservations recommended. 363.3000

Coyaba ★$$ This island version of the Orient features fish and seafood. The attractive decor enhances the traditional menu of delicacies such as Triple Dragon (pork, chicken and shrimp). ♦ Chinese ♦ Tu-Su 6:30-11PM. 363.3000

Gulfstream ★★$$$ Fish and seafood, especially local offerings, are prepared in various ways. Grouper and snapper are popular choices. ♦ Seafood ♦ Tu-Su 6:30-11PM. Reservations recommended. 363.3000

Cafe Martinique ★★★$$$ This is probably the most famous Paradise Island restaurant—**James Bond** ate here in the film *Thunderball*. The views and soufflés are both breathtaking. The restaurant was built on the site of Swedish developer **Dr. Axel Wenner-Gren's** boathouse. Seafood, steak, and breast of pheasant round out the menu. All in all, dining here is a memorable experience. ♦ Continental ♦ M-Sa 7-11PM; Su 11:30AM-2:20PM, 7-11PM. Reservations required. 363.3000

9 Sheraton Grand Hotel and Towers $$$ Opened in 1983, the hotel's 360 rooms are beautifully decorated in a tropical theme: bright flowers, lots of citrus colors, and an ambience that says "let's enjoy." The towers offer VIP comforts, including personalized check-in (that

Paradise Island

means no standing in line). All water sports are on site, there are others nearby. ♦ Casino Dr, west of the casino. 363.2011, 800/325.3535

10 Club Land 'or $$$ There are fully equipped kitchens in the 72 tastefully decorated one-bedroom apartments set around the pool or on the lagoon overlooking the beach. The resort is quiet and serenely beautiful (ideal for family vacations) yet only minutes away from the hustle and bustle of the center of the island. ♦ Paradise Island Dr, west of the casino. 363.2400

Within Club Land 'or:

Blue Lagoon Restaurant ★★$$ Classic fish and seafood items are done well and served graciously. Enjoy fine dining in a beautiful tropical setting. ♦ Bahamian/Continental ♦ Daily 6-10PM. 363.2400

11 The Pink House $ Owner **Minnie Winn** and her partner **Kevin Smith** operate this Georgian cottage on the grounds of **Club Med** as a bed-and-breakfast. The **Duke** and **Duchess of Windsor** enjoyed brunch in the lovely pickled-pine lounge in the charming home built in the 1920s for a **Huntington Hartford** family member. Minnie serves "Pink House Punch," a concoction of rum, fresh lime juice, Angostura bitters, syrup, and water. (Caution: Her punch can lead to sightings of pink elephants.) This is the smallest hotel (with only five rooms) in the Bahamas. Guests enjoy private access to the beach, the nearby casino, and a number of restaurants. ♦ West end of the island. 363.3363, 800/327.0787; fax 393.1786

12 Club Med $$$ When Club Med says activities, they mean activities. Club Med resorts are geared to folks with active lifestyles, the kind who play tennis, then swim, and then take an aerobics course. The restaurant (a cafeteria, really) is for guests only. No cash is permitted at the all-inclusive resort, and guests pay for things with beads they wear around their neck or wrist. The beach programs are go-go-go—not for everyone, but very popular with honeymooning couples. ♦ Paradise Beach Dr (Casuarina Dr). 363.2640, 800/258.2633

13 Paradise Paradise Beach Resort $$ This casual resort on the ocean places a strong emphasis on water sports. Located on the original, beautiful white sand Paradise Island Beach, the hotel is an addition to those resorts that made the island rich and famous. ♦ Casuarina Dr, west end of the island. 363.2541, 800/321.3000

14 Paradise Pavilion ★★$$ The sunsets are dramatic and quite romantic viewed from this attractive oceanfront terrace restaurant. Bahamian cracked conch is close to perfect and other specialties include a 16-ounce T-bone with a baked potato and corn on the cob. The service here is among the best on the island. ♦ American/Bahamian ♦ Far west end of the island. Daily 7PM-midnight. 363.3000 ext. 4622

15 Pirate's Cove Holiday Inn $$$ Set on a crescent-shaped beach, one of the island's best, the hotel's 515 rooms are quite comfortable. The newest addition is a replicated wreck of a pirate ship in the beautifully landscaped pool area. The huge, high-ceilinged lobby is a busy place throughout the day. The rooms are standard Holiday Inn fare, but the view from the covelike beach is special ♦ Casuarina Dr (Pirate's Cove). 363.2100

Restaurants/Clubs: Red   **Hotels:** Blue
Shops/ 🌳 **Outdoors:** Green   **Sights/Culture:** Black

158

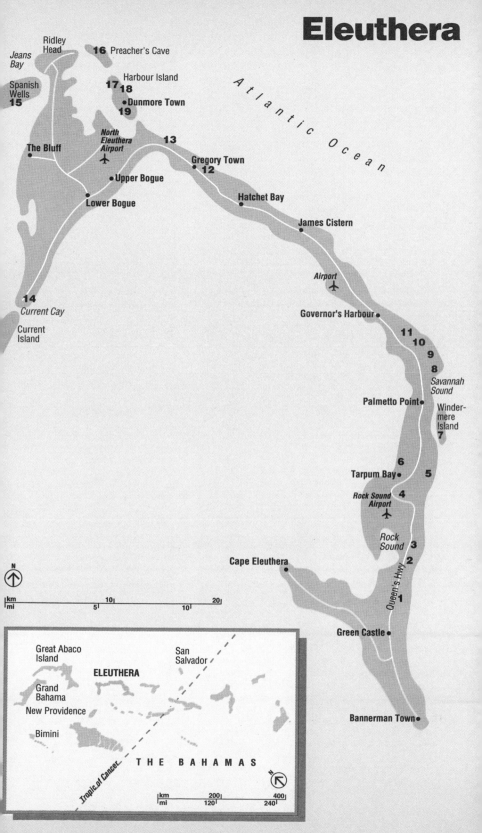

Eleuthera

Atlantic Ocean

Ridley Head
Jeans Bay
16 Preacher's Cave
Spanish Wells
15
Harbour Island
17 18
• **Dunmore Town**
19
North Eleuthera Airport
The Bluff
13
Gregory Town
• **12**
• **Upper Bogue**
Lower Bogue
Hatchet Bay
James Cistern
14
Current Cay
Current Island
Airport
Governor's Harbour •
11
10
9
8
Savannah Sound
Palmetto Point •
Windermere Island
7
6
Tarpum Bay •
5
Rock Sound Airport
4
Rock Sound
3
Cape Eleuthera •
2
Queen's Hwy
1
Green Castle •
Bannerman Town •

N

| km | | | 10 | | | 20 |
| mi | | 5 | 10 | | | |

THE BAHAMAS

Great Abaco Island
San Salvador
ELEUTHERA
Grand Bahama
New Providence
Bimini

Tropic of Cancer

N

| km | | 200 | | 400 |
| mi | 120 | | 240 | |

The three major communities of **Eleuthera** are **Rock Sound,** in the southern portion of the long, skinny island; **North Eleuthera,** the ferry point to Spanish Wells and Harbour Island; and **Governor's Harbour,** a beautiful bay at midpoint. Until the middle of the 20th century, agriculture was the major industry on Eleuthera, with dairy farms around Rock Sound, chicken ranches farther north, and lots of pineapple plantations scattered about. Now most locals have turned to tourism, serving the vacationers drawn to the island's pink-hued coral beaches.

Eleuthera was discovered in 1648 when **William Sayles,** the former governor of Bermuda, brought a band of settlers here in search of religious freedom. They named the island (*eleutheria* is Greek for freedom) and spent the winter at **Preacher's Cave.**

The **Eleutherian Adventurers,** as they were called, colonized the island and to this day at least 95 percent of the population of **Spanish Wells,** a little town off the island's northern tip, are descendants from Adventurers or **Loyalists,** the next influx of Eleutherians.

Area code 809 unless otherwise noted.

1 Cotton Bay Club $$$ Pan Am Airlines founder **Juan Trippe** not only brought electricity to the island, he created this outstanding resort as a getaway for his rich and famous contemporaries. Business execs originally sought rest and relaxation here and current management still keeps distracting telephones and television sets out of rooms. Former **President Richard Nixon** and the late **Sammy Davis Jr.** have been guests here. This is a grand resort with only 77 large rooms, plus a posh six-bedroom, six-bath villa with a panoramic view of the Atlantic that's ideal for family reunions and corporate meetings. The resort's water activities are varied and an 18-hole **Robert Trent Jones** golf course and **Peter Burwash** tennis courts keep visitors active and entertained. Laid-back beach aficionados can enjoy one of the prettiest white sand beaches in the Bahamas. ♦ Powell Point, Rock Sound. 334.6101, 800/223.1588

2 Sammy's Place ★$ Long-time Cotton Bay maitre d' **Sammy Culmer** and his wife have opened a restaurant that features Bahamian specialties such as deep-fried grouper and cracked conch. Fresh home cooking goes well with the basic coffee-shop ambience and traditional island fare. ♦ Bahamian ♦ Daily 8AM-10PM. Queen's Hwy, 1 mile south of Rock Sound Airport. 334.2121

Eleuthera

3 The Haven Restaurant and Pastry Shop ★$$ A favorite among sweet tooths, this place specializes in baked goods (island style) and local favorites. ♦ Bahamian ♦ M-Sa 7:30AM-7PM. Rock Sound. Dinner reservations required. 334.2155

4 Ocean Hole Park Locals and tourists bring bread to feed the many angelfish, snapper, and grouper that swim free and grow fat in this 600-foot-deep pit. The strictly no-fishing hole is fed by deep underground access to the Atlantic. Dedicated in 1970 by **Prime Minister Lynden Pyndling,** the Ocean Hole is where youngsters swim when school's out. ♦ Queen's Hwy, Rock Sound

5 Winding Bay Resort $$$ Each of the 36 large rooms features a patio and a great island view. Set on 40 acres of palm grove, the resort offers water and land sports galore in a lush tropical landscape. ♦ Queen's Hwy, 7 miles north of Rock Sound Airport. 334.4054, 800/835.1017; fax 334.4057

6 Mal Flanders Art Gallery A resident of more than two decades on the island, Flanders' works of art combine objects of the past and present. He developed his unique style of art about 35 years ago when he lived in Key West and painted Bahamian work boats. ♦ Daily 9AM-5PM. Tarpum Bay, Rock Sound. 334.4187

7 Windermere Island Club $$$$ Privacy and exclusivity are offered in 21 rooms on the ocean. The resort has five miles of beaches where guests can do as little or as much as they like in the way of water or outdoor sports. An **Orient Express** resort, the Windermere stresses luxury and elegance.

Hotel rooms and 42 privately owned residential units are available ranging from one-bedroom suites to five-bedroom villas. The restaurant on the premises (open only to guests) is known for fine dining. The Continental and island cuisine includes chicken with snow crabmeat and red pepper sauce, and pork fillet kabobs with bird pepper and peanut sauce. ♦ Deluxe ♦ Rock Sound. 332.6003, 800/237.1236; fax 332.6002

8 Club Med $$$ Newspapers, television, and even money are banned during your stay at Club Med. The mother of all all-inclusive resorts, this one offers 300 rooms, an outstanding beach, and a broad range of programs. ♦ Governor's Harbour. 332.2270, 800/258.2633

9 Wykee's World Resort $$ There are six fully equipped homes on the private estate along with a pool, pink sand beaches, water sports, and fishing. ♦ Governor's Harbour. 332.2701; fax 332.2123

10 Richard and Carmen's Tuckaway Motel $ Lush landscaping and privacy are the key notes here and visitors are only minutes away from wonderful beaches and restaurants. ♦ Governor's Harbour. 332.2005

11 Rainbow Inn $ Set on three acres of landscaped property, many of the six double rooms and one-, two-, and three-bedroom units at Rainbow Inn (pictured above) look out on one of the Bahamas' favorite ports of call, **Hatchet Bay Harbour.** The inn encourages relaxed, restful vacations. The excellent restaurant on the premises features island favorites. ♦ Governor's Harbour. 322.8593, 800/327.0787

12 The Cove $$ Swim in a freshwater pool or off the beautiful white sand beach, unless you'd rather stroll past vast the pineapple fields nearby. The choice is yours.

The Cove's 28 rooms—four to a building—are tastefully furnished and each boasts a patio or terrace. ♦ Gregory Town. 332.0142, 800/552.5960

13 Glass Window Bridge Little more than the width of a car, the Glass Window Bridge faces the Atlantic Ocean on one side and the Gulf of Mexico on the other. ♦ Located just north of Gregory Town

14 Current Club and Lodge $ Choose from 18 villas or a cottage on one lovely crescent beach. They're only minutes away from one another. Divers love the nearby reefs. There's no charge for children under 12 sharing a room with adults. ♦ North Eleuthera. 333.0264; fax 333.0199

15 Spanish Wells Beach Resort $$ Right on the beach, this renovated resort with 21 beachfront rooms and six cottages is a super destination for those who want to get away from it all. The sense of privacy is a major selling point and the natural beauty of the resort another. There's tennis, deep-sea fishing, snorkeling, and scuba diving, among other activities. ♦ Take the ferry from North Eleuthera Airport, 1 mile off the island. 333.4371, 800/327.0787

16 Preacher's Cave This is where the first religious services were held on the island by the **Eleutherian Adventurers.** ♦ Just north of Glass Window Bridge

17 Valentine's Yacht Club and Inn $$ You're practically on the doorstep of this newly renovated 20-room hotel when you step off the ferry from North Eleuthera. In a friendly setting that could be Key West or the south of France, the hotel offers bike and boat rentals and fishing on the premises. ♦ Harbour Island, take the ferry from North Eleuthera Airport. 333.2080, 800/327.0787; fax 333.2135

18 Coral Sands Hotel $$ This 33-room resort lets you think pink while you unwind and lay back in truly relaxing surroundings. The Coral Sands Hotel is set on 14 acres in the heart of 300-year-old **Dunmore Town,** an early capital of the Bahamas. The three-mile pink beach has enjoyed a long popularity among honeymooners. ♦ Harbour Island, take the ferry from North Eleuthera Airport. 333.2350, 800/468.2799

19 The Harbour Lounge $ Feast on snacks,

Eleuthera

salad, and the ever-popular grouper and conch. The view from the front terrace of the Harbour Lounge offers a fine opportunity to people-watch while you await the ferry to North Eleuthera. ♦ Seafood ♦ Daily 11AM-11PM. Harbour Island, take the ferry from North Eleuthera Airport. 333.2031

Restaurants/Clubs: Red   **Hotels:** Blue
Shops/ 🌴 **Outdoors:** Green   **Sights/Culture:** Black

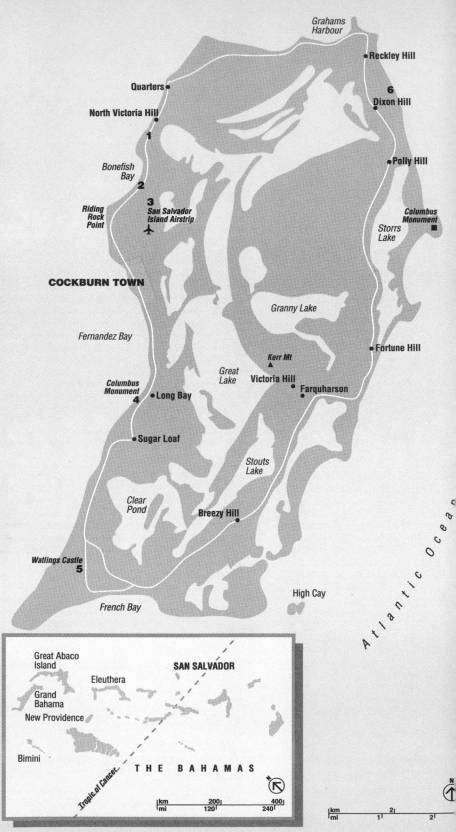

Grahams Harbour

Reckley Hill

Quarters

6

Dixon Hill

North Victoria Hill

1

Bonefish Bay

Polly Hill

2

Riding Rock Point

3

San Salvador Island Airstrip

Columbus Monument

Storrs Lake

COCKBURN TOWN

Granny Lake

Fernandez Bay

Fortune Hill

Columbus Monument

Kerr Mt

4

Long Bay

Great Lake

Victoria Hill

Farquharson

Sugar Loaf

Stouts Lake

Clear Pond

Breezy Hill

Watlings Castle

5

High Cay

French Bay

Atlantic Ocean

Great Abaco Island

SAN SALVADOR

Eleuthera

Grand Bahama

New Providence

Bimini

THE BAHAMAS

Tropic of Cancer

km
mi   200   400
             120   240

km
mi   1   2

N

San Salvador

On 12 October 1492 **Christopher Columbus** discovered an island the resident **Arawaks** called **Guanahani**. Columbus claimed the land for Spain and named it *San Salvador* (Spanish for "Holy Savior").

The island is fairly unchanged from the day Columbus arrived. Luckily, it escaped the great building booms that took place on New Providence and Paradise islands. San Salvador's claim to fame is its outstanding water sports, which include diving, swimming, and snorkeling.

Area code 809 unless otherwise noted.

1 Ocean View Villas $ The four efficiencies sleep a total of 10. Water sports can be arranged. To get in touch with someone at this "hotel," call information and ask for Cockburn Town (pronounced *co-burn*). Ocean View Villas will be alerted to your call. ♦ N. Victoria Hill

2 Club Med $$ Brand new for the 500th anniversary of Columbus' voyage, this Club Med offers the typical sports-intensive program with lots of water, diving, and fishing programs. ♦ Between Riding Rock Point and N. Victoria Hill. 323.8430, 800/258.2633

3 Riding Rock Inn $ The newly renovated resort is geared to meet the needs of dedicated divers. Visibility exceeds 150 feet and reveals magnificent coral groupings and a few shipwrecks. There's a pool for those who don't know how to scuba dive. ♦ Riding Rock Point. 800/272.1492

4 Columbus Monument This was built in 1956 to commemorate the landfall of **Christopher Columbus** in the New World. ♦ Long Bay

5 Watlings Castle The ruins of a 17th-century plantation house offer an outstanding photographic opportunity. Englishman and pirate captain **George Watling** took over San Salvador and built this mansion during the buccaneer days. The castle is also known as **Sandy Point Estate.** ♦ Daily dawn-dusk. Located near Clear Pond

6 Dixon Hill Lighthouse This kerosene-burning, manually operated lighthouse is the last of its kind. It has a visibility of 90 miles. ♦ Daily dawn-dusk. Dixon Hill

Apparently no one can make up their mind exactly where Christopher Columbus arrived when he came to San Salvador in the Bahamas on 12 October 1492. Markers on three different parts of the island claim to be resting on Columbus' arrival spot.

More than 600 years before Columbus came to the Bahamas, the Arawak Indians and the Caribs (their warlike cousins) called the islands home. Two Arawak words still used today are cannibal and barbecue; both words were inspired by the fierce Caribs.

The pirate Blackbeard, who frequented the Caribbean shores, reputedly spiked his rum with a sprinkle of gunpowder.

Bests

Stella Hayes
Tour and Activities Director, Sonesta Hotel, Oranjestad, Aruba

Jamaica is the place for a fun-filled crazy time. Get swept up in the island spirit with its reggae music and spicy foods.

St. Lucia is a lovely, lush island. And a weekly street party reveals the true spirit of the locals.

If you want to get away from it all, go to **Bonaire,** where you don't have to speak to a soul if you don't want to. Life is simple in this paradise that's still unspoiled by tourism, and the marine life is incredible.

Edward Seaga
Former Prime Minister of Jamaica, Owner of The Enchanted Garden resort in Ocho Rios

Hunting in the mangroves, away from telephones, concrete, and crowds.

Watching the sun go down. The Jamaican sunset is a spectacle—a flash of brilliant green as the last bit of orange disappears over the horizon.

A relaxing day at a cricket test match, the only game where the artistry of stroke play is as important as the outcome. Choose the day the great "bats" are at the wicket.

Carnival in **Trinidad** and now in **Jamaica,** for those who can indulge in abandonment to "wicket" music.

Roy C. Brown
Retired Airline/Public Relations Executive, San Juan, Puerto Rico

Old San Juan in **Puerto Rico.** Just to walk the streets of this restored historic city is a treat.

The 18-hole golf course at **Rio Mar** is the toughest, most scenic, and the best course in **Puerto Rico.**

Fairview Inn, on the leeward island of **St. Kitts,** is a small, family run hotel with good food and service. It's great for relaxing and doing nothing.

San Salvador

Frenchman's Reef hotel, on **St. Thomas** in the **US Virgin Islands,** is a resort that has everything, including a staff that knows how to please.

The island of **St. John,** in the **US Virgin Islands,** is still relatively unspoiled, and **Caneel Bay** resort is a fine place to stay. This island also has the best beaches.

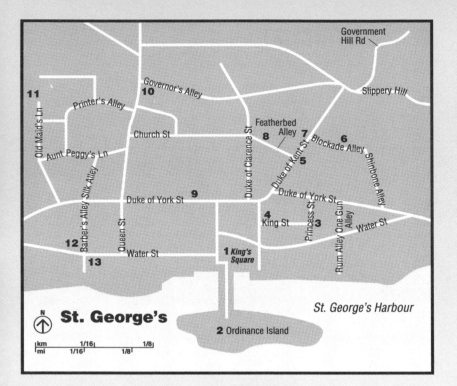

St. George's

1 King's Square
2 Ordinance Island

St. George's Harbour

Old Maid's Ln — 11
Printer's Alley
Governor's Alley — 10
Government Hill Rd
Slippery Hill
Aunt Peggy's Ln
Church St
Featherbed Alley — 8 — 7
Blockade Alley — 6
Shinbone Alley
Barber's Alley / Silk Alley
Duke of Clarence St
Duke of Kent St — 5
Duke of York St — 9
Duke of York St
Princess St — 3
Rum Alley / One Gun Alley
Water St
Queen St
King St — 4
12
Water St — 13

N
km
mi   1/16   1/16   1/8   1/8

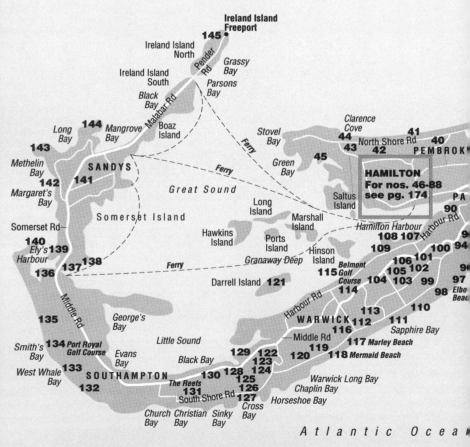

Ireland Island Freeport
145
Ireland Island North
Pender Rd
Grassy Bay
Ireland Island South
Parsons Bay
Black Bay
Matabar Rd
Boaz Island
Long Bay
144 Mangrove Bay
Stovel Bay
Clarence Cove
44 North Shore Rd **41**
43 **42** **40**
45 PEMBROKE
Green Bay
143
Methelin Bay
SANDYS
Great Sound
Saltus Island
HAMILTON
For nos. 46-88
see pg. 174
PA
142 **141**
Margaret's Bay
Somerset Island
Long Island
90
Somerset Rd—
140
Ely's **139**
Harbour
137 **138**
136
Hawkins Island
Ports Island
Marshall Island
Hinson Island
Hamilton Harbour
108 **107**
109
106 **101**
105 **102**
104 **103** **99**
Harbour Rd
9
100 **94**
9
97
98 Elbo Beac
Belmont Golf Course
115 **114**
Darrell Island **121**
Granaway Deep
Middle Rd
135
George's Bay
134 Port Royal Golf Course
Smith's Bay
Evans Bay
Little Sound
Black Bay
WARWICK
113
112 **111**
116
110
Sapphire Bay
West Whale Bay
133
SOUTHAMPTON
132
130
The Reefs
131
South Shore Rd
129 **122**
123
128 **124**
125
126
127
Cross Bay
119
120 **118** Mermaid Beach
117 Marley Beach
Warwick Long Bay
Chaplin Bay
Horseshoe Bay
Church Bay
Christian Bay
Sinky Bay

A t l a n t i c   O c e a n

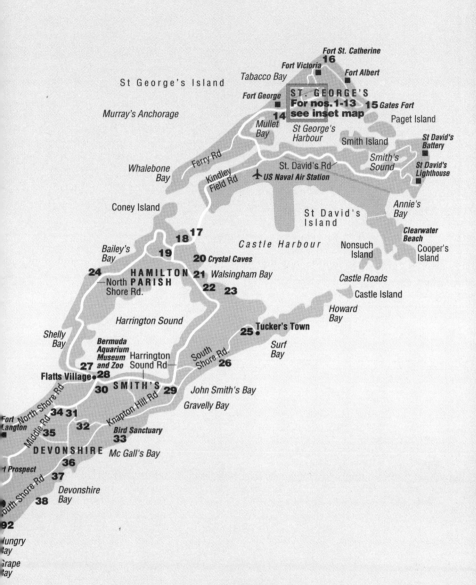

Bermuda

Less than half of Bermuda's nearly 150 tiny islands are actually big enough to build a house on. The archipelago's seven largest islands are connected by bridges or causeways, and the subsequent body of land is divided into nine parishes, each with its own personality and attractions. **St. George's Parish** anchors the east end and **Sandys Parish** the west end, and the capital city of **Hamilton** sits in between.

Unlike many other Caribbean islands, Bermuda's seven principal islands have been completely tamed. Its 21 square miles are almost suburban in character, with pastel-colored cottages fronted by manicured lawns. Even the natural landscape is unremarkable compared to some of the other islands; for example, you won't find the rain forests or mountains that are characteristic of Puerto

Rico on this island. But just offshore and beneath the water's surface is a fantasylike seascape made up of the world's northernmost coral reefs. The coral's brilliant colors and exotic shapes attract scores of snorkelers, scuba divers, and glass-bottom boats. And bits of coral mixed in with grains of sand create Bermuda's renowned pink beaches.

Bermuda's culture is likewise exceptionally civilized, a direct influence of its English heritage. Not only is cricket the national game, the judges wear white wigs and tea is served every afternoon in this self-governing British colony.

In the interest of maintaining the island's serenity, the maximum speed limit for motorized vehicles is 20 miles per hour. And because of its tiny size, rental cars are not allowed on Bermuda. The pink public buses, however, are convenient and economical, as are the ferries that cross the **Great Sound**. If public transportation doesn't appeal to you, hail one of the island's taxi drivers, commonly referred to as Bermuda's "ambassadors of goodwill."

To explore the island on your own, scooters, mopeds, and bicycles are available for rent by the hour, day, or week. The roads, however, are narrow and winding, and often lined with stone walls—and don't forget that the people here drive on the left side of the street, English style.

Area code 809 unless otherwise noted.

Getting to the Island

Airlines

American	800/433.7300
Bermuda Aviation	253.2500
Civil Aviation	293.1646
Continental	800/525.0280
Delta	800/221.1212
United	800/538.2929
USAir	800/428.4322

Airport

Civil Air Terminal Bermuda's only airport serves the major airlines and a multitude of charter flights. Located on the east side of the island, in St. George's Parish, the airport is on Kindley Field Road, just off St. David's Road, approximately nine miles north-west of Hamilton. For more information, call 293.0030.

Cruise Lines

Chandris Celebrity Cruises	800/621.3446
Royal Caribbean Cruise Line	800/327.2055
Royal Viking Line	800/422.8000

Getting around the Island

Bicycles and Mopeds

If you like to bike, you'll have plenty of company here. Wheeling around Bermuda is the most pleasant way to see its towns, beaches, and parks. Mopeds rent for $25 daily, or $105 per week. Bikes cost $10 to $15 for the first day, and $5 thereafter. Recommended rental agencies include:

Devil's Hole Cycles	293.1240
Eve's Cycle Livery	236.6247
Georgiana Cycles	234.2404
Oleander Cycles	236.5235, 295.0919

Buses

Modern, brightly colored buses traverse Bermuda's main roads in 15-minute intervals; they are dependable, convenient, and, in comparison to taxi service, inexpensive. The **Central Bus Station** in Hamilton is the nexus of most bus travel, but buses stop just about everywhere on the island. Newcomers may find it difficult to find the bus stops at first. They're indicated by pink-and-blue poles at the roadside, but many are so weather-beaten that the paint has completely worn off. A blue top indicates that the bus route heads out of Hamilton, while a pink top means the route will take you toward the capital.

Pick up a copy of the bus schedule, which also includes ferry timetables, at the airport or your hotel; fares are determined by the number of Bermuda's 14 bus zones you are traveling through, and drivers require exact change or tokens. The Central Bus Station is at the intersection of Washington and Church streets in Hamilton. For more information, call 292.5854.

Several private minibus companies serve the outer ends of the island. They are more akin to taxis than buses, as you can call for pick-up or flag one down in the street. In Somerset Parish, call **Sandys Taxi Service** at 234.2344; in St. George's Parish, contact **St. George's Transportation** at 297.8199.

Ferry Service

Ferries cross the Great Sound from Hamilton to Paget and Warwick parishes ($1) and to Somerset Island ($2) daily; they run until 11PM. They depart from the Ferry Terminal on Front Street in Hamilton. Call 295.4506 for more information.

Taxis

Bermuda Taxi Operators	292.5600
Radio Cabs Bermuda	295.4141

FYI

Accommodations

The choices of where to stay in Bermuda are delightfully varied, ranging from the sand-in-your-shoes, carefree kind of atmosphere to basking in the lap of luxury. The gamut is covered from large resorts to smaller hotels, private residence clubs, cottage colonies, housekeeping cottages and apartments, and guest houses.

The largest resort hotels usually have their own beach and freshwater pools, and several have their own golf course. Most feature the usual luxury-resort amenities: porters, bell and room service, planned activities, sports, a social desk, shops, a beauty salon, cycle livery, restaurants, nightclubs, and on-premises entertainment. The smaller hotels offer much of the same, though their services and activities are less extensive and the entertainment is limited. Several, however, do have their own beach or waterfront.

The cottage colonies, a uniquely Bermudian institution, feature a main clubhouse with a dining room, lounge, and bar. The individual cottages are spread throughout the landscaped grounds, offering privacy and luxury. Most have kitchenettes that are convenient for beverages or light snacks, but are not suited for cooking full meals. You won't go hungry, though, as many of the cottage colony restaurants are among the best on the island. All have their own beach or pool, usually accessible via private patios.

You can also stay at the housekeeping cottages and apartments, which are essentially efficiency units. Usually situated in landscaped estates with their own beach and small pool, they're downscale equivalents of the cottage colonies, without any sort of main clubhouse or restaurants of note on the premises. Most offer daily, though minimal, maid service.

The guest houses are old Bermuda homes in garden settings that have been modernized and made comfortable. A few have their own waterfront and/or pool. Most offer bed-and-breakfast rates and are generally informal, with kitchenettes or shared facilities for the preparation of snacks.

Dress Code

Proper attire in Bermuda is often defined as "smart casual"—a term that remains open to definition. As such, it is better to err on the casual side rather than on the "smart."

Casual sportswear is acceptable in restaurants at lunchtime, but many restaurants and nightclubs require a coat and tie for men in the evenings. It's best to inquire about the dress codes when making dinner and nightclub reservations.

Swimsuits, short shorts, and midriff tops are not permitted in public spaces or hotel dining rooms in Bermuda. Beachwear is strictly for the beach, and it is an offense to be topless in public, especially on a motorbike, in which instance the offender will not only be stopped, but cited. Ditto for women wearing bathing-suit tops.

Drinking

The legal drinking age in Bermuda is 21.

Money

The Bermudian dollar is interchangable with the United States dollar. American money can be used anywhere, and most of the larger shops, restaurants, and hotels accept American credit cards and American traveler's checks. The **Bank of Bermuda** has 10 branches; all are open M-Th 9:30AM-3PM, F 9:30AM-4:30PM. They also have automatic teller machines open 24 hours, but for access, you must have a credit card. **Bermuda Commercial Bank** is open M-F 11AM-4PM.

Phone Book

Ambulance	236.2000
Directory Assistance	411
Emergency	911
Fire	900
Police	292.2222
Weather	977

Publications

The *Royal Gazette* is published daily in Hamilton, while *Mid-Ocean News,* with an emphasis on arts and entertainment, is issued every Friday. Major United States newspapers are delivered to Bermuda on the day of publication.

Taxes

For passengers arriving by air, there is no arrival tax; however, there is a departure tax of $15 per adult, $5 for children under 11, and those under the age of two travel free.

For travelers arriving by sea, there is an arrival tax but no departure tax. The fee for passengers on cruise ships is $60 per person. However, the arrival (landing) tax is generally included in the cost of the cruise ticket, so in effect, it's nothing "extra." Those coming to the island via private yacht pay a $30 tax upon clearing immigration and customs.

St. George's

This parish is comprised of two large islands, St. George's and **St. David's.** The town of St. George's is the second-oldest English town in the New World, and for almost two centuries, was the capital of Bermuda. It is named for both **Sir George Somers,** the founder of Bermuda, and **Saint George,** the patron saint of England.

Area code 809 unless otherwise noted.

1 White Horse Tavern and Restaurant $
This establishment, formerly a private home dating from 1815, is pretty grungy, but then again, St. George's is and always has been a

seaport; and being right at the water's edge, this is the type of place that one might expect to hear some sea chanteys being sung after a couple of drinks too many. But, because it's

Bermuda, the seafarers mostly arrive on yachts, the atmosphere is upbeat, the drinks tall, and the mood jovial. The best vistas are viewed from the terrace. As for the food, you pay for what you get. ♦ International ♦ Daily 10AM-1AM. King's Square. 297.1838

1 King's Square Known as the center of St. George's, this is where the town hall, the old stocks and pillory, and several gift shops, taverns, and the **Visitors Information Office** (297.1642) are located. It's fun to take some souvenir photos of modern-day cutups in the stocks and pillory, formerly used as devices for punishment. ♦ Duke of York St-Convict Bay

2 Ordnance Island If you find the stocks and pillory at King's Square aren't punishment enough, try the ducking stool here, once a way to punish nagging wives and suspected witches. The ship you'll see is the *Deliverance II*, a full-scale replica of the Bermuda-built pinnace *Deliverance I*, constructed in 1609 by the survivors of the *Sea Venture*. The bronze statue of **Sir George Somers** is by **Desmond Fountain**. ♦ Admission. Ducking demonstrations: M 10AM-3:30PM. Self-guided tours of *Deliverance*: daily 10AM-4PM. Across King's Bridge from King's Square

3 State House This is the oldest stone building in Bermuda, dating back to 1620. It was formerly the seat of government, but is now rented to a **Masonic Lodge** for one peppercorn annually. The interior is open to the public only one day a week, but the exterior is worth checking out any time. ♦ Free. W 10AM-4PM. Princess St

4 Bridge House Built in the early 1700s, this house was formerly the home of several royal governors of Bermuda. It houses the island's best all-Bermudian art gallery, with fine works from the 18th and 19th centuries. Its name is derived from a bridge that once spanned a muddy creek flowing from **Somers Garden** to the harbor. ♦ Free. Daily 10AM-5PM Mar-Dec; W, Sa 10AM-5PM Jan-Feb. King St. 297.8211

5 Somers Garden When **Sir George Somers**, the founder of Bermuda, died in 1610, his body was returned to England for a proper burial; but at his request, his heart was allegedly buried in this garden. ♦ Free. Daily 7:30AM-4:30PM. Shinbone Alley (Blockade Alley)

6 Unfinished Church Construction began on this church in 1874, but, due to financial problems, church politics, and storm dam-

age, it had been abandoned by the turn of the century. Imagine what it might have been had it ever been finished. ♦ Blockade Alley (Church Folly Lane)

7 St. George's Historical Society Museum This typical, small-town museum displays artifacts from Bermuda's early days. Dating back to the early 18th century, the building is worth a visit. Its staircase is an excellent example of Bermuda's welcoming-arms architecture. ♦ Admission. M-F 10AM-4PM. Featherbed Alley (Duke of Kent St). 297.0423

8 Featherbed Alley Printery As the old saying goes, "If it's not broken, don't fix it." The printing press here has been in continuous use, with a few changes, for more than three and a half centuries. It was invented by **Johannes Gutenberg** in the 1450s. ♦ Free. M-Sa 10AM-4PM. Featherbed Alley. 297.0009

9 St. Peter's Church This is the oldest Anglican church in the New World, built on the site of Bermuda's first church. The first house of worship, constructed of posts and palmetto leaves in 1612, was destroyed in a storm. This church was completed in 1713, and the galleries were added in the 1830s. Of special note is the silver communion service, a gift of **King William III** in 1689. ♦ M-Sa 10AM-4PM; Su and evening services vary. Duke of York St (Church St). 297.8359

10 Old Rectory Located directly behind St. Peter's Church is an old Bermuda cottage that, as the story goes, was the home of a one-time pirate who was inspired by God and donated the cottage to the church for use as the rectory. It's now administered by the Bermuda National Trust, but was owned as a private home. ♦ Free. W noon-5PM, except holidays. Broad Alley. 297.0879

11 St. George's Club $$$$ This 61-unit timeshare cottage colony/hotel is set high on a hill overlooking the town and the oceanfront. The two-story cottages are luxurious, complete with fine china, marble bathrooms, and Jacuzzis. The main building houses offices, game and recreation rooms, a club shop, pub, and the **Margaret Rose**, a tasteful hotel restaurant. If you're a golfer, the club is adjacent to the **St. George's Golf Club**. ♦ Rose Hill. 297.1200

12 Tucker House **Henry Tucker,** president of the Governor's Council, lived in this limestone house from 1775 to the turn of the century. His furniture (most of it is cedar) is still here, as is his beautiful mahogany dining table. Just to the side of the dining room you'll see the miniscule wig rooms where guests adjusted their wigs. The house is now owned by the Bermuda National Trust. ♦ Donation. M-Sa 10AM-5PM. Water St. 297.0545

More than 27,000 couples celebrated their honeymoon in Bermuda in 1990.

When the flagship *Sea Venture* headed for Virginia and shipwrecked on Bermuda's reefs in 1609, it gave William Shakespeare the inspiration to write his play *The Tempest* in 1610.

Restaurants/Clubs: Red   Hotels: Blue
Shops/ Outdoors: Green   Sights/Culture: Black

13 Carriage Museum This small museum is dedicated to the history and romance of horse-drawn carriages on the island ♦ Free (donations accepted). M-Sa 9AM-5PM. Water St. 297.1367

14 Wharf Tavern $$ This is a real find amidst the touristic atmosphere of central St. George's. The menu is diverse, ranging from pizza to steaks, chops, and plenty of fresh fish dishes, but the food is tasty, the service prompt, and the ambience unexpectedly good. ♦ American ♦ Daily 11AM-2:30PM, 6-10PM. Somers Wharf. 297.1515

15 Gates Fort There isn't much to see at this reconstruction of a small fort from the 1620s. It was named after **Sir Thomas Gates,** the first of the *Sea Venture* survivors to make it to shore. The view from here is quite spectacular. ♦ Free. Daily 10AM-4PM. Cut Rd

16 Fort St. Catherine This fort has the most impressive collection of cannons and underground passageways of any of the fortifications in St. George's. The restored structure dates from the 1640s. If you are not excited by military displays, there's a collection of replicas of the crown jewels of England. ♦ Admission. Daily 10AM-4:30PM. Barry Rd. 297.1920

Hamilton Parish

Located around the eastern end of Bermuda, Hamilton Parish is named after the second **Marquis of Hamilton,** a 17th-century nobleman who was an original member of the Bermuda Company (a British land trust). Don't confuse this with the capital city of Hamilton, which is located in Pembroke Parish.

17 Grotto Bay Beach Hotel and Tennis Club $$$$ One of the first hotels to be seen on the way in from the airport, this expansive complex of sparkling white buildings is spread across a 21-acre waterfront estate. Unfortunately, the hotel has been experiencing hard times in recent years and in late 1991 embarked on a no-tipping policy (unique to Bermuda) they claim will either revitalize the hotel or close it down due to the staff's opposition to the new plan. Regardless, you're guaranteed to enjoy it, as it has excellent facilities, including four tennis courts, a private beach, and a gracious

swimming-pool complex. ♦ 11 Blue Hill Hole, across the causeway from the airport. 293.8333, 800/225.2230

18 The Swizzle Inn $$ If you're over the age of 30 and under 70, chances are you made it to one or more of the old-time "College Weeks in Bermuda." But even if you didn't, a couple of minutes spent at this emporium of fast food and strong drink will bring back vivid memories of salad days.

As everyone knows, the "Swizzle" is the national drink of Bermuda. But how many know that the Swizzle was first created and served at the Swizzle Inn (illustrated above) back in 1902? Of course, the building predates those times by centuries, having been built about 350 years ago. Today, the Swizzle Inn is a Yuppie hangout with a fun-filled atmosphere. The outside windows are plastered with stickers from around the world, and the ceiling is covered with thousands of business cards. Happy-hour drinks are priced according to a spin at the "wheel of fortune." Caribbean themes happen on most Saturday nights, though it just as easily could be Irish, American, or Polish. It's true nostalgia, Bermuda-style, and there's plenty of room out front to park your moped or scooter. Reservations? Just push yourself in through the crowd and shout your drink order to the bartender. ♦ American ♦ Daily 11:30AM-1AM. Blue Hole Rd (N. Shore Rd). 293.1854

19 Bermuda Perfumery Guided tours explain the history and production of the famous **Lili Bermuda** perfumes and men's colognes, including exhibits on old and new methods of extracting fragrances from native flora. The actual factory is set off to the rear in an 18th-century cedar-beamed cottage surrounded by acres of picture-perfect gardens, so bring your camera and be prepared to test your sense of smell—there's an aromatic nature trail walk through the orchids. ♦ Free. M-Sa 9AM-5PM; Su 10AM-4PM. 212 N. Shore Rd (Bailey's Bay). 293.0627

20 Crystal Caves The underground caves are full of white crystal stalactites and stalagmites and pontoon walkways to cross over sparkling, clear lakes. Note: There are steep, narrow stairs that might be difficult for some

people. ♦ Admission. Guided tours daily 9:30AM-4:30PM, except holidays. Harrington Sound Rd (Harrington Sound-Castle Harbour). 293.0640

21 Tom Moore's Tavern ★★★★$$$$ In 1804 the Irish poet **Thomas Moore** was appointed Registrar of Vice-Admiralty to the Court of Bermuda. His name became attached to the old Walsingham House, site of this restaurant and tavern, because he was a frequent guest over the years. The house actually became a tavern almost a century ago, and was named **The Poet Tom Moore's House.** Today it is Bermuda's oldest restaurant and one of the best, constantly vying with **Fourways** for the No. 1 spot. Executive chef **Benon Leszkowski's** innovative creations include such succulent vitals as *petite caille chaude en pate à la Benon* (quail filled with goose liver, morels, and truffles, and baked in puff pastry) and *cannett de barbaris au franboises* (crisp duckling roasted with its natural juice and a touch of raspberry vinegar). For the record, the calabash tree that poet Moore makes frequent references to in his songs and poems still exists some 200 yards behind the tavern. ♦ French ♦ Daily 7-9:15PM. Harrington Sound Rd (Washington Bay). Jacket and tie required. Reservations required. 293.8020

22 Plantation Restaurant ★★★★$$$$ Owners **Christopher** and **Carol West,** who have owned and personally operated the restaurant since 1979, put their philosophy not only right on the line, but on the front cover of their menus: "the secret of good cuisine is first-class products, time, love, and innovative ideas." And that's exactly what their delightful, eclectic, and ever-so-popular restaurant is—first-class, loved by all, and extremely innovative.

For instance, over the years the restaurant has become so popular that they had to expand the dining area. What better way than to erect a circus-sized tent on the lawn for a unique dining experience. As for the food, luncheon favorites include sautéed chicken livers served on a bed of fresh spinach, topped with croutons and served with vinaigrette; or perhaps sliced, steamed wahoo with tomato and

lettuce on wheat bread, served with the Plantation's own cocktail sauce.

Dinner might include a duck Harrington (duck sautéed with a julienne of fresh vegetables and

bacon, wrapped in puff pastry and served with duck sauce). And of course, their unbeatable, though sometimes unbearably hot, Bermuda fish chowder. Fun as it is, the Plantation is an excellent restaurant and a favorite of most Bermudians. It started as a tearoom for the adjacent Amber Caves of Leamington, also owned by the Wests, and eventually began to serve spirits to the officers from the nearby naval base, which became their watering hole of choice. The rest is history, and a treat in every way. ♦ Continental ♦ Daily noon-2:30PM, 7-9:30PM. Harrington Sound Rd (Bailey's Bay). Jacket required. 293.1188

22 Leamington's Amber Caves The amber-tinted grotto covers about two acres, with crystal formations and subterranean pools that form a large underground lake. If you have lunch next door at the Plantation Restaurant, admission is free. ♦ Admission. M-Sa 9:30AM-4:30PM; Su noon-3PM. Harrington Sound Rd (Bailey's Bay). 293.1188

23 Marriott's Castle Harbour Resort $$$$ The quintessential Bermuda resort is situated on 250 acres of the most valuable land on the island. This is classic Bermuda. Forget the name Marriott, and simply think of this grand hotel as being the castle by the sea that it actually is. As if to prove a point, you'll be treated like royalty by the almost exclusively Bermudian staff. Castle Harbour is like no place else. The hotel is divided into three major areas—the main building with high-ceilinged rooms, the golf wing adjacent to and overlooking one of the world's most famous courses, and the marina wing beside the pool and Castle Harbour. Most rooms in the latter two wings have private balconies. There are three pools, and two private beaches, one of which is reached by a shuttle bus. In the evenings, there's live entertainment daily, with country-club-type dinner-dances held in the **Windsor Room** most Friday, Saturday and Sunday nights. Of course, one of Castle Harbour's biggest draws is its legendary golf course, whose signature first and 18th holes are said to offer the most expensive vistas in golfdom. Hotel guests enjoy special golfing rates with numerous golf packages available throughout the year, even during high season. ♦ Castle Harbour (S. Shore Rd). 293.2040, 800/228.9290

Within Marriott's Castle Harbour Resort:

Windsor Room ★★★★$$$$ European-style food in a Euro-style setting, with, of course, prices straight out of Paris or Berlin. Pasta dishes are heart-stopping in the southern Italian tradition, but the Prime Rib atop Yorkshire pudding is the real killer. Do not come here if you are interested in becoming, or remaining, svelte. ♦ Continental ♦ Daily 7-9:30PM. Jacket and tie required. Reservations required. 293.2040

Mikado ★★★$$$$ The colorful fish in the reflecting pool are not the same ones served in the sumptuous sushi bar, although both are rare, expensive, and eye-catching. The real show here, however, is the martial-artist chefs who slice, dice, flip, and fillet your spicy, sizzling steaks and seafood right at your table. Seven-course prix fixe dinners are the best bets, as they sample widely from a cuisine known for its variety. However, everything from *tori* soup to fancy imported sake is available à la carte, if you want to do your own mix and match from the long-winded menu. ◆ Japanese ◆ Daily 6:30-9:30PM. Reservations recommended. 293.2040

24 Clear View Suites $$ Located midway between Hamilton and St. George's, this cluster features 12 modern housekeeping cottages with two pools and a tennis court right on the oceanfront. Added attractions include a small art gallery and weekly workshops given by **Otto Trot,** a local painter. ◆ N. Shore Rd (Sandy Lane). 293.0484, 800/468.9600

Tucker's Town

This residential area is Bermuda's answer to Grosse Point, Beverly Hills, and Greenwich: very exclusive and strictly controlled by the local landowners, all of whom, by law, are members of the **Mid Ocean Club,** a private country club and golf course.

25 Mid Ocean Golf Club $$$$ This private club is à la carte if you've been introduced by a member and are staying in one of the 14 guest rooms that are actually compact efficiency units. Of course, if you happen to be staying at the right hotel or cottage colony and the manager is on friendly terms with the manager of the Mid Ocean, you could be allowed to play their magnificent 18-hole golf course. It's worth a try, but if you strike out, remember that neighboring Castle Harbour's course is equally as good. ◆ S. Shore Rd, 6.5 miles east of Hamilton. 293.0330

First-time visitors passing Hamilton's north roundabout on a weekday between 6AM and 10AM are always surprised to be greeted by the enthusiastic waves, blown kisses, and joyous salutations of white-bearded Johnny Barnes. Years ago, Johnny got a job near the roundabout that required him to arrive promptly at 7AM. The only bus he could take dropped him off at the roundabout at 6:05AM, leaving him almost an hour to hang around waiting for his shift to start. To kill time, he often waved to friends who passed by. Strangers who saw him frequently waved back, and in no time, Johnny was greeting everyone who traveled by between 6:05AM and 7AM, at which time he would walk across the street to his job. By the time Johnny retired, he had become so accustomed to this morning routine that he decided to continue to get on the bus and arrive at 6:05AM, waving until the end of the rush hour at 10AM. You can find him there to this day.

Bermuda's waters are considered the cleanest in the Atlantic, providing some of the best underwater visibility in the world. In fact, scuba divers have reported visibility as far as 200 feet.

Smith's

Named after **Sir Thomas Smith,** a charter member of the Bermuda Company, which bought the island in 1612 for £2,000, the charms of this sparsely populated parish include its parks and geographic wonders. **Flatts Village,** a smugglers' port that had its own vigilante justice and law-enforcement system is certainly worth a visit.

26 Pink Beach Club and Cottages $$$$ For decades, **W.A. "Toppy" Cowen** has been both a Bermuda institution and the manager of this 81-unit cottage colony gracing 18 acres on the south shore. In 1991 Cowen announced he was going to retire and speculation began immediately that he would enter politics. If so, perhaps he'll be able to bring all of Bermuda up to the exalted standards he's achieved over the years at the Pink Beach Club.

This resort, like a handful of other truly fine cottage colonies, is both traditional and up-to-date, favored by those who come back year after year for its serenity and friendliness. It has two exquisite pink beaches and a main clubhouse where dinners are served overlooking the Atlantic. Lunches are served poolside, while breakfasts are on one's cottage terrace. From April to November there's live entertainment six nights a week, with a dinner-dance each Friday. Guests have access to two tennis courts on the premises and golf privileges at nearby Castle Harbour and the Mid Ocean Club. ◆ S. Shore Rd (Devil's Hole Rd). 293.1666, 800/422.1323; fax 293.8935

27 Flatts Village One of the Smith's first settlements, this quaint parish town was the meeting place of wealthy landowners and political powerbrokers who came to shape Bermuda's future. For 200 years, smugglers from the West Indies used to sneak ashore at night to illegally deposit their goods. ◆ Off N. Shore Rd

27 Bermuda Aquarium, Museum, and Zoo The aquarium displays most of the species of fish found in Bermuda's waters in their natural habitats. These include barracuda, many varieties of shark, mighty grouper, and a family of harbor seals. There is a zoological garden with tropical birds, monkeys, turtles, and alligators and a deep-sea diving exhibit devoted to **Dr. William Beebe** and the bathysphere that took him on his historic 1930s dives. ◆ Admission. Daily 9AM-5PM. Flatts Bridge (Harrington Sound). 293.2727

28 Palmetto Hotel and Cottages $$$ Take an old Bermuda mansion at the water's edge and turn it into a stately hotel, replete with an English-style pub (called the **Ha' Penny**).

Then add a cluster of tidy cottage suites. What do you have? This cozy, casual 42-room complex—a favorite of many. ◆ Flatts Bridge, 2.5 miles northwest of Hamilton. 293.2323, 800/982.0026

29 Devil's Hole Aquarium This pool, open as a natural aquarium since 1847, is formed naturally in the coral rocks and fed by streams of underground water from more than half a mile away. These days, it is chock-full of fish of all sizes, including sharks. Baited, but hookless, lines are available for children to try to "catch" the big one. ◆ Admission. Daily 10AM-5PM, except holidays. Harrington Sound Rd. 293.2072

30 Brightside Apartments $$$ Conveniently located on the major bus line, sandwiched between the Harrington Sound and the north shore, this is about as nice as Bermuda's housekeeping apartments come. Each of the 17 self-contained, one- and two-bedroom units has a private porch or patio right on Flatts Inlet. ◆ N. Shore Rd (Flatts Inlet). 292.8410

31 Cabana Vacation Apartments $$ Built in the 18th-century by fishers but used as a farmhouse for most of its history, this home has been remodeled to include seven housekeeping apartments, each with its own private entrance, ceiling fan, kitchen, and private bath. The original cedar ceilings, a well-preserved common room, and a deep pool make this spot user-friendly. ◆ Verdmont Rd (St. Mark's Rd). 236.6964

32 Verdmont Museum This vintage Bermuda house, built in 1662 by **William Sayles**, then governor of the island, is now a Bermuda National Trust property. The home blends Bermuda and New England elements of design, enhanced by an extensive collection of antique-cedar furniture, portraits of the manor's 18th-century inhabitants, and a delightful old nursery. ◆ Admission. M-Sa 10AM-5PM. Collector's Hill (S. Shore Rd). 236.7369

33 Spittal Pond Nature Reserve This is Bermuda's largest wildlife sanctuary, encompassing more than 60 acres. The scenic walkways wend along the high shoreline cliffs, passing through woodlands and meadows. The pond itself is fenced off, but bird-watchers can get close enough to see waterfowl land and take-off. The best viewing times and most activity takes place on the pond from November to May. Also within this Bermuda National Trust property, on a cliff facing the sea, is the famous **Spanish Rock** on which there is a cipher dated 1543, believed to have been carved by a Spanish or Portuguese mariner. ◆ Daily dawn-dusk. S. Shore Rd (Knapton Hill Rd). No phone

Bermuda

Since there are relatively few natural sources of drinking water, Bermudians collect raindrops from their whitewashed rooftops and store it in underground cisterns.

Devonshire

The first Earl of Devonshire in England, **William Cavendish**, a patron of several of the original settlers, inspired the naming of this parish. What sets it apart from the rest of the island is its lack of hotels, shops, and restaurants. Instead, there are rolling hills, marshes, and nature preserves.

34 Burch's Guest Apartments $$ This complex of 10 self-contained apartments features good views of the ocean, is located on the main east-west bus line, will rent bicycles, and is within a stone's throw from the Clay House Inn, a popular nightclub. There's also a pool on the premises. ◆ 110 N. Shore Rd, 2 miles east of Hamilton. 292.5746

35 Old Devonshire Church Some claim this has been sacred ground since an original church was built in 1624, though the present foundation dates back to 1716. The church was virtually destroyed by an explosion in 1970, but has since been totally reconstructed. ◆ Daily 9AM-5:30PM. Middle Rd (Brighton Hill Rd). 236.0537

36 Palm Grove Garden Set behind an old mansion, this private estate is open to the public and home to many species of birds. It's also the setting for one of Bermuda's most romantic Chinese moon gates. Another feature is a map of Bermuda created from plants in the middle of a pond. ◆ M-F 9AM-5PM. S. Shore Rd (Brighton Hill). No phone

37 Edmund Gibbons Nature Reserve Along with the nearby arboretum, this marshland park is a welcome break from sand, brine, palm trees and sunbathing. Audubonists delight in the flocks of marsh birds who preen and mutter among rare native flora. The land conservatory is maintained by the Natural Trust; they ask you to remain on the walkways. ◆ Free. Daily dawn-dusk. S. Shore Rd (Collector's Hill)

38 Ariel Sands Beach Club $$$$ This is one of Bermuda's most popular cottage colonies, right on the South Shore. It features an exceptional beach for snorkeling due to a large and varied resident population of colorful fish. There are 51 units with a common main clubhouse, restaurant, and bar. ◆ S. Shore Rd, 2.5 miles east of Hamilton. 236.1010, 800/468.6610

39 Arboretum The quiet, tasteful oasis contains endemic trees and innumerable indigenous plants of Bermuda in an open setting. The Bermuda Department of Agriculture and Fisheries supervises the upkeep of this park. If one of their staff happens to be around, do not miss the opportunity to gather important information about Bermuda's quickly disappearing native plant and wildlife. ♦ Free. Daily dawn-dusk. Middle Rd (Montpelier Rd). No phone

Pembroke

While most people equate Pembroke with Hamilton, the island's capital, the residential neighborhoods extend beyond the city toward the north shore, offering peninsular vistas of both busy Hamilton Harbour and the great Atlantic. Pembroke Parish is traditionally the first stop on any royal visitor's tour. The **Governor's House,** wherein dwells Bermuda's governor (appointed by the Queen of England), has lodged a variety of world leaders, including **John F. Kennedy** and **Sir Winston Churchill.**

40 La Casa del Masa $$ You can see the ocean and myriad fishing vessels, yachts, and cruise ships upon it from these three small housekeeping units. Each suite has two double beds, a color TV, a private telephone, and air-conditioning. A separate kitchen with complete cooking and dining facilities is available to guests. ♦ N. Shore Rd, 1 mile north of Hamilton. 292.8726

41 Mazarine by the Sea $$ Each of the seven rooms in this small guest house has a private bath, a kitchenette, and air-conditioning. Families with small children may want to think twice about staying here, however, because there isn't a beach, just an immediate drop off into 10 feet of water. ♦ N. Shore Rd, 1 mile north of Hamilton. 292.1659

42 Hi-Roy $$ The six-room guest house provides a complete homemade breakfast (bacon and eggs) every morning and a view of the ocean from the front porch. The air-conditioned rooms feature wall-to-wall carpeting, color TVs, private baths, and two twin-sized beds. ♦ Pitts Bay Rd (St. John's Rd). 292.0808

43 Robin's Nest $$ Each air-conditioned apartment in this three-unit minicottage colony is decorated differently (one's done completely in wicker) and comes with a phone and complete kitchen facilities. Sunbathers will enjoy the large pool on the premises. ♦ 10 Vale Close, less than 2 miles north of Hamilton. 292.4347

44 Spanish Point Park This is perhaps the first acre of Bermuda to be visited by European visitors, as some historians are convinced that **Captain Diego Ramirez** landed here briefly in 1503. Just more than a mile across the mouth of the Great Sound lies **Ireland Island;** the view of its shoreline from this quiet park is unmatched. ♦ Daily dawn-dusk. Spanish Point Rd (N. Shore Rd)

45 Marula Apartments $ The five hurricane-proof, housekeeping apartments are right on the protected waters of **Mill Creek Cove.** There's also a large swimming pool. ♦ Mariner's Lane (St. Johns Ave), 1.5 miles west of Hamilton. 295.2893

Hamilton

This is the capital of Bermuda, and it's one of the prettiest ports in the world. Most of Hamilton's main attractions are within easy walking distance of each other, and **Front Street's** elegant shops are among the island's biggest draws, but the boutiques in the side alleys of Front Street offer the best bargains.

46 Fort Hamilton This restored Victorian fort has a moat filled with stately Bermuda olive-wood bark trees, an underground passageway from the 1870s, and 18-ton guns. Built by order of the **Duke of Wellington** in 1868 to defend against suspected American attacks, it offers the best panoramic view of the city and harbor. There is a tearoom for your own internal fortification. ♦ Free. M-F 9:30AM-5PM. Happy Valley Rd (King St). No phone

47 Showbiz $$ If you're into the sixties scene, this restaurant is for you, complete with an old jukebox full of hits from that era. The dress code is bobby socks casual. ♦ American ♦ M-Sa 11:30AM-2:30PM, 5-10PM; Su noon-3:30PM, 6-10PM. Bar open until 1AM nightly. King St (Reid St). 292.0676

48 Ye Olde Cock and Feather ★$$ The second-floor pub has a dining terrace overlooking the harbor and ferry dock. Known for its soups and chowders, it also features pub fare such as kidney pie, prime ribs, and barbecued ribs. Popular with locals as well as visitors, it offers entertainment nightly, and has been known to be just a tad boisterous at times. ♦ British ♦ Daily 11AM-5:30PM, 6-10:30PM. Front St (Court-Union Sts). Reservations recommended. 295.2263

49 Bombay Bicycle Club ★$ Bermuda's only Indian restaurant features New Delhi-style delicacies from its tandoor oven. The daily luncheon buffet is a delicious change from the standard island offerings, but also a good buy. A caveat: it's located on the third floor of the **Rego Furniture** building, and may prove hard to find. ♦ Indian ♦ M-Sa noon-3PM, 6:30-11PM. Reid St (Church St). Reservations recommended. 292.0048

49 Rosa's Cantina $ Feast on nachos, black bean soup, Lone Star chile, guacamole, and almost every other known Tex-Mex dish. Wear jeans and cowboy boots if you have them;

you'll feel right at home. ♦ Mexican ♦ M-Sa noon-2:30PM, 5:30PM-midnight; Su 5:30PM-midnight. Happy hour: 5-7PM, 10PM-1AM. Reid St (Court St). 295.1912

Restaurants/Clubs: Red **Hotels:** Blue
Shops/ 🌳 Outdoors: Green **Sights/Culture:** Black

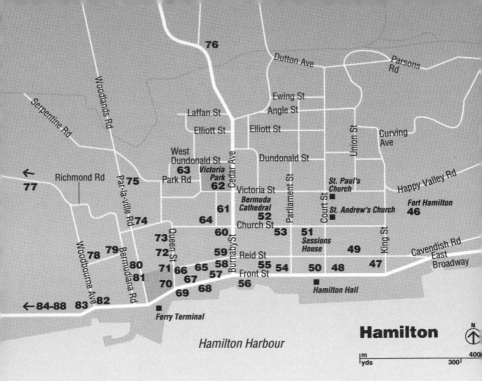

Hamilton

Hamilton Harbour

50 The Cabinet Building Bermuda's **Senate** (the upper legislative house) meets here on Wednesday at 10AM, except during summer recess. The two-story building also houses the offices of the island's premier. The monument in the front, known as the **Cenotaph,** is Bermuda's memorial to its dead in WWI and WWII. ◆ M-F 9AM-5PM. Front St (Parliament-Court Sts). 292.5501

51 Sessions House/House of Assembly Look for the **Victoria Jubilee Clock Tower,** which has been marking time since 31 December 1893. Bermuda's **House of Assembly** (the lower house of parliament) meets every Friday on the second floor. One should visit if only to see the wigged speaker preside over this august body of island lawmakers. The **Supreme Court** of Bermuda meets on the first floor, and a visitors' gallery is open to the public (call 292.1350 for times of assembly). Proper attire is mandatory for both. ◆ M-F 9:30AM-4:30PM. Parliament St (Reid-Church Sts). 292.7408

52 Cathedral of the Most Holy Trinity Better known as the **Bermuda Cathedral,** this impressive Gothic-style edifice is the seat of the Anglican church on Bermuda. The first church built on this site—**Trinity Church**—burned to the ground 12 years after its com-

Bermuda

pletion in 1872. Construction on this cathedral wasn't finished until 1911. Its 143-foot-tall tower is one of the dominant features of Hamilton's skyline. The pulpit and lectern are

replicas of those in the St. Giles Cathedral in Edinburgh, Scotland. ◆ Daily 8AM-5PM. Church St (Cedar Ave-Parliament St). 292.4033

53 Romanoff ★★★★$$$$ Owner/maitre d' **Antun Duzevic** has created what has to be the island's most surprising dining experience. Truly haute cuisine is served in a regal setting of red and gold velvet. Old World recipes for such timeless classics as *fillet de boef* stroganoff (as originally created in the 19th century for a Russian count), *paupiettes de sole Jacqueline* (stuffed fillet of sole with salmon mousse, served in champagne), and *tournedos flambé Alexander* (beef tenderloin flamed at the table with cognac, topped with a secret sauce) are among the specialties. Romanoff is mouth-watering testimony to Duzevic's training at Zurich's fabled Dolder Grand Hotel. ◆ French ◆ M-F noon-2:30PM, 7-10PM; Sa 7-10PM. Church St (Burnaby St). Jacket and tie required. Reservations required. 295.0333

54 Port O'Call ★★★★$$$$ With its distinctive nautical decor and upscale ambience, the Port O'Call is more like the dining room of an exclusive yacht club than a restaurant. As a result, this relatively new addition to the

Hamilton gourmet scene has become an overnight sensation. Nothing has been overlooked, including the fancy china. The luxurious setting is surpassed only by the excellence of the cuisine and the realistic prices (though deservedly pricey at dinner, lunch can be a real bargain). ♦ Seafood ♦ M-F noon-2PM, 7-9PM; Sa 7-9PM. Front St (Burnaby-Parliament Sts). Reservations required. 295.5373

54 Loquats ★$$ This sister restaurant of the **Hog Penny** and **Fisherman's Reef** is likewise informal, relatively inexpensive, and upbeat. The fare is an eclectic blend of Mexican, American, Italian, and Bermudian served in a setting that provides panoramic views of the harbor. A children's menu is available until 7:30PM. ♦ Bermudian ♦ M-Sa noon-2PM, 6-10PM. Front St (Parliament St). 292.4507

55 Chancery Wine Bar ★$ What better setting could there be for a wine bar than a former wine cellar? There's also a courtyard. ♦ Daily 11:30AM-2:30PM, 6:30-10:30PM. Bar service: 11:30AM-1AM. Chancery Lane (Front St). 295.5058

56 Passenger Terminals Several times each week during the peak tourist season, cruise ships arrive and depart from here. If expecting someone on a ship, be advised that St. George's and the Dockyards also have terminals. A favorite tourist attraction is watching these sea behemoths maneuver around the small crafts that share the extremely tight berthing area. ♦ Front St (Queen-Court Sts)

57 English Sports Shop This isn't quite Saville Row, but it's nevertheless noted for fine English menswear, woolens, and sports jackets, as well as designer suits, blazers, and **Harris** tweeds. They also feature women's sportswear from such leading firms as **Liberty**. ♦ M-Sa 9AM-5:30PM. 49 Front St (Queen St). 295.2672

57 Archie Brown and Son, Ltd. Sometimes called the **Pringle Shop** for being the exclusive outlet for famed **Pringle** of Scotland, this store is known for its superb selection of the finest quality sweaters and woolens. Cashmeres, Shetlands, and lamb's wools, plus almost all of the Scottish tartans and distinctive Irish knits, are carried here. ♦ M-Sa 9AM-5:30PM. Front St (Queen St). 295.2928

57 A.S. Cooper and Sons, Ltd. One of the most complete collections of European dinnerware, crystal, figurines, and gifts, all priced substantially below US prices, can be found here. **Wedgwood, Orrefors, Bing & Grondhal, Lladro, Waterford, Royal Doulton**, and **Swarovski** are among the prestigious names. They also have some of the best in British and

European clothing and accessories for ladies, gentlemen, and youngsters. ♦ M-Sa 9AM-5:30PM. Front St (Queen St). 295.3961

57 Pink's Delicatessen ★$ Even in Bermuda, a good deli is a good deal. The sandwiches here are hefty and reasonably priced, and the service is fast and attentive. Continental breakfasts are available, and you can select from more than 15 salads. Boxed lunches will be prepared for you on a day's notice. ♦ Deli ♦ M-F 7:30AM-4:30PM; Sa 8:30AM-4:30PM. 55 Front St, 2nd floor. 295.3524

58 Hog Penny Restaurant and Pub ★$$ Ask any Bermudian about "hog money" and they'll quickly tell you that it was the island's earliest British Colonial currency, having been issued in 1615 to take the place of tobacco (the first *real* currency). Hog money was issued in four denominations: twopence, threepence, sixpence, and shilling. One side of these coins bore the inscription "Sommer Islands," a wild boar, and Roman numerals reflecting the value. The reverse side had a ship with the cross of St. George at each masthead. Oddly enough, there was never an actual Hog Penny coin.

It wasn't until 1962 that the Hog Penny was conceived in the shape of a restaurant and pub. Since its opening, the establishment has become a part of Bermuda's heritage and culture, and a favorite meeting, eating, and drinking place for locals and tourists alike. The food is typically British, with steak and kidney pie, bangers, and hot, tasty mash. ♦ British ♦ Daily 11:30AM-5:30PM, 6-11PM. 5 Burnaby Hill (Front St). Reservations recommended. 292.2534

58 Fisherman's Reef ★$$ The popular seafood spot right over the Hog Penny is under the same management. Don't let its name deter you from having a delicious beef or veal dinner. And unlike most local fish restaurants, which feature the spiny or clawless lobsters, this one specializes in the Maine variety. ♦ Seafood ♦ M-F noon-2:30PM,

6:30-10:30PM; Sa-Su 6:30-11:30PM. 5 Burnaby Hill (Front St). Reservations recommended. 292.1609

Bermuda is the world's northernmost coral reef.

59 Bermuda Railway Company Although they don't openly admit it, these fun apparel stores, with their flip railroad station themes, are the brainchild of **Trimingham's**, and are indeed owned by them as well. They feature modestly priced men's and women's sportswear, mostly cotton, and generally with a BRC logo on it. ♦ M-Sa 9AM-5:30PM. Reid St (Burnaby St). 295.4830

La Trattoria

60 La Trattoria ★$ This is definitely not your typical deli, any more than Bermuda is a typical island. It's pure *la dolce vita,* and dirt cheap in the bargain. The choices include everything from hot homemade pasta and pizza to cool and creamy ice cream. ♦ Italian ♦ M-Sa 11AM-6PM. Washington Ln (Church-Reid Sts). 295.1877

61 Central Bus Terminal All of the government-owned pink buses serving Hamilton arrive and depart from this open-air terminal. The buses, along with the ferries, provide the most economical way to get from one point to another on Bermuda. For instance, a bus ride from the terminal to the **Royal Naval Dockyard** costs less than two dollars (as does a ferry trip). Both take about an hour. A taxi, which would cost about $24 for up to four people, takes 30 to 40 minutes. ♦ M-Sa 5:30AM-12:30AM; Su 9:15AM-4:45PM. Washington St (Church St). 292.3854

62 Monte Carlo ★★$$$ The artsy bistro named for the principality of the same name serves an eclectic mixture of French and Italian fare in an upbeat atmosphere. The featured dishes include piping hot focaccia with fresh rosemary and excellent carpaccio (thinly sliced raw beef) doused with shaved parmigiana and extra-virgin olive oil. ♦ French/Italian ♦ M-Sa noon-3PM, 6-11PM. 9 Victoria St, behind City Hall. 295.5453

63 Once Upon a Table ★★★★$$$$ Don't let the out-of-the-way, almost industrial setting deter you from a gustatory experience in this restored 18th-century home with tables lit by candles, windows draped in white lace

curtains, and several small intimate dining rooms. Starting with homemade herb-scented rolls, the menu includes such inventive entrées as grilled salmon trout with pink peppercorns, calves' liver with pears and black

currant sauce, and thinly sliced mignonettes of lamb in dark red currant sauce. ♦ French/Bermudian ♦ Daily 6:30-9:30PM. 49 Serpentine Rd, west of City Hall. 295.8585

64 Hamilton City Hall You'll recognize it as the building with the circular driveway and the six-foot-tall bronze weathervane, a replica of the *Sea Venture,* a ship closely tied to the island's early history. The *Sea Venture* wrecked on Puerto Rico (then uninhabited) in 1609. Besides municipal offices, City Hall also has a small auditorium for musical, dance, and theatrical performances, as well as an art gallery. ♦ M-F 9AM-5PM. Church St (Main Bus Terminal-Wesley St). 292.1234

65 Arcade Restaurant in Walker Courtyard ★$ This is Hamilton's top spot for the burger of your choice in a trellised garden setting. The arcade also serves breakfast all day, and will do box lunches for a picnic or day of sight-seeing. ♦ American ♦ M-Sa 7AM-9PM. Walker Arcade (Front-Reid Sts). 295.5130

65 Flying Chef's Biergarten ★$ If you're looking for a genuine German *oompah-pah* band, look no further than this beer garden cum ice cream parlor, serving "authentic" Bermudian-German fare. ♦ German ♦ M-Sa 10AM-1AM. Walker Arcade (Front-Reid Sts). 292.5516

66 Fourways Grill and Gourmet Shop ★★★$$ In the rear of a building called **The Windsor,** which is really an indoor shopping arcade, is one of the best places in town to have lunch. It's an offshoot of the **Fourways Inn** in West Paget and is rated as one of the finest of Bermuda's restaurants. An informal gourmet deli with table service can be found at street level, and one flight up is a proper dining room (actually a Continental grill) with bar service and more than one hundred wines on its list. The local movers and shakers can be seen lunching here, resplendent in their Bermuda shorts. A different multicourse luncheon special is featured daily. ♦ Continental ♦ M-Sa noon-2:30PM, 6-10PM. Queen St (Front-Reid Sts). 295.4086

67 Gosling's Wine and Spirit Merchants If anything can be said to be synonymous with Bermuda, it's rum, and nobody is more closely associated with Bermuda rum than Gosling's, founded in 1806. Their **Black Seal Rum** is the most well known and, indeed, the best selling of all the island's rums. It is a smooth, dark, full-flavored beverage, blended on the island according to a centuries-old Gosling family recipe and, until 1900, was called **Old Rum** and was available only on draught out of ancient wooden barrels. Shortly after WWI Gosling's began to bottle Old Rum in the most widely available empty bottles in Bermuda—used champagne bottles. However, labels were not put on the bottles, so the rum was identified by the black color of the sealing used to cover the cork (hence the origin of the name Black Seal). ♦ M-Sa 8:30AM-5:30PM. Front St (Queen St). 295.1123

67 New Harbourfront Restaurant ★★$$$
For many years, one of Bermuda's most popular restaurants was the **Tavern on the Green** at the **Botanical Gardens** just outside of Hamilton. However, the government recently took back the space in order to operate a souvenir shop, and the restaurant closed. Fortunately, much of the ambience of the former restaurant has shifted to this second-floor establishment overlooking the harbor and Front Street. The cuisine is a combination of French, Mediterranean, and Bermudian served in a casual, comfortable atmosphere accented by blue velvet, starched linen, and fine crystal. ♦ Bermudian ♦ M-Sa 11:45AM-3PM; 6:30-10:30PM. Front St West. 295.4207, 295.4527

67 Bird Cage The funny little structure in the middle of the intersection of Front and Queen streets is not a piece of sculpture, but rather where, prior to the installation of traffic lights, a helmeted constable would direct traffic. Nowadays, however, it's rarely occupied. ♦ Front St (Queen St)

67 H.A. and E. Smith Ltd. Like so many of the fine stores on Front Street, Smiths is a Bermuda institution, having been founded in 1889 by **Henry A. Smith** and his wife, **Edith**, and so its official name. After the turn of the century it was taken over by their son **Alfred Blackburn Smith**, and subsequently incorporated in 1922. Today, the company is still 100 percent Bermudian owned, with the Smith family retaining a substantial interest. Best described as a smart specialty department store in a uniquely Bermudian fashion, Smiths first specialized in ladies' clothing and accessories, and has since expanded to feature almost everything from fine crystal and bone china to perfumes, luggage, fine jewelry, all at considerable savings over US prices. ♦ M-Sa 8:30AM-5:30PM. 35 Front St (Queen St). 295.2288

Trimingham's

67 Trimingham's Just as Queen Elizabeth visited New York's Bloomingdale's, so should you visit Trimingham's, Bermuda's landmark store that has been family owned and operated since 1842. The island's largest store is an exceptional place to shop for European imports at considerable savings over state-side prices. The world's finest china, crystal, perfumes, jewelry, sweaters, fashions, and accessories are featured throughout the four floors. ♦ M-Sa 9AM-5:30PM. Front St (Queen St). 295.1183

Bermuda is the oldest self-governing British colony.

Restaurants/Clubs: Red	**Hotels:** Blue
Shops/ ⚜ Outdoors: Green	**Sights/Culture:** Black

68 Crisson Jewelers Someday, somebody is going to get an exact count of how many branches this prestigious chain has in Bermuda; it seems as if every other store in Hamilton is a Crisson branch. One might think it was New York's 47th Street at Sea. Few jewelers anywhere, regardless of how many stores they have, feature so many fine names in jewelry, or carry such an extensive selection, all at prices considerably below those in the states. ♦ M-Sa 9AM-5:30PM. Queen St (Front St). 295.2351

68 Bermuda Buggy Stand The legendary Bermuda buggies can be hired from here. It should be noted that the government oversees the care and condition of the horses and sets the rates that are clearly posted. If the buggies aren't around, wait a few minutes; one will return shortly. ♦ Front St (Queen-Burnaby Sts)

69 Visitors Service Bureau Operated by the government's Department of Tourism, the bureau offers everything you'll ever need to know about the island—maps, brochures, free information, and plenty of helpful advice. Ferries to Paget and Warwick parishes and across the Great Sound to the West End depart from the docks behind the **Ferry Terminal.** **Albuoy's Point,** a small grassy park, and the **Royal Bermuda Yacht Club,** the sponsor of several ocean races to and from the states, are also nearby. ♦ M-Sa 9AM-5PM. Front St (Par-la-Ville Rd). 295.1480

The Irish Linen Shop

70 The Irish Linen Shop True, there are Irish linens galore, double damask, and other handwork from the Emerald Isle sold here. But there are also laces from Belgium; embroidery from Madeira; and tableware from Italy, France, and England. The second floor is brimming with bolts of fine fabric, especially those of France's famous designer, **Souleiado.** ♦ M-Sa 9AM-5:30PM. 31 Front St (Queen St). 295.4089

71 Perot Post Office This mid 19th-century post office is a good place to buy stamps for friends. Note the architectural beauty and charm of the white-shuttered building. ♦ M-F 8AM-5PM; Sa 8AM-noon. Queen St (Reid St). 295.5151

72 Par-la-Ville Park This refreshing parcel of Bermuda's Old World charm has been fastidiously preserved as a park in the heart of the city, offering a delightful respite from sightseeing and shopping. It was formerly the home of Bermuda's first postmaster, **William**

B. Perot, in the early 1800s. Today, it houses the **Bermuda Public Library** and the **Bermuda Historical Society Museum.** ♦ Queen St (Front-Church Sts)

Within Par-La-Ville Park:

Bermuda Historical Society Museum Among the treasures in the museum are furnishings from the 18th and 19th centuries, an interesting collection of Bermuda's early "hog money," cedar and whalebone crafts made by prisoners of the **Boer War,** and some Bermuda silver. Public restrooms are located at the Front Street side of the library, accessible from Queen Street. ◆ Donation. M-Tu, Th-Sa 9:30AM-4:30PM. 295.2487

73 Kentucky Fried Chicken $ Like everywhere, the chicken served here is "finger lickin' good." For the record, there's also a **McDonald's** in Bermuda, but it's only open to the general public on Tuesday (when visitors are allowed on the US Naval Air station in St. George's where the Golden Arches are located for the "exclusive benefit of navy personnel and their dependents"). ◆ Fast Food ◆ Daily 11AM-10PM. Queen St (Front St). 295.5887

74 New Queen Restaurant $ This restaurant features both Cantonese and Szechuan fare, as well as an array of American and English dishes. The decor is nothing special, but the food is superb. ◆ Chinese ◆ M-Sa 11:30AM-midnight; Su 5:30PM-midnight. Par-la-Ville Rd (Church St). 295.4004, 292.3282

75 M.R. Onions ★$ With a name like that, you'd expect such menu items as "Attack a Rack" (baby back ribs) and "Two for Tuna Thursdays." The restaurant's name is derived from the expression "Them are Onions" (Bermudians refer to themselves as Onions, for the sweet red onion grown on the island) meaning "he's one of us." Not only is it fun and economical, especially the three-course, early-bird dinner specials, but the fare, including a wide range of seafood offerings, is quite good. ◆ Bermudian ◆ M-F noon-3PM, 5:30-10PM; Sa-Su 5:30-10PM. Bar: daily until 1AM. Par-la-Ville Rd North. 292.5012

76 Government Tennis Stadium You can rent a tennis court here if your hotel or cruise ship doesn't have one. Choose between clay and asphalt courts, both of which go for about five dollars an hour. They light the courts at night, which is a great way to beat the heat, but an additional fee is charged. ◆ M-F 8AM-10PM; Sa-Su 8AM-7PM. Cedar Ave, just blocks north of Hamilton. 292.0105

77 Edgehill Manor $$ The totally refurbished guest house offers nine rooms, most with private balconies or terraces. There aren't any beaches nearby, but you can take a dip in the swimming pool. Breakfast is served buffet-style, with plenty of muffins and scones. ◆ End of Rosemont Ave. 295.7124

Bermuda

Bermuda's first permanent settlers were shipwrecked victims of British Admiral Sir George Somers' flagship, *Sea Venture,* which crashed on Bermuda's reefs in 1609 while en route to settle the Jamestown colony in Virginia.

78 Oxford Guest House $$ The 12-room family owned and managed guest house is smack dab in the middle of town. Built in 1938, each room is unique and private; a sun-drenched lounge is accessible from all accommodations. For early risers, a nutritious breakfast is included, featuring healthy slices of homegrown citrus. ◆ Woodbourne Ave. 295.0503

79 Lobster Pot and Boathouse Bar ★★$$$ This, Bermuda's oldest and most popular place for seafood, seems to have been transported directly from Boston's waterfront. The service is friendly, the atmosphere salty, the ambience pure "Mudian," and the prices more than fair. The lobsters are fresh from a giant saltwater tank and the fish are caught right off the docks. For energizing lunches, the chowders, whether the traditional fish variety or the succulent conch, are unbeatable. ◆ Seafood ◆ M-Sa 11AM-1AM, except holidays. 6 Bermudiana Rd. Reservations required. 292.6898

80 The Little Venice Restaurant ★★$$$ This popular restaurant offers an extensive menu of veal, seafood, fish, and pasta flavored with fresh ingredients such as piquant Bermuda lemon, basil, and fragrant rosemary. Somewhat more formal than other Italian restaurants on the island, the dress is "smart casual," meaning ties and jackets for men and dresses for their ladies. After dinner, many go upstairs to **The Club,** a disco, for a nightcap and dancing into the night. ◆ Italian ◆ Daily 11:45AM-2:30PM, 6:30-10:30PM. Bermudiana Rd (Gorman Rd). Reservations recommended. 295.3503

81 Portofino ★★$ Almost every night there's a line in front of this 45-seat, totally informal Italian bistro, as popular for its 14 varieties of fresh-baked, nine-inch pizzas as it is for pasta, fish, and meat specialties. And somehow, each night, more than 200 people manage to dine here. It's fun, intimate, and inexpensive. More important, it's probably the best Italian food at any price on the island and has been for 13 years. ◆ Italian ◆ Daily noon-3PM, 6PM-midnight. Bermudiana Rd (Pitts Bay Rd). 295.6090, 292.2375

82 William Bluck and Company If it's fine European china and crystal you're after, look no further. Even if you're just looking, plan to spend at least half a day browsing through this 140-year-old emporium's huge selection. There's china from **Richard Ginori, Royal Worcester, Wedgwood, Hermès, Spode, Aynsley, Royal Crown Derby, Royal Doulton,** and **Chase,** and **Herend** porcelain from Hungary. There's also crystal by **Waterford, Baccarat, St. Louis, Maroolin, Daum, Hoya,** and **Lalique.** ◆ M-Sa 9AM-5:30PM. Front St West. 295.5367

83 Woodbourne Guest House $$ This four-bedroom guest house with a lounge/breakfast room is within walking distance to the center of town. ◆ Woodbourne Ave (Front St). 295.3737

84 Rosedon $$$ The meticulously maintained Bermuda manor is set on well-manicured grounds just steps from the center of Hamilton. Seventeen rooms, a heated swimming pool, and complimentary tennis and beach privileges are provided for guests at the Elbow Beach Hotel. ◆ Pitts Bay Rd, across from the Princess Hotel. 295.1640, 800/225.5567

85 The Princess Hotel $$$$ Sometimes called the Pink Palace by the Sea, the Princess is a gracious blend of classic European elegance and a traditional Bermudian atmosphere right at the harbor's edge. It is also the largest in-town resort hotel, offering complete exchange facilities with its sister hotel, the **Southampton Princess,** via a complimentary boat shuttle. Named for Princess Louise, **Queen Victoria's** daughter who visited the island in 1883, the Princess has a heated freshwater pool, as well as a smaller saltwater one. There is also a putting green. ◆ Pitts Bay Rd. 295.3000, 800/223.1818

Within the Princess Hotel:

Harley's ★$$ Lively day and night, this grill is popular for its indoor/outdoor terrace. The poolside garden setting would not be out of place in Florence or Nice, and neither would the food, which ranges from rum-laced fish chowder and sandwiches to Greek cashew chicken and fettuccine with fresh wahoo in a white garlic sauce. ◆ Mediterranean ◆ Daily 7-11AM, noon-4:30PM, 6-10PM. 295.3000

The Colony Pub ★$$ The cedar-paneled bar off the main lobby has food and grog in the tradition of an Old English bar, though juicy American-style burgers are available all day. ◆ British ◆ Daily 10-11:30AM, noon-4PM, 6:30-10PM. 295.3000

Tiara Room ★★★$$$ With harbor views from every table, an all-encompassing menu that features half a dozen flambé creations, and accordingly fiery chandeliers and tiara-shaped candle displays, this is one of Bermuda's most popular gourmet dining rooms, and the site of many galas and banquets, including the awards dinner for the

Newport to Bermuda Ocean Race. The dinners are elaborate five-course endeavors, with an emphasis on seafood and succulent meats such as roast duck and chateaubriand. The buffet-style breakfast served each morning is equally comprehensive but much less formal. ◆ International ◆ Daily 7:30-10:30AM, 6:30-9PM. Reservations and jacket required. 295.3000

86 Waterloo House $$$ One of Bermuda's favorite and finest small hotels, a refurbished 19th-century house, is located directly on the harbor. It's also among the few places in Hamilton where one can enjoy breakfast, lunch, and dinner (alfresco if you wish) at the water's edge. There's a swimming pool tucked away in one of its several cozy, flower-filled courtyards, and guests also enjoy full privileges at Waterloo's sister hotels, **Newstead** and **Horizons and Cottages,** as well as access to the tennis courts and ocean beach at the exclusively private **Coral Beach Club.** ◆ Pitts Bay Rd. 295.4480, 800/468.7100; fax 295.2585

Within the Waterloo House:

The Waterloo ★★★$$$$ This fine establishment provides a cosmopolitan array of Swiss, French, native Bermudian, and Continental cuisine. Zurich-born and trained chef **Bruno Heeb** serves nouvelle cuisine, combined with a changing menu of native fish creations, including Bermuda rockfish and tangy mussel pie. ◆ Continental ◆ Daily 8AM-2:30PM, 6:30-10PM. Reservations recommended. 295.4480

87 Ristorante Primavera ★★$$$ It's too bad that this excellent restaurant, recognized for its fine cuisine, can't be satisfied being what it is, namely a great place for Italian food in a comfortable atmosphere. Instead, its upstairs **Oyster Bar,** accessible through the restaurant, has a raucous happy hour on weekdays, then becomes a sushi bar, and finally, in the wee hours, an eardrum-splitting Latin nightspot. ◆ Italian ◆ M-F 11:45AM-2:30PM, 6:30-10:30PM; Sa-Su 6:30-10:30PM. Happy hour: M-F 5-7:30PM. 69 Pitts Bay Rd. 295.2167

88 Royal Palms Club Hotel and Restaurant $$ A turn-of-the-century private home surrounded by lush, blooming flower gardens has been turned into a 12-room hotel, complete with a casual restaurant and cocktail lounge. ◆ 24 Rosemont Ave. 292.1854

Paget
Bordered by Hamilton Harbour on the north

and the Atlantic on the south, Paget is one of the most desirable residential areas in Bermuda, with beautiful historic homes, as well as many of the island's finest hotels and restaurants.

89 King Edward VII Memorial Hospital

One of the silent reminders of Bermuda's wealth and high standard of living is its modern, efficient, and exceptionally well-staffed hospital just outside the city limits of Hamilton. The hospital has complete around-the-clock, outpatient emergency services. ♦ Point Finger Rd (S. Shore Rd). 236.2345

89 Botanical Gardens and Camden

A natural and national treasure of Bermuda, its manicured grounds are ablaze with hundreds of flowers, shrubs, and trees. Special tours of the 36-acre gardens are held on Tuesday, Wednesday, and Friday mornings; they leave at 10:30AM from Tavern on the Green. A very special feature is the **Garden for the Blind,** a collection of foliage selected for individual scents. **Camden,** once a gracious private residence, is now the home of Bermuda's premier. The house is also open for tours. ♦ Gardens: daily 8:30AM-sunset. Camden: T, W noon-2PM. Point Finger Rd (S. Shore Rd). 236.4201

90 Waterville

The headquarters of the **National Trust,** a nonprofit organization dedicated to the preservation of historic buildings and wildlife preserves throughout the island, is located in this 18th-century home. Unfortunately, tours of the building are not permitted, but its gift shop on the lower level, appropriately called **Trustworthy,** is a good place to do some souvenir shopping. ♦ Shop: daily 9:30AM-4:30PM. S. Shore Rd, just west of the Foot-of-the-Lane roundabout. 236.6483

91 Que Sera

$ This centrally located, three-unit guest house has all of the necessary efficiency amenities, plus a swimming pool that is just steps away from both the Botanical Gardens and the hospital. ♦ Point Finger Rd (S. Shore Rd, 1 mile south of Hamilton). 236.1998

92 Grape Bay Cottages

$$ Two small, pink two-bedroom housekeeping cottages, each with its own fireplace, overlook Grape Bay and the beach. They're reasonably remote, yet close to Hamilton and golf. ♦ S. Shore Rd (Grape Bay). 236.1194, 800/541.7426

93 Glenmar Holiday Apartments

$ This small cluster of five housekeeping cottages on the South Shore is available for rent to large parties—perfect for family reunions. ♦ Mission Rd (S. Shore Rd). 236.2844

94 Dawkins Manor

$ This seven-room guest house was formerly known as Serenity. It's a hike to the nearest beach, but the casual friendly atmosphere (and air-conditioned rooms) are worth it. ♦ 29 St. Michael's Rd (S. Shore Rd). 236.7419

Bermuda

95 White Sands and Cottages

$$$ Just a five-minute walk to the beach at Grape Bay, this 35-unit luxury hotel is well maintained and holds to many of the ageless traditions of Bermuda, such as requiring gentlemen to wear a jacket and tie to dinner. It's ideally suited to those who want a convenient location and a relatively low-key atmosphere. ♦ S. Shore Rd (Grape Bay). 236.2486

96 Stonington Beach Club

$$$ This is a most interesting situation, since the property is owned by the government of Bermuda and staffed by students studying to be tomorrow's hoteliers at the Hotel Technology Department of **Bermuda College.** The result is a beachfront, modern hotel, with each of the 64 rooms outfitted with a balcony facing the ocean and one of the most ambitious and anxious-to-please staffs anywhere. The hotel's restaurant and kitchen, both maintained by supervised students, is not only an excellent place to dine, but modestly priced considering the quality, service, and ambience. ♦ S. Shore Rd (Middle Rd). 236.5416, 800/223.1588

97 Elbow Beach Hotel

$$$$ Over the years, it's been said that Bermuda enjoys what's almost a "progression" among its visitors, many of whom were first introduced to the island during the legendary "College Weeks in Bermuda." Elbow's expansive beach serves as the College Weeks' headquarters, with dawn-to-dusk activities for thousands of collegians, all of whom were treated to a complimentary lunch, day after day and week after week. Many of these students would return to the island's large resort hotels on their honeymoons, and later to the smaller hotels and cottage colonies with their own families.

As such, the Elbow Beach Hotel has become synonymous with Bermuda to legions of college graduates. It is a large hotel, set on a 35-acre oceanfront estate, with 298 rooms and suites and almost everything else except golf, which can easily be arranged. Its beach is second to none on the island, and the motel-like lanais, especially those on the lowest tier directly in front of the beach, are extremely desirable.

A complimentary shuttle service operates around the clock, taking guests up and down the hill. You may want to ask for a room on an upper floor to minimize the daytime noise from the swimming pool. Dining at Elbow is a treat regardless of where its done. The resort also has one of the best ongoing tennis programs on the island, with five courts. ♦ S. Shore Rd (Elbow Beach). 236.3535, 800/223.7434; fax 236.8043

Within the Elbow Beach Hotel:

The Terrace Room ★★$$$$ Like most posh resort dinner clubs, this is expensive, expansive, exuberant gourmet dining. The fixed-price menu rotates around rich meats: roast veal, hearty duck, butter wahoo, and monkfish. A la carte meals are also available, but there's not much of a price break, considering the missing soup, salad, and dessert. ♦ International ♦ Daily 6:30-10:30PM. 236.3535

The Sea Horse Grill ★$ The long luncheon hours allow plenty of time to peruse the variety-filled menu, which emphasizes cheap finger-foods such as burgers, fish and chips, and healthy pita-pocket creations. During the summer months, there's dancing under the stars on the beach terrace and live entertainment in the **Sea Horse Pub**. ♦ American ♦ Daily 11:30AM-3PM, 6:30-9:30PM. 236.6060

98 Coral Beach and Tennis Club $$$$ This is a private club, unless, of course, you've been introduced by a member or just happen to belong to another club which has a reciprocal agreement. Chances are good to excellent, however, that by using the right travel agent, you'll be able to book one of the 66 guest units in traditional Bermuda-style cottages and suites. Another way to gain access to the best of Bermuda's tennis facilities, with eight Har-Tru courts and two squash courts, is to be a guest at one of its sister properties (Horizons and Cottages, Newstead, or Waterloo House), and simply come and go at will, with all charges billed to your hotel room.

You can even have dinner at the club, enjoying the almost nightly music and dancing and weekly specials such as their fabled buffet, Calypso night, and black-tie dinner dance. If you do, a jacket and tie is mandatory, with ladies attired in cocktail dresses. Oh yes—don't let the "club" deceive you. This is a first-class hotel with all of the services one might expect, including room service en suite breakfasts, a splendid afternoon tea, and one of the friendliest bar-lounges on the island. ♦ S. Shore Rd, 4 miles south of Hamilton. 236.2233

99 Horizons and Cottages $$$$ If you know Bermudian architecture, you're familiar with the unique "welcoming arms" that are generally outside the entry stairs. Nothing could be more fitting for Horizons, a very special place for those who demand and appreciate the best, be it in accommodations, food, service, or company.

As the island's sole member of the prestigious Relais and Chateaux, this 50-unit cottage colony personifies that organization's five C's—character, courtesy, calm, charm, and cuisine—with a rarely experienced grace and style. Its success is primarily due to the talent and efforts of its long-time managing director, Austrian **Wilhelm Sack,** who has himself become a Bermuda institution, and in 1991 was named Bermuda's "Hotelier of the Year." Small in stature but big at heart," Willie," as he's universally known to all, presides over everything at Horizons, assuring only the best for his guests, about 65 percent of whom return year after year.

A sister property of Waterloo, Newstead, and Coral Beach Club, Horizons has its own tennis courts, a nine-hole pitch-and-putt golf course, an 18-hole putting green, and a large swimming pool and patio with fantastic ocean views. Guests have full privileges, including use of the beach and restaurants at the Coral Beach Club just across the street. ♦ S. Shore Rd (Tribe Rd 4-Tribe Rd 5). 236.0048; fax 236.1981

Within Horizons and Cottages:

Horizons

Horizons ★★★$$$$ Because of its Relais and Chateaux affiliation, there's good reason to expect superior cuisine at Horizons, and the kitchen lives up to all expectations, including the weekly barbecue party held on the lower terrace, featuring everything from filet mignon to tangy ribs and whole lobsters. Most nights, though, sublime French-country cuisine is served; book early and often, for non-resident seating is limited. ♦ French ♦ Daily 8-9:30AM, noon-3PM, 7:30-9PM. Reservations required. 236.0048

100 Harmony Club $$$$ If one is into "all-inclusives," this 71-room, couples-only hotel is the place for you. Actually, the idea of going to a resort where everything, including drinks and gratuities, is included in the room rate (a concept that originated in Jamaica) and

is becoming more and more popular, as it affords vacationers the opportunity to know their precise expenses in advance. The club has a pool, on-site tennis, and golf privileges at its sister hotel, the **Belmont.** Unfortunately, the all-inclusive plan tends to detract from the overall Bermuda experience, since visiting the numerous fine restaurants around the island is an integral part of the charm. ♦ S. Shore Rd (Middle Rd). 236.3500, 800/225.5843

101 Valley Cottages and Apartments $$ All of the nine housekeeping cottages have TVs and telephones. ♦ Middle Rd (Valley Rd). 236.0628

102 Loughlands $$ The stately Bermuda mansion astride nine acres of manicured grounds has been converted into a 25-room guest house. It features a large swimming pool and a tennis court. The bedrooms feature high-post beds and antique chests. ♦ 79 S. Shore Rd (Elbow Beach). 236.1253

102 Paraquet Guest Apartments $$ Nine quaint Bermudian cottages with kitchenettes are clustered amiably across a verdant slope, making this a good choice for family vacations. The rooms are air-conditioned and comfortably furnished. And it's only a five-minute walk to Elbow Beach. ♦ S. Shore Rd. 236.5842

103 Sky Top Cottages $$ Perched upon a hilltop with views of the ocean, its 11 modest units offer a traditional British atmosphere at a modest cost. Half of the English-style cottages date from the early 20th century, and all of the cottages are air-conditioned, with private baths and full kitchenettes. ♦ Southcote Rd (S. Shore Rd). 236.7984

104 Barnsdale Guest Apartments $$ The compact five-unit complex of self-contained studio units has its own swimming pool. ♦ Middle Rd (S. Shore Rd). 236.4709

105 Fourways Inn $$$$ Years ago Mark Twain said, "You go to heaven, I'll go to Bermuda, which is heaven on earth!" Chances are he knew that cottages would be built behind the even then popular **Peg Leg's Tavern**. Actually, Fourways (pictured above) traces its heavenly roots back to 1727, but it's only been since 1976, that famed Czechoslovakian hotelier **Walter Sommer** purchased the property.

Sommer, the former president of the Princess Hotel chain, set about to create one of the most upscale resorts on the island. The result was an almost immediate success. The regis-

ter brimmed with the names of notables from around the world: **President George Bush**, **King Faud** of Saudi Arabia, **Margaret Thatcher** and **John Major** from the United Kingdom, and a host of celebrities from

around the world. In a word, Fourways' cottages have become Bermuda's showplace, setting an island-wide standard for excellence. Guests receive Fourways famous Continental breakfast either ensuite or on their terraces. ♦ 1 Middle Rd (Cobbs Hill). 236.6517, 800/962.7654

Within Fourways Inn:

Fourways Inn Restaurant ★★★$$$$ Bermudian food at its best is part traditional British simplicity and part imaginative island creativity, with more than a little European flair for the exquisite and a dash of Yankee ingenuity. The Fourways epitomizes this ideal quartet, harmonizing in delicious tones. On any given night, you might encounter something on the level of the *Sole de Douvres*: imported Dover sole sautéed with prawns and capers and seasoned with lemon and parsley. Don't miss the chef's special smoked-salmon bisque served cold with dill, or the roast beef on its own juice-soaked Yorkshire pudding. ♦ Bermudian ♦ Daily 6:30-9:30PM. Jacket and tie required. Reservations required. 236.6517

106 Pretty Penny $$ This is one of the more attractive and better appointed groups of housekeeping cottages. Secluded, yet close to the ferries and South Shore beaches, it has nine fully equipped units. ♦ Cobbs Hill Rd (Harbour Rd). 236.1194, 800/541.7426

107 Newstead $$$$ Like its sister properties (Waterloo House, Horizons and Cottages, and the Coral Beach Club), Newstead (illustrated above) represents an era that Bermuda and its aficionados refuse to forget. It's small, having but 500 rooms and cottage suites that are grand, traditional, and extremely proper. The grounds and gardens are exquisite, as are the buildings, especially the former manor house where the main lobby, library, lounge, dining room, and bar are located. There are two tennis courts, a heated pool, a sauna, and swimming from the bulkhead. In addition, guests have privileges at both Horizons and the Coral Beach Club. ♦ 27 Harbour Rd (Chapel Rd). 236.6060, 800/468.4111; fax 236. 7454

108 Glencoe Harbour Club $$$ Not that many years ago, there were "two" Bermudas—one for the general public, the other for a privileged few. A small hotel on its own peninsula at the head of Hamilton Harbour, many of those "few" would make Glencoe their home in Bermuda. When sailors arrived on racing yachts, they too would head for Glencoe. And so it was that Glencoe became a bastion of upscale elegance, overseen by its legendary owner/host **Reggie Cooper.**

Bermuda has changed, and with it Glencoe. All are now welcome within its hallowed walls. Glencoe has two swimming pools with patios and gardens, a small private beach, a restaurant, a bar, and what has to be the most delightful and scenic terrace on the island, regularly patrolled by an ever-so-friendly cat and its constant companion, a "killer duck" who will peck at one's leg until offered a morsel of food. Best of all, no two of the spacious, breeze-cooled, mostly harbor-view rooms are alike. ♦ Harbour Rd (Salt Kettle Rd). 236.5274, 800/468.1500

Within the Glencoe Harbour Club:

Glencoe ★★$$$ As might be expected, the kitchen is superior, offering imaginative fare such as avocado soup with crabmeat and almonds, a seafood *mille feuille* (a combination of rockfish, scallops, mussels, and shrimp served in a puff pastry shell with tangy seafood sauce), and turkey Argenteuil (scallops cut from the breast of turkey, topped with ragout sauce, ham, and fresh tomatoes, baked with Swiss cheese). ♦ French ♦ M-Sa 8-10AM, noon-2:30PM, dinner seating 7PM, 8:30PM; Su 8-10AM, noon-3PM, dinner seatings 7PM, 8:30PM. Dinner reservations required. 236.5274

109 Palm Reef Hotel $$ Old-timers will remember it as the **Inverurie Hotel,** right at the water's edge. Unfortunately, few reminders of the gracious ambience of those earlier days remain, except perhaps for the menu covers that read "Inverurie" (pronounced in-ver-roor-ee) and are still being used (the management claims they haven't gotten around to printing new ones, even though the Palm Reef has been open for more than a year). As a matter of fact, they don't seem to have done much to update the hotel, which had been shuttered for some time prior to the reopening. ♦ Harbour Rd (at the intersection of Paget and Warwick parishes). 236.1000

Warwick

On the south shore, Warwick Parish is the site of Bermuda's longest uninterrupted stretch of beach, running more than three miles from **Astwood Park** to **Horseshoe Bay;** on the north, it's noted for the fine homes lining the harbor and the plethora of agreeable hotels and cottages. Indeed, unless you're going the deluxe-hotel route, chances are you'll spend a night or two in this lovely, well-situated parish. Most of the accommodations are located within blocks of one another, so if you don't happen to like what you see, just look across the street or up the road.

110 Surf Side Beach Club $$$ Planned and constructed with much care, this hillside complex contains 35 housekeeping cottages spread evenly among terraced gardens overlooking a private beach. Choose from the oceanside efficiencies or hilltop penthouse suites. An open-air coffee shop serves light meals poolside. ♦ S. Shore Rd (Tribe Rd 1). 236.7100

111 Marley Beach Cottages $$$ If you're a movie buff, you'll immediately recognize these 17 tidy housekeeping cottages as locations where scenes from **Peter Benchley's** movie *The Deep* were shot. The views from the cliff-edge swimming pool are spectacular, high above the expansive, though boulder-dotted private beach. ♦ S. Shore Rd (Marley Beach). 236.1143, 236.8910

112 Sandpiper Apartments $$ Situated happily between several beaches, this complex provides an ideal compromise between comfort and cost. There are nine studio apartments among the 14 housekeeping units, each of which accommodates either single or double occupancy. ♦ S. Shore Rd, across the street from the Flamingo Beach Club. 236.7093

113 Astwood Cove $$ Built in 1720 to headquarter a dairy farm, the homestead's transformation into vacation lodging has not destroyed its charm. Modern, bright studio-apartments are clustered around a pool at the edge of a subtropical nature park filled with birds and lush fruit trees and shrubbery. ♦ S. Shore Rd, just east of Long Bay Beach. 236.0984

114 Granaway Guest House and Cottage $$ This is a great spot to do absolutely nothing but watch Hamilton Harbour and swim off the sea wall. It's a circa 1734 homestead, since modified to house five peaceful guest rooms. ♦ Harbour Rd (Hamilton Harbour). 236.1805

These Shorts Were Made for Walking

The first people to wear short trousers on Bermuda were British military personnel, who created them around 1900 as a tropical adaptation of their uniforms. Bermudian business executives and affluent visitors to the islands were quick to copy the look, which called for knee-length trousers accompanied, always, by a pair of knee-high socks with their tops turned down.

During the 1930s, students from Ivy League colleges brought their Bermuda shorts back to the

states, wearing them primarily on campus, though without the knee-high socks. Over the years, the length of Bermuda shorts crept up from being just above the top of the knee to anywhere between the knee and mid-thigh.

115 Belmont Hotel, Golf and Country Club
$$$$ Over the years, this once regal country-club resort has slipped in elegance and popularity. However, in anticipation of Bob Hope's 1990 stay there while taping his annual Christmas special for television, the hotel underwent a quick (if superficial) refurbishment. Hopefully, these renewed standards will be maintained, since Belmont has enjoyed an excellent reputation in the past. Situated on a 110-acre estate with a championship 18-hole golf course, three tennis courts, and a swimming pool with unique underwater windows, about half of its 154 rooms and suites offer outstanding views of Hamilton Harbour and the Great Sound. Though it doesn't have a beach, all water activities can easily be arranged and shuttles leave frequently to the hotel's nearby **Discovery Bay Beach Club.** There's a main dining room as well as light food service in the **Terrace Cafe and Golf Club,** in addition to exchange privileges with its sister property, **The Harmony Club.** ♦ Harbour Rd (Middle Rd). 236.1301, 800/225.5843

116 South View Apartments $ The three compact Bermudian housekeeping cottages include a moderately priced penthouse with a garden terrace and ocean views. ♦ S. Shore Rd, next to the Mermaid Beach Club. 236.5257

117 Longtail Cliffs $$$ Thirteen modern two-bedroom, two-bath housekeeping apartments are perched on dramatic cliffs with a private beach. If possible, opt for a second-floor unit with stratospheric ceilings and wonderful views of the ocean and the hundreds of longtail seagulls that inhabit the cliffs. ♦ S. Shore Rd. 236.2864

118 Mermaid Beach Club $$$ Most of the 83 rooms in this crescent-shaped hotel offer ocean views and private balconies. A few units have kitchenettes, as well. **Miramar Restaurant** and a heated swimming pool are on the premises. Best of all is the private beach right at one's doorstep. ♦ S. Shore Rd, 4.5 miles west of Hamilton. 236.5031, 800/441.7087

119 Syl-Den Guest Apartments $$ There's nothing fancy here, just five modest housekeeping units, with the requisite swimming pool and adequate ocean views, about 200 yards from the beach. ♦ S. Shore Rd, 4 miles west of Hamilton. 238.1834

120 Clairfont Apartments $$ The eight housekeeping apartments (two studio and six loungable duplexes) offer ceiling fans, gas stoves, a central swimming pool, and easy access to the South Shore beaches. ♦ S. Shore Rd (Long Bay Beach Rd). 238.0149

121 Darrell Island This was the site of Bermuda's first airport. It also served as a quarantine station for arriving ships, a site for a prisoner-of-war tent camp during the Boer War and as a refueling station for the trans-Atlantic clippers during WWII. ♦ Great Sound, reachable only by boat

Southampton

If one word could be used to describe Southampton Parish, it would have to be views, since many of Bermuda's most spectacular ocean vistas are from its south shore.

Bermuda's Best Bets for Basking on the Beach

Bermuda's beaches are perfect for strolling, jogging, snorkeling, horseback riding, and just plain sunbathing with a good book and box lunch. Turquoise waters lap at their pink shores (the pink cast of the sand comes from minuscule particles of seashells and coral mixed with fine grains of sand). Some are sheltered and have calm waters, while others, depending on the tides and winds, can be rough.

You can travel by taxi, bus, ferry, or bicycle to the beach of your choice; however, always wear casual clothing over your bathing suit because it's against the law here to wear your bathing suit in a public place other than the beach.

These are Bermuda's public beaches, from the west to the east portions of the island:

Bermuda

Astwood Park. This Warwick Parish beach provides some of the best views of the south shore, as well as hiking trails and picnic groves. Astwood also has excellent inshore snorkeling areas. Public conveniences are available, too.

Elbow Beach. In reality, there are two Elbow beaches. One is the public beach, accessible from Tribal Road No. 4 between the Coral Beach Club and the Elbow Beach Hotel. (If you're lucky, you'll find a lunch wagon there.)

The other is the private beach at the Elbow Beach Hotel, where you can use the facilities for a modest three dollars a day per person, which includes not only the expansive beach, but use of the changing rooms, towels, chairs, freshwater showers, and access to the informal Surf Club restaurant. This beach is also where Bermuda's legendary College Weeks activities take place during spring break.

Horseshoe Bay Beach. This is far and away Bermuda's most popular and best-known beach because of its symmetry, vegetation, and the brilliant colors of its waters. Full beach facilities are available, including a snack bar, souvenir shop, and snorkeling gear rentals. A lifeguard is on duty during the summer months. It's located in Southampton Parish along the south road.

Jobson Cove Beach. A tiny rock-encircled bay in Warwick Parish that is ideal if you're looking for a secluded spot with calm waters.

John Smith's Bay Beach. If you were drawn to Bermuda by pictures of beautiful pink sand beaches,

122 Sound View Apartments $$ Not far from the lighthouse sits this modest, but cozy complex. Three housekeeping units provide definitive views of the sublime, subdued Great Sound. ♦ S. Shore Rd (Astwood Park). 238.0064

123 Ocean Terrace $$ Three small housekeeping units feature 360-degree panoramic views from their knoll-top location. There's also the radiant, inevitable swimming pool. ♦ S. Shore Rd, behind the Southampton Princess. 238.3240

Southampton Princess

124 Southampton Princess $$$$ This is Bermuda's answer to the Taj Mahal, a luxury resort in the Princess Hotel tradition, offering everything except relative peace and tranquillity (such as that found at the smaller Princess Hotel in Hamilton). There's always something happening, and groups of people coming or going. But if that's your bag, then "South P" is the place for you.

Guests have a choice of six on-site restaurants, with the option of using those at the in-town Princess resort as well. At night, there's a Las Vegas-type revue in the **Empire Room**, disco dancing in the **Touch Club**, and a small combo in the **Neptune** bar, amounting to almost unlimited nightlife. The public rooms in the Southampton Princess are huge, spanning two levels connected by a sweeping circular staircase that seems right out of a Hollywood production. Almost without exception, each of the guest rooms, which range from sublime to modest, has an expansive view of the water.

The hotel's grounds are best described as magnificent. They include an 18-hole, par 3 executive golf course and two pools, one indoors and another on the sundeck. And just a short shuttle ride away, in a rock-bound secluded Atlantic cove, is the sports club and private beach, complete with 11 all-weather tennis courts, a restaurant, and a bar. The Southampton Princess is the best on Bermuda, if for no other reason than it offers the most. ♦ Deluxe ♦ S. Shore Rd (Middle Rd). 238.8000, 800/223.1818

Within the Southampton Princess:

Windows on the Sound ★★★$$ A breakfast buffet and an à la carte dinner are served in the tastefully done salmon-colored dining room overlooking the Great Sound. Steaks and Bermuda fish are among the dinner specialties. ♦ Continental ♦ Daily 8-10:30AM, 6:30-9:30PM. Jacket and tie required at dinner. 238.8000

Whaler Inn ★$$$ You can dine inside or on the terrace of this restaurant nestled high above the boulders overlooking the South P's beach. The Whaler Inn is fairly informal, with a menu that centers around the local fishers' catch of the day. ♦ Seafood ♦ Daily 6:30-9:30PM. 238.8000

Rib Room Steak House ★★$$$ Located above the golf pro shop, this fine restaurant

chances are they were taken at this popular south shore beach in Smith's Parish. Its nearby rocks and reefs are home to large schools of colorful parrotfish, who make picturesque snorkeling companions. During the summer months, there's a lifeguard on duty and often a lunch wagon with light refreshments.

Natural Arches Beach. This sandy stretch in St. George's Parish was one of Bermuda's earliest tourist attractions, and the rock formations, formed by the action of the surf against the rocks, still draw swarms of sightseers and picnickers. Other nearby beaches include **Tobacco Bay,** with refreshment stands and changing facilities available, and **Achilles Bay Beach.**

Shelly Bay Beach. On the western side of Harrington Sound in Hamilton Parish is Shelly Bay Beach, a favorite among families with young children and nonswimmers because of its calm, shallow water. About 200 yards long, it's also the largest beach on the rocky north coast. And if you're into sunsets, they tend to be beautiful here.

Somerset Long Bay Beach. Located on Ireland Island in Sandy's Parish, the waters at this beach are both shallow and tranquil, making it ideal for children. Exposure to the midday and afternoon sun is excellent. Public restrooms are available.

Spanish Point Park. There are no beaches in the city of Hamilton; the nearest one is Spanish Point Park on the north shore in Pembroke Parish. Besides having public conveniences and sheltered waters, it also affords superb vistas of the Royal Navy Dockyards across the bay.

Stonehole Bay Beach, Chaplin Bay Beach. These beaches, though near Horseshoe Bay, are relatively deserted. They're favored by rock climbers, and provide no public facilities.

Warwick Long Bay Beach. This Warwick Parish beach is one of the island's longest beaches and is popular with picnickers and bodysurfers. Public camping is allowed here.

West Whale Bay Beach, Church Bay Beach. Both of these beaches are along the south shore in Southampton Parish and are easily accessible, although relatively secluded. Public facilities are available at each beach.

Restaurants/Clubs: Red   Hotels: Blue
Shops/ 🌳 Outdoors: Green   Sights/Culture: Black

is the logical choice after a day on the greens. The fare is hearty, but not necessarily good for your heart, especially when your meal is started off with the "Dark and Stormy," a black rum and ginger beer concoction. ◆ Steaks ◆ Daily 7PM-closing. 238.8000

125 Pillar-Ville $ Near fabled **Horseshoe Beach**, this Mediterranean-style cottage colony also has access to a hideaway beach of its own. ◆ S. Shore Rd (Lighthouse Hill). 238.0445

126 Henry VIII ★★$$$ If pushed, most Bermudians will say that this is one of the most popular watering holes on the island. Its location, midway between the Princess and the Sonesta resorts, guarantees a never-ending stream of upscale customers. The reasons are many. For starters, it's as close as Bermuda comes to having a *real* British Isles-type pub with sing-along entertainment. The menu offers selections for every palate and budget. And those serving wenches, dressed in period costumes, add just the right amount of bawdiness to allow everyone, including themselves, to have a jolly good time. ◆ British ◆ Daily noon-4PM, 7-10:30PM. Bar: 11AM-1AM. S. Shore Rd (Southampton Princess-Sonesta Beach hotels). Jacket and tie required. 238.0908

127 Sonesta Beach and Spa Hotel $$$$ Like the South P, this is a b-i-g hotel with more than 400 rooms, yet it doesn't appear as such when one looks down on it from S. Shore Rd. Seen from the water, however, it's a totally different story, with a gracefully arched main building rising from a rocky peninsula and cove-shaped beaches on either side. The tennis complex forms the background for one beach, and a row of modern guest buildings the other.

The main entrance is short of spectacular, with a pedestrian bridge leading from the circular drive to the expansive lobby. To the left is what they call a **Solar Dome Pool** complex, which is a swimming pool enclosed in a glass bubblelike structure (there's also an outdoor pool and sundeck).

Guests have a choice of above-average restaurants within the hotel, with **Lillian's** heading the list. Diners not only enjoy European-style cuisine, but dancing as well. The **Boat Bay Club**, usually referred to as the BBC, offers casual dining, dancing, and nightly entertainment. The **Port Royal** has a variety of theme-night buffets that are always fun. There's even an Italian seafood restaurant, **La Sirena.**

The hotel has recently added a full-service spa, offering everything from a Universal-style gym, an exercise area, whirlpools, saunas, and steambaths. Complete full-day programs for skin and body care with European facials, inch-reducing treatments, massages, aromatherapy,

salt-glo loofas, manicures, pedicures, and hairstyling are also available. ◆ Deluxe ◆ S. Shore Rd, 9 miles west of Hamilton. 238.8122, 800/343.7170

Within the Sonesta Beach Hotel and Spa:

Lillian's ★$$$ A jazz trio keeps time to the clanking of silverware and improvises on the melodies of laughter and conversation during dinner in this airy, good-humored seafood emporium. Spicy grilled swordfish is just an inkling of the possibilities and combinations of fresh fish and mollusk dishes that round out their weighty menu. ◆ Seafood ◆ Tu-Sa 7-9:30PM; closed Nov-Mar. Jacket required. Reservations recommended. 238.8122

La Sirena ★$$ While seafood restaurants abound in Bermuda, and Italian food is certainly vogue on the island, few put the two together as delightfully as does La Sirena. Festive appetizers are a must; they range from baked clams capping artichoke hearts to crunchy Bermuda mussel pot pies. Entrées include monkfish brochette and wahoo fettuccine. ◆ Italian/Seafood ◆ Daily 6:30-9:30PM. 238.8122

128 Royal Heights $ This six-room guest house near **Horseshoe Beach** overlooks the Great Sound. The rooms are comfortably furnished, with private baths, balconies, and refrigerators. The Continental breakfast is complimentary. ◆ Gibb's Hill, 15 miles west of Hamilton. 238.0043, 800/247.2447

129 Waterlot Inn ★★$$$$ Claiming to be Bermuda's oldest inn (circa 1670) the restaurant was rescued after a disastrous kitchen fire, and is now run under the auspices of the Southampton Princess, which provides shuttle service from the resort. Its waterside terrace is one of the island's most romantic settings, and Sunday brunch, Bermuda's oldest and best, has been frequented by locals and visitors alike for decades. Luminaries who have broken lobster claws here include **Eugene O'Neill** and **James Thurber.** ◆ French ◆ M-Sa 7-10PM; Su noon-2PM. Middle Rd, 8.5 miles west of Hamilton. Jacket required. 238.0510

130 Gibbs Hill Lighthouse Southampton's prime tourist attraction was built between 1845 and 1846 on the highest point in Bermuda. The need for a lighthouse was established after 39 ships wrecked here within 15 years. The lighthouse (the oldest of its kind still functioning) is made almost entirely of cast iron, towering 362 feet above the water. The bird's-eye view of the Bermuda archipelago will make your eyes thank your legs for climbing 185 steps to the lookout balcony. ◆ Admission. Daily 9AM-4:30PM. Lighthouse Rd (Gibbs Hill). 238.0524

131 The Reefs $$$$ It would be hard to find a more picturesque resort in Bermuda than this charming 65-room hotel nestled atop coral cliffs and, located at the island's southernmost point, overlooking its own vast private beach. Imagine waking up to breakfast on a private lanai with a view of the ocean. Then, it's on to the beach, and perhaps an alfresco lunch and tall drink at **Coconuts** (★★$$), or at the **Sandtraps** snack bar. The **Clubhouse**

(★$$), as the Reefs' main restaurant is known, is where buffet-style breakfasts are served, as are off-season lunches, afternoon tea, and dinner (ties and jackets are required for gentlemen). There's also an on-site fresh-water pool and tennis, with golf just up the road. ◆ 56 S. Shore Rd, 12 miles southwest of Hamilton. 238.0222, 800/223.1363; fax 238.8372

132 Chance It Cottage $$ From the time you get off the airplane to the moment you dip your toes in the whirlpool or nearby ocean, the friendly managers will customize your stay here to fit your needs. The five simple housekeeping apartments are near the **Port Royal Golf Course,** and package deals can be arranged for golfers. ◆ 43 Grenaway Heights Rd (S. Shore Rd). 238.0372

133 Whale Bay Inn $$ This is one of the best-kept secrets on the island for budget-priced hotels. The five housekeeping units are adjacent to the **Port Royal Golf Course** and **Whale Bay Beach.** The Bermuda-style pink building is surrounded by beautifully landscaped grounds. The rooms are furnished in rattan, and feature small, fully equipped kitchens. The only drawback (for some guests, anyway) is that the inn isn't particularly close to Hamilton and the great beaches. ◆ Whale Bay Rd (S. Shore Rd). 238.0469, 800/541.7426

134 Munro Beach Cottages $$$ Sixteen modern duplex cottages offer peace, quiet, and fully equipped kitchens; each has a private entrance and an equally private exit onto the secluded beach. ◆ Port Royal Beach. 234.1175

135 Pompano Beach Club $$ What better location could golfers ask for than this relatively small (just 54 suites and rooms) hotel nestled between the ocean and **Port Royal Golf Course?** Besides a small private beach, it has an oceanside freshwater pool and Jacuzzi. Breakfast and dinner are served in the **Cedar Room Restaurant** overlooking the sea. Lunch is catered on the sunny pool terrace. There are two bars that sometimes feature nightly entertainment. ◆ Pompano Beach Rd (Middle Rd), 10 miles west of Hamilton, with access through the Port Royal Golf Course. 234.0222, 800/343.4155

Within the Pompano Beach Club:

Cedar Room Restaurant ★★★★$$$$
Every night prix fixe five-course meals are served in this radiant, elegant dining room. Built on a cliff facing due west, patrons can watch miraculous sunsets as they dine on cornish game hens or Bermuda's tangiest rum-laced chowder. All pastries, breads, and desserts are baked daily by an Austrian master chef. The menu offers five entrées daily, none of which are repeated during the week. ◆ International ◆ Daily 8-10AM, 7-9PM. Jacket required at dinner F-Sa. Reservations recommended. 234.0222

Sandys

Located at the westernmost end of Bermuda, Sandys Parish is actually comprised of several islands—Somerset, Watford, Ireland North, Ireland South, and Boaz. Though easily reached by taxi or bus, the nicest way to travel to the parish is on a 45-minute ferry ride across the **Great Sound** from Hamilton. Sandys' two major areas are the quaint village of **Somerset** and the recently restored **Dockyard** (which the **Royal Navy** occupied for nearly 150 years, until 1951). The parish is known more for its sights than for its resorts, which are few in number, but include two of Bermuda's finest: the **Lantana Colony Club** and **Cambridge Beaches.**

136 Garden House $$ Five small apartment units are set on a three-acre estate with lovely flower gardens showcasing oleander, orchid, and mariposa varieties. Privacy and informality are among its attributes. ◆ Middle Rd (Wreck Rd). 234.1435

137 Somerset Bridge This is claimed to be the world's smallest drawbridge, with an opening of just 18 inches to allow a sailboat's mast to pass through (the draw is actually the wooden planks in the road). ◆ Somerset Rd, north end of Sandys Parish, 12 miles around the Great Sound from Hamilton

138 Lantana Colony Club $$$$ Billing itself as a "living museum" because of its art collection, especially bronze sculptures, this cottage colony is about as posh as they come in Bermuda. The 20 acres of lawns and gardens are perfectly manicured. Unfortunately, as good as Lantana is, the excellence of the 64 suites and cottages varies considerably, so it's best to inquire about the one you'll be in. Life centers around the main clubhouse with its outdoor patio, atrium dining room, formal dining room, and Carrousel Bar. Luncheon is served pool and beach side at **La Plage,** on the water's edge. A Continental breakfast is served en suite. There's upscale entertainment almost every evening, and, of course, croquet matches are held daily. ◆ Middle Rd, north of Somerset Bridge. 234.0141

Within the Lantana Colony Club:

La Plage ★★★$$$ They serve only one meal a day here, but it's a humdinger. Imagine if you will the Mediterranean, where lunch is the main meal of the day. Fountains, terraces, and statues surround you as delicacy after delicacy is placed on your table: pâté, mousse, mussel stew. Life couldn't be better. ◆ Continental ◆ Daily 1-2:30PM; closed Jan-Mar. 234.0141

139 Somerset Bridge Hotel $$ Located on the shore of **Ely's Harbour** (pronounced ee-lees), this 24-room hotel is the perfect hideaway for snorkelers and scuba divers, with trips available

twice daily. All of the apartments have kitchenettes and most have Murphy beds. ◆ Middle Rd (Somerset Bridge). 234.1042, 800/468.5501

Within the Somerset Bridge Hotel:

Blue Foam Restaurant ★$$ While the name sounds decisively unappetizing, the amazingly fresh seafood within will never make you blue. Lunches are grab-bag affairs, everything from vinegary fish and chips to chicken-salad sandwiches with nutmeg and mustard. Dinners are more sophisticated, succulent, and fresh: wahoo steak, scallops, and the irrepressible fish chowder. ♦ Seafood ♦ Daily 8-10AM, 11:30AM-2:30PM, 6:30-9:30PM. 234.1042

140 Cathedral Rocks This unique formation of cathedral-like vaulted rocks can be found on the shore of Ely's Harbour. Unfortunately, the best vistas of them are from the boat. ♦ Middle Rd, just east of Somerset Bridge

141 St. James Church Somerset's Anglican church is set back from the road. Look for its graceful spire, added in 1880, and spend a moment in thanks for the beauty of Bermuda. ♦ Daily dawn-dusk. Middle Rd, Somerset. No phone

142 Willowbank $$ This old Bermuda manor house has been converted into a small hotel with 60 units for those who literally want to make a Christian religious retreat in Bermuda. There's an optional morning devotional daily. The evening activities include sharing the fellowship of other guests through family and Christian films, hymn singing, and entertainment by local gospel groups. ♦ Somerset Rd, near Soundview. 234.1616

143 Scaur Hill Fort This late 19th-century fort, built to defend the Royal Naval Dockyard from an attack by the Americans, provides superb views of both the Great Sound and Ely's Harbour. Picnic tables are available, walking trails amble through 22 wooded acres, and shoreline docking and fishing areas are provided. ♦ Free. Daily 9AM-4:30PM (grounds open until sunset). Middle Rd, 1 mile north of Somerset Bridge

143 Somerset Long Bay Park and Nature Reserve The Bermuda Audubon Society owns this nature reserve adjacent to crescent-shaped Long Bay Beach. It abounds with a wide variety of birds, and walking its trails is a treat for the entire family. ♦ Free. Daily 9AM-5:30PM. Middle Rd (Long Bay Ln). No phone

144 Cambridge Beaches $$$$ If someone told you this spectacular resort enjoyed a repeat factor of more than 65 percent for returning guests, you might think that figure to be somewhat excessive—unless, of course, you were familiar with this most sybaritic of

Bermuda's cottage colonies. For starters, Cambridge Beaches was the first of the lot, and it's only gotten better through the ensu-

ing decades, artfully providing true quality without the commercialism.

Its location on a private 25-acre peninsula is unmatched, with six beaches, numerous coves, three tennis courts, a health facility, a full-service marina, and a putting green. It should be noted, however, that this delightful, romantic hideaway is not for everyone, since it purposely has none of the hustle and bustle of a major resort. What it does offer is a combination of freedom from everyday cares and ultimate relaxation. The executive chef, **Jean-Claude Garzia**, formerly of the Hamilton Princess and Ritz-Carlton in Atlanta, has become a legend on the island for his innovative cooking. The cottages, each of which has been individually decorated to resemble a private dwelling rather than a hotel or lodge, have all been named, providing additional charm. Breakfast is generally served on the terraces of the cottages, though it is available in the main dining room from 8AM to 10AM. There's live entertainment nightly, dancing under the stars, and barbecues and swizzle parties weekly. ♦ Deluxe ♦ Somerset Long Bay (Mangrove Bay). 234.0331, 800/468.7300

144 Springfield Library The restoration of this former plantation turned library was done by the National Trust, which also restored the outbuildings. It borders the two-acre, hibiscus-filled **Gilbert Nature Reserve,** one of the most beautiful spots on the island. ♦ Free. Nature Reserve: daily dawn-dusk. Library: M, W, Sa 9AM-1PM, 2-4PM. Main Rd (Somerset Rd). 234.1980

145 Royal Naval Dockyard The government of Bermuda spent millions to restore the dockyard, and then did little to follow up. Britain started construction of the dockyard in 1809, and the Royal Navy called this home for 150 years. What a shame, as the tourism department spends a great deal of time, effort, and money promoting this former military stronghold, it is now a park and shopping complex at the westernmost tip of Bermuda on **Ireland Island**. It takes a good half day to get out to the island and return to Hamilton. It's best to plan ahead and take the ferry across the Great Sound. ♦ Extreme west end of the island.

Within the Royal Naval Dockyard:

Bermuda Maritime Museum Rich and historic exhibits of Bermuda's nautical history are housed in an authentic Victorian fortress setting, protected by a moat. Its primary attraction is the permanent display of the buried treasure found by deep-sea diver **Teddy Tucker,** who located the wreck of the *San Antonio,* perhaps the most significant

Restaurants/Clubs: Red   Hotels: Blue
Shops/ ♣ Outdoors: Green   **Sights/Culture:** Blac

(and wealthy) underwater archaeological discovery in British history. ♦ Admission. Daily 10AM-5PM; closed Christmas. 234.1333

Crafts Market Local artists peddle their handmade cedarwork, candles, caned articles, jewelry, and miniature doll-house furniture. There are also craft demonstrations. ♦ Free. Daily 11AM-5PM. 234.3208

Bermuda Arts Centre This art gallery showcases works by local and international artists. **Princess Margaret** presided over its opening in 1984. The exhibitions change monthly. ♦ Admission. Tu-F 10AM-4:30PM; Sa-Su 10AM-5PM. 234.2809

Neptune Theater Deep within the historic Cooperage building, this one-screen theater, one of very few in Bermuda, shows one-week runs of the latest popular films. ♦ Admission. 234.2923

THE BLUE OYSTER

The Blue Oyster Restaurant ★★$$
The California-style bistro is popular with Bermudians, especially in the evenings. During the day, it's filled with tourists and passengers from the cruise ships that berth at the dockyards. Start your meal off with fresh Blue Point oysters on the half shell. The poached salmon rosette or the roast rack of lamb with rosemary sauce are distinguished entrées. ♦ Seafood ♦ Daily 11AM-2:30PM, 6:30-10PM. 234.0943

Tee Time

Bermuda has more golf courses per square mile than any country in the world (eight 18-hole courses on 21 square miles). Three of the courses are maintained by hotels: the Belmont Hotel, the Marriott's Castle Harbour Resorts, and the Southampton Princess. Two of the courses are private: the Mid Ocean Golf Club and Riddell's Bay Golf and Country Club; you can play them if you are sponsored or introduced by a member or a hotel manager. The remaining three are government owned and are open to the public: Port Royal Golf Course, St. George's Golf Club, and the Ocean View Golf and Country Club in Devonshire (sometimes called the Queens Park Golf Club).

Belmont Golf Club. Renowned for its elevated and double-tiered greens, blind second shots, tight fairways, and narrow putting surfaces, the Belmont's 5,777-yard course has an almost unrealistic par of 70 strokes. The course is in Warwick, about two miles from Hamilton. For a reservation, call 236.1301.

Marriott's Castle Harbour Golf Club. The two signature holes, the first and the 18th, claim to have "the most expensive vistas in golf" because of the multimillion-dollar homes seen from their tees. Veterans say the 6,440-yard, par 71 course never plays exactly the same due to the ever-changing winds that sweep over the fairways. Call 293.2040 for more information.

Mid Ocean Golf Club. This is not only Bermuda's best-maintained and least-crowded course, it's also the most exclusive. An orientation by a club member or hotel manager is necessary if you want to play on the two days a week it's open to non-members. Suffice it to say that good shots along its 6,547-yard course (with six par 4 holes exceeding 400 yards) are rewarded. A bad shot could land your ball over a cliff and into the Atlantic. The course is in Tucker's Town, about seven miles from Hamilton. Call 293.0330 for more information.

Ocean View Golf and Country Club. This nine-hole, par 35, 2,956-yard course offers visitors a chance to play a fast, though somewhat unexciting round of golf. The pro shop at the Devonshire course can be reached at 236.6758.

Port Royal Golf Course. Designed by golf architect **Robert Trent Jones,** the Port Royal contends with the Mid Ocean Golf Club as Bermuda's best. However, several of the holes along its 6,465 yard, par 71 fairways have a nasty habit of feeding one's golf balls to the fish in the adjacent Atlantic. The course is approximately six miles from Hamilton. Call 234.0974 for reservations.

Riddell's Bay Golf and Country Club. This club has the toughest opening hole on the island, a 418-yard par 4. This course is a par 69, and it covers just 5,588 yards, but is hilly and has extremely narrow fairways. Darron Swan is the pro at this Warwick course. To play here, you must be introduced by a member or a hotel manager. For information, call 238.1060.

St. George's Golf Club. Also created by the hand of **Robert Trent Jones,** St. George's is just a few minutes walk from the town and harbor, ideal for cruise-ship passengers arriving on the island. Be forewarned, however, that the island's blustery winds will play havoc with your game along the entire 4,502-yard, par 64 course. Located approximately eight miles from Hamilton. The pro shop at this course can be reached by calling 297.8353.

Southampton Princess Golf Club. This is Bermuda's shortest and quickest 18 holes, requiring about two and a half hours to play its 2,684 yards, par 54. But

don't let its small size fool you. It's hilly, full of water hazards, and has 60 bunkers (sand traps). Ron Wallace and Bruce Sims are the resident pros here; for more information, call 238.0446.

Timeline

AD 120

Archaeologists generally believe the Caribbean islands were populated by the **Tainos, Arawak,** and **Carib Indians,** who had paddled their way north from South America until they reached **Puerto Rico.** The Arawaks were fishers and farmers who worshiped spirits of nature. Archaeologists have found carvings and cave paintings of these spirits on some islands, including **Aruba.** The fierce Caribs, for whom the region is named, were cannibals.

1492

Christopher Columbus makes the first of four voyages to the New World, landing on an island the natives call Guanahani (now known as **San Salvador**) in the **Bahamas** on 12 October. The welcoming party includes Indians, probably Arawaks.

1493

Columbus drops anchor off the east coast of an island he calls **St. Martin,** named after the Bishop of Tours (the warrior Saint Martin), on 1 November. Spain takes possession of all the **Antilles Islands,** and Columbus brings Africans to work as slaves to find the gold he sought for Spain. The slaves work in the fields and mines with the Indians Columbus captured from other Caribbean islands.

1498

On his third trip to the New World, Columbus discovers the island of **Grenada** (which he names Concepción). The bay where Columbus anchored (now known as **Levera Bay**) is located on Grenada's northern shore.

1503

Columbus reaches the mainland of Central America and stops at the **Cayman Islands.**

Spanish navigator **Juan de Bermudez** discovers **Bermuda** (some historians believe this did not occur until 1511).

1536

Navigator **Pedro a Campo** of Portugal discovers **Barbados.** The Portuguese stay a short while. After they leave, the British take over the island in 1627.

1571

English navigator **Sir Francis Drake** sails through the passage between the **British** and **United States Virgin Islands** (the passage now bears his name).

1600

Piracy becomes big business in the Caribbean, and Welsh buccaneer **Henry Morgan** sets up shop in the **Bahamas,** making **Nassau** on **New Providence** island his home base.

1625

The first British settlers come ashore at **Holetown** on **Barbados,** claiming the island for **King James I** of England. **Antigua, St. Kitts, Nevis,** and **Barbuda** are taken under the protection of Great Britain.

1630

The Spanish leave **St. Martin/Sint Maarten,** and the French take over the island. Their government is short-lived, however, and when the Dutch arrive in 1631 they find the island deserted. In 1633 the Spaniards return and drive the Dutch away.

1631

The Dutch, seeking outposts for their ever-expanding West Indian trade, settle on **St. Martin/Sint Maarten** again.

British settlers from **St. Kitts** claim **Antigua** for the crown.

1644

A Dutch fleet under the command of **Peter Stuyvesant,** the West India company director of **Curaçao,** arrives at **St. Martin.** During a three-week-long battle with the Spanish (who again occupy the island), Stuyvesant loses a leg.

1648

The French are booted out of **St. Martin** by the Dutch; eventually an agreement between the two nations is signed on 23 March dividing the island in half, and their peaceful co-existence continues to this day.

British settlers land on **Eleuthera** in the Bahamas.

1655

British forces capture **Jamaica** from Spain as **Oliver Cromwell** sets the stage for Britain's imperial role in the region.

1670

The **Bahamas** become a British colony and England formally takes control of **Jamaica** and the **Cayman Islands.**

1684

The number of slaves in **Barbados'** sugar trade increases from 5,680 in 1645 to 60,000; the slaves outnumber their owners three to one.

1796

French soldiers storm **Rendezvous Bay** in **Anguilla** in a futile attempt to reclaim the island from England. The island remains British and in 1825 becomes a single crown colony, along with **St. Kitts** and **Nevis**.

1824

A young sheepherder finds gold deposits on **Aruba's** north coast, prompting the birth of the island's first industry. Within months, more than 25 pounds of gold is collected.

1833

The **Emancipation Act** is passed in the **Bahamas** and by other British islands on 1 August.

1834

Slavery is abolished on **Barbados** and slaves become "apprentices" who work for their masters for the next four years.

1838

The French islands abolish slavery and complete emancipation is achieved.

1859

The **Royal Victoria Hotel** is built in **Nassau** on **New Providence**.

The **Bahamas** become a base for blockade runners during the **War between the States**.

1872

Smelting begins at the **Aruba Inland Gold Mining Company** on the island's north coast. Another smelting company opens at **Balashi** in 1899. The Netherlands government sends troops to Aruba to guard the fields and dry creeks.

1898

The United States lays claim to **Puerto Rico** in the **Spanish-American War**.

1917

The United States grants citizenship rights to **Puerto Ricans**.

1949

The Hilton hotel chain opens its first Caribbean hotel, the **Caribe Hilton**, in **San Juan**, boosting tourism in the Puerto Rican capital.

1951

Puerto Rico elects its first native-born governor, **Luis Muñoz Marín**.

1959

The Cuban revolution places **Fidel Castro** in power, and the door is effectively closed on tourism to the Caribbean's largest island.

1961

A&P supermarkets heir **Huntington Hartford II** buys Hog Island (now called **Paradise Island**) in the **Bahamas** from Swedish industrialist **Axel Wenner-Gren** for $9.5 million.

1962

Jamaica becomes an independent member of the Commonwealth of Nations.

1966

Barbados becomes an independent state within the British commonwealth.

1973

The **Bahamas** become an independent nation on 10 July.

1981

Antigua becomes an independent state within the British commonwealth.

1986

Aruba becomes a separate entity within the **Kingdom of the Netherlands**.

1988

Hurricane Gilbert hits **Jamaica,** causing hundreds of millions of dollars of damage. It takes two years before tourism gets back on track.

1989

Hurricane Hugo strikes in the Caribbean, devastating **St. Croix** in the **United States Virgin Islands**, which takes three years to recover. **Puerto Rico** is spared when **El Yunque** rain forest takes the brunt of the storm's force.

1991

The 500,000th visitor arrives on **Aruba**.

Sandals, the first couples-only resort in the Caribbean, opens on **Jamaica**.

Index

Hotel Ratings

Each island's hotels are listed alphabetically in the following island indexes. The hotels are also indexed according to their price ratings. The dollar signs reflect general price-range relationships between other hotels on the islands; they do not represent specific rates.

$$$$ A Month's Pay
$$$ Expensive
$$ Reasonable
$ The Price is Right

Restaurant Ratings

Each island's restaurants are listed alphabetically in the following island indexes. Restaurants with star ratings are also indexed according to their ratings. Always call in advance to ensure a restaurant has not closed, changed its hours, or booked its tables for a private party. The dollar signs reflect general price-range relationships between other restaurants on the islands; they do not represent specific rates.

★★★★   Extraordinary
★★★   Excellent
★★   Very Good
★   Good
$$$$ A Month's Pay
$$$ Expensive
$$ Reasonable
$ The Price is Right

194

Index

197

St. Martin/Sint Maarten Hotels

$$$$

$$$

$$

$

St. Martin/Sint Maarten Restaurants

★★

★

Index

Index

206